Ex Líbrís

Lotte x

Hans Christian Andersen

Also by Alison Prince

The Witching Tree
Kenneth Grahame: An Innocent in the Wild Wood

a&b

Hans Christian Andersen

The Fan Dancer

Alison Prince

First published in Great Britain by
ALLISON & BUSBY Limited
114 New Cavendish Street
London W1M 7FD

A catalogue record for this book is available from the British Library

ISBN 0 74900 346 4

Design and cover illustration: PEPE MOLL

Edited by Alba Editorial, S. L.

Printed in Great Britain by
Biddles Limited, Guildford and King's Lynn

To all my Danish friends,
with love and thanks

Acknowledgements

I am immensely grateful to the Scottish Arts Council for financial help in the form of Travel and Research grants. Without this support, the book could not have been written.

In Denmark, I met with marvellous co-operation and friendship. Roger Leys and Brigitte Sedoc were endlessly hospitable and helpful, ever willing to cast an eye over my translations and solve practical problems. Trine Skjoldan Nielsen has been an invaluable researcher, always available at the end of a fax line, and I am much indebted to her for her perceptive work. Ivan Bartolo did some enlightened Internet trawling, and I am grateful both to him and to Johan de Mylius of Odense University who gave me his time and his specialised insight. Jacob Wisby, whom I met through my utterly brilliant agent, Jennifer Luithlen, brought a whole new dimension to the book through his warmth and originality of viewpoint.

Research is inevitably dependent on the skill and goodwill of librarians, and I would particularly like to thank the staff of my local public library, whose inspired efforts brought so many books into my hands, and also the Danish Cultural Institute in Edinburgh. Audrey McCrone was tireless in finding rare second-hand books, and I am grateful to all those people, too many to count, who have contributed newspaper cuttings, old postcards and scraps of personal expertise.

Finally, a huge thank-you must go to Vanessa Unwin of Allison & Busby, a pearl among editors, to whom it was never necessary to explain anything.

ALISON PRINCE
1998

Contents

LIST OF ILLUSTRATIONS, between pages 224–225

Grateful acknowledgement is made to the following for permission to reproduce illustrations:

To the Hans Christian Andersen Hus, Odense City Museums, Copenhagen, for Plates 1, 2, 3, 4, 7, 8, 9, 10, 12, 13, 14, 16; to Det Kongelige Bibliotek, Copenhagen, for Plate 5; to Forlaget Hovedland, Højbjerg, and Det Nationalhistoriske Museum, Frederiksborg Slot, for Plate 6; to Ny Carlsberg Glyptotek, Copenhagen, for Plate 11; and to Det Berlingske Bogtrykkeri for Plate 15.

Introduction

In a long, low house by a fjord, I was given coffee in a delicate, daffodil yellow cup which had belonged to Napoleon III. Dusty chandeliers hung from the wooden ceiling. 'So you see,' said my host, 'Hans Christian Andersen really was a prince.'

The contention was not a new one. Jens Jørgensen, a Danish MP and ex-headmaster of Slagelse Grammar School (once attended by Andersen himself) had in 1987 suggested in his book, *En sand myte* (*A True Myth*) that Denmark's most famous writer had been an embarrassing offshoot of the royal family. The thesis came in turn from the work of Hans Brix, writing in 1907 – and now it was being stated again.

Nevertheless, I was sceptical. Andersen's own accounts of his childhood dwell almost obsessively on the poverty of his upbringing, and the parish records confirm his baptism and christening as the son of a shoemaker and his older wife, an illiterate washerwoman. This story of hidden nobility, revealed in a Danish paperback and now told on a strange afternoon in Jutland, must surely be wishful thinking. It was not until I returned home and looked at the almost-complete manuscript of my own book that I realised, with the greatest reluctance, that the theory could not be discounted.

The known facts are scant but fundamental. On 2 April 1805 or a day or two earlier, at Broholm Castle on Funen, owned by the French count, Hofjaegermester Frederik Severin, a baby boy was born to the young countess Elise of Ahlefeldt-Lauernvig, daughter of a General who later rose to be Field Marshal of the Danish army. The child's father was Prince Christian Frederik, then nineteen years old, son of King Frederik V. Such a scandal could not be allowed to touch this Crown Prince of Denmark who would rule as Christian VIII, and so the child was whisked away by Severin's wife and given to her maid, Anne Marie Andersen, to be brought up as her own son. Anne Marie, who rather conveniently could not read or write, was not a woman to insist on any formalities. She had just two months previously married a young shoemaker, possibly as part of a paid arrangement. This lad,

Hans, was employed at Tranekar Castle, owned by the family of the child's aristocratic young mother.

This baby was not the only offspring of the Crown Prince. Only a few months previously, a daughter, Fanny, had been born at Ludwigslust Castle near Schleswig to Princess Charlotte Frederikke von Mecklenburg-Schwerin, whom he subsequently married in 1808. The couple then produced their only officially sanctioned child, 'Fritz', the son who became King Frederik VII. For reasons which can only be guessed at, Anne Marie Andersen used frequently to bring her boy to play with this royal child (who could have been his half-brother), at Odense Castle.

Objections to the theory of noble birth leap to mind at once. Why should the son of a Crown Prince, illegitimate or not, be allowed to grow up in abject poverty, particularly if a payment had been part of the deal? Why did he receive no real education until, at seventeen, he made such a nuisance of himself in Copenhagen that something had to be done about him? Why do his diaries show no sign that he was aware of a royal origin? The answers creep in like shadows cast by the presence of something solid but invisible. Hans and Anne Marie Andersen could not tell him what they did not know. Aware only that their boy must be of high birth, the honour of being entrusted with him also carried overtones of secrecy and fear. At a time when the monarchy was still absolute, any indiscretion or disrespect was, to say the least of it, unwise.

It may well be that the secret was not totally kept. A sense of dazzled privilege and a spillage of hints could be the factors which lay so potently behind the family myths of vanished grandeur and which caused the boy to dream, as his autobiographies show, so constantly of castles and the trappings of power. The Andersens were part of a deeply romantic outlook.

For a royal family trying to maintain secrecy, dealing with the foster parents could have presented some difficulties. Any ostentatious favours shown to this lowly tribe would at once have caused awkward questions to be asked. The poverty-stricken could not be given even small amounts of money without this being very evident to all friends and neighbours – and Anne Marie in particular, with her garrulousness and her liking for alcohol, would never be a discreet manager of money. There was indeed a hoard of coins given into the trust of Hans Christian's paternal grandmother, who seems to have been the only one among them to have any shrewdness. She referred to this as 'a fortune', and kept it intact for so long that at last it became worthless.

Even the most casual reading of Andersen's autobiographies reveals a certain royal interest in the boy, expressed through closely connected Court officials and their families. His early account, unpublished in his life time, is unguarded about the trips to the Castle to play with Fritz and reveals nonchalantly that his rather casual early school attendances were undertaken on the strict understanding that he should never be beaten. What ordinary child or ordinary poverty-stricken parents would dream of making such a stipulation?

All this is of course circumstantial. Nothing exists in writing, though the gradually emerging archive of the Wulff family letters with fresh evidence of what Andersen confided to his close friend, Jette Wulff, may yet produce conclusive proof. Meanwhile, Johan de Mylius, currently Denmark's leading authority on Andersen, remarked dismissively of Jørgensen's book that it was '*fup minus fakta*' – a piece of baseless trickery, fiction minus fact.

Negation must always work both ways. If the theory of royal birth cannot be proved, neither can it be disproved; and once it lodges in the reader's mind, all sorts of small pointers in Andersen's life leap into new significance. Not least is Anne Marie's attitude of craven respect to the boy she brought up as her son. Countess Elise, in complete contrast, was a lively, unconventional girl, born into the same liberality of treatment as her elder brothers. She shared Andersen's passion for the theatre, frequently appearing in amateur productions. She was on the stage at Odense Theatre shortly after the birth (and hushed-up disappearance) of her illegitimate child in April 1805.

Whether Andersen himself ever knew the truth about his origins awaits conclusive proof. Hints abound, but his diaries became ever more circumspect as he grew older and more famous, recognising that every word he wrote would one day be public. In view of that, one may look again at his phrasing in *My Life's Fairytale*, his later autobiography. He states only that 'there lay here on April 2nd 1805 a living, weeping child.' He does not say, 'was born'.

Whatever the facts, it is obvious that Andersen struggled throughout his life with a painful sense of greatness and of being different from others. This was partly due to the suppressed homosexuality which set him apart in loneliness and forced him to take refuge in the safer and more conventional image of the talented and hypersensitive poet, but it is possible that his high self-esteem was partly due to inheritance. During his early days he was baffled by his own romantic arrogance – and if the kings and queens who watched him and later welcomed him did so with a secret smile, the secret was theirs to keep. If they ever revealed it, they did not do so until they were sure that he could become one of themselves, controlled by total loyalty. To this day, one can do no more than look at Hans Christian Andersen's complex, difficult life with an open mind, and try to perceive where his constant dance of self-protection ended, and where the truth began.

The tiny house in Odense where Hans Christian Andersen is said to have lived as a child has been absorbed into a large museum. The teller of wonderful tales is now part of Denmark's heritage industry with all its trappings of credit-card logos and guidebooks in a dozen or more languages, but far from resenting this, Andersen would probably have loved it. Throughout his life, he behaved like the curator of his own existence, preserving every letter and gift, every diary and notebook, as if consciously collecting these things for display. In the most literal meaning of the phrase, he made an exhibition of himself.

Andersen's behaviour, too, was a constant exhibition of what he could do. From an early age, he was always ready to recite, sing, dance or read aloud to anyone who would listen; he worried endlessly about what people thought of him and whether his performance had been successful. He resembled a fan-dancer whose feathers are in perpetual bewitching movement, hiding the naked self from the watching eyes which both admire and are filled with prurient curiosity, for he was at a fundamental level a pretender.

He had much to hide. All questions of his possible royal birth aside, he was even in childhood effeminate and the butt of cruel jokes from the village boys, and learned early to keep his true nature concealed behind a performer's exterior. He was happy to be thought a conceited show-off if this prevented any closer investigation.

The earliest experiences of which he was aware encouraged pretence, for he seemed to have been born into a family of confirmed fantasists. His parents and his paternal grandmother laid claim to an inherited grandeur which, though notably lacking in any discernible reality, cast a theatrical light over their poverty. It gave young Hans Christian a strong sense that the unattractive actual world could easily be disregarded in favour of the more magical one to which people of superior spirit had access. He was proud to remark later that the bed on which Anne Marie claimed to have given birth to him on 2 April 1805 had been contrived from the framework on which the body of a count had lain. Jens Jørgensen's book, *En sand myte*, points out that no count had died at about that time, but mythology is never troubled by tiresome details of that sort. For Andersen, the scraps of black fabric which hung about the rough structure confirmed that family sense of being in some way special.

The established facts give no grounds for such romantic self-deception. Hans Christian's father – if such he was – a shoemaker who owned nothing but the tools of his trade, was twenty-two years old when the boy was born, and went by the name of Hans Andersen. He had married Anne Marie Andersdotter, who was about eight years older, exactly two months previously, on 2 February 1805, at St Knud's church. Hans Christian was christened at two weeks old in a different church, St Hans, and while this could have no significance, it might also indicate that the priest who had married the couple might have been surprised had they turned up with a baby two months later. Nobody will ever know whether Anne Marie was pregnant at the time of her marriage, and if she and her young husband were both working as palace servants, and were only installed in Odense's slum cottages after the arrival of Hans Christian, nobody ever did know except a small circle of aristocrats and the royal family itself.

The Andersens moved at least twice during the first two years of Hans Christian's life, and arrived at number 646, Klingenberg, now known as Munkemollenstraede, the site of the museum, in May 1807, the year of the bombardment of Copenhagen. Three families were housed in the small building, twelve people in all, and the Andersens occupied a tiny room and kitchen. Though inadequate by present-day standards, few working-class people would have expected any more at the time, and an almost identical set-up is preserved in Copenhagen's Museum of Work as a sample of nineteenth century living conditions.

Hans Christian's paternal grandparents had come to Odense in 1788 as smallholders dispossessed of their peasant holding by the enclosures of the late eighteenth century. Anders Andersen, like his son, was a shoemaker, but it was probably the loss of the ancient rights to grazing and free access to peat and firewood which had forced them, like so many others, into the town as part of a virtually destitute underclass. Their situation was made worse by a rapid inflation resulting from the ailing national bank's 'print money' policy, thought necessary in the wake of the protracted and ever-more alarming revolution in France which had made all Europe's rulers desperate to consolidate their authority. This bleak family history was translated by

Hans Christian's paternal grandmother into a series of exotic tales of how a big farm and extensive lands had been lost. Fire and cattle disease and failed crops were cited as a liturgy of disaster which had robbed them of their heritage and caused her poor husband to lose his reason.

The madness of Anders Andersen, if nothing else, was visibly true. He sang to himself as he wandered back along the village street from the woods, decked in green like Ophelia and pursued by cat-calling boys, and occupied his days in whittling strange figures. They were 'men with beasts' heads and creatures with wings', his grandson remembered, which Anders carried with him in a basket and gave away to anyone who would stop and talk to him.

A fear of insanity haunted Andersen throughout his life, stemming from the day when he hid behind a flight of steps from the jeering lads who followed the old man. He was horrified to think himself to be 'of his flesh and blood', as he admitted in his first autobiography, and knew that the boys would be more than ready to hurl the same accusations at himself, given the slightest cause. 'Mad Anders' seldom addressed a word to young Hans Christian, but when he did suddenly speak to him one day, he used the formal second-person-plural address rather than the '*du*' of family intimacy, and this frightened the child even more. It is tempting to wonder whether the old man in his confusion inadvertently let slip the respect he felt for this high-born boy whose arrival was such a dark but exciting family secret, for Anders was a simple man, sharing none of his wife's wild − or shrewd − imaginative power.

Born Anne Cathrine Nomensdatter in 1745, Hans Christian's grandmother claimed, despite her non-aristocratic Danish surname, that she had come from a noble German family in Kassel, from which her mother had been banished because she ran away with an actor. In fact, Anne Cathrine's mother, Karen Nielsdatter, had been a penniless Danish girl who married a long-distance postal rider, bore him eight children and was left destitute when he died in the year of Anne Cathrine's birth, about 1745. It may have been purely coincidental that Andersen's beloved grandmother, 'a quiet and most likeable old lady with mild blue eyes and a fine figure', as he called her, dwelt so constantly on a superior family background which seems entirely illusory. She could have been merely exercising a private daydream to soften the sense of loss which would quite reasonably have attended her move away from the frail independence of country life; on the other hand, her insistence on a background of grandeur might well be seen as an effort to assure her strange grandson that the family into which he had been given was worthy of him.

Education – or the lamented lack of it – was a major topic in the blue-eyed grandmother's mythology. She shook her head over the undiscovered brilliance of her son and claimed that when they came to the town, wealthy people had talked of clubbing together so that he might be sent to the grammar school, though nothing had come of it. Hans Christian's father, perhaps correctly, believed this tale of his own deprivation to be true, and resented his lost chance bitterly. He, too, in his own way, strove to give Hans Christian the best he could. Possessing a few books – La Fontaine's *Fables, The Arabian Nights* and a volume or two of Holberg's plays – he lost no time in sharing with the little boy his enthusiasm for reading. Family legendry had it that he read aloud to the squalling newborn baby, telling it either to go to sleep or be quiet and listen. The works of Ludwig Holberg (1684–1745) particularly appealed to the frustrated longings of the shoemaker, perhaps in part because of their author's extraordinary and totally self-made success. A Norwegian, he had come as a penniless eighteen-year-old to Copenhagen, demanding access to the university to study. Granted this, he later went on foot across Europe to Rome and walked back across the Alps after a narrow escape from the Inquisition. Although appointed professor of Latin Eloquence at Copenhagen University, he had written comic plays which had effectively laid the foundations of a Danish theatre, ousting the French adaptations which had held sway until then. Holberg's history was interwoven with that of the Andersen father and son to such an extent that the little boy could quote long sections of his plays from an early age, and accepted without question the idea that present circumstances could quite easily give way to something better.

Young Hans Christian found in his shoemaker father a companion who was more than ready to lead him into the world of imagination. The cobbler built a toy theatre for his son and peopled it with puppets dressed in costumes made from scraps of silk and velvet, and together they made up plays which were a garbled mixture of Holberg and their own fancies. The magic of this small world lived in the boy's mind for ever. On Sundays when Hans was free from his cutting and stitching of leather, he would take the little boy with him to the woods, where, as

Hans Christian Andersen later remembered, he would often 'sit silently, sunk in deep thought' while his son ran and played.

The brooding silences were nevertheless oppressive, and Andersen recorded that his father 'was never really happy in his life as a craftsman'. Once, a boy from the Grammar School came to be measured for a new pair of boots, and Hans Christian saw tears come to the cobbler's eyes as he looked with envy at the books the lad carried. 'That was the path I should have followed,' he said, and his son recalled afterwards how his father had kissed him 'passionately, and was silent the whole evening'.

By contrast with the romantic intensity of the relationship between father and son, Andersen's feeling for his mother seems to have been one of simple, loving dependence. Anne Marie, unable to read or write, had no share in the toy theatre and the play-making, but while her husband dreamed and brooded, she dealt with all the practicalities, washing bedlinen and curtains in the river to keep them fresh and white and treasuring the few pretty cups and ornaments which brightened the tiny room. A ladder led to the roof where, in the gutter between one sloping pitch and the next, she planted a box of soil with chives and parsley, for her a useful source of cooking herbs, but a magical garden in the eyes of her small son.

For all her domesticity, Anne Marie, too, had her secrets and pretences. Six years before her marriage, she had given birth to an illegitimate daughter, Karen Marie, the child of a grenadier known as Rosenvinge who already had several children by local women. Karen, clearly a deep embarrassment to her mother, was never mentioned in the house, and it was some time before Hans Christian discovered that he had a half-sister.

Alternatively he might have had a royal half-sister, Fanny, baptised Franziska Enger and, like Hans Christian, given away to a servant at the Castle Ludwigslust in Schleswig shortly after her birth on 31 August 1804. Fanny was the child of Prince Christian Frederik and the sixteen-year-old Princess Charlotte Frederikke von Mecklenburg-Schwerin, the result of a wild fling when the prince, then eighteen, had stayed at Schwerin on his way to visit his grandmother at Ballestedt Castle in Hessen. Quite a lot is known about her; she and her foster-mother lived in Persillegade in Aabenrna, with remarkably little discretion. Miss Enger paid her bills with gold coins, just once a year, and her little girl went to school with the Prefect's daughters at the castle. Tongues wagged, but nobody seemed to care; the child, after all, was a girl, with no claim to the throne even if her father *was* the Crown Prince.

No such cavalier attitude encompassed the presence of Hans Christian's known half-sister, Karen Marie. The family furtiveness and unease about her existence gave her a nightmare quality, and also sowed in the boy the seeds of a lifetime's fear of the half-understood sexuality of women, that dark power which the boys made jokes about, and which could produce a living creature so illicit and embarrassing that she had been sent away and was never spoken of.

Karen Marie was being brought up in Bogense by her maternal grandmother, Anna Sørensdatter, which must have at least partly explained why Andersen had no recollection of his mother's mother. She was on the inferior side of the family, with no tall tales to tell of lost land and property. Anna Sørensdatter had produced three illegitimate daughters, of whom Anne Marie was the eldest. Her next-youngest sister, Christiane, was still living, but the youngest had died as a baby, and Anna was at that point thrown into prison for the crime of unsanctioned motherhood. When released, she was thirty-eight years old and dutifully married a Jens Pedersen, by whom she had a fourth child, which also died. Little is known about Pedersen except that he had served a term in Odense Gaol for shooting a gamekeeper, but this scrap of family history added to the disturbing store which was building up in Hans Christian's mind and which would find its way so powerfully into his writing, notably in the novel, *O.T.* Here the initials stand for the eponymous hero's name and also for the prison which looms so large in his history. After Pedersen's death eleven years later, Anna had married again, this time to a glove-maker fifteen years her junior, Jorgen Rasmussen Sievert, and, by now in her fifties, had taken on the task of bringing up Karen.

That his mother's mother had led a life of extreme hardship did not seem to strike Hans Christian, either then or later, as unusually pitiable. He was growing up in surroundings where everything was hard, and what mattered most to him, as to his father, was the private retreat into the world of books and imagination. His mother's family entered that world only with tales of fear and squalor which were an unwelcome though haunting addition to his growing stock of fantasies. Anne Marie told him how she was sent out to beg while still very young and how, fearing the beating that awaited her for going home empty-handed, she had sheltered under a bridge for a whole day. The image surfaced later in 'The Little Match-Girl', but other elements in the family saga were less easy to incorporate. Hans Christian had been only a year old when the Poor Law Inspectors had come to the door demanding to know the whereabouts of Christiane, Anne Marie's surviving sister, and whether she was married or single. His mother either could not or would not tell them, and secrecy hung over this as well. A few years later, Christiane came to visit her sister, and gave Hans Christian a silver coin. He remembered afterwards how angry his mother had been at this gift, and her inexplicable fury with Christiane for showing off her silks and fine clothes – but it was not until many years later that he discovered the truth. His aunt was running a brothel in Copenhagen.

Anne Marie, in her primitive way, added to Hans Christian's sense that reality was multilayered and far from straightforward. Despite her Lutheran faith, she was deeply superstitious, consulting the wise woman rather than the doctor when anyone was ill – though it must be remembered that doctors cost money – and never failing to carry out rituals and customs which long predated Christianity. She came with her husband and son to the woods only on the first day of spring, wearing her best dress of flowered brown calico, and brought back armfuls of fresh, green birch branches, and she set sprigs of St John's Wort into the chinks in the house walls, watching the way they grew as a sign whether the human lives of the household would be long or short.

After the disgrace of Karen's birth, Anne Marie gloried in her legally married state and in the son who seemed so wonderful, clever and sensitive. She watched, awestruck, as Hans Christian entered with no apparent difficulty into the stories contained in the books which were so baffling to her. The boy was becoming a foppish, fastidious lad, tall for his age but with no taste for the rowdy street games of the other boys. He was content to sit in the corner and stitch at his dolls' clothes while his father was busy with his cobbling, or play in the little yard behind the house, draping his mother's apron over a stick propped between the wall and the solitary gooseberry bush to make an improvised tent.

The single small room offered no privacy. Hans Christian's little bed could not be put down in the limited floor space until the parents had retired for the night, so in the evenings he would lie in their curtained double bed, 'in a waking dream', aware of what went on outside the curtains and yet detached from it. He was by his own admission an unusually dreamy child, walking about with eyes that appeared to be half shut so that people sometimes asked Anne Marie if her son was blind. In fact a restriction of the eyelids which a simple operation would nowadays rectify gave him a hooded, small-eyed look which he never outgrew.

In time, the vast gulf of difference between Hans Christian's mother and father began to affect their relationship. Hans, burdened by his mother's constant lamentations about what might have been, retreated further into the bitterness of his own thoughts, and sometimes came out with statements which shocked his superstitious wife. Essentially a free-thinker, he closed the Bible one day with the remark that Christ may have had exceptional abilities but he was a man like any other man. Anne Marie burst into tears at such blasphemy and made Hans Christian join her in an immediate prayer for her husband's soul. She was further alarmed when Hans revealed three scratches on his arm, probably, as his son later admitted, caused by the rough timber of the bed, and she had no hesitation in declaring them to be the mark of the devil. Hans had rashly stated that the only devil was the one men carry in their hearts, and his wife was convinced that the Evil One had come to claim his own.

The wider background to Hans Christian's life was no more reassuring than his domestic circumstances. Napoleon, having subdued Italy and rampaged through Spain, began his process of closing European ports against the British, resulting in a pre-emptive bombardment of the Danish fleet in Copenhagen. In two days of intensive attack on 3–4 September 1807, the city had been virtually destroyed and the remaining Danish ships carried off to prevent them from falling into French hands. Not unnaturally, on 20 February 1808 the Danes threw in their lot with Napoleon, and the little emperor marched without opposition through Denmark in order to invade Sweden, then Britain's only remaining ally. French soldiers under the command of Marshall Jean-Baptiste Jules Bernadotte, together with a ragged corps of Spaniards reluctantly conscripted after the taking of Barcelona and Madrid, poured into the streets of Odense, to the fascination of the three-year-old Hans Christian.

The troops must have come as a dramatic interruption to the lives of Danish peasants who had seen nothing more military than the marching guilds who would turn out at Whitsun with flying banners and harmless swords decorated with lemons and ribbons. Suddenly, as

Andersen remembered in his autobiography, *Mit livs eventyr* (*My Life's Fairytale*) the village was full of horses and cannon and 'dark brown men'. The soldiers slept where they could, sprawled on the footpaths or between the guns or on bundles of straw in the scant shelter of a half-ruined church. A foreign and wickedly exotic Catholicism was suddenly manifest, with Mass being said in the open air, at the roadside or in the leafy natural cathedral of a group of trees.

The villagers began to discriminate between the French soldiers, said to be haughty and arrogant, and the unenthusiastic Spanish conscripts, who hated Napoleon's troops far more than the notional enemy in the northern land that lay ahead of them. These good-natured, dark-haired lads endeared themselves to their involuntary hosts by their friendliness, and the villagers sympathised with the Spaniards for having been hauled into a fight which was not of their making. A memory which stayed for ever in Andersen's mind was of being snatched up impetuously by a young Spanish soldier who danced with the little boy in his arms, kissing him with tears in his eyes as if missing a small son of his own. He pressed against Hans Christian's lips the 'silver image which he wore on his naked breast', and Anne Marie was outraged, knowing this to be to 'something Catholic'.

More briefly touched on in the autobiography is Andersen's memory of seeing a Spanish soldier led away for execution, having killed a French soldier. Imprisonment, with all its implications of pain and punishment, was already a familiar part of his background, for his godfather, Nicholas Gomard, was a porter at Odense Gaol, a fact which added much to Andersen's later obsessive use of prisons as a theme in his work. A long-established theory suggests that it was Gomard who was actually Hans Christian's father, and while this cannot be totally ruled out, it seems a little unlikely. Gomard was fifty-nine at the time of the boy's birth – an old man by the short life-expectancy standards of the time – and it is more probable that he was merely pressed into service at the christening service, there being no male relative of sound mind available. While Hans Christian was still small enough to be carried in his mother's arms, he was taken to 'a family party', probably at the invitation of Gomard, in the gaol. He may not have known that his grandmother's husband had been incarcerated there, but he knew it later, and his account of it in *Mit livs eventyr* makes much of the iron-barred gate and the key produced from a rattling bunch as the gaoler led them up a steep stairway to an upper room. They were served a meal by two prisoners, but Andersen recalled being too scared to eat anything. His mother made the excuse that he wasn't well and laid him on a bed in the corner. The gaol, as all local people knew, had come into being as a workhouse, founded in 1752 in an effort to clear beggars from the streets. Both then and when it housed criminals, the inmates were used as forced labour to supply the neighbouring cloth mill, for which reason the place was still referred to as 'the spinning house'. As Hans Christian lay there, fancying himself in a castle of robbers, he was uneasily certain that he could hear the whirr of spinning wheels, and felt 'afraid and on edge'.

His blue-eyed grandmother, whom Andersen adored, worked as a gardener in Odense's other institution, Greyfriars Hospital, which housed the old and insane. Once a week she brought flowers home for her grandson to arrange in a vase. 'She loved me from the bottom of her heart', he claimed. Even though the flowers were ostensibly to decorate his mother's chest of drawers, 'they were my flowers', he said firmly. 'She brought everything to me.' Sometimes in the autumn, when there was a lot of work to be done, the grandmother would take Hans Christian with her for the day, and he recalled his pleasure in playing in the garden and romping on the great heaps of pulled-up pea-haulm. The food, he said, was much better than anything he was given at home. He mingled with the less seriously afflicted patients who were allowed to walk in the courtyard, chattering cheerfully, and he sometimes ventured into the building itself.

On one occasion, he had a bad fright. He records how he found himself in a long corridor with doors on either side and, crouching down to peer through the crack in one of the doors, saw a naked woman sitting on a bed of straw. Her long hair covered her shoulders and she was singing in a most beautiful voice. And then, as if sensing the boy's presence, she leapt up and hurled herself against the door with such violence that the little trap-door of the food-hatch flew open and she pushed her arm through it, reaching down to try and touch him. Prostrate on the floor and screaming with terror, he was, he said, half dead with fear when an attendant came to rescue him.

His explorations of the asylum were not always so traumatic. Near the boiler-room where his grandmother was feeding garden rubbish into the furnace was a spinning room used by the more able-bodied inmates, and here he found a splendid audience for the garbled snippets of knowledge he had picked up from a biology book shown to him by his father. Delighted to entertain, he launched into a lecture on what he imagined to be the workings of the human body, illustrating his talk with drawings of internal organs scrawled in chalk on the door. The old women thought him 'too clever to live long', he recorded in *My Life's Fairytale*, with no hint that they might have meant it with some sarcasm. They then took over the flow of story-telling, silencing the cocky little boy with their old tales of ghosts and dark deeds and frightening him so much that he became afraid to go out after dark, feeling safer in the curtained haven of his parents' bed, where his own thoughts and dreams could be so real that the outside world hardly seemed to exist.

The Odense of the early eighteenth century was indeed a darker and more bogey-filled place than the brisk city of today. With about five thousand inhabitants, it was a teeming, overcrowded village rather than a town, and the ancient superstitions were not far below the surface. The very name, Odense, comes from *Odins vi*, meaning a place of sacrifice to the god Odin, and the powerful spirits of land and water were still very real. There was, for instance, a terrifying figure called the River Man, said to dwell in the depths of the Odense river, who demanded the annual toll of a human life as payment for his work in turning the water mills that stood along the banks. When Hans Christian was eight years old, a boy called Tyge Josias was drowned, and the local women nodded their heads and said the River Man had taken him. The unforgotten legend made a shivering appearance in Andersen's story called 'The Bell Deep'.

For all its poverty and its odd quality of slightly unhinged secretiveness, Hans Christian's home life was not loveless. Anne Marie, according to his own accounts, worshipped him, and missed no opportunity to point out his cleverness and special sensitivity to her friends. In the harvest time of one year when she and her son were gleaning corn after reaping – one of the few rights left to common people after the enclosures – an over-officious bailiff started to drive the women and children off, using a long dog-whip. Hans Christian stumbled and lost one of his wooden shoes. Unable to run barefoot over the spiky stubble, he turned to face the man and said, 'How do you dare to hit me when God may see what you do?' To everyone's astonishment, the unnerved man patted the boy on the head and gave him a coin, and Anne Marie again pointed out her son's astonishing powers.

At the age of five, Hans Christian was sent to the dame-school in the village, on his mother's strict stipulation that he was not to be beaten. Despite his familiarity with his father's books, the boy had little ability to write or spell, and the brief time he spent at the school seems to have been spent mostly in watching the clock on the wall, from which small mechanical figures emerged on every striking of the hour. Inevitably, he was given a clout for some piece of misbehaviour or inattention, and ran crying home to his mother, who promised he should never go there again.

He was sent next to a school for Jewish children, run by a young man called Fedder Carstens, then twenty-six years old, and this left strong emotional impressions which lasted throughout his life. Andersen was always easy in the company of Jews, and he shared their ready expression of feeling which he was later to find so notably lacking in many of his Lutheran compatriots. There was absolutely nothing phlegmatic about Andersen; he was impatient and passionate, never content with the low-key courtesies and kindnesses which for most people are enough to assure affection. Even as a small child, his expectations were high, and he went to school in search of unstinting admiration.

The children at Carstens' establishment were all boys except for one little girl, Sara Heimann, who was slightly older than Hans Christian, and by far his favourite among his fellow pupils. As he wrote in his first autobiography, *Levnedsbog* (*Book of My Life*):

> I still remember a beautiful little girl of about eight who kissed me and told me she wanted to marry me; this pleased me, and I always let her kiss me although I never kissed her, and I allowed nobody else apart from her to kiss me.

This aversion to being kissed is Andersen's first mention of the antipathy to females which was to be an underlying characteristic throughout his life, and he sandwiches it between equally emphatic statements about his dislike of the rough games played by the boys and his preference for the company of little girls – but only those below the age of puberty. 'I felt a strange dislike of grown-up girls aged twelve or more, they really made me shudder.'

Mr Carstens, however, was a different matter. His young pupil was happy to record as a grown man that the teacher 'always held my hand lest I should be knocked over. He was fond of me and gave me cakes and flowers and patted me on my cheeks.' In these days of hypersensitivity about child abuse, warning bells ring in any parent's mind, but it is abundantly clear that Andersen had no feeling that these attentions were unwelcome. In his first novel, *The Improvisatore*, he details an episode in which a man called Federico (which could not be much closer to Fedder Carstens) lures a young boy into a cave for what is obviously a sexual encounter. The boy, speaking as the first-person narrator, recounts this with nostalgia as if remembering a first love, and the incident (including Hans Christian's mother's outraged reaction to it) is written in such detail that one cannot help suspecting it to have been based, as most of his adult novels were, on fact. Erik Ulrichsen, in his book *H.C. Andersen og Hjertetyven* (*H.C. Anderson and the Ladykiller*) insists that Hans Christian suffered sexual abuse as a child.

The facts perhaps speak for themselves, for within a year of Andersen's attendance at Carstens' school, the establishment was abruptly closed down and Carstens left the town. He never taught again, and eventually found an occupation as manager of the telegraph office at Thorseng. Andersen, far from being traumatised, evidently had a great affection for the teacher, claiming in *Mit livs eventyr* that Carstens had been proud to have taught a boy who became a famous poet. In fact, when he looked the ex-schoolmaster up twenty years later, Carstens said he did not remember him – but that did not prevent Andersen from sending him a copy of his autobiography in 1856 or, almost at the end of his life, from sending a bust of himself to the teacher on 9 September 1872.

Sara Heimann, the little girl who befriended Andersen at school, remained as a substantial presence in his mind, acting as model for a number of beautiful young Jewish heroines in his novels. In fact, their friendship had been short-lived. Sara told Hans Christian that she wanted to be a dairy-maid when she grew up, preferably in a big manor-house – and he promptly assured her that she could have a job at his castle when he became a nobleman. When Sara laughed at the preposterous idea, he insisted that he was the child of nobility, and had been taken away from his rightful parents.

Andersen plays this down in *Mit livs eventyr*, remarking merely that he 'wanted to impress her like the old women in the hospital'. Perhaps, indeed, it was just a childhood fantasy, but equally, an incautious word at home or a repeated element in his grandmother's tales could have planted an idea which he half believed to be true. Either way, his attempt to impress Sara failed abysmally. She stared at him, then remarked to one of the other boys, 'He's mad, like his grandfather.'

'I shuddered at these words,' Andersen wrote. To be like mad Anders was his deepest dread, and at five years old, he knew already that the other children thought him odd. It did not help that his mother dressed him with all the dandyism she could muster in his father's cut-down clothes supplemented by a square of bright silk pinned across his chest to look like a waistcoat, and topped off by a kerchief tied into a floppy bow. With his gawky thinness and curly yellow hair, he must have looked something of a popinjay, the natural butt of his more roughly and comfortably dressed fellows. She seemed to be trying to dress him like a prince, though for what reason must remain conjectural.

After the closure of Carstens' school, Andersen stayed at home, happy with the company of his father and the imaginary characters of the toy theatre. At six years old, his schooling was over. At about this time, however, he went with his parents to a performance of Holberg's *The Political Tinker*, arranged as an opera and sung in German. He did not understand a word, but the lights and costumes and music enchanted him, fanning his love of the theatre into a passion which never left him.

In 1811, a great comet arrived in the sky, raising fears that it heralded the Day of Judgement and the end of the world. Andersen remembered how his mother, herself full of terror, took him with her to stand with the awestruck crowd in the square in front of St Canute's church, gazing skyward with no more hope of averting disaster than Canute the king had had of turning back the tide. When Andersen's father came out to join them, he explained that the shining fireball overhead was unimaginably far away, set on a course that could do the world no harm – but heads were shaken and Anne Marie feared again that she had married a heretic who would be punished for his sins.

The year of the comet saw Napoleon pursuing his equally invincible way northward towards the disaster that awaited him in Moscow, but its presence was marked in countless smaller ways. The exceptional quality of the grape harvest that year caused vintners to mark their corks with a comet, and the same fiery sign gave its name to Henry Bell's first ever steam-driven river boat launched on the Clyde. And for the Andersen family, it brought a bright new hope.

One of the big landowners on Funen – that part of Denmark which includes Odense – wanted a shoemaker who would settle in the village by the manor house and undertake all the cobbling needed by the noble family and its staff. In return, the successful man would be given a rent-free house, together with pasture for a cow. Such an existence would be a dream come true, a triumph which would at last silence the family lamenting. Hans Christian's father applied for the post and, as a test-piece, was given some silk to make into a pair of dancing shoes. He was to provide the leather for the soles at his own cost, but this was a small price to pay for the paradise which the job offered. When the shoes were ready, he wrapped them in a handkerchief and set off on the long walk to the manor house.

He came back white with fury. The lady had not even tried the shoes on, he said – just looked at them and said sourly that he had wasted her silk. He had taken his knife and hacked off the soles there and then, retorting that if she had wasted her silk, so had he wasted his leather. The dream lay in ruins and the family wept. Long afterwards Andersen consoled himself with the thought that, had his father passed the lady's test, he himself would probably have settled into a comfortable peasant existence and never written a word, but at the time, the disappointment was crushing.

Should it be true that Hans Christian was of royal birth, there is a strong possibility that the lady of the manor realised only after Hans senior had been given the silk – probably not from her own hands – that this particular cobbler was best left in obscurity. The secret was safe in Odense, where any wild claims on the family's part were dismissed as madness, but once brought into contact with the aristocracy, goodness only knew what chickens might come home to roost.

Whatever the cause of his abrupt dismissal, the shoemaker was in despair. His marriage to the illiterate, superstitious Anne Marie, whether as a royal shotgun affair or not, clearly left him dissatisfied, and the one frail hope of escape from the squalid pettiness of his life in the slums of Odense had been snatched away. At that low point, the last chance of the desperate presented itself. A local landowner, due for military service by virtue of his rank, was looking for some common man whom he could pay to stand in for him. Hans offered himself, and took the money. Anne Marie wept, and the neighbours said her husband was mad. Why go off and get himself shot when he had a family and a trade? They could see no glory in joining that dirty, underfed rabble, the members of which pillaged and scrounged in order to stay alive, and were only whipped back into some semblance of discipline by the brutal dominance of their officers. Napoleon's own diaries, for all their confidence, have a practical man's eye on the life of the troops, and unwittingly confirm the villagers' opinion.

Andersen afterwards romanticised his father's decision to join up, claiming that he had long admired the little emperor and wanted to serve him, but his novel *Only a Fiddler* contains a detailed account of the tempting amount of money that changed hands during an evening in the local inn.

On the morning when his father went away, Hans Christian was ill in bed with measles. There was determinedly cheerful singing and talking as the preparations for departure were made, but in *Mit livs eventyr* Andersen recalled the underlying anguish. His father

> was deeply agitated at heart; I could see it from the passionate way he kissed me goodbye. I lay in bed . . . and was alone in the room when the drums beat and my mother, weeping, went with him as far as the city gate. When they had marched off my old grandmother came in and looked at me with her gentle eyes and said it would be a good thing if I could die now, but God's will was always best. That was the first morning of real sorrow I can remember.

Hans senior was away for two years. He was perhaps fortunate that his division never managed to meet up with Napoleon's main body of troops as they went northwards in 1812. He got as far as Holstein, but the advance guard was by then well ahead, and the Danish conscripts remained scattered and uncertain.

The child he left behind had lost the only person of valuable influence in his life. His mother, for all her love, could teach him nothing, and now he was aimless and unoccupied. The money Hans had taken for his army service would be needed to buy basic essentials – which doubtless included an occasional bottle of brandy, since Anne Marie's drinking was becoming an established habit.

The only remaining place of education which Andersen could have attended was the Poor School, but there is no evidence that he went there. Anne Marie saw little value in book-learning, considering her son too clever to need to be taught anything further, as her later behaviour showed when education became compulsory. Between the ages of six and eight, the boy played in the house with his model theatre and was also fascinated by the real thing. He hung round the doors of the playhouse in Odense, begging discarded posters from Peter Junker, whose job it was to distribute them. Even though he was no more than seven, he managed to get in to see *Das Donauweibschen*, Ferdinand Kauer's light opera *The Little Lady of the Danube*. Again, the words eluded him, since the only German words he knew were *Schwester* and *Brüder*, but, undeterred, he began to make up plays for his puppets in a polyglot language of his own devising, and, stored away in his mind from that magical operatic evening was a first awareness or that mythical being, the little mermaid.

In 1814, the treaty of Kiel brought an end to the war, and the troops came home, badly defeated. Denmark had been forced to yield Norway, which it had previously ruled, to the authority of Sweden, and the Danish Crown Prince, Christian Frederik, who had for a brief while been King of Norway, returned from his northern empire to a much-reduced status as Governor of Funen. This young man, who could so possibly have been Hans Christian Andersen's father, took up residence in Odense Castle, and at about the same time, in January 1814, Andersen's shoemaker father came back as well, a sick man, broken in mind and body. Although only thirty-one, his bookish, sensitive nature had not stood up well to the crude barbarity of army life. He talked as any ex-soldier does, of the things he had done and the comedies and horrors he had witnessed, throwing in the scraps of foreign languages he had picked up and assuring the small boy who listened that he, too, would learn much from the great world which lay out there, waiting to be discovered. Hans Christian took his father's advice seriously, but Anne Marie said that if she had anything to do with it, her boy would stay here at home and not go gadding about, ruining his health.

For two years, the shoemaker tried to settle back into the life he had left, but he was haunted by the war, and in the spring of 1816 developed a high fever in which his delirious ramblings were all of Napoleon and the campaign, coupled with the delusion that he himself was in charge of the regiment, taking orders directly from the emperor. Anne Marie sent her son to seek advice from the wise woman who lived a couple of miles outside the town, and when the boy got there, the woman, having questioned him, tied a woollen thread round his arm. She made signs over him and pressed a green twig against his heart, telling him it came from the tree on which Christ had been crucified. On the way home, she said, he must walk along the river bank; if his father was going to die, he would meet his ghost.

It was a terrifying journey. When he reached the house, Anne Marie asked anxiously, 'You didn't see anything, did you?' The boy shook his head – but on the third evening after that, on 26 April 1816, his father died. Throughout that night, his corpse lay on the bed that was said to have been a count's bier, and Anne Marie and her son slept as best they could on the floor. A cricket chirped throughout the dark hours, and Andersen remembered his mother saying to it, 'You needn't call him – the Ice Maiden has taken him.' He knew what she meant. In the previous winter, when the windows had been covered with frost, one of the patterns had looked like a girl with her arms outstretched. 'She has come to fetch me,' the sick man had said.

Hans Christian's shoemaker father was buried in St Canute's churchyard, not far from the place where the awestruck crowd had watched the comet blaze in the sky. The boy he left behind was eleven years old.

The shoemaker's death left Anne Marie and her son destitute. Hans Christian was alone in the one-roomed dwelling for most of the day while his mother went out to earn a little money as a washerwoman. While he still played with the toy theatre, he had moved also into the idea of being an actor himself, and nine years later described in a long letter to his benefactor, Jonas Collin, how he used to stand before the mirror with his mother's apron round his shoulders in place of a cloak, fancying himself the knight in *Das Donauweibschen*.

Not far from the house lived two old ladies, the widow and the sister of a minister by the name of Bunkeflod who had at the time been moderately well known as a poet. His sister in particular was immensely proud of this fact, and spoke almost with awe of 'my brother, the poet'. The word she used, *digter*, like the German *Dichter*, carries overtones of *gravitas* for which there is no English equivalent, and the eleven-year-old Hans Christian was deeply impressed. That a person could become an actual *digter* was a totally new possibility. He gazed with reverence at the shelves of books in the Bunkeflod house, and the two ladies, touched by his excitement, took him under their wing. They introduced him to Shakespeare, whose name he never managed to spell, even as an adult, and he promptly started writing sub-Shakespearian dramas for his puppets.

His first effort was derived from *Pyramus and Thisbe*, and although the Bunkeflod ladies were amused when he read it aloud to them, his mother's neighbours were not. He had called his piece *Arbor and Elvira*, but the woman who lived next door cut him off very firmly when he started to declaim it to her. Arbor was a bore, she said. Anne Marie consoled him, remarking that the neighbour was only jealous because her son couldn't have written it – but her reassurance was a little half-hearted. The boy who lived next door might not be as clever as her Hans Christian, but at least he went to work in the clothmill and brought home a wage each week.

Andersen was always tall for his age, and by the time he was twelve, his idleness became something of a local scandal. Anne Marie defended him, but with decreasing conviction. She was dismayed by his infatuation for the real-life theatre, and things came to a head when he performed for her benefit an entire ballet-pantomime of his own devising. According to his thinly disguised recall of this in *Only A Fiddler*, she threatened to apprentice him to a tightrope acrobat who would feed him on oil to make his limbs supple, but her son accepted this idea quite happily, thus calling his mother's bluff.

Anne Marie made what money she could as a washerwoman, up to the knees for long hours in the cold river, lifting and twisting the wet, heavy sheets and increasingly often sending Hans Christian to fetch her a drop of brandy. Any other mother would have set her son to work – but Anne Marie shrank from flinging her special, sensitive boy into the rough world of employment. The neighbours scorned her reluctance and at last, persuaded by their nagging, she sent the lad, now as tall as a man, to work in the clothmill. It was partially staffed by prisoners from their neighbouring Odense Gaol, but it also took workers from the town, including about twenty children of between nine and twelve years old, whose job was to keep the machines supplied with raw wool.

Andersen's autobiography is frank in admitting that the idea of working in this place horrified him. He 'wasn't suited at all to being put with other wild boys and girls'. On the first day, his grandmother escorted him to the factory gate where she wept and kissed him, saying that this would never have happened had his father still been alive. It was the worst possible send-off, for the boy must have gone in feeling hard-done-by and without any real intention of working as the others did. Half-hearted about his tasks, he began to sing instead. The bored workers were only too ready to listen, for the new boy had a clear soprano voice and a great repertoire of songs. They egged him on – but when he came to the end of all he knew, he turned to reciting scenes from Holberg instead, which went down much less well. On the following day, he was told curtly to get on with his work, which he did with fumbling clumsiness, deeply embarrassed by the dirty stories exchanged by the mill-hands. At last he began to cry. This, combined with his effete appearance and his soprano voice, provoked one of the workers to say he didn't believe young Andersen was a boy at all – perhaps they'd better make sure. He was grabbed and stripped of his trousers, and when he managed to tear himself free, he ran home in floods of tears. The guilt-stricken Anne Marie caved in at once and said he should never go back.

She made one more effort to get him into employment, this time in a tobacco factory in Vestergade. Here, by Andersen's account, his singing was a longer-lasting success, largely because he took care never to run out of material. When his repertoire was exhausted, he simply improvised words and tunes of his own. 'Meanwhile,' he added, 'I was taken ill, and my mother thought it might be the tobacco affecting my lungs, which it wasn't, for I've always had good lungs; however, she removed me once again, saying she was afraid I might die from it.'

Whether Anne Marie suspected, as her beloved boy approached puberty, that his natural inclination was very different from her own robust heterosexuality, cannot be proved. Certainly she saw that he was effeminate and vulnerable to attack from young males who sensed his oddness and would not tolerate it, but she had no means of even starting to approach the probable truth. The taboo of the day was manifest in profound ignorance, and while Anne Marie had a rough, farmyard knowledge of sex and reproduction, the idea of something different from the male-female coupling came into the category of half-understood jokes about the unthinkable. If her son showed signs of approaching this unknown, appalling area, it could only – must only – be because of his brilliance. Genius and eccentricity went hand-in-hand; everyone said so. Hans Christian was different from the others, yes, but only because he was refined and sensitive and clever.

Andersen accepted his mother's catch-all excuse without reservation. Clearly aware that he was a canary among sparrows, he sheltered behind a public presentation of himself as the boy who was going to be a *digter* – or, as he believed at the time, an actor. Relieved of any more attendances at a place of work, he went back to his pleasant days of cutting and stitching clothes for his puppets and reading the books at the Bunkeflods' house. He made a white satin pincushion for Mrs Bunkeflod's birthday, and was always on the hunt for scraps of bright silk or velvet, and Anne Marie suggested with a flash of inspiration that he might like to be apprenticed to a local tailor, Mr Stegmann. She was met with a firm refusal. Hans Christian wanted to be an actor.

This was too much. Actors were well known to be shiftless and immoral – the idea was unthinkable. Perhaps nudged by the rumour that elementary education was about to become compulsory (which it did the following year, in 1818), Anne Marie sent her son back to school. This time, there was no choice. He went to the Poor School, housed in what used to be the old workhouse, where a solitary Norwegian called Welhaven did his best to instil the rudiments of literacy, arithmetic and Holy Scripture. Andersen admits in his recollections of this period that he could hardly spell a single word – and yet he was dilatory about his studies, not bothering to open his homework book except to try to scramble some sort of work into his head as he walked to school. It may well be that Anne Marie, clinging to her determination that he must be brilliant, did not want to concede that there was much he did not know. She pointed out with pride to her friends that Hans Christian had no need to do homework, his glance at the book on the morning walk was enough.

Welhaven was no Carstens, and young Andersen's attempts to curry favour did him no good. The teacher was merely irritated when the gangling boy presented him with a garland of flowers and a poem of his own composition on his birthday. It did not endear him to his schoolmates, either. They knew how he stood on the patch of ground between his house and the mill-stream, singing in his high voice in the summer evenings for anyone who would listen. They knew, too, that the people next door, a Mr Falbe and his ex-actress wife, brought their friends out to listen to 'the little nightingale of Funen' as he was starting to be called. Sometimes he was given a few coppers for singing at people's houses, and the town notabilities began to take in interest in him. Among them was the influential Colonel Christian Høegh-Guldberg, whose father, Ove, had been personal tutor to King Frederick VI as a boy and later his Cabinet Secretary. Quite why Guldberg should have interested himself as closely as he did in the welfare of a boy from the Odense backstreets is not clear. Because of his long-established and very intimate family connection with the Court, it could be possible that he knew more about young Andersen than the boy himself did.

Hans Christian was not doing well at school. Brought up by Anne Marie to think himself too perfect to need the benefits of education, he took little interest in anything other than the Old Testament stories which Welhaven used to deliver with apocalyptic fire. In the playground Andersen persisted in telling his own tales, always featuring himself as the hero, and he became increasingly unpopular. On one occasion, he was chased home by the other boys, pelted and shouted at like his mad grandfather before him.

Høegh-Guldberg came to see Anne Marie, perhaps a little disturbed to hear of the boy's arrogant behaviour, and advised her to get him settled into a trade apprenticeship. It was easier said than done. Reading between the lines of Andersen's own accounts of his childhood, Anne Marie's attitude to her son had from the start been one of boundless admiration and protectiveness. Seeking to reassure him that his delicacy and vulnerability were signs of special talents, she had failed completely to establish any authority over the boy, and it was too late now to make him do anything against his will.

In the autumn of 1817, an invitation – or command – came from the owners of a manor house in which Anne Marie had once worked, requiring her and her son to join the workers in the annual hop-picking. It is not known through what mechanism contact was made, or why a woman who lived so far from the manor should be specifically selected. Andersen himself seemed to regard it as a kind of holiday, but it is not impossible that Guldberg or some other go-between was making it possible for the boy to be seen and inspected by a titled family which knew the truth about him.

The manor house was two days' walk from Odense, so presumably south or west of the town, since the sea was relatively close in other directions. Andersen himself recorded that the lady of the house was generous with good food, and he seemed to find the work in the big barn pleasant enough as the hops were stripped from the bines, accompanied by the singing of songs and telling of stories. On this occasion he was a listener rather than a performer. Fate and superstition featured constantly in what he heard, and one old peasant observed that God knew everything, both what had happened and what lay in the future.

The boy was much struck by the words. That evening, wandering alone and gazing at the countryside, he found himself thinking again about the omnipotence of God. He came to a deep pond and made his way out to a large stone which stood in its centre, staring down into the water. Was everything predestined? As far as he knew, God planned that he should live long, but what if he should jump into the water now, and prove God wrong by drowning? The obvious corollary that this action, too, might be planned by the Almighty did not seem to occur to him, and for a moment, the desire to challenge this highest power was so overwhelming that he turned to the deepest part of the pool, determined to plunge in. He was stopped by a mental voice which seemed to say clearly that this temptation was the work of the Devil, and ran in a panic back to the barn, where he flung himself hysterically into his mother's arms and could not explain what had happened. The peasant women shook their heads and said he must have seen a ghost.

In the following year, on 8 July 1818, Anne Marie, now in her mid-forties, married again. Her new husband, Niels Jørgensen Gundersen, was ten years younger than her and, like the dead Hans, a shoemaker. In every other way, he was very different, blunt and unimaginative, with little sympathy for his new wife's peculiar son. His family did not like Anne Marie, who had brought nothing whatever to the marriage in terms of money or possessions, and Niels did not like Hans Christian's blue-eyed grandmother. She became, Andersen said afterwards, 'a stranger in the house; I was the bond which kept her there, and I often cried with grief at her silent suffering, for she had suddenly turned old with sorrow.' In *Only A Fiddler* he depicts the marriage (similar in almost every respect) as a strain on the wife, torn between her new husband and her son. Increasingly, as probably happened in reality, it was the husband who had his way.

To a thirteen-year-old boy, sharing a tiny room with his mother and her newly wed husband must have brought embarrassingly intimate evidence of their sexual activity. Andersen's father had died only two years previously, and it must have seemed to him at this particularly vulnerable stage of his own development that his mother's appallingly audible lovemaking with this new man was a betrayal. It can only have added to the revulsion for female sexuality which was to become a dominating factor in his life.

The problem of what to do with her son became more pressing for Anne Marie in her new marriage. Gundersen had no sympathy for an overgrown lad of approaching fourteen who still behaved like a dependent child, and time was running out. At fourteen, boys and girls were confirmed and then began their adult lives, seeking apprenticeships or, if necessary, leaving home to go into service. Anne Marie again pointed out the magnificence of Mr Stegmann's tailoring shop with its big windows through which one could see the apprentices and journeymen sitting cross-legged on tables, but apart from a passing thought that it might be a good source of offcuts, Hans Christian showed no interest. He was in a sense already engaged in the writer's informal apprenticeship of observing and imagining, and liked nothing better than to play in the mill-race behind the house.

In this slightly spooky place, three great water-wheels turned in the river, stopping abruptly when the sluice-gates were closed and the mill-pond drained away, and in that eerie moment, fish jumped in the remaining puddles and water-rats came out of their holes. Hans Christian would venture out across the river bed, catching the slippery fish in his hands, fearful that at any minute the sluice-gates would begin their creaking rise and let the pent-up water rush out in a foaming torrent that sent him scrambling back to the bank as fast as he could. One of the women who washed her clothes in the river alongside Anne Marie said the Empire of China lay under the river bed, and the boy fancied – or so he later claimed – that as he sat there one moonlit night, singing, a Chinese prince would swim up through the water and take Hans Christian back to his own country, to be installed in a magnificent castle. On return to Odense, he promised himself, he would build a castle there, too.

Such fantasies may have been no more than the normal dreams of a spoiled boy who could not face the come-down of living in the world inhabited by ordinary people, but it is just possible that there may have been a more specific explanation. When Crown Prince Frederik Christian returned to Odense and took up residence in the Castle, he made contact with the boy. The usually accepted explanation has been that this happened through a mild interest in this lad with the fine soprano voice, and that the interview was arranged by Colonel Guldberg, but Andersen's two biographies show an interesting variance in their reporting of the episode. The early and somewhat artless *Levnedsbog* reveals that it was Andersen's mother who first started going to the castle, taking her twelve-year-old son with her to play with Prince Fritz (later King Frederik VII) and various other 'bourgeois children' in the big courtyard. This record details how Fritz's father, Frederik Christian, came out to sit with the children as they played, watched by the princess from the window, and how it was only after a break in the visits that Colonel Guldberg set up a personal meeting to discuss Hans Christian's future. The later account in *Mit livs eventyr* is far more circumspect, making no mention of this early, casual-sounding contact – and it must be remembered that the first autobiography was never published in Andersen's lifetime. If he learned later that the Crown Prince's interest in him was truly a fatherly one, it may have explained why, despite his passion for publication of everything he wrote, this first, faintly indiscreet life story was never made public. Whereas *Mit livs eventyr* is ingratiating, constantly stressing the friendship and generosity of the royal family, the earlier book is filled with the unselfconscious petulance of a young man who does not know he has been favoured. Guldberg, it admits, advised him to say, should the prince ask his intentions, that he wanted to go to the Grammar School. But Andersen's real intentions were very different:

> I acted some scenes from Holberg for him and sang something improvised, and when he asked me if I wanted to go on the stage, I freely admitted it, but told him that people had advised me to *say* I wanted to study. The prince, finding this unacceptable, said that *as a poor child* I should instead learn a good trade as, for instance, a wood-turner. But I didn't want to do that. "Decide on such a course and tell me so, then I will consider you." I was not at all amused by this, and afterwards would not talk to him. He on the other hand often talked of me at the Colbiørnsens' . . .

The emphases are Andersen's own, revealing his indignation and the fatal over-confidence which had led him to blow his chances with the man who, father or not, could have rescued him from ignorance and poverty. Poor Anne Marie had nurtured in her boy all the trappings of empty grandeur, but she could not teach him the first essentials of how to be a gentleman. The Crown Prince must have seen that this turbulent, arrogant creature was in no frame of mind to benefit from education, and perhaps never would be. Safer by far to tuck him away in decent obscurity, even if to 'consider' him would cost years of quiet support.

Hans Christian went back to his uneasy life at home, idling his time away at the Poor School and growing fast into the beanpole lankiness which must in the early nineteenth century have been quite unusual. (A report on the physique of conscripted men in 1799 states that 72% were less than 1.50 metres – about 5ft 2ins – tall.) At thirteen, the problem of his future became acute. Anne Marie had been hoping he would settle for a tailoring apprenticeship, considering his love of silks and velvets, but whatever he did, he must first go to confirmation classes, for no boy could be accepted as an apprentice until he had been confirmed. After that, his childhood would be officially over, and he really would have to make some kind of move.

To this day, confirmation remains a rite of passage for many Danish families, but in the nineteenth century it was also a distinct division of the young people into their appropriate social classes. In Odense, the grammar school children, a select group from richer homes, went to the dean for their instruction, whereas the poor ones with little or no education were catered for by the curate. Andersen, claiming perhaps with truth that he was terrified of the rough boys in the curate's class, presented himself to the dean. He admitted afterwards that the man must have thought this an act of colossal vanity – and, of course, it turned out to be a mistake. The grammar school children were affronted to have such a guttersnipe pushing his way in, and made it clear that he was not welcome. His usual singing and reciting made things worse, and when Dean Tetens caught him declaiming a scene from a play in front of an astonished audience of fellow-students, he threatened him with expulsion from the class. One girl, Laura Tønder-Lund, the daughter of a Privy Councillor, might well have been aware that the strange boy had been the playmate of the Crown Prince's son, for her sister was married to P.N. Møller Holst, tutor to Prince Fritz. Laura befriended Andersen and gave him a rose, but the rest of the group remained hostile.

The confirmation ceremony demanded presentable clothes. Hans Christian wore a suit made from his dead father's overcoat and in place of his usual wooden shoes, was given his first-ever pair of leather boots. He was so impressed with these that he tucked his trousers inside them, so that everyone could admire them, and creaked his way up the aisle on 18 April 1819 to be confirmed in the Christian faith. Years later, he recorded in a story called 'The Bell' – perhaps the best thing he ever wrote – how guilty he felt about allowing the new boots to fill his mind rather than the spirit of God.

A month went by, and still he remained at home – and then a touring company from the Royal Theatre of Copenhagen came to Odense. Hans Christian, with no money for a ticket, hung round the stage door continually, talking to any actor who would listen about his passion for the stage, and, good-naturedly, they let him in to watch the performances from backstage. They even gave him a walk-on part as a page in the operetta *Cendrillon*, with a line to say. His days passed in breathless anticipation of the wonderful evening, and he was always the first of the company to arrive, eager to put on the red silk costume, enchanted by the make-up and the general air of practical magic which

makes the theatre so irresistible to its devotees. By the time the
company went on, Andersen's mind was made up. He would go to
Copenhagen and become an actor.

The Greek chorus of neighbours bewailed such folly, and Anne
Marie was utterly dismayed. She predicted hardship and ruin from this
devilish occupation but Hans Christian was too used to getting his own
way to be deterred now. In a stormy confrontation he wept and prayed
and promised that fame would come, even though actors first had to
'suffer terribly' – it said so in the books he had read. The illiterate
Anne Marie was unable to counter this, and there can be no doubt that
she wanted to get this great boy, now six feet tall, out of the tiny
dwelling where he, she and her husband were uncomfortably close.

An actress called Helene Hammer who happened to be visiting the
town said she would take young Andersen with her when she went
back to Copenhagen, but the promise came to nothing. Although
Hans Christian made himself useful by carrying notes to the young
man with whom Miss Hammer was in love, the actress finally admitted
that she was heavily in debt and could not afford the coach fare to
Copenhagen. The lad would have to go by himself.

Andersen had saved up thirteen rixdollars by hoarding the coins
people had given him for singing. At a time when an unskilled worker
earned two rixdollars a week, it was a considerable achievement. Even
so, it was not enough for the coach fare, but the driver could be bribed
for three rixdollars to let a passenger ride as a 'stowaway'. Anne Marie
accepted the inevitable. He'd soon turn back, she told her neighbours,
when he saw the stormy sea that lay between Funen and Zealand. Then
he'd be home again, and settle down as a tailor's apprentice. His
grandmother said he might even become a clerk, but nobody took that
seriously. Clerks had to be able to write and spell, and Anne Marie's
boy, for all his much-vaunted cleverness, was no good at that.

The wise woman was consulted about the adventure which lay
ahead. Coffee dregs were studied and the cards laid out – and the
pronouncement, according to Andersen's account of it, was exactly
what he wanted to hear. 'Your son will be a great man,' the woman told
Anne Marie, 'and in his honour all Odense will one day be
illuminated.' It is tempting to wonder whether such a confident
prediction was based on overheard gossip about the boy's reputedly
noble origins, but whatever the truth, it brought Anne Marie's
objections to an end. Her concern was now to find a travelling

companion for Hans Christian, and she hit on Sophie Charlotte Hermansen, who had come to Odense as a nurse to the infant Prince Ferdinand twenty-seven years ago and was now returning to Copenhagen. Again, Anne Marie's informal intimacy with the domestic doings of the Court suggests that she had, at the least, a long-established servant relationship with it.

Hans Christian himself was looking ahead with as much practicality as he could muster. He knew that he needed a letter (or preferably letters) of introduction, for no properly equipped person would venture abroad without the means of contact with people who would offer help and hospitality. He had already approached Colonel Høegh-Guldberg, who had promised to contact the director of the Royal Theatre on his behalf, a Colonel F. von Holstein, but Guldberg was now himself away on a tour of Denmark and Norway. In some desperation, Andersen went to see the local printer and bookseller, Christian Henrik Iversen, who had been on hobnobbing terms with the touring troupe of actors, and asked him for a letter of introduction to Madame Schall, Denmark's leading ballerina, whose name he had heard mentioned with reverence.

Iversen did not know Madame Schall. Neither did he know Andersen, and his first reaction was to try to talk the boy out of the whole idea. He should stay in Odense and learn a trade, he said but Hans Christian retorted angrily that to do so would be 'a shame'. The fierceness of his answer, as the Iversen family later admitted, so impressed the printer that he determined to do what he could to help. He wrote the letter as asked, and Andersen bore it away like a talisman, worthless though it was. Far more valuable, though he did not know it at the time, would be the lasting friendship of the Iversens.

On 4 September 1819, Hans Christian's mother and grandmother went with him, weeping bitterly, to where the coach stood waiting at the city gate, complete with the motherly Mrs Hermansen. The boy said his goodbyes and climbed up to his outside 'stowaway' seat, and the horses moved off. He would not see his grandmother again, for she died the following year and was buried in a pauper's grave.

It was, he remembered, a bright, sunny afternoon as the heavy coach rumbled out of Odense on the long drive to the ferry boat, and his spirits soon lifted after the sad farewell. At last he was on his way to the fulfilment of his dreams. Only when he stood on deck and watched the island of Funen recede across the widening strip of water did his resolution waver as his mother had predicted. In a frightening moment, he realised how alone and friendless he was, and knew, too, that it was too late to turn back. When the ship docked in Zealand and the passengers went ashore, he crept away behind a hut where he could not be seen, and fell on his knees and prayed.

Andersen came to Copenhagen in the early morning of 6 September 1819, a date which he was to celebrate for the rest of his life. The city was in a state of uproar, for the anti-Semitic rioting which had originated in north Germany had now spread across the border into Denmark. It was to be the country's last pogrom but, having flared up on 4 September, it ran for ten days, with appalling violence against Jewish people. The boy from Funen had no idea what was happening, and wondered if these were the normal wicked ways of the city that he had been warned about. Having descended from the coach on Frederiksberg Hill with his little bundle of clothes, he walked through the park and down the long avenue to the town centre. He found himself a room at the Guards Inn, one of the first small hostelries he came to, then made his way to his mecca – the theatre.

On that Monday morning, its doors were still closed, but Andersen walked round the building several times, gazing up at this place which, he was sure, was going to be a home to him. A ticket-tout noticed him and came up to ask if he wanted a ticket for the evening's performance, and Andersen in his simplicity thought the man was offering to give him one. He accepted with glad thanks, and was startled by the resulting torrent of abuse.

Madame Schall remained his best hope. He arrived on her doorstep later the same day, wearing his confirmation suit and the squeaky boots, plus a hat which was too large for him and slipped down over his eyes. Before daring to ring the bell, he fell on his knees to pray that this interview might bring him success and was found there by a housemaid who came up the area steps. Taking him for a beggar, she put a small coin in his hand and waved aside his protests. 'Oh, keep it, keep it,' she said.

The door was opened, and Andersen produced his treasured letter. After some delay, he was ushered into the presence of Madame Schall, who gazed at him in astonishment. She had never heard of a printer in Odense called Iversen, but nevertheless asked the gawky boy what role he thought he could play.

'Cinderella,' he said at once, since it was *Cendrillon* in which he had spoken his solitary line on those dizzy theatrical nights. He asked permission to take off his boots because they impeded his dancing, and then burst into the leading-ballerina role, singing and leaping about, using the large hat as a tambourine.

Madame Schall admitted to Andersen years later that she had thought he was mad. She offered him a free meal in her kitchen but got rid of him as quickly as she could, adding that he might like to approach Bournonville, the Royal Theatre ballet-master, but the boy was inconsolable. He had hoped for nothing less than instant recognition and acceptance, and left the house in tears.

The next day, he was back at the theatre, trusting that whatever Colonel Høegh-Guldberg had said to the director would weigh in his favour. Holstein looked at the gangling lad and said bluntly that he was too thin to be an actor. He was not won over when Andersen promised that he'd get fatter if he could just be taken on and paid ten rixdollars a week, and delivered the unvarnished truth. The theatre did not employ uneducated people. Snatching at the faint hope offered by Madame Schall, Andersen asked if there might be an opening in the ballet school, but learned that this, too, was unlikely. No new dancers would be taken on until May, eight months hence, and even then, there could be no question of any payment. Once again, Andersen left in tears.

This time, all hope seemed to have gone. He toyed, as he would so often do, with ideas of suicide, then remembered from his experience at the hop-picking that such a challenge to God's will would be a sin – and spent the last of his money on a gallery ticket for that night's performance of *Paul et Virginie*. The tragic plot reduced him to tears again, and the women sitting beside him pointed out that it was only a play and he shouldn't upset himself. One of them gave him a sausage sandwich, and as he ate it he explained that Paul, the hero of the operetta, was like himself and Virginie was his beloved theatre, lost to him. He told them the whole story of how he had come penniless, from Odense, and they gave him another sausage sandwich and a cake and some fruit.

When he had paid his bill at the inn the next day, he had only one rixdollar left. The choice was stark. He must either go down to the harbour and try to find a skipper who would let him work a passage back to Funen or seek an apprenticeship in Copenhagen. The latter was slightly less humiliating; at least in the capital city, nobody knew him and there would be no gloating over his failure.

He turned in desperation to Mrs Hermansen, his coach companion, who had put up for a few days in the same inn, and she obligingly bought him a meal and paid for a further night's lodging. With robust common sense, she took him out the following day to buy a newspaper, and helped him peruse it in search of apprenticeships offered. Somewhat gloomily, Hans Christian picked a carpenter by the name of Madsen, living in Borgergade, and went to see him. Madsen seemed a pleasant man, but before he could enter into the binding agreement which apprenticeship demanded, he would need certificates from Odense to prove that the lad came of a respectable family and had been baptised and confirmed. Until these had been obtained, he was willing to take the boy on trial to see how he got on. He would live in the master's house with the other apprentices.

Andersen was ready for work at six the next morning, earlier than anyone else, but his fear and dread returned as he watched the other apprentices and journeymen come in, talking and laughing among themselves. As he admits in *Mit livs eventyr*, their ribald humour left him 'as bashful as a girl'. The embarrassing incident at the cloth-mill had added to his terrors, and as he stood there blushing, his distress was noticed by his fellow-workers and freely commented on. The taunts worsened, and after a few hours he burst into hysterical weeping and rushed to Madsen to pour out his confession of how he could not bear the jokes and foul language. He could not become a carpenter, he said, it was impossible. Madsen tried to calm him down and assure him that it would be all right, but the distraught boy thanked him for his kindness, and fled.

Utterly forlorn, he wandered through the streets in the late autumn afternoon, all his high hopes in ruins. Even the kindness of Mrs Hermansen, his one friend in this entire city, had proved to be of no help – and he now knew that he would never be able to fall back on the taking up of a trade. His strange appearance and hypersensitive nature made it impossible.

Mulling over the day's events, he remembered how, looking through the paper for an apprenticeship, he had seen a report about Signor Siboni having been appointed as the new director of the Academy of Music in Copenhagen. It had been a disapproving notice, since the appointment of foreigners to leading posts was not popular in

Denmark, but for Andersen, the opinions expressed were not important. His soprano voice was still unbroken, and to sing for this man Siboni was the last faint chance of opening the doors which seemed so firmly locked against him.

The housekeeper explained to the gaunt boy who stood on the doorstep that the master was holding a dinner party and could not be disturbed, but Andersen was too desperate to be put off by such protests. He poured out his story, and the woman listened in mounting concern. She took him in and sat him down, and said she would have a word with Signor Siboni.

She was away for some time, and when she returned, she brought not only her master, but his assembled company of guests, including the poet Jens Baggesen and Professor C.E.F. Weyse, a leading composer of the time. Andersen had burst in at just the right time, for their meal was over, and after a few questions, they led him into the drawing room, where Siboni sat down at the piano and invited the strange boy to sing.

Knowing that his whole future depended on this impromptu audition, Andersen sang song after song, then recited several poems and a couple of scenes from Holberg then burst into tears. The sympathetic audience applauded, and he perhaps cheered up a little too readily, for Baggesen cautioned him not to be vain when receiving applause. Siboni, with Italian impetuosity, declared the lad to be an extraordinary find and promised to train him, predicting that he would sing in the Royal Theatre.

Andersen was in a tumult of laughter and tears. When the housekeeper let him out, she patted his cheek and advised him to go and see Professor Weyse the next morning, because the composer intended to do something for him.

Christophe Weyse had come from a poor background himself, and understood the practicalities of the boy's needs. On the night at Siboni's, he collected seventy-six rixdollars from his fellow-guests, enough to meet Andersen's needs for about six months, with care. Weyse would give him ten rixdollars from this fund each month, and he must find himself cheap lodgings and go to Signor Siboni's house each day for singing lessons.

The grant was pitifully small, but anyone more skilled in such matters than Andersen might have spent it more wisely. He took a windowless room little better than a cupboard, opening off the kitchen of an apartment owned by a midwife, Mrs Thorgesen, in a street where almost every dwelling was a brothel. Once installed in this unsalubrious place, he wrote his first letter home. It said nothing of his trials and disappointments, and when Anne Marie had it read to her, she was so proud that she showed it to everyone. Some smiled, Andersen recorded in his autobiography, and others shook their heads, doubting where all this would lead.

While living at Mrs Thorgesen's house, Andersen hunted up his aunt Christiane, whose silken finery had so unaccountably annoyed his mother on that long-ago visit. He found out that she was now called Mrs Jansen, having reputedly married a sea-captain, and perhaps thought she might offer him accommodation, for his account of the meeting certainly suggests that Christiane felt put-upon. He recorded the episode only in *Levnedsbogen*, deleting all mention of it from the later autobiography. Receiving her nephew in an elegant sitting-room, Christiane launched into a tirade about Anne Marie's coarseness and ignorance. 'And she now saddles me with her child!' she added indignantly, having detailed her sister's shortcomings – 'a boy, at that! If only you'd been a girl!' Andersen understood what she meant when, a few minutes later, a man was ushered into the room, where a well-dressed girl had sat throughout his meeting with his aunt. Christiane hustled her nephew out, concluding the interview in an attic room where she said without enthusiasm that he could come and see her whenever he liked.

Fuller information on the running of a brothel was supplied by Andersen's landlady, Mrs Thorgesen, who explained in plain terms exactly how his aunt lived. The sea-captain, it turned out, was merely a boatswain, and was a lover rather than a husband but Andersen wanted no further details. His suspicion that female sexuality was monstrously corrupt had received an appalling confirmation. His mother had a secret, embarrassing daughter hidden away, and she had brought a new man into the bed she had shared with Andersen's beloved father, and now his aunt was found to be catering for the depraved needs of men, and making good money at it. He never contacted Christiane again, and even in his first cautious account of their one meeting, claimed that he had forgotten her name.

Later on, he found that Mrs Thorgesen herself was not above a little dabbling in the sexual trade. A young woman who took the room above Andersen's cubby-hole had a night-time caller, an older man in a

high-buttoned coat and a hat pulled down over his eyes whom Mrs
Thorgesen said was the girl's father, come to take a cup of tea with her.
She warned her young lodger that the couple were on no account to
be disturbed, as the father was very shy. Andersen, who sometimes let
the man in through the back door, wondered why the girl wept on
evenings when his visit was due, but it was only years later, recognising
the man at some glittering event, in evening dress and with medals
across his chest, that he realised the reason for the shyness, and for the
girl's tears.

Each morning, he walked from his lodgings to Siboni's house and
stayed there all day, though his individual singing lessons happened
only about twice a month. There was a major snag in that the maestro
spoke only the most rudimentary Danish. Most educated Danes could
get by in German, and it was in this language that Siboni
communicated with his students but Andersen's knowledge of
German was limited to the few phrases picked up by his father, and his
failure to understand irritated Siboni and turned the lessons into a
nightmare of incomprehension and bad temper. He went again to Mrs
Hermansen, whose son was a student, and begged for help, and she
arranged for him to have German lessons free of charge with a Jens
Worm Bruun.

He could not learn fast enough to understand Siboni's increasingly
impatient instructions, and grew more and more frightened of him.
The opera singers from the theatre company came to rehearse each
day at the house, and Andersen was often asked to attend the session,
but it only intensified his panic to hear how even these accomplished
professionals were bellowed at by the temperamental maestro. Siboni,
crimson-faced, would rant at them in his imperfect German or in the
Italian which none of them understood, and Andersen grew to dread
his private lessons. He cringed and trembled, and when asked to sing
scales, was so terrified that his voice shook and tears came to his eyes.
Siboni tried to be kind to the boy, pressing a few coins into his hand
and telling him in execrable Danish to be 'no fright', but increasingly
often, the lessons ended with an exasperated shrug and a wave of
dismissal.

Andersen was happier in the kitchen quarters, running errands for
the maids and the Italian cook and enjoying their undemanding
friendship. He fitted in so easily that he began to seem like one of the
staff, but on the day when he carried a dish of food to the table of the

Siboni family, the maestro raged into the kitchen to inform the cook that his pupil was not in the house to be used as a waiter.

After that, Andersen was forbidden to go into the kitchen and had to spend his time in the drawing-room, with little to do except attend the rehearsal sessions and go to his German lessons. He was pressed into service as a model by Siboni's niece, Marietta, who was doing sketches for a portrait of her uncle in the title role of Achilles in Paer's opera, *The Revenge of Achilles*, being required to wear the costume so that she could draw the drapery of tunic and toga. Siboni was of vast operatic girth, and Marietta went into peals of laughter at the sight of Andersen's lanky scarecrow figure swamped by the folds of cloth, but she, unlike her uncle, was not frightening.

Siboni himself was having a difficult time. His Italian flamboyance was going down badly with the reticent, sober Danes who already resented the fact that a foreigner was running their premier music school, and his determination to introduce Italian opera to the Copenhagen stage was received with hostility, even though Rossini and Bellini were all the rage in the rest of Europe. Siboni's productions were unpopular, and public taste was a long way from the Verdi-fever which would later grip the country. Unfortunately for him, Siboni's salary partially depended on the proceeds of a benefit performance with himself in the leading role, and whereas this had produced handsome results in other countries, the Danes refused to be impressed. Even Napoleon had admired his rendering of Achilles – hence the portrait by the niece – but at the benefit performance in Copenhagen, the audience hissed and catcalled until the curtain had to be brought down.

Siboni's authority, both as performer and teacher, was effectively destroyed. Copenhagen's cultured circles cackled with delight over his humiliation, and his students felt free to laugh openly at his linguistic errors. The maestro's temper shortened even further, and he was less inclined to bother with the tremulous, weepy boy whose voice, in any case, was beginning to show its first signs of roughness. In April 1820, a few days after Andersen's fifteenth birthday, Siboni called him in and told him bluntly that he would never be any use on the stage. Neither his appearance nor his manners were suitable, and his voice was starting to break. It would be three or four years before it settled into a tenor or bass range, and Siboni was not prepared to keep him on for that length of time. He had better go back to Odense and learn a trade.

The blow fell at the point when the fund collected by Weyse and his friends had run out. The winter had been a hard one; Andersen's boots were leaking and he had no warm underwear which, he claimed, was the reason for the loss of quality in his voice. He went to Weyse to plead for further support, but the composer, well aware that Siboni had discarded the lad as hopeless, saw no point in any further efforts. He gave Andersen a little money, and paid scant attention to his suggestion that he might stay in Copenhagen and become apprenticed to a watchmaker. The boy had been given his chance, and he had muffed it, and Weyse could only hope that he was not going to become an embarrassing nuisance.

After only six months, it seemed that Andersen's luck had run out. Again, he cast about desperately for someone who might help him, and hit upon Colonel Guldberg's brother, a Copenhagen-domiciled academic, Professor Frederik Høegh-Guldberg. He sat down and wrote the professor a careful letter. Ironically, it was his many mistakes in spelling and syntax which moved Guldberg to do something about him. How much the professor had heard about the boy from his brother in Odense must remain speculative but he was extraordinarily generous in terms of both time and money. He took Andersen on as a pupil in German and in basic Danish grammar, and raised a subscription for his further support. Contributors included the composer Friedrich Kuhlau and the eminent author, councillor and president of the Royal Society of Arts, Just Mathias Thiele.

Andersen was punctilious in going to thank each of his benefactors personally, and Thiele's autobiography, *Af mit livs aarboger*, left an evocative description of the strange figure which presented itself in his office:

> I was surprised to see a lanky boy, of a most extraordinary appearance, standing in the doorway, making a theatrical bow right down to the floor. He had already thrown his cap down by the door, and when he raised his long figure in a shabby, grey coat, the sleeves of which did not reach as far as his emaciated wrists, my glance met a couple of tiny, Chinese eyes, badly in need of a surgical operation to give them a free view, behind a large, protruding nose. Round his neck he wore a gaily coloured calico scarf, so tightly tied up that his long neck seemed to make an effort to escape; in short, a truly surprising figure, who

became even more peculiar when, with a couple of steps forward and a repeated bow, he began his high-flown speech with these words; 'May I have the honour of expressing my feelings for the stage in a poem written by myself?'

To stop Andersen in mid-flow would have taken a sheer unkindness which few people could muster, for all those who knew him agree that he was, above all, innocent. He had no idea of the amusement and exasperation he caused wherever he went – and he could not see, either, why his well-wishers seemed so determined to deflect him from his beloved theatre into the dull discipline of education. However, he was in no position to quibble. Totally dependent on the charity of individuals, he could only be grateful.

Daniel Friedrich Kuhlau, the German composer who had been resident in Copenhagen since 1810, was particularly sympathetic because, like Weyse, he had known what it meant to be poor. In his own impoverished childhood, he had been sent out to fetch a bottle of beer and had fallen and broken it, losing the sight of an eye. But Andersen was perhaps most touched by the promise of two of Siboni's kitchen-maids that they would pledge a few coins each quarter out of their small wages. They only made one actual payment, but their kindness warmed him. Professor Guldberg took over the administration of the fund, and agreed to continue the metered supply of ten rixdollars a month, plus basic board and lodging.

Following his exclusion from Siboni's house, Andersen's situation was more difficult. No midday meal was provided, and no friendly servant girls would slip him some left-over food to take home for the evening. Andersen put his problem to Mrs Thorgesen, who was happy to feed him but at a cost of twenty rixdollars a month, payable in advance. Professor Guldberg had stipulated that he must on no account pay more than sixteen, otherwise there would be nothing in the maintenance fund for other necessities, and confronted with the landlady's terms, Andersen burst into tears and begged for a reduction.

Mrs Thorgesen, well aware that there were few tenants willing to pay good money to sleep in a windowless cupboard, was unwilling to let Andersen go. She knew about the new fund raised for his support – very probably he had told her himself – and retorted that the eighty rixdollars that had been subscribed would buy him four months' board and lodging, after which, 'Mr Guldberg' would doubtless get hold of some more. She told the weeping lad she was going out shopping, and if he didn't give her the twenty rixdollars when she came back, he could pack up and go.

Andersen, at only fifteen years old, was helplessly distraught. With all its shortcomings, the house seemed like home to him, and he had no inclination to go and look elsewhere. In a rush of superstition, he touched a tear-wet finger to the portrait of Mrs Thorgesen's deceased husband which hung on the wall, hoping the dead man would intercede for him, for he had only ten rixdollars in his pocket, a mere half of the twenty she wanted. On her return, the landlady conceded that he could pay ten rixdollars a fortnight rather than twenty a month, and he gladly thrust all the money he had into her hand, regardless of the fact that he had wildly exceeded the sum stipulated by Guldberg.

Mit livs eventyr, the later autobiography, alters his first account of this episode, claiming that Mrs Thorgesen came back with an offer to reduce her price to sixteen rixdollars, but the original version, in all its touching ineptness, is the one with the ring of truth. From that time on, Andersen, like Kuhlau, ran little errands, hoping thus to earn a small reduction in the rent so that he could buy paper to write on, and an occasional play-script.

At about this time, he made contact with Laura Tønder-Lund, the girl in his confirmation class who had given him a rose. Now resident in the house of her influential uncle in Copenhagen, when she heard her ex-classmate's story she made a collection for him among her friends and contributed some of her own pocket money. Through her, he met several notable people, including the dean of Holmen's church, Frederik Carl Gutfeld, who took a benevolent interest in him.

Andersen did not settle easily to a life of study. After only a few weeks, he was twitching with anxiety to resume contact with his beloved theatre, and decided to try to get into the ballet school for the coming year. He went to see Bournonville, only to be told by Carl Dahlén, the company's leading solo dancer, that the director and his son, August, were away in Paris. Once again, Andersen's timing was perfect. Dahlén, left in charge, took pity on the boy and agreed to accept him as a pupil. It was an act of pure kindness, for there was no chance that the over-tall lad with his oddly quirky movements would make a dancer, but Dahlén and his wife welcomed him into their home, providing a family's warmth and an occasional meal. It must have been a welcome change from Mrs Thorgesen's establishment, where Andersen never accepted the landlady's invitation to share her sitting-room, preferring to carry his supper to bed and then lie reading for the rest of the evening.

The problem of money was again becoming acute. Guldberg's fund would run out in August, and benefactors could not be expected to provide for him indefinitely. Andersen had begun work at the ballet school and had renewed hopes that the Theatre might help him financially, and Guldberg drafted petitions for him to send to potential benefactors, including the king himself. None of these had any effect, though they constitute the first documents preserved in Andersen's own hand, dated 2 June and 3 July 1820.

The royal petition was dated 6 August, and three weeks later, the request to the Theatre produced a devastating response:

> When the suppliant presented himself before the board about nine months ago with a wish to be employed in the Theatre, he was found, after having been tested, to lack both the talent and the appearance necessary for the stage. None the less, Mr Siboni had the kindness voluntarily to give him lessons in singing in the hope that it might be possible to train him to sing in the choir of the Theatre, but he was forced to abandon even this. He then took refuge in Mr Dahlén's dancing school to be trained in this subject, for which, according to Mr Dahlén, he also lacks the ability and outward appearance.
>
> In view of the fact that the board regard it as their duty to advise against employing him in any subject in the Theatre, they cannot recommend that he be given any financial support from the Theatre's chest.

In spite of this, Andersen stayed on at the ballet school. The other dancers befriended him, letting him come into the wings to watch performances or sometimes taking him with them to reserved seats if the were not dancing. Looking back on it, he observed that despite his great height, the girls seemed to regard him as a child to be looked after.

That summer, he got the chance to set foot on the stage himself. A light opera called *The Children From Savoy* included a scene which demanded a big crowd of people, and all spare bodies were pressed into service, including seamstresses, stage-hands and all the pupils. Andersen was included, but only because Ida Wulff, an actress whom he had met at Siboni's, put in a word for him. She may have regretted it, for his appearance was a disaster. The crowd players wore their ordinary clothes, and Andersen, still in the grossly outgrown and outworn garments which were all he had, looked grotesque. The confirmation suit had, in its previous incarnation as his father's overcoat, already been well worn and was now grey with age, hopelessly short at the wrists and ankles. The waistcoat rode halfway up his chest, leaving a great gap, and his boots were dilapidated. The hat, however, was still too big, and fell continually over his eyes.

Acutely aware of these shortcomings, Andersen clowned about, overacting outrageously. In his later novel, *The Two Baronesses*, he recreates the episode, complete with the falling-down of the over-small trousers; whether or not this happened, he is writing autobiographically in *Mit livs eventyr* when he recalls that one of the principals, while taking a bow, grasped him by the hand and said ironically, 'May I present you to the Danish public!' There was a roar of laughter, and Andersen rushed off the stage in tears.

This was not his only dramatic disaster. His first autobiography (but not the second) records a similar episode in a production called *Lanassa*, for which Crown Princess Caroline happened to be in the audience. Caroline was not, as her title suggests, the wife of Crown Prince Christian Frederik, but the elder daughter of the reigning monarch, Frederik VI, whose six sons had all died in infancy. Technically she was thus the heir to the throne but, as a female, could not inherit. Twelve years older than Andersen, she was evidently on easy terms with him, as his account in his *Levnedsbog* of the *Lanassa* fiasco reveals:

> When I was talking to the Crown Princess shortly afterwards, she told me I had looked like a skinned cat and Nielsen a scalded pig. But in her remarks to the originator of the piece, I remember that she said, "Will you also write a sad play like Oehlenschläger; no, let it be! One can have sadness enough in the world, better to give people something to laugh at, something like Holberg." She was always so affectionate towards me, joked about my naïve utterances, and when she came in once as her lady-in-waiting was drawing my profile and I was not pleased with the expression, she sketched in a crooked nose and big eyes, and said, "He will look like Schiller!" And I completed the picture. A pity I have lost that; I've never had a more interesting page from the past.

Caroline's lady-in-waiting was Olivia Colbiørnsen, a daughter of the Privy Councillor mentioned earlier by Andersen as a confidant of the Crown Prince, and it is evident that at one level he was moving easily in royal circles. At the same time, if his own accounts are to be believed, there was no question of any hand-outs from on high. It was Guldberg and his friends who supported him through another winter of cold and hunger and increasing shabbiness, and his efforts to secure further patronage constantly failed. In October 1820 he petitioned Denmark's towering figure of nationalistic theology, Nicolai Frederik Severin Grundtvig, again without success. At the Theatre, there were no further chances to appear as a dancer, but on 25 January 1821, Andersen was given a non-dancing part as a musician in the ballet, *Nina*. The title role was danced by Madame Schall, and he was delighted when she recognised him.

During that winter, Professor Guldberg persuaded a well-known actor of the day, Lindgreen, to come and hear the boy recite. Despite the actor's advice to try something comic, Andersen plunged into a passionate speech from a drama about the life of Coreggio, and was so moved by his own oratory that he burst into sobs at the end. Lindgreen patted him on the shoulder and said he certainly had feeling but he was hopeless as an actor. Giving the verdict which Guldberg had probably hoped for, he advised the boy to stick to his studies, adding that he really ought to learn some Latin.

Dutifully, Andersen consulted his friend, Mrs Hermansen, who had been so helpful about finding a German tutor, but this time she shook her head. Latin was an expensive language, she said. The ever-patient Guldberg, however, arranged with a friend, Vilhelm Bentzien, to give the boy some grounding in Latin without charge.

Andersen found the language extremely difficult. Danish is uninflected and totally non-Latinate, the Romans having failed to spread their influence so far north, and the concept of declensions and conjugations baffled him. He was bored by the lessons, and could not see that they had any relevance to his purpose in life, which remained firmly rooted in the theatre.

By mid-winter, the fund collected for him had once again run out. Professor Guldberg, with a generosity which seems to indicate an obstinate faith in the boy's rather deeply hidden worth, made Andersen a present of the proceeds from a pamphlet of verse and prose, the preface to which dedicated any profits to 'a hopeful young scholar deprived of almost any other support'. It was as if Hans Christian had entered a testing period, during which those interested in him watched to see if stick-and-carrot tactics could induce him to stop frittering his time away in grandiose dreams and accept the educational discipline which lay ahead of him. Guldberg advised Andersen to approach a newly appointed director of the theatre, Jonas Collin, with a request for help. There was no response, and when Andersen sent a revised petition on his sixteenth birthday this, too, was ignored. He was asking for the wrong thing; no official approval would ever be forthcoming for his self-deluding theatrical ambitions.

Meanwhile, on 12 April 1821, Hans Christian appeared at the Royal Theatre as one of a band of eight trolls in Dahlén's new ballet, *Armida*. Masked and comic, the role was far from a starring one, but for Andersen the ecstasy of seeing his name on a programme for the first time was enough. There was, he said, 'a halo of immortality about it.' All day, he gazed repeatedly at the magical piece of paper, and when night came, he took it to bed with him and stared at the Gothic letters by the light of his candle. Only his surname appeared, but he inscribed a heavily inked asterisk against it and added his initials, H.C., and was filled with happiness.

For a while, Andersen's luck held. In the month following the *Armida* production, he was taken into the Theatre's choir school by the singing master, P.C. Krossing. As a sworn enemy of Siboni, Krossing may have picked up his discarded pupil in order to discredit the maestro's hasty judgement, but it does also seem that Andersen's voice had returned. In his very autobiographical novels he several times refers to the regaining of a treble voice, but in fact, at approaching sixteen, it seems more likely that he had settled into a tenor. As a chorus member, he appeared as a shepherd and as various halberdiers and warriors, which suggests that he was no longer a soprano, but in other ways he was slow to mature, showing no signs of facial hair until he had turned twenty-five.

Stage appearances brought him a little money, and he was entitled to attend all performances in the pit, free of charge, so Andersen entered into a period of bliss, at last accepted (no matter how reluctantly) by his beloved theatre. He began to make connections with people who would be useful to him throughout his life. In the same production of *Armida*, for instance, had appeared a little girl called Johanne Pätges – her name wrongly spelt in the programme as Petcher – who would later marry the immensely influential writer and critic, Johan Ludvig Heiberg. As Johanne Heiberg, she was to become Denmark's leading actress, and her husband would be the director of the Royal Theatre.

During the summer recess of 1821, Andersen made closer acquaintance with the Colbiørnsen family. Christian Colbiørnsen, who had been the presiding judge of the Superior Court as well as a Privy Councillor, was now dead, but his widow, Engelke Margrethe and her daughters made Andersen welcome. Their house was a meeting-point for Copenhagen's literary and intellectual élite, and their continuing royal connections were close. Angelique, whom Hans Christian almost certainly knew through previous contacts with Crown Princess Caroline, took him with her to Frederiksberg Castle, where he sang and recited for the Princess. She praised his voice and gave him ten rixdollars as well as fruit and sweets. Andersen was ecstatic. He records in *Levnedsbogen* how he carried his booty into a park and sat down under a tree to eat some of the grapes and peaches (though he kept some for the undeserving Mrs Thorgesen). Out of sheer joy he began to sing 'to the birds and flowers, for there was no one else to whom I could express my happiness.' A stable boy stared at him and asked if he was mad. 'I sneaked away,' he confessed, 'silent and embarrassed.'

The Colbiørnsens invited him to join them for some time at Bakkehuset, (The Hill House), a country house owned by the poet Lyhne Rahbek, who was also in residence there. Rahbek never spoke to the boy, though he once approached and stared at him, then turned away. The women, however, mothered him. Mrs Colbiørnsen gave him a blue coat that had belonged to her husband – very fashionable in the days when every young blade wanted to wear the romantic blue topcoat of Young Werther – and Andersen was immensely proud of it. The garment was far too big for him, but he padded it out with old play posters, refusing to unbutton it lest this secret should be revealed.

While at Bakkehuset, Andersen finished off a play he had begun to write as an exercise in Danish for Professor Guldberg, who had stipulated that he was not on any account to offer it to the theatre. The play was based on a story Andersen had read in a magazine, and he called it *The Forest Chapel*. While nominally obeying Guldberg's instructions, he insisted on reading from his creation to anyone who would listen. Thiele, the benefactor who had recorded such a disillusioned description of the young man, was also at Bakkehuset but told Andersen firmly that his play was a terrible mishmash of bad German novels. It had its good points, he added to the crestfallen playwright and Andersen's crushed spirits promptly lifted again. Without seeming to realise their eminence, he begged an audience with the great writers of the day, presenting himself and his play to Ingemann, Grundtvig and Oehlenschläger, all of whom were extraordinarily forebearing even though his idea of writing was to cobble together a pastiche of other people's work. Mrs Rahbek, who was his most sympathetic listener, felt obliged to point out that he had lifted whole scenes unaltered from Ingemann and Oehlenschläger, but he was undisturbed. 'Oh, I know,' he said, 'but they're so lovely!'

If the Colbiørnsens were a little appalled by their protégé's cockiness, they refrained from letting him see it, and Andersen's confidence swelled dangerously. He began to think himself a real *digter* and did not smile when Mrs Rahbek gave him some roses to take up to her husband, saying she was sure he would like to receive them from the hands of a fellow poet. Self-deprecation was not in his scheme of things. He even allowed himself to think that Guldberg's embargo on submitting work to the theatre was caused by professional jealousy because the professor himself had never had a play produced. On return to Copenhagen for the next theatrical season, he began to cut the Latin lessons which Guldberg had organised for him. He had always found the subject boring, and most of his fellow chorus-members assured him that there was no need for it in a theatrical career.

When, in mid-September, his tutor reported his absence to Guldberg, the professor finally lost patience. He had expended a vast amount of time and money on the boy; but Andersen had utterly failed to get down to study. He had still not mastered the correct use of his own language, let alone any other, and he was now spurning the Latin lessons which had been provided as a personal favour, without so much as a word of excuse. That was the end, Guldberg told his friends. The wretched boy could expect no further help from him.

It was a couple of weeks before news of the professor's displeasure reached Andersen, but then he rushed in panic to his benefactor's house, desperate to make amends. It was too late. The pigheadedness with which he had pursued his theatrical enjoyments had irritated the professor so much that he would not even let his erstwhile pupil into the house. He berated him savagely as he stood on the doorstep, and would listen to no excuses or apologies. It was the first time, Andersen admitted in *Mit livs eventyr*, that anyone in his entire life had severely reprimanded him, and he was as shocked as a criminal receiving a death sentence. His stricken face merely annoyed Guldberg further, for such an extreme reaction looked like more play-acting. He'd heard all these protestations before, he said, but this time was the end. Thirty rixdollars remained in the current fund, of which Andersen might collect ten a month until it was finished. He slammed the door.

Badly shaken, the boy retreated in a state of shock. He was no good, Guldberg had said. Worthless – a waste of anybody's time. He wandered along by the Peblinge Lake and stopped to look into its dark water. Disaster stared back in the form of his own reflection.

It was the beginning of a very bad time. Mrs Thorgesen, who had been conducting an affair with a sailor, got married and left Denmark, handing Andersen's tenancy on to her upstairs neighbour, Mrs Henckel, who let him have a similar airless, unlit room in her apartment but with Guldberg's support gone, there could be no question of board as well as lodging. Between his lessons in singing and dancing, he wandered the streets, cold and hungry and virtually barefoot, as his boots were now hopelessly worn out. He let his new landlady think he was eating with friends, but usually he bought a small loaf of bread and devoured it in the park, or just occasionally went to a cheap cafe called The Plane, sitting in a quiet corner where nobody would notice his raggedness.

Of his own accord, he went back to Dean Bentzien who had been teaching him Latin and begged his pardon. Bentzien took him back without complaint, and although Andersen still found the subject a struggle, it was at least an occasional respite from the street.

At the theatre, Andersen's singing and ballet lessons continued, but neither Dahlén nor Krossing offered him any more parts. From being an appealing lad, he was turning into a perpetually derelict young man, embarrassingly ragged and hungry and with no apparent promise whatever. One of the actresses had dubbed him 'the little declaimer', and the mocking title still clung to him although few people now would listen to his recitations. As the days shortened into winter, Andersen turned back to his childhood consolation of the toy theatre. Once again, he cut and stitched clothes for his puppets, scrounging samples of silk and satin and small lengths of ribbon from the shops in Ostergade. Writing years later, he remembered standing in the street to gaze at the passing ladies in their finery, calculating how many miniature cloaks and robes he could make from all that opulence of silk and velvet.

He read all the books he could lay hands on, and made contact with the librarian of Copenhagen University, Rasmus Nyrup. Having himself come of a poor peasant family, Nyrup took a liking to the tall lad with the odd, ugly face, and once assured that he would be careful with the books, he let him take illustrated volumes home with him. In December, Andersen met the great physicist, Hans Christian Ørsted, the discoverer of electromagnetism, and the unlikely pair took a strange liking to each other. Ørsted, too, lent him books, and was in time to become by far the strongest influence in Andersen's life – but all that lay in the future. As the year of 1821 ended, the boy could see no hope of any relief from his dire situation. On New Year's Day, he walked through the empty streets to the Royal Theatre, his mind full of the superstitious need to see some sign for the year that lay ahead. The theatre was closed, but the stage doorman did not see the ragged boy who ducked past and made his way into the darkened auditorium. Alone on the stage, Andersen fell on his knees and offered up a mental ultimatum. If this new year intended to bring him the gift of paid performance, it must be foreshadowed now in whatever words should come to his mind and be spoken aloud.

No words came. His thoughts remained obstinately empty; not a single line from any play presented itself. It must have been a dismaying portent, but he fought back well, declaiming the Lord's prayer in a ringing voice. He left the theatre reassured, telling himself that such an entreaty could surely not be ignored.

In the months that followed, there was no sign of his prayer being answered. He wrote a 'patriotic tragedy' called *The Robbers of Vissenburg*, completing it in only two weeks, and without the restraining authority of Guldberg, decided to submit it to the Theatre's directors. Conscious that his handwriting was barely legible, he took the manuscript to Laura Tønder-Lund, who paid a scribe to copy it out in a more regular hand but the copyist faithfully reproduced every spelling mistake and grammatical error. Andersen duly submitted this in March.

It was, of course, a further irritation to the Theatre's directors, who were finding it extraordinarily difficult to get rid of this tiresome boy. They turned it down with an exasperated letter which insisted that work betraying such an abysmal lack of education should not be submitted. Hard on the heels of this came a further letter, dismissing him forthwith from the schools of ballet and singing. The directors hoped that his friends would look after him and procure the education without which any form of talent was useless.

Whether all this was orchestrated by the royal powers which controlled public funds and might just possibly have been keeping an eye on young Andersen's progress must remain a matter of guesswork, but the effect was a co-ordinated cutting off of all routes except the desired one. Whether he liked it or not, Hans Christian was being urged steadily towards the grammar school education for which he had proved himself to be so unready when given his first chance by Colonel Guldberg and the Crown Prince.

At seventeen, Andersen himself was still not thinking in terms of education. He continued to believe that he could write a successful play, and had embarked on a five-act tragedy called *Alfsol.* He showed this to Dean Gutfeld, who saw some virtue in it despite its manifest faults, and thought there was no reason why it should not be submitted to the theatre. However, he too advised the young man to go and see the new director, Jonas Collin.

Andersen was reluctant. Two petitions to Collin had already failed, and there had been no response to a poem which he had sent Collin on his own sixteenth birthday, expressing the hope that he might one day take his place in 'the garden of Art'. Collin was in fact a shrewd and experienced civil servant, an administrator whose position on the theatre board owed nothing to creative imagination. Asked for an interview, he consented to see the troublesome young man, and when they met, showed no sign of being impressed. Andersen for his part saw only a dry and unsympathetic businessman, and shied away in search of more congenial figures to whom he could appeal.

He went to see Captain P.E. Wulff, famous as the first translator of Shakespeare into Danish verse. Armed with the mis-spelt pages of *Alfsol,* he plunged into reading even though Wulff had courteously invited him to join the family for lunch – and yet, for all his unmannerly haste, there was something about his eagerness and vulnerability which the Wulffs found endearing. Although the Captain did nothing on that occasion to encourage the young writer's unrealistic hopes, he and his family became long-lasting friends to him.

In the summer, a scene from *The Robbers of Vissenburg* was included in *The Harp,* a magazine owned by A.P. Liunge, and this threw Andersen into a desperate effort to achieve more publication and prove his credentials as a writer. Through an actor who put him in touch with a typesetter in a Copenhagen printing works, he managed to produce a booklet called *Youthful Attempts,* consisting of *Alfsol* and a story which was directly imitative of Scott's *Heart of Midlothian.* He published it under the pseudonym of Villiam Christian Walter, being a compilation of the forenames of Scott and Shakespeare with his own – and, with stunning effrontery, he wrote to Professor Guldberg to ask if he might dedicate the booklet to him. The response was so outraged that it stung Andersen for years, He reproduced the letter word for word in his first novel, *The Improvisatore.*

> While I believed that you were availing yourself of the opportunity which I gave you to learn something and become a useful member of

society, nothing of the sort is happening; you are going in a direction quite different from the one I had intended.

If he insisted on pursuing this idea of calling himself a writer, the professor went on, then he might make his debut in what way he chose:

> but give me this one proof of your much-vaunted gratitude, never to connect my name, my care for you, with your public life. The very great service you might have done me by learning something, you refused; the very small one of naming me as a benefactor is so repugnant to me that you could not do anything I would find more offensive.

This hefty crack across the rump from a man who, through his brother's royal connections, would have been privy to any secret about Andersen's origins, effectively ended Hans Christian's headstrong inclinations. All hopes were rapidly crumbling. *Youthful Attempts* was a total failure. The printer offloaded the stock to a bookshop, but even when offered under a different title, it did not sell. The copies were eventually pulped or used as wrapping paper, and the book disappeared so completely that hardly a single copy remains today.

In a last, desperate gamble, Andersen sent *Alfsol*, via Dean Gutfeld, to the Theatre directors, and on 3 September it was rejected, with a letter to the Dean pointing out once more that its author lacked basic education. The piece had been nothing but a 'collection of words and tirades without any dramatic action, without character . . . in short, completely unsuitable for the stage.' On 6 September, exactly three years after Andersen' s arrival in the city, the directors confirmed their decision, but added a recommendation that he be sent to grammar school. He was called to an interview the following week, on 13 September. Jonas Collin had evidently not been idle. As the administrator of the fund *ad usos publicos*, which was directly under the control of the king, he was in close contact with royalty while himself being solidly middle-class and discreet – the perfect man to act on behalf of a higher power while appearing to have great authority in his own right. He proposed that Andersen should be sent to Slagelse Latin School, all costs to be met from the public fund.

Hans Christian, slightly stunned, had no choice but to accept. Collin then made formal application to the king, and received his assent, which came as no surprise to anybody. Collin himself would be in charge of all disbursements and would act *in loco parentis,* making himself responsible for the lad's welfare. Andersen would start in a month's time at the school in Slagelse, which lay fifty-six miles south-west of Copenhagen. It had been attended by the poets B.S. Ingemann and Jens Baggesen, and its newly appointed headmaster was Dr Simon Meisling.

Andersen wrote to his mother to tell her of this upturn in his fortunes, and received a letter back, as always written by a scribe, in which she said how sorry she was that neither his father nor his grandmother were alive to see this triumph. He himself was 'strangely thrilled', although there was a slight sense of being exiled from the scene of all his hopes. He went to see Jonas Collin as instructed, and found him strictly dispassionate. 'He gave me this help without a word or a glance which might make it weigh heavy on me,' he recalled in his *Levnedsbog.* Money would be sent every three months, and the young man was to write regularly with news of his progress. He must not be afraid to impart any difficulties. For all its kindness, the undertaking was made without emotion.

On Saturday, 26 October 1822, with his few possessions tied in a bundle as they had been three years ago, Andersen got on the early morning coach to Slagelse. He was seventeen-and-a-half years old, and by his side there sat a lad of about his own age who, rather than just beginning his education, had with a sigh of relief ended it. Grammar school, he said, was dreadful, and if he had to go back there, he would be the most unhappy person in the world. Andersen tried to take no notice. This was his future, and he intended to make the best of it.

When the coach rumbled into Slagelse late that night, Andersen got out with the other passengers and went across to the inn to put up for the night. He asked the innkeeper's wife what there was of interest in the town, and received a discouraging reply. There was the new English fire-engine, she said, and Pastor Bastholm's library – really not much else.

The next day, he was invited to Sunday afternoon tea at the headmaster's house, together with a couple of sixth-form students, and made his first big mistake. He insisted on reading, first from *Alfsol* and then from his Scott-derived story. Meisling, a short-tempered man at the best of times, told him there was to be no further reference to himself as a writer. He was here to study, and there would be no time frittered away on stories or plays or poems.

Andersen found himself neatly boxed in by his anti-bohemian benefactors. Meisling, Collin, the theatre directors and maybe the king himself were united in the determination to make him become a respectable citizen, free of unpleasant artistic tendencies, but the combined forces had a harder fight on their hands than they realised. The lanky boy, older by far than most of his fellow-pupils, quickly discovered that there was a local theatre. Maidservants from the houses of the town were allowed to attend rehearsals free of charge, and so were the schoolchildren, when Meisling chose to permit it. However, where Andersen was concerned, Meisling seems to have put the theatre firmly out of bounds. The diary which Hans Christian kept later in his school career makes no mention of any such treats.

He soon began to realise that the townspeople of Slagelse took a great interest in the grammar school – or 'Latin school' as it was more commonly called. They knew what pupils had arrived and what class they had been put into, and this caused Andersen deep embarrassment, for although he was seventeen and taller even than most of the teachers, he was put in the class next to the lowest, to sit with boys of eleven or twelve. Perched among his small classmates like a stork caged among sparrows, the pain of his situation began to come home to him. The image of the caged bird was one which he used himself in describing his schooldays, and it occurred again and again in his stories.

Very quickly, he became the butt of the headmaster's sarcasm. Andersen had no grounding whatever in academic work, and floundered helplessly in the unfamiliar concepts of Greek and geometry, Hebrew and the ever-difficult Latin. Meisling, a classical scholar, taught Andersen's lowly class only once a week, but as the time for that lesson came round, the lanky boy would pray that some heaven-sent mishap would prevent the master from attending. Meisling's sarcasm was of the blistering kind which forces the rest of the class into complicity lest any one of them should become its new victim – and yet, he continued to ask the seventeen-year-old round to his house and let him walk to church with the senior boys on Sundays, so that the watching villagers would not see that he had been put with little boys far his junior.

Some of the assistant teachers did their best to be helpful. Mr Quistgaard, the divinity master, had been a poor boy himself, and was sympathetic, and others perhaps meant well, though Andersen's hypersensitivity flinched from heavy-handed jokes such as the history master's comment that if you cut him in half, you could make two puppies out of him. Andersen was, indeed, extremely tall, but he was far from being grown-up. As the school had no boarding facilities, he lodged with a widow called Mrs Henneberg, sharing a small bedroom and sitting room with another tenant who occasionally came home drunk. When this happened, Andersen would creep in alarm up to the landlady's flat and ask to be allowed to spend the night on her sofa. Letters continued to arrive from his mother, and within a month of his attendance at the school, one of these brought disturbing news. Andersen's half-sister, Karen Marie Rosenvinge, wanted to get in touch with him. Anne Marie had stalled over whether or not to reveal her son's whereabouts, and now wanted to leave the decision to him. Karen, now twenty-three, was about to cross to Zealand herself, and knew that Hans Christian had gone to Copenhagen three years ago. She would stop pestering, Anne Marie said, if he would just give her his address.

Andersen's answer is unknown, but another letter came from his mother, thanking him and implying that the purpose of Karen's trip was to find a certain Lieutenant Martens who had left Odense the previous year. Maybe Hans Christian could see the lieutenant, Anne Marie went on hopefully, and make him fulfil his promise.

Karen had evidently been jilted, but Andersen was horrified at the idea of being involved with her in any way. He had grown up in the tacit assumption that this sinful earlier product of his mother's sexual urges was not to be mentioned, and the threat of her arrival at the grammar school was a nightmare. Whether he had ever met Karen as a child is doubtful, and the only hint that Hans Christian knew her by sight came long after his initial panic had abated. Three years later, he would note in his diary for 3 November 1825 that the Meislings were about to take on a new maid, and he was certain it would be Karen. The next day, he noted with relief that he had seen the new girl, whose name was Maria, and didn't know her at all.

Andersen was punctilious about writing to Jonas Collin as instructed, but in all his detailed reports of school life, he made no mention of his panic about Karen. It is hardly surprising. Collin, for all his kindness, was still a stranger, and Andersen, confused as he was by the secrecy and furtiveness in which he had grown up could not be sure how such an eminently respectable man would react to a hint of squalor. Anne Marie, hampered by having to use another person for her communications, told him in a December letter that Karen was in Copenhagen and that he need not worry 'about either her virtue or her youthfulness, for it has all been well preserved here in Odense.' The coded message was obscure, but it seemed to mean that there would be no scandal, and Andersen's fears began to subside.

At Christmas, the headmaster included his new pupil, presumably by arrangement with Collin, in a family trip to Copenhagen. The Meislings, their three children, their maid and Andersen were all packed into Slagelse's single available coach, with a big eiderdown tucked round them for warmth during the day-long journey. Mrs Meisling, who fancied herself as an opera singer, regaled them with arias from Mozart's *Don Juan*, and they played cards and ate sweets and pancakes.

Andersen was invited to dine with the Collin family, and produced his school report for inspection. Jonas professed himself satisfied, but warned the boy again that he must forget all about writing poetry. He made it clear that his protégé's obsession with writing and the theatre was a major obstacle to his progress, a silly aberration from which he must be liberated before he could hope for success and respectability.

Back at school, Andersen did his best to be dutiful, but news arrived that Dean Gutfeld had died, and he felt impelled to write a memorial poem for this man who had believed in him and helped him so much only a few months previously. Pleased with the result, he recklessly sent the poem to the local paper, where it was printed on 1 February 1823. Meisling was furious, and perhaps remonstrated with the editor, Pastor Bastholm, for having accepted it, as the pastor wrote Andersen a reproving letter, regretting his own decision to publish the poem and advising him to concentrate on his studies. In an odd passage of internal debate, he admitted that the young writer clearly justified the financial support he was receiving (Meisling, again, must have told him about this) but added Andersen must avoid 'the snares of vanity'. Despite these dutiful words, he then offered the boy some valuable literary advice:

> Look at nature, mankind and yourself with an attentive eye, for that will give you original material for your works. Choose small subjects taken from the things that surround you; contemplate everything you

see from all points of view before you take up your pen. Become a
poet as though no poet had ever lived in this world before you, and as
though you had to learn from no one.

Such wisdom ran utterly against all Meisling's teaching, but Andersen
was beginning to realise that he was serving two very different masters
in the work he did for the school and the attention he paid to his
struggling and forbidden talent.

During this time, the poet B.S. Ingemann, whom Andersen already
knew, was appointed to the post of senior master at Sorø Academy,
about ten miles from Slagelse. On a Sunday, Andersen would
sometimes walk over there, sure of a kindly reception from the poet
and his young wife in their house by the lake, and this refuge helped to
make the days of school more bearable. Ingemann, deeply influenced
by Oehlenschläger, wrote with an artless religious enthusiasm about
nature, and enjoyed his life in the country enormously. He and his
wife, Lucie, took Andersen sailing with them on the lake, an aeolian
harp fixed to the mast so that the wind made its own strange music in
its strings, and their flower-filled house was a centre to which all the
poets and musicians of the Romantic movement came.

Such an influence was far more attractive than Meisling's ferocious
advocacy of academic discipline, specially as Ingemann's writing was
popular and successful. His hymns were widely sung and translated
into other languages; among others, 'Through the Night of Doubt and
Sorrow' was his, translated into English by S. Baring-Gould. Ingemann
also turned out numbers of flamboyant, Scott-inspired novels which
were standard reading for Danish adolescents and, perhaps most
significantly, had just produced a collection of fairy tales and fantasy
stories, predating those which his young visitor would write by more
than a decade.

At Easter, Andersen asked Meisling for permission to go to Odense
to visit his mother, whom he had not seen for over three years.
Reluctantly, Meisling agreed, stipulating that the boy should not be
away for more than a week, because at the end of that time, Meisling
himself had to go to Copenhagen, and he wanted Andersen in the
house to keep his children occupied.

This time, there was no money for a coach-ride. Andersen got up at
three in the morning and walked to Korsor, where he took the ferry to
Funen, then walked again from Nyborg to Odense, a distance of some

thirty miles. He did not stay with his mother, although her second husband had died in the previous year. The visit had been suggested by Colonel Guldberg, now a General, who had sent some money and invited the boy to stay in his house.

Marie Shoemaker, as she often called herself, was of course immensely excited by the return of her successful son, and came round to the Guldbergs' house to collect him every time she wanted to show him off to an acquaintance. For all the initial head-shaking, the neighbours were now deeply impressed, and Andersen was treated as quite a notability. He went to see all his old friends, Iversen the printer and the Bunkeflod ladies, and claimed in *Mit livs eventyr* that all along the narrow streets, people opened their windows to have a look at him, the famous boy who had got himself sent to Grammar school at the king's expense.

Since the death of Andersen's grandmother, her gently insane husband had been unable to cope with living alone and had been taken into Greyfriars Hospital, where his wife used to burn the dead leaves. This removal may have been the underlying reason for Hans Christian's insistence on a visit to the family home, for he had been assured throughout his boyhood that his grandparents were keeping a fortune for him to inherit when they were gone. There was indeed a small hoard of coins in the tiny dwelling which the old couple had inhabited but it was in pre-1813 currency, now worthless. At the collapse of the state bank in that year, new, devalued coinage had been issued, but Mad Anders and his wife had not converted their 'fortune' into the new money.

It may have been that the money was, as the grandmother had claimed, the last remnants of the lost farm – but why, in that case, had she not used it to ease the poverty in which she and her family had lived? An alternative explanation is impossible to ignore. If the money was a cash settlement which arrived with the infant Hans Christian, the respect in which it was held is instantly explicable, and so is the choice of its keeper. Anne Marie, ignorant, garrulous and heavy-drinking, could be relied on to give unstintingly of her motherly love and admiration, but she was not a woman to be entrusted with money. Brains and a certain primitive business acumen lay on the paternal side of the family, in the book-loving, uncommunicative shoemaker and in his mother whose legend-making could so easily have been a cover-up for a truth which could not be revealed.

The facts will probably never be proved. For Andersen, the small hope died without much pain, having never been more than a wraith of frail possibility. A few possessions were retrieved and sold before the little house was sold by the bailiffs to meet outstanding debts, and Anderson was able to buy a pair of boots with the proceeds. There remained about twenty rixdollars, little more than the small sum he had scraped together through his singing as a child, and his grandparents' house was demolished by its new owners as soon as they had bought the site.

Andersen was enjoying himself too much to be unduly bothered. Søren Hempel, owner of the town's bookshop, took him up to the tall tower he had built on the side of his house as an observatory, and there he stared through a telescope at the astonishingly close details of things far away. He saw an old woman from Greyfriars Hospital point up, and could not resist the thought that she could have known him as a child and was impressed by his elevation in the world. One afternoon the Guldbergs took him out on the river together with the family of the bishop, and Anne Marie was in tears of joy to see her son mixing in such exalted company.

For all her delight, Anne Marie was entering into a dependence on alcohol which would prove fatal. From very early days, Hans Christian had remembered being sent to fetch a nip of brandy for his mother, and later recorded the adverse local opinion of her in a bitterly defensive story, 'She Was No Good'. Like many drunks, she suffered from the abutting of a private world – in her case centred round the wonderful boy she had brought up – against the harshness of reality. Whether Hans Christian was her own son or a royal foundling makes little difference; he had been too big for her in every way. She had nothing now but pride in his achievements, and pride did not help to warm cold hands or fill an empty heart.

For Andersen, the return to Slagelse was a cold blast of unwelcome reality. He continued to find Latin and Greek extremely difficult, and Meisling constantly exploded in irritation. Any small incident added to the tension. A silly rhyme scrawled on a Latin grammar was not, Andersen protested, in his hand, but Meisling raged that whether or not he had written it was immaterial; it was just the kind of thing he would do. He was a stupid boy who would never be any good, and even if he should one day scribble a lot of rubbish, nobody would ever read it and it would be sold as pulp – 'and for God's sake don't start weeping, you overgrown lump!'

Andersen was now eighteen, tall and craggy, with big hands and feet, and his hypersensitivity and readiness to cry clearly infuriated the headmaster. He called him 'Shakespeare with the vamp's eyes', and would sometimes send a younger boy to fetch a brick for the weeping young man to use as a handkerchief. None the less, when the time came at the end of the summer term for Meisling to be formally installed as headmaster of the school, the music master asked Andersen to write the words of a celebratory hymn.

No glorying in this request was permitted. Andersen was not even allowed to attend the ceremony, and wandered instead in the little churchyard as the organ pealed and the words of his hymn were sung. He found the grave of a poet called Frankenau, whose work he knew, and stared at it in depression, wishing either to achieve success or lie similarly deep in the earth. He sent a copy of the hymn to Jonas Collin, who wrote back to say that it was not bad, but he must on no account resume any ideas of being a poet.

That autumn, Professor Guldberg, no doubt after communication with his brother about Andersen's summer visit, relented from his long silence and began to write to the boy, but this small comfort was lost in Andersen's increasing fears that he would not pass the annual examination necessary for promotion to the third year. He wrote an appeal to Mr Quistgaard, the friendly divinity teacher, saying he suspected himself to be too dull to go on studying, and asking what he should do.

If Andersen had hoped for confirmation that he should abandon his studies, he was disappointed. Quistgaard wrote back with kindness, pointing out that he himself had been twenty-three years old before he started full-time education, so he understood the problem but he offered no escape. While admitting that Andersen needed a very different educational approach from the one current at Slagelse, he could only advise endurance. The headmaster's violence of expression, he said, did not necessarily reflect his true opinion.

Andersen managed to scrape into the third year, but the work was now harder, and relationships with the headmaster continued to deteriorate. In desperation, Andersen wrote a letter to Meisling himself, asking pardon for any offence he might have committed and protesting that he did not, as accused, read 'entertaining books' instead of pursuing his studies. He offered an ultimatum; if at the end of three months he was not considered capable of progress, he would remove himself from the school where he caused 'nothing but dissatisfaction'.

This taking of the bull by the horns did him no good at all. Meisling was doubly irritated, and when he heard that Andersen had recited a poem at a party held by friends in Slagelse, he was so angry that he threatened to report the offence to Jonas Collin, which would probably result in the ceasing of his support and Andersen's consequent expulsion. He was in any case a useless pupil, he added, and he, Meisling, would be glad to get rid of him.

Hysterical with despair, Andersen wrote a pre-emptive letter to Collin himself, declaring this to be the end. He would emigrate to America and be no more trouble to anyone. He sent letters in a similar vein to all his acquaintances, and while Collin and Guldberg sent soothing replies, there were some who lost patience. Mrs Wulff, wife of the Shakespeare translator, wrote back with brisk, housewifely reproof which Andersen found deeply hurtful. He reproduced her letter in *Mit livs eventyr.*

> For Heaven's sake, do not imagine yourself to be a poet just because you can write a few lines of verse. It is a mania with you. What would you say if I went about believing I was going to be the Empress of Brazil? You would think it insane, and that's just what it is when you fancy that you will be a poet.

At least during his escapes to Sorø, Andersen's poetic ambitions were taken seriously. In the safety of that bohemian house, he had written a poem to his mother and another entitled 'The Soul', and felt himself to be almost on a level with the other young writers who went there. Carl Bagger and Fritz Petit were of his own age-group though Ingemann himself was sixteen years older, and the friendships formed at that time were to be lasting ones.

In late December, Crown Princess Caroline sent Andersen a gift of money and this, additional to his grant from the public fund, enabled him to go to Copenhagen for Christmas. Again, Meisling demanded a prompt return so that Andersen could take up his unpaid au pair duties with the children, and this meant leaving the city on Saturday night, as there was no coach on Sunday. Andersen was unwilling to do this as he had a ticket for the theatre, so he attended the performance and got up at dawn on Sunday morning to walk the fifty-six miles back to Slagelse. Snow was falling heavily, and the journey took him two days.

1824 proved to be a year of unrelenting difficulty. In the qualifying exams that autumn, Andersen came fifth out of eight, but only the first four were promoted to the fourth year, and he, with the others, was kept back to repeat the work. In a way, the failure, though ignominious, was a relief. The lessons, being already familiar, were less demanding, and his improved marks kept him out of trouble with Meisling, although he continued to live in terror of the headmaster's unpredictable temper.

In May 1825, the older boys were given a day's leave so that they could go to see a public execution carried out in Skjelskør. Meisling thought the spectacle would 'do them good', Andersen remarked in *Mit livs eventyr*. The boys travelled through the night in an open coach, and arrived on the hillside chosen for the execution in the first light of dawn. A vast crowd had assembled, for the case was an exciting one to the prurient imagination. A seventeen-year-old girl, pregnant by her lover, had persuaded him and a domestic servant to collude with her in the killing of her husband, and now the three of them were to be beheaded. Andersen watched, sick with horror, as the condemned trio were driven up in an open cart, 'the deathly pale girl leaning her head on her lover's breast'. The dark-haired servant who sat behind them had a squint, and nodded to acquaintances who shouted goodbye to him. The three were made to stand on the scaffold beside their waiting coffins, where they sang a hymn together with the priest, 'the girl's voice sounding high above the others'. This, for Andersen, was worse than the actual deaths, and he felt that his knees were going to give way. In a horrible follow-up, a couple of superstitious parents hustled their half-paralysed son, the victim of a stroke, up to the scaffold and forced him to drink a bowlful of the blood which ran from the bodies. This gave Andersen nightmares for long afterwards, and he dwelt with horror on the barbaric 'cure' in *Only A Fiddler*. It did not help that the other spectators were so phlegmatic. 'Pity to waste good clothes,' one of them observed, glancing at the headless corpses.

That summer, Andersen again went back to Odense. Anne Marie, by now about fifty, had been taken into a charitable institution called Doctors Boder as a hopeless alcoholic, and he again stayed with Guldberg. When he returned to school he began, as if feeling newly alone, to confide his feelings and opinions to a diary, and this became a habit which he kept up with some gaps, throughout his life. His first entry, on 16 September, contained a prayer in the forbidden form of a poem, and on the following day, he wrote a brief two lines:

> Listless and tired from reading – φ – studied – because of listlessness, went to bed before ten o'clock.

The Greek letter, *fi,* was a symbol he used at that time to indicate masturbation, though later this changed to a small upright cross.

He passed the qualifying exam to get into the fourth year, the result being whispered to him by Mrs Meisling, who tended increasingly to take him into her confidence. She told him also that her husband had applied for the post of headmaster at Elsinore grammar school, and was likely to get it because he had already worked there as a classics master some years previously. This would of course necessitate a move, since Elsinore lay on the other side of Copenhagen, on the narrow strait between Denmark and Sweden, and Mrs Meisling was sure Andersen would want to remain with the family. Since the move might take place at short notice, she suggested that when his quarter's rent elapsed with Mrs Henneberg, he should move into the Meisling household as a lodger, ready to come with them to Elsinore.

Unfortunately for Andersen, Jonas Collin approved the idea. He could hardly do otherwise, since, he was in effect an administrator of a scheme devised for the boy's welfare by people other than himself. Andersen, who always tended to think emotionally, never understood this and expected Collin to behave towards him with the care of a genuine father. It was a misconception which coloured his entire relationship with the Collin family and was to cause him much grief but for the time being, Andersen turned with relief from Collin's severity to the company of the Ingemanns who invited him to their house for the two-week break which followed the exams. There, he began to write a long story which is referred to in his diary in anonymous terms as 'my novel', but was probably a first attempt at *The Dwarf of Christian II.* This historical romance occupied him for a long time as a half-formed idea but never came to fruition. Taking advantage of the Ingemanns' books, Andersen read voraciously, discovering the genre of travel books for the first time. He was particularly taken by Christian Molbech's cumbrously titled *Journey*

Through A Part of Germany, France, England and Italy In the Years 1819 and 1820, which caught his imagination. He followed it with maps and geography books to hand, realising for the first time that these places were real. On return to school on 27 October, he moved into the Meisling household.

Andersen had tried to persuade himself that he would be better off with the Meislings than he had been with Mrs Henneberg, but he soon realised that he now had no refuge from the headmaster's bad temper. He found, too, that the household was extraordinary. Mrs Meisling, whom he described as 'a fat woman with false red curls' was on aggressively bad terms with her servants, and as a result, the house was filthy. She accused the kitchen and parlour maids of immorality, but the shocked Andersen discovered that she herself was of dubious reputation, causing much scandalised gossip in the town. Being fond of punch, Mrs Meisling would instruct her maid to steal rum from the bottle which her husband kept for his own use, but did not scruple to lay the blame on the girl if Meisling should complain.Convinced that the servants stole from her – which they probably did – she would lock leftover food such as meatballs in a cupboard along with domestic tools and laundry starch, and with even scanter regard to hygiene, kept her pickles and preserves in the privy, along with a live pig. The poor creature died before it could be turned into sausages, and the Meislings buried it in the garden.

Simon Meisling would retire to bed by eight o'clock in the evening with a supply of strong punch, and liked his wife to read to him from the novels of Walter Scott. Once he was asleep or, as not infrequently happened, the reading had ended in a quarrel, Mrs Meisling spent the remaining hours in the town, reputedly at the local garrison where she amused herself with the young officers of the regiment. She dressed up as a peasant woman for these expeditions, so as not to be recognised – but it was a dangerous game. On one occasion she came back to the house with such a noisy group that her husband woke and looked out of the window but, short-sighted and dependent on his thick glasses, did not recognise his disguised wife. Andersen recorded that on another night when she was entertaining some guests with a song, an officer who recognised her voice knocked on the window. Meisling sent his pupil to see who it was, and when Andersen reported innocently that it was an army officer who had run away at the sight of

him, Mrs Meisling shot him a furious glance. She later scolded him for
being so tactless. 'You don't know how jealous Meisling can be,' she
said.

Andersen, for all his dislike of the headmaster, had cause to think
his jealousy might be justified, for Mrs Meisling had made an attempt
to seduce Andersen himself, coming into his room one evening to ask
if he had noticed how much weight she had lost recently. He could feel
for himself, she said, how loosely her dress hung on her. She was
offended by his horrified retreat, and retorted that he was 'not really a
man' – an accusation she was to throw at him several times during his
stay in the house. Andersen, at twenty years of age, had lost none of his
long-held aversion to the female sex, and used Mrs Meisling's
attempted seduction in *The Improvisatore* a few years later, dwelling on
the 'shame and indignation' which it had caused him.

The reputation of the headmaster's wife was such that the
respectable matrons of the town would have nothing to do with her.
They refused to allow her to sing in the choir, and in retaliation,
Meisling, to Andersen's chagrin, would not allow any of his pupils to
join it. Despite this token support of his wife, it is obvious that the
marriage was a mockery, and the personal strain must have added
considerably to his irritability.

Things worsened for Andersen as the autumn went on. On 4
October, his diary made a first mention of the toothache which was to
plague him throughout his life, and as an old man he remembered
having had a tooth extracted while still at the Slagelse school.
Although his work was improving, Meisling refused to be satisfied, and
on 10 December made the pettish comment that a person like
Andersen would get bad marks in exams no matter how much he
knew, 'just because of the way he was'. Having read a biography of
Byron, he wrote that 'my soul is ambitious like his, happy only when
admired by everyone, even the most insignificant person who refuses
to do so can make me miserable'.

At Christmas, Andersen was invited to stay with the Wulffs, and
accepted gladly despite Mrs Wulff's flattening letter about his poetic
ambitions. He set off with Meisling and another teacher by coach at
half past three in the morning on 19 December, and was indignant at
being made to pay for his share of the refreshments when they stopped
to change horses. H.C. Ørsted had sent him two rixdollars on 11
December, but apart from that, he was virtually penniless. Arrival in

the capital, however, lifted him into a different world. Captain Wulff, who apart from his literary work was a naval officer, had been appointed head of the Naval Academy and was now living in an apartment in the royal palace, Amalienborg Castle, and Andersen stared out from his warm room in this glorious place on Christmas night, clutching the three volumes of Wulff's Shakespeare that he had been given as a present, and felt that this was the way life should be.

The next day, he went to see Jonas Collin and met two of his children. Ingeborg, the eldest daughter, was cheerful and relaxed, but Edvard, the middle one of the five children and three years younger than Andersen, seemed lofty and did not bother to speak to the visitor. Jonas spoke encouragingly about the good reports he had received from Meisling, and was evidently disinclined to think that his protégé's complaints had any firm foundation – or, at least, any importance.

For the next few days Andersen rushed round the city, renewing his acquaintance with everyone who had befriended him. It was an impressive list, including Professor Guldberg and Oehlenschläger and the Ørsteds, with whom he spent Christmas Eve. There were theatre people, too – the Dahléns and his fellow-students and the actress, Mrs Birgitte Andersen (no relation) who had written to him often. The Colbiørnsens gave him theatre tickets and so did the Wulffs, and two days before Christmas, he was present at the naval cadets' ball held by the Wulffs at the castle.

That occasion was an embarrassing one. The royal family was present, and among the evening clothes and glittering decorations, Andersen's shabbiness was appallingly evident. He was still wearing the blue coat given to him four years previously by Mrs Colbiørnsen, and when gently advised by the Wulffs that he should be in a tail coat, could only fall back on the threadbare grey garment he wore at school. Among the people present, nobody spoke to him except Oehlenschläger, who came up to shake hands with the self-conscious young man lurking by a curtain in the corner of the room, and by nine o'clock Andersen had retreated to his own quarters, explaining to the Wulffs the next morning that he had had a headache. He was particularly mortified to be seen at such a disadvantage by the fourteen-year-old Lotte Oehlenschläger, whom he liked for her lively wit and admired as the daughter of such a famous poet. He was aware that, at twenty, people would assume that he showed an interest in girls, but the distaste which he had felt since childhood still prevented him from any sexual response to females over the age of puberty. For him, love was inextricably bound up with the idea of purity, and its nature was spiritual rather than physical. While his own sexuality troubled him constantly, and was expressed in frequent masturbation, he was still revolted by the despoiling and ugliness which to him were always linked with the idea of carnal love.

While at the Wulffs', Andersen formed a close friendship with their daughter, Henriette, known, like all Henriettes, as Jette. A year older than himself, she had been born with a spinal deformity which made her severely hunchbacked, and it may have been this very deformity which made him feel so safe with her. Jette Wulff was highly intelligent, possessed of great courage and humour, and she was also a gifted artist, but nobody could regard her bent body as conventionally attractive in sexual terms. Physically, she could be thought of as a perpetual child.

Andersen watched with a kind of baffled respect as other young men fell in love. Christian Werliin, a teacher at his school, was standing outside the Wulff's house in the week before Christmas, convinced – wrongly – that their younger daughter, Ida, was the same Ida Wulff as the opera singer for whom he had conceived a wild passion, and this amused Andersen – but his diary is taken up with his own concerns, of which the opposite sex formed no part. Meisling had instructed him to report to his house every morning while in Copenhagen, and the young man had done this faithfully, often running small errands, but the headmaster remained stern and disapproving. 'I go to see him every day and yet he never gives me a friendly glance,' Andersen wrote on 23 December. 'I would like to be truly fond of him, but it's not my fault that I feel the way I really do.'

Visits to friends, by contrast, were warm and rewarding. Andersen was encouraged to read out loud, and Oehlenschläger in particular listened attentively and gave him good advice on avoiding triteness and elaboration. In this circle, reading and reciting were as accepted a part of a social evening as singing and playing musical instruments – but when Meisling heard of his pupil's performances, he was furious. To make things worse, Oehlenschläger, with the best of intentions, had written to the headmaster to suggest that he might be a bit more sympathetic to the young man who longed so much for a word of encouragement. Since Meisling himself was a poet, he went on, Andersen could as usefully consult him about his verses as he could consult Oehlenschläger.

If Meisling did indeed write poetry, he kept it to himself, and that Andersen should have tried to enlist support in this insolent way was intolerable. Actually, Andersen knew nothing of Oehlenschläger's letter, and he was stunned to receive an outraged note from the headmaster on Boxing Day, berating him for 'wasting time'. As a punishment, on return to Slagelse he was not to 'take part in decorating the children's Christmas tree, crêches, masquerades or God knows what else has been planned'. Meisling had already insisted that his pupil should return to Slagelse as soon as the holiday was over, and he duly went back on 28 December, getting a lift in a private coach belonging to a Lieutenant Thane. With the children in their decorated sitting room, he realised that their father had meant what he said, for they looked at him silently. 'A hell is awaiting me,' he wrote in his diary on New Year's Eve.

1826 was, he said afterwards, 'the darkest, bitterest time of my life'. From 12 April, he gave up writing his diary, though letters to friends give a clear picture of the events. In May, the Meisling family moved to Elsinore, and that, at least, was a joy to Andersen. His account of the journey was very lively, begun in a letter to Jonas Collin while waiting for the heavy baggage to arrive by sea. The rough roads and horse-drawn carts could not possibly cope with a house removal and, like many other maritime countries, Denmark relied on ships for all heavy transport. Rasmus Nyerup, the librarian of Copenhagen University who had lent Andersen books, was so impressed by the description he received that he published it anonymously in a newspaper, but this annoyed the various other correspondents who had received identical versions of the same letter and assumed it to be personal to them. This duplication was a habit Andersen kept up throughout his life. Letters seem to have been as conscious a form of writing as any other, and his set-piece descriptions were widely circulated among his friends.

The move to Elsinore was Andersen's first essay in travel-writing, and he realised at once that recording what he saw was a pleasantly direct form of literature, needing only an acute eye and a neat turn of phrase. He escaped from school whenever he could, and took a great pleasure in the coastal scenery and in the busy dock-life of the town:

> What traffic! What liveliness on the wharf, here some fat Dutchmen speak their hollow language, there I hear musical Italian, further

down coal is being unloaded from an English brig so I can imagine I am smelling London.

The teachers at the new school were patient and kind, and for a while, things seemed better. Meisling's report to Jonas Collin at the end of the term emphasised that Andersen was worthy of continued public funding, though his desire to hang on to a senior pupil who was so useful in the house as a child-minder may have had something to do with it. Andersen himself would have been startled by the glowing terms:

> His natural aptitude is extremely good, indeed in certain spiritual disciplines even brilliant, his diligence constant and his behaviour, due to his lovable good nature, is of a kind that may serve as a model to the pupils of the school.

During the summer break, Andersen turned down an invitation to stay with Colonel Guldberg in Odense. Meisling had offered extra coaching in Greek, but there was also the chance to go into Copenhagen and see friends from time to time. It meant getting up at three in the morning and a walk of forty miles, but the Wulffs were always willing to put him up, and Jette's good-humoured teasing was a welcome change from the serious atmosphere of the school. While there, he wrote a self-mocking poem called 'The Evening', here translated for its frivolity rather than literal exactness:

> Yonder on the hill there stands
> A lanky, Werther-pale young man,
> His nose is vast, a cannon-sneeze,
> His eyes as tiny as green peas.
> He sings a wistful German song
> And gazes at the sunset, long
> And yearningly. What does he want?
> Lord knows, I'm not omniscient;
> He's mad, a lover, or – I know it!
> Yes – the stupid chap's a poet.

A visit to the Collin family was less relaxed, and Andersen wrote to Jonas on return, 'I feel I can speak much more freely and warmly to you by letter than in speech; I don't feel half so embarrassed.'

With the resumption of school, the honeymoon period in Elsinore came to an end. Local opinion of Mrs Meisling rapidly became as bad as it had been in Slagelse, and domestic tension mounted. The house was again filthy and the Meislings quarrelled with each other and with the servants. Meisling raged at Andersen, telling him that the two hundred rixdollars paid for his board and lodging annually were not enough, and he wished he had not brought him to Elsinore. Andersen struggled to understand his failings, admitting to Collin that there was something 'restless and hasty' in his nature which the headmaster was perhaps trying to cure. His meekness did him no good. Meisling shouted at him that he was insane and therefore quite ineducable, and Andersen wrote in distress to Jonas Collin, who, knowing nothing of the truth, assured him that the headmaster's opinion of him was not as bad as he thought. Mrs Wulff, though concerned about his evident unhappiness, was still inclined to tell Andersen not to fuss, and bade him remember the Cinderella story, and how patiently the girl put up with her lot.

It was no comfort. The constant assertions that he was stupid and would get nowhere and that his so-called writing was fifth-rate rubbish wore down his resistance, and he was near breaking-point. In Elsinore there was no Ingemann to escape to at weekends, and Meisling forbade him any further expeditions to Copenhagen. In the October exams, Andersen's Latin and Greek results were a disaster. He wrote in distress to a Mrs Jürgensen, widow of the royal watchmaker whom he had met in Copenhagen before leaving for Slagelse, admitting that he had been 'grounded' because of his poor results and thus must turn down her invitation to visit her and her son. Meisling was going with his wife and children to the city, but had stipulated that Andersen must remain at the school during the two-week break, and would have no further time off until Christmas. With winter coming, it was a bleak outlook. Elsinore seemed daily closer to the North Pole than to Copenhagen, Andersen said in his letter to Mrs Jürgensen, and he was in a mood 'à la Werther'.

Goethe's *The Sorrows of Young Werther* had since its publication in 1774 captured the imagination of half the young men in Europe with its suicidal, deeply romantic hero, and in Denmark the book had for a while been banned as a pernicious influence, which naturally

increased its popularity. Andersen, while feeling that his anguish had a
poetic precedent in Goethe, could see no way out of his depression.
He wrote on 14 October to a schoolfriend from Slagelse, Emil
Hundrup, 'the only one to think of me a little' with a torrential
outpouring of his miseries. 'I have never felt as unhappy as now, never
despaired like this.' A fortnight later he wrote again, telling Emil he
wished his father had burned every book in the house so that 'this
madness' would never have occurred and he would not have ended up
as a disappointment to those who tried to help him – but, with
endearing wryness, he ended his letter by bidding his friend
remember, if he thought it a little pompous, that he, Andersen, 'had a
screw loose'. (The idiom is the same in Danish.)

During this time, he wrote 'a heartfelt little poem' called 'The Dying
Child', which he sent to Mrs Jürgensen, written on the reverse side of
his letter, cautioning her not to let any stranger see it. The poem
embodied not only his despair, but the longing for a pure, spiritual
love which had been with him since childhood. A new translation is
offered here:

> Mother, let me sleep, my eyes are heavy,
> Let me drift away in your embrace.
> Hush, my mother, why should you be weeping?
> I can feel your hot tears on my face.
> I am cold, so cold, the rough wind scares me,
> But in my dreams I float in tranquil skies
> And mingle with the other angel children
> Standing round me as I close my eyes.
>
> Mother, look; here comes the great Arch-angel!
> Listen how the glorious music plays!
> Now he spreads his mighty wings, God-given,
> Broad and white before my wondering gaze.
> Look, he brings green leaves and fresh, sweet flowers,
> Floats them, red and yellow, round my head.
> Mother, can I have my wings while living
> Or must I wait until I, too, am dead?
>
> Why, my mother, do you hug me tightly
> And press your burning cheek so close to mine?

In a while, I'll be with you for ever –
There will be no need for you to pine.
Do not mourn, or I too will start crying,
And I am tired, so deathly tired – oh, see –
Sweet mother, dry your eyes – see how the angel
Come flying through his skies – he kisses me!

Despite his warning to Mrs Jürgensen, Andersen sent copies of the poem to various other friends, including Collin and Guldberg, explaining that he could not help having written it, the impulse was too strong to withstand – and, he added, he had wasted no school time on it, since it had been composed in what was supposed to be a holiday period. He also, in desperation, showed the verses to Meisling himself, realising that 'The Dying Child' was the best thing he had done. The poem was destined to be immensely popular, and can be seen to have marked Andersen's debut as a serious writer, but Meisling declared it to be sentimental rubbish. The telling-off which followed again reduced the young man to trembling misery, and on Professor Guldberg's advice, he decided to have the whole thing out with the headmaster. He wrote Meisling a very polite letter in which he explained that the angry attacks produced such panic in him that he could not give a coherent answer, and begged for a more moderate approach.

Meisling assured him that his severity was only in order to make sure that Andersen did well in his exams, as this was the final year before the public *examen artium* which qualified for University entrance, but within a short time, his savagery was redoubled. Close to a complete breakdown, Andersen poured out the headmaster's actual words in a frantic letter to Jonas Collin:

You think it doesn't matter about a single letter, that it's all the same whether you write an e or an i . . . You are the most narrow-minded person I have ever met, and yet you believe yourself to be worth something. If you were really a poet, you would drop your studies, devote yourself entirely to poetry. If you couldn't make a living out of it in Denmark, there's the whole of Germany for you. But you are no good at all! You may be able to write an occasional drinking song, turn out some rhymes about the sun and the moon, but such things are nothing but childish pranks. I, too, can write, probably just as well as you can, but it is only tomfoolery . . .

Meisling's insistence that Andersen could not spell adds credence to the well-established theory that the young man was, in fact, dyslexic. An article by Axel Rosendal in the Danish periodical *Ordblindebladet* (*The Journal of the Word-blind*), June 1975, gives numerous examples of his letter substitution and misconstructions, and there can be little doubt that Meisling's ferocity only increased his difficulties.

Collin received his letter with scant patience:

> Do not lose heart, my dear Andersen, compose yourself, calm down and be sensible, then you will see that things are really all right. The headmaster means well. His method may be somewhat different from that of others, but it will lead to the desired goal all the same. More of this later, perhaps, as I am pressed for time just now. May God give you strength!

Mrs Wulff, becoming worried about the increasing desperation of Andersen's letters, went to see Jonas Collin and told him that something must be done. She wrote to Andersen on 16 November, telling him of her action and promising that a plan to improve things had been devised but Collin was still reluctant to believe that anything was amiss. He wrote Meisling a cautious letter, saying he had not heard anything from his protégé for some time and that he had been sounding despondent. He added that some information from another person which he had previously ignored led him to believe the headmaster might be dissatisfied with Andersen, and asked for further information.

The letter was utterly inoffensive, but Meisling, who seems to have been in a state of some mental instability himself, responded with a roar of rage, pointing out that a pedagogue, like an artist, worked best when ignorant bystanders refrained from poking their fingers into his business. He accused Collin of having listened to malicious gossip and ended by saying that he would be quite happy to leave Andersen's education in other hands.

Nothing could have proved the substance of Andersen's complaints more conclusively, but Collin, though insulted, was still not convinced. He wrote back a stiff letter:

> Without finding occasion to engage in an analysis of pedagogy and

art, I will with respect to your communication of the 25th merely remark that I, as you will recall, have never intruded into your method of handling Andersen.

He had, he added, kept his fingers to himself, and would be glad if the headmaster would have the courtesy to make a proper reply to a legitimate letter.

Meisling, needless to say, had berated Andersen for complaining, and demanded to know who it was that had gossiped to Collin. He instructed Andersen to write to his benefactor and ask whether he should remain in the school until 27 January of the coming year, 1827, when the quarter already paid for came to an end; obviously he could not remain in the house any longer than that. Andersen duly retailed these queries to Collin, adding some of his own:

> Is there no possibility that I can get private tuition? The meals I can get somehow, and the money which is saved could then be used to pay a teacher. It goes without saying that I will be diligent, for my life is at stake.

Jonas Collin was not a man to be hustled into precipitate action, and emotional appeals merely increased his caution. He wrote back to say that a change of some kind might be considered, and sent a dignified letter to Meisling, asking to be informed 'some weeks in advance' if Andersen was in fact no longer to lodge with the Meislings. He then seemed to feel that the whole thing had blown over. Andersen wrote to Emil Hundrup and suggested that he might move back to Slagelse, but Emil warned him strongly against it.

By the middle of February 1827, things were at crisis point again. Andersen sent a wild letter to Mrs Wulff in which he said that everything was lost and he now had nobody to turn to, and she, having put herself out to try to help him, wrote back with a flash of impatience:

> You certainly do your utmost to be trying to your friends, and I can't believe you get much fun out of it yourself – all because of your constant concern with yourself – your own self – the great poet you think you'll be – my dear Andersen! Don't you realise that you are not going to succeed in all these ideas and that you

It was better to be good at something small than bad at something great, she insisted, but Andersen could not accept any such idea.

Salvation came at last through Christian Werliin, the young teacher who had mistakenly stood outside the Wulffs' house in hopes of seeing Ida Wulff the opera singer. Employed as a Hebrew teacher at the Elsinore school, he was only one year older than Andersen, and had struck up a friendship with him. He was also well aware of the true situation, and at Easter, accompanied Andersen to Copenhagen. Andersen stayed with the Wulffs, but on the first morning after his arrival, strongly prompted by Werliin, he went to see Jonas Collin and told him how bad things were at the school. Collin still insisted that the young man must put up with it but when Andersen reported this to his friend, Werliin took the matter into his own hands. He went to see Collin alone, and whatever he said to him had a dramatic effect. That same day, Andersen was told he must leave Elsinore at once. He could complete his studies with a private tutor in Copenhagen, and would take his *examen artium* as an independent student at the University the following year. Collin wrote immediately to Meisling, withdrawing Andersen from the school.

Werliin had almost certainly revealed details of Mrs Meisling's promiscuity. He, being on the staff of the school and sharing none of Andersen's sexual naïvety, would have been well aware of what was going on – and those in charge of Hans Christian's moral and physical welfare would have been horrified to hear that they had placed their protégé in the care of a woman who was to all intents and purposes a prostitute.

Mrs Meisling left her husband some years later, and took up residence in Vestergade. Happening to meet Andersen one day, she was outspoken about how much she had loathed her husband, and invited the young man to pay her 'a tender visit' which he hastily turned down. He never gave any sign of understanding why his school career had come to such an abrupt end, but whatever the cause, he was profoundly relieved. 'I could breathe and live again,' he wrote in his *Levnedsbog*. 'My old happiness returned, I could hardly sleep the next night.'

Not even waiting for the holiday to end, Collin sent Andersen back on the steamer to Elsinore on Easter Sunday, telling him to pack his things and say goodbye to the Meislings. He was then to come back to Copenhagen, where Werliin had already arranged for an academic friend, L.C. Müller, nicknamed 'Hebrew Müller' by those who knew him, to act as tutor. Meisling had gone away for Easter. Andersen waited dutifully for his return on the Wednesday, only to be asked, 'Haven't you gone yet?' He explained that he would be off on the mail coach early the next morning, and when he climbed aboard on Thursday 18 April 1827, he made his carefully prepared farewell, thanking the headmaster for all the help he had been given. Meisling's last words were not mollified. 'You can go to hell,' he said.

On 18 April 1827, a couple of weeks after his twenty-second birthday, Andersen moved into an attic room in Vingaardsstraede. He went daily to Müller for coaching in all subjects except mathematics, in which he found no difficulty, a common characteristic of dyslexics. He found his new tutor pleasant to work with, and disagreed with him only on religious grounds. Müller, a strict Christian who was later to enter the ministry, believed absolutely in judgement and hellfire, whereas Andersen, always inclining towards his father's humanitarian views, found this impossible to accept. A strong influence in the opposite direction came from H.C. Ørsted, with whom Andersen dined every Friday. The physicist saw the detailed totality of life as an immanent expression of the holy spirit, and this was far more to Andersen's taste than the fierce disciplines of the Lutheran church.

As he had assured Collin, meals could indeed be got 'somehow'. Andersen had no compunction whatever in accepting hospitality on a regular basis, as he had done in the days before he went to Slagelse. Mrs Wulff had been right when she pointed out his total obsession with himself; since childhood, he had been assured by the doting Anne Marie and his grandmother that any shortcomings and discomforts he experienced were to be blamed on the failure of the outside world to understand him and cater for his special needs. He himself had been cosseted and protected, his strangeness explained away as genius, and throughout the harsh years of belated schooling he had clung desperately to this belief. Now that he had attained the privileged status of student, it seemed more than ever natural that other people should play their part in supporting him.

This was not mere arrogance. Andersen knew that study was normally only undertaken by the sons of gentlemen who could afford the costs. For a poor boy to fight his way into this privileged situation was exceptional, and in the absence of a grant structure, it was left to private individuals to help in what way they could. Accordingly, Andersen again took up his routine of meals with his various well-wishers; Monday with the Wulffs,Tuesday with the Collins and on Wednesday, G.H. Olsen, Councillor and Theatre director. On Thursdays he went to Frederikke Müffelmann, widowed sister of the Meisling's housekeeper in Slagelse, and on Fridays to the Ørsteds. Saturdays were earmarked for Jonathan Balling, a warehouse manager with whom he had stayed sometimes during brief escapes from school, and Sundays were left free in case of other invitations. When none was forthcoming, he reluctantly ate at a café.

In his new happiness, Andersen abandoned his gloomy poetry and wrote satirical, flippant verse, influenced to some extent by Heiberg, whom he met at the Ørsteds. Johan Heiberg was the darling of the Copenhagen public at the time, having triumphed in a battle with the directors of the Royal Theatre over the introduction of vaudeville to the Danish stage. Irreverent, funny and above all, written in the language of the people, his productions were instantly popular; effectively, he had broken through the convention which regarded the theatre as exclusive to upper-class culture, and flung it wide open. Andersen, too, was moving into fresh fields. He had discovered the fantasy stories of E.T.A. Hoffmann, now only known through Offenbach's *Tales of Hoffmann*, and these imaginative stories ran in his mind as he walked every day to his lessons. Müller had now moved over the bridge to Christianshaven, on the Copenhagen island of Amager, and the longer distance gave his student ample time to let his imagination run. His mind was buzzing with long-suppressed imagination, and now his thoughts flew out 'like a swarm of bees'. He began to put together a series of fantasies centred around the fictional young poet who was himself, and let his fancy take him to meet St Peter, who held the keys to Amager as well as the heavenly gate. He explored the future and talked to giants – and he took his revenge on Meisling, who had been known to the Slagelse pupils as 'the monster', in a highly recognisable portrait, purportedly of the Devil:

> His hair stood out bristling and uncombed round his purple face; his eyes had a greenish gleam, and his whole person looked like something that belonged in a pond.

Andersen even rewrote some of his earlier and somewhat morbid poems in a mocking style and included them in the book which resulted from this new exercise of his fancies, *A Journey on Foot from*

Holmen's Canal to the Eastern Part of Amager in the Years 1828–1829. It was not a time of snappy titles, but this one contained a joke at Molbech's expense. His travel book, with an equally lengthy title, covered the experiences of two years, whereas Andersen's imaginary wanderings all take place on the single night of New Year's Eve, thus spanning two years in a few hours. Writing afterward in *Mit livs eventyr*, he was disparaging about this early work, referring to it as 'a new mannerism' adopted to conceal his diffidence – and yet, it was closer in tone to the stories which would make him famous than much of the longer work which he himself thought impressive.

Long before the book was completed, Andersen was anxious to appear in print and establish some credentials as a writer. From his return to Copenhagen in April 1827, he had eighteen months before the *examen artium* which would qualify him for university entrance - and he did not want to go on to a degree course. He needed to pass the exam, otherwise Jonas Collin might well feel that his help had been wasted, but he was not a natural academic. More years spent in study would simply defer his main aim in life, which was to be a writer.

On 17 August 1827, Heiberg printed several of Andersen's comic poems in the paper he edited, *Københavns flyvende Post*. They were signed only with a capital H and a couple of dashes, and most people assumed them to have been written by Heiberg himself which, Andersen admitted wryly, accounted for much of their popularity. The following month, Ludolph Schley, whom Andersen had met at Elsinore, translated 'The Dying Child' into German, and after appearing in a German paper it found its way into a Copenhagen publication and Heiberg reprinted it. In January 1828 the poem, together with two others, appeared in Schley's Swedish translation in *Scandinavian New Writing*, and Andersen began to feel that he was getting somewhere.

Jette Wulff cheerfully dismissed 'The Dying Child' as sentimental, though she was, Andersen said:

> the only person who understood me at that time; she encouraged the humour in my poems; she won all my confidence, defended me boldly against all the small attacks to which I was subjected in her circles, especially because of my personality . . .

Despite her deformity, Jette was lively and irreverent and full of courage, and Andersen found the Wulffs by far the easiest and most relaxed of the hosts who gave him a daily meal. Although – or perhaps because – he owed Jonas Collin a great debt of gratitude, the brisk, unemotional tone of the household chilled him a little. In *Levnedsbogen* he is frank about his first impressions:

> I was in some way really afraid of the father, though I loved him with all my heart; my fear was due to the fact that I regarded him as my life's destiny, indeed; my whole existence depended on him. The eldest daughter Ingeborg Drewsen was married and had left home, she was the one who had spoken to me most, the other children did not do so at all, in fact, Edvard seemed to me so cold, so forbidding, that I really believed he could not stand me, that he was arrogant, even my enemy.

Edvard Collin admits that his father's odd protégé made little impression on him at first. He remembered Andersen at about seventeen as an overgrown boy with a long, old-looking face, blue eyes and fair hair, with a pair of yellow nankeen trousers that reached only halfway down his shins. Five years later, he was struck by 'the change for the better which had taken place in his physical development', but there was still no sign of the close friendship which was to develop between them. Andersen's most frequent companion at this time was Carl Bagger, the young poet he had met at the Ingemanns' house in Sorø and who had just come to Copenhagen, but the relationship seems to have been founded on admiration rather than real warmth. Bagger was, Andersen said, 'one of the soundest and most gifted poets' of his time.

In April he moved to number 33 Store Kongensgard, and in August he met at the Wulffs' house two young Portuguese brothers, the wonderfully named Jorge and Carlos Torlades O'Neill. He was not greatly impressed, and confided in a letter to Jette that he found the elder one 'a little serious and silent'. Their only subject of real mutual interest was the libretti of some Italian and Portuguese operas, and apart from this, 'we didn't talk to each other much, I don't know why'. Since they were aged only eight and eleven at the time, they may have found Andersen a little alarming, but years later, they were to make him welcome in their own country.

Andersen meanwhile was beginning to panic about the *examen artium* which would take place in October, and confessed in a letter to Jette Wulff that he was sure he would fail. As it turned out, the experience must have been a strange one, for people he knew as personal friends suddenly appeared in the guise of examiners. Adam Oehlenschläger, as Dean of the Faculty of Arts, shook Andersen by the hand when he presented himself and wished him luck, but the gawky lad was still filled with dread. The mathematics examiner turned out to be a shy young man called von Schmidten, to whom Andersen had chatted over dinner at the Ørsteds, taking him for a fellow-student. Both of them were embarrassed, and von Schmidten was so reluctant to come to the business in hand that Andersen had to suggest that there should be some mathematical questions. 'But do you know anything?' the young man asked anxiously. He must have been relieved to find that Andersen in fact had a good grasp of the subject though the nervous candidate was by now in such a state that several of von Schmidten's pens snapped in his shaking fingers during his replies.

Latin, as ever, was his poorest subject, but although Andersen did badly in the paper, his overall result was a pass. After six years of belated full-time education, he could at last feel that he had justified Jonas Collin's faith in him. His grant from the public fund was extended for a further year so that he could take the two-part examination in philosophy and philology, necessary for those intending to take an honours degree, but Andersen persuaded Collin that he could study for this final qualification on his own, thus saving the fifteen rixdollars paid monthly to Müller. Such a sum, Andersen felt, could be much better used.

His main aim was to get something into print. His *Journey On Foot* had not yet found a publisher, and the need to make some sort of mark as a professional writer was pressing. In the autumn, Heiberg printed some excerpts from the *Journey* in the *Københavns flyvende Post*, which laid down a useful preliminary appearance, but Carl Reitzel, the leading publisher of the day, was still cautious. He would not pay the hundred rixdollars Andersen asked, and offered only seventy for an outright purchase of all rights. Andersen turned this down, and instead took the huge risk of publishing the book himself, using the money saved from Müller's fees. Five hundred copies were printed, to sell at one rixdollar per book – and, helped by the publicity Heiberg had given it, the edition sold out. Reitzel, impressed, offered a hundred rixdollars for rights to a second edition, which Andersen was happy to accept.

Despite its popularity, the book was full of small errors. Nobody had edited the manuscript, and Andersen's misspellings and grammatical lapses were pounced on gleefully by those who thought him a conceited young puppy. His friends were embarrassed for him, but Andersen was now unstoppable. Full of admiration for Heiberg, he rejigged his earlier effort at play-writing, *The Forest Chapel*, converting it into a vaudeville, full of self-parody and mock heroics. Quite possibly through Heiberg's continued influence, the Royal Theatre accepted it, and although the play had only three performances, from 23 to 25 April 1829, Andersen was hysterical with delight:

> When the play was staged it was acclaimed by my fellow-students and they shouted out, "Long live the author!" . . . I could not contain my happiness but rushed out of the theatre and along the street to Collin's; his wife was at home alone; in a state of near-collapse I fell into a chair and burst into tears. Mrs Collin was full of sympathy but had no idea what was the matter, so she began to comfort me, saying, "Don't be upset, you know Oehlenschläger and many other great poets have been hissed before now." "Yes, but they didn't hiss," I sobbed, "they clapped and shouted 'Three cheers!' "

This account from *Mit livs eventyr* is unguarded in admitting that it was a student claque who supported him so loyally. In fact the play was not well received – hence its rapid replacement – but Andersen hardly cared. For the first time in his life, he was part of a group of young men who were thoroughly enjoying themselves, and went about in what he later called 'the poetical intoxication of youth', finding delight in friendship and shared enthusiasms. Carl Bagger proposed that he and Andersen should publish a joint book of verse and others wanted to start a weekly review, and while these ideas never actually came to anything, they added to the general ebullience. They read Byron together in a romantic ecstasy, dreaming of Greece and the Grand Tour of Europe's cultural capitals, and Andersen discovered Heine, that dark and revolutionary figure who was to flee the political repression in Germany and live in exiled sin. Andersen and Bagger recited his poetry continually, and the high romanticism of Scott, Byron and Heine, Andersen said, 'went spiritually into my blood'.

Also in his blood – though whether through heredity or from sheer enthusiasm cannot be proved – was a fervent royalism. Shortly after the *examen artium* Andersen joined the second company of the King's Life Corps as a private. His unusual height may have helped considerably to get him into this rather exclusive regiment, but it was evidently on a territorial basis rather than as full-time service, for on 29 June of the following summer, while still a member of the corps, he set out on a six-weeks' tour of Denmark, moving from one hospitable household to another.

At the start of his journey, he crossed on the country's first steamship, the *Caledonia*, to the small island of Møn, where he stayed with Laura Tønder-Lund's married sister, Anna. The steamer had been unkindly nicknamed 'Splashy Molly' by the resentful captains of the sailing vessels, and in *Mit livs eventyr* Andersen recalled the forebodings of an old sailor who happened to be a relative of H.C. Ørsted. Since the beginning of time, he lamented, people had been satisfied with sensible ships that sailed with the wind, but now they had to go and meddle with things. Every time he saw the 'smoke-ship' go past, he would shout abuse at it through a megaphone until it was out of earshot.

Andersen moved on to Petersgaard, the home of Jette Wulff's uncle, Commander Christian Wulff, then spent a few days in Odense, where he visited his mother and stayed with the now-widowed Mrs Iversen in her country house, Marieshøj. He broke the return journey with a stay at Hofmansgave, a manor-house belonging to Niels Hofman-Bang, whose brother, Christian, was friendly with the Collin boys, and this visit was in many ways a crucial one. It gave Andersen a first taste of the gracious country living which was to become a cherished part of his annual pattern, and at the same time sharpened his sense of the social divide. To be named for one's own estate was a mark of privilege unattainable by those whose surnames ended with the humble '*sen*', a relic of the old patronymic system which named the commoner's child merely as the son or daughter ('*sen*' or '*datter*') of the father. In a story called 'Children's Prattle', written years later, the chip on the shoulder still shows as Andersen reflects with bitter triumph that the great sculptor Thorvaldsen, had triumphed over the handicap of his common name.

The stay at Hofmansgave was also significant because Andersen was joined there by Edvard Collin and his younger brother, Theodor. Six months previously, Andersen had sent Edvard a copy of his early poem,

'The Soul', with a brief and self-conscious note excusing this 'poor first-born' effort, but since then, the letters exchanged between them had become easier and more personal. From Odense, Andersen had written to tell Edvard how he had blundered into a private house where a man and his wife were eating their supper, having mistaken the house for a pub – but he had also been discussing with Edvard such weighty matters as the nature of the human spirit. It was obvious that a close friendship was developing.

Andersen at this time was evidently interested in his own nature and the working of the human mind, for a month later, on 18 September, he read the whole of F.C. Sibbern's *Psychological Pathology*, published the previous year, and was immediately moved to write a poem about it. This, entitled 'The Moment of Death', was published in *Københavnsposten* the following week, and incorporated many phrases from a letter Andersen had written to Edvard on 19 September, including the wish articulated by Robert Burns that we could see ourselves as others see us. In that pre-Freudian age, the study of psychology was still much concerned with human feeling and behaviour as an expression of the soul, and this metaphysical approach cannot have enlightened Andersen much, though it no doubt reinforced his mother's assurances that he was a person of exceptional spiritual quality.

On 21 October and 14 November, he sat the final exams in philology and philosophy and was again questioned by men well known to him. H.C. Ørsted, though friendly, floored him completely by asking what he knew of electromagnetism, and Andersen pointed out with a trace of indignation that there was no mention of the subject in Ørsted's own textbook. The physicist, who had discovered the principles of electromagnetism only a few years previously, reminded him that it had been covered in one of his lectures, and Andersen had to admit that he must have missed it. The omission cost him a mark, but he passed the exam as a whole, and at the Ørsted's house later, was fascinated to be given an insight into the new discovery.

The year of 1830 began well, with the publication of a book of Andersen's poems which also included a story entitled 'The Corpse'. This, though not well resolved at its first appearance, was later reworked as 'The Travelling Companions', one of his first and best-known fairy tales. At that time, however, the writing of brief stories did not greatly interest him. Still anxious to impress the reading public, he had set his thoughts on a full-length novel in the style of a Scott or Ingemann romance, historically based. He had been toying with this idea ever since his schooldays, proposing to call the book *The Dwarf of Christian II* and set it in sixteenth-century Jutland. Jonas Collin, concerned about the young man's welfare now that his last exams had been taken and his grant had ceased, encouraged him. Serious historical research might well attract a further bursary.

Andersen clung to the suggestion as his only hope. Even without financial support, he could at least write up an account of the trip for publication in a newspaper, as he had done with his journey the previous summer – and Copenhagen was offering him little comfort. On 30 March, he had been promoted to corporal in the King's Life Corps, but his poems brought no real income, and his one semi-successful book, the *Journey On Foot* had been mercilessly satirised by Carsten Hauch in a comedy which had featured a very recognisable Andersen, as a clown who had built 'a mad-house' of pedestrian fancies. Andersen had been unwise enough to write a rhymed riposte in Heiberg's paper, which did not improve his reputation. To cap it all, his mother had begun to send him importuning letters, assuming that he was now an educated gentleman who must also be rich. Andersen knew she wanted money to support her alcohol dependency, and at first sent his small contributions via the Guldbergs, asking if they would use it to buy clothes or other necessities for her use, but his mother wanted none of that. Her next letter demanded cash in her own hand, and Andersen evidently complied, for on his twenty-fifth birthday in April of that year, she thanked him for his support, without which she would, she said, have died.

The situation was a depressing one and, as so often, Andersen took refuge in flight. Accompanied by a young artist called Martinus Rørbye, he set off on 30 May for the major Danish island of Jutland, taking the steamer Dania across to Århus. To his delight, people in this north-westerly area had heard of his *Journey on Foot* even though his poems were unknown to them. He made his way westward, keen to see this wild part of the country where gypsies still roamed. It was a barren landscape at that time, useless as farm-land, and so had escaped the enclosures, remaining a wilderness very attractive to Andersen's romantic spirit – but the weather turned wet and windy after he left Viborg, and the 'biting sea-mist' affected him so badly that he abandoned his plan to explore the coast and headed back to Skanderborg. Rørbye's destination had been the manorhouse of Tjele, so Andersen was now travelling alone, recording his progress in letters to friends. On 15 June, he wrote optimistically to Edvard Collin, reporting that Jutlanders were full of enthusiasm for his work, and had promised to contribute to a subscription list for the publication costs of his proposed new novel. Edvard wrote back without illusion. Such assurances were a response to Andersen's pressure, he said, and would quickly be forgotten when he had moved on.

Andersen was indeed moving on. The account of the bleak north-west which he later published was based on pure hearsay, for he was heading south again, down to Funen and his friends in Odense. He stayed again with Mrs Iversen, and this time found the house full of lively girls, for an Iversen granddaughter, Henriette Hanck (who, like Henrietta Wulff, was known by the diminutive, Jette) was there with some friends and cousins, and this 'flockof charming and intelligent' young things flattered and teased their tall visitor. Jette Hanck, who was to become the author of several books herself, became a frequent correspondent. It was Edvard Collin, however, who seems at this time to have been most central to Andersen's thoughts, and on 30 June, about ten days after his arrival at the Iversens', Andersen wrote:

> There is no-one to whom I feel more closely attached than you, and if you are willing to forget the conditions of birth and always be to me what I am to you, then you will find in me the most candid and cordial friend.

The delicate allusion to social status found its mark, and his next letter was delighted:

> This was the first time you have signed yourself as my 'friend', though you have often proved yourself to be that in real life, and this little occurrence was infinitely dear to me, because I feel drawn to you, not only through gratitude but from the depth of my heart.

The mid-ninetenth century was a time of passionate friendships between young men; in the absence of any real public knowledge of homosexuality, degrees of affectionate intimacy were permissible then which nowadays would automatically be taken as evidence that the relationship was a gay one but Edvard's caution gives a strong indication that he found Andersen's fervour embarrassing and wanted to keep it within decent conventional bounds. Even at the time of these first overtures, he was inclined to be severe, and wrote back in July to warn his impetuous friend that some people in Copenhagen found him impossibly conceited, feeling that he rated himself even above Ingemann and Oehlenschläger. The insistence on reading his poems aloud wherever he went was making him a laughing-stock, and if he wished to preserve a good reputation, he must be more careful about his behaviour. Andersen did not listen. His response on 28 July made it clear that he treasured every word Edvard spoke, almost regardless of its meaning:

> Avidly I swallow every letter I receive, even though it may occasionally taste like medicine, but then medicine is intended to help the sick person, and if offered by a friend's hand, one accepts it gratefully.

From the Ingemanns', he went on to Hofmansgave, the manor-house where he had stayed the previous year with the Collin boys, and Niels Hofman-Bang added to his enjoyment of the great house by letting him look through a microscope at a drop of water. In a long letter to Ludvig Laessøe, one of the three children of Mrs Signe Laessøe, Andersen was excited about the infusoria he saw 'tumbling about each other, the big ones swallowing their smaller neighbours'. Hofmann-Bang, a biologist, had opened a new world to him, and in a later story called 'A Drop of Water', Andersen saw the teeming microbes as an analogy for the crowded streets of Copenhagen.

While in Funen he also visited his inebriated mother and, more strangely, hunted up Fedder Carstens, the teacher at the Jewish school who had been so affectionate twenty years ago. He found Carstens in charge of the telegraph office at Tåsinge, but the ex-teacher claimed to have no recollection of him.

The next port of call was Fåborg, where a student friend, Christian Voigt, had invited him to stay at his parents' house. Andersen arrived in the town on 5 August and put up at the inn, having made contact with Christian and arranged to go round the next morning. That evening, he wrote an impassioned letter to Edvard:

> I repeat what I have told you before, that you are the only person I

regard as my true friend, and my heart is sincerely attached to you. This is something I may never be able to say to you personally, but you can be certain that I attach the greatest importance to your every word, so please do not ever push me away – but I am becoming sentimental; you will know what I mean.

He also wrote a comment in the diary which he had reopened the previous day for the first time in four years, and this betrays an anxiety, not only about his uncertain future, but concerning the erotic urge which now constantly troubled him:

Almighty God! I have only got you, you govern my destiny, I must give myself to you! Please give me a living! Please give me a bride! My blood wants love, as my heart wants it.

As far as Andersen could see, marriage was the only permissible route to sexual fulfilment. There is no sign that he had yet, or ever would, overcome the distaste for women which he continued to articulate, but the diary entry shows very clearly that he could see no alternative. For all the evident passion he felt for Edvard, he was too ambitious and too insecure to risk revealing the forbidden self which he kept so well disguised.

Whether the missing diaries for his years between twenty-one and twenty-five years old had really not been written is doubtful. It had been a time of much angst, and throughout his life Andersen turned readily to writing down his feelings on paper – but it may well have been that he saw his early outpourings as indiscreet, and destroyed them. Towards the end of his life, on 9 May 1870, he wrote, 'If this diary should be read at some time, people may find it empty and non-committal. What happened within me and around me I don't put on paper out of consideration for myself and many others.' Edvard, too, covered his tracks to some extent, omitting from his later account of Andersen and the Collin family the most passionate of Andersen's early letters.

In this turmoil of contradictory emotion, Andersen made his way round to the Voigts' house on the morning of 7 August. He arrived too early and Christian was still in bed, but the door was opened by his sister, Riborg Voigt, who invited Andersen in and joked easily about her brother's laziness. After a stay of two days, Andersen remarked in a letter to Edvard that 'one of Mr Voigt's daughters is quite beautiful, and very natural, which I particularly like.' Twenty-four years old and dark-eyed, she had been wearing a simple grey gown that morning, and on the boating trips with the family which followed, she told the visitor how much she admired his poetry. This, he admitted in *Levnedsbogen*, 'tickled my vanity and at once made me interested in her'.

Riborg asked him for a poem written out in his own hand, and he obliged with one of his self-mocking verses about a poet who, while seeking a wife, stipulates that she must constantly praise his poems. Andersen was pleased that this pretty girl sat beside him and chatted throughout a dance one evening (for Andersen, despite the years at ballet school, could never manage a waltz or polka), but showed little real interest. All else apart, Riborg Voigt was about to announce her engagement to a local apothecary, and in her long talk to Andersen, would hardly have left this unmentioned.

From the Voigts', Andersen returned briefly to Mrs Iversen's house before going back to Copenhagen, and must have behaved in a moonstruck way, for the girls immediately accused him of having fallen in love. According to his account in *Levnedsbogen*, he was not sure whether to feel pleased or embarrassed:

> I began to long for her; the others made jokes about me; I did not like it and wanted to get these thoughts out of my head altogether. I found it ridiculous that I, who had always been so mocking about love and *Schwärmerei*, should now fall victim to it.

His thank-you letter to Mrs Iversen written on 3 September gave a broad hint that he was thinking in terms of love and its consequent domesticity, saying that he was finding it hard to settle back into his small room in Copenhagen and had a strong feeling of wanting a home of his own. He sent his greetings to the children, adding 'Pardon me, I mean the big girls', and said he missed them very much. Jette Hanck, who was only two years younger than himself, merited a letter of her own, and in this Andersen ran with irritating archness through the names of the young women whom his friends supposed him to be in love with. Riborg Voigt was included, but of her he said, 'The last guess is rather silly, as she is engaged, and I dare almost swear that she is no more to me than I to her. We have only seen each other for a few days, and she will soon be a bride.'

This was to be a constantly recurring pattern in Andersen's relationships with women. It seemed almost a prerequisite that any girl to whom he professed himself attracted would already be committed to someone else. In the case of Riborg Voigt, it was clear from the start that she was not for him, but this fact appeared to add to her charms. Like young Werther, Andersen could declare himself romantically and hopelessly in love, but he was at the same time incapable of wanting physical involvement with a female person. The situation was a genuinely sad one, for all hopes of a home and family were bound up with the institution of marriage, and these were beginning to seem as unattainable as Riborg herself.

Following the two days with the Voigts and the repeat visit to the Iversen household, Andersen went back to Copenhagen and worked for a while on a competition paper set by the university on Greek and Norse myths and their current implications. His ideas came straight from Ørsted, and centred round the notion of universality as encompassed by the human soul but Andersen was no academic. His writing was essentially about himself, and he began to produce increasingly gloomy poems, plunging deeply into a much-publicised state of unrequited love. Christian Voigt was back at the university, and Andersen visited him frequently. When Riborg came to the city for a three-week visit that autumn, Andersen saw her several times and gave her a poem entitled 'To Her', and then confessed to Christian that he loved his sister. Christian said cautiously that he thought Riborg quite liked Andersen, but offered no further encouragement.

Towards the end of Riborg's stay, on 10 October, Andersen sent her a letter which simultaneously declared his love and backed out of it, on the pretext that he had only just heard of her engagement – which, of course, was untrue:

> If you really love the other person, then forgive me! Forgive me for having dared to do this, which must then seem an effrontery. I wish you both happiness! And please do not forget someone who can never, never forget you.

He saw her that night with her family at the Royal Theatre, looking, he said, 'deathly pale and yet very beautiful, extremely beautiful'. Riborg sent him a brief note of farewell via Christian and returned to Fåborg the next day. Six months later, she was married to the apothecary.

It had been an insubstantial affair, but Andersen continued to write anguished letters to Ingemann and other literary friends, stressing his lovelorn state. Jette Hanck told him briskly that he was not nearly as unhappy as he made himself out to be, and he wrote back with offended hauteur. Jette Wulff was away in Germany, which was perhaps just as well,for she, too, never encouraged Andersen's self-pity. And Edvard Collin was not told a word about it.

Riborg Voigt was only one aspect of a time which seemed full of difficulties. The July revolution which had broken out in Paris had sent shock waves as far as Denmark, where demands for a liberalising of the system were gathering momentum, and Andersen found himself torn between what seemed irreconcilable sympathies. In his *Journey on Foot* he had expressed a satirical democratic instinct and throughout his writing there is a strong identification with the underprivileged, and yet his royalism was never far below the surface – and his public persona as the potentially great *digter* demanded an assiduous 'keeping-in' with persons of influence. At this time, Andersen was very friendly with Orla Lehmann, the lively young National Liberal who had remarked scathingly that a complaint in the local paper about a missing gutter-pipe was the full extent of free speech in Denmark. Lehmann, five years younger than Andersen, later rose to become a Cabinet Minister, but in 1830, the two young men were reading Heine together, and Andersen warmed to the way his friend gave such free and eloquent expression to his convictions. He himself had no such certainties, and was deeply vulnerable to any kind of criticism.

In December, the young playwright, Henrik Hertz, published *Letters of a Ghost*, a blistering attack on his contemporary writers which threw Copenhagen's literary circles into a state of twitter and caused Andersen the deepest of anguish. The book, published anonymously in the first instance, purported to be a beyond-the-grave communication from the dead poet, Jens Baggesen, complaining about the current obsession of writers with form as opposed to any real content. It was in fact a call for courage in a climate of political repression, urging writers to express themselves clearly instead of taking refuge in mannered triviality. Andersen, hit in his most vulnerable area, was accused of being 'drunk on the ale of fantasy' and of failing even to be linguistically competent. A child at school being guilty of such grammatical howlers as appeared in *Journey on Foot*, Hertz went on, would be spanked and stood in the corner.

The book drove a deep wedge between the opposing literary schools of thought. Heiberg, as a close friend of Henrik Hertz, took up an aggressive position in the resulting hostilities, insisting that drama and novels should be concerned with the realities of life rather than escapist fantasy, while Ingemann and Oehlenschläger, together with the younger Carsten Hauch, who had been specifically attacked in the book, clung to the view that human truth could be told in more allegorical ways.

Andersen vacillated. Caught in the crossfire, he could not bear to abandon allegiances to his friends on either side. Heiberg had been a tremendous help to him, giving advice on his poetry and publishing his early work when nobody else would – and yet, Ingemann and Oehlenschläger, too, had supported Andersen since his earliest days, and he was on closer personal terms with them than with Heiberg – and besides, he, like Hauch, was a victim of the venom of the 'Ghost'. Heiberg was not a man to tolerate political dithering, and events subsequently proved that he had lost patience with the uncommitted and increasingly self-obsessed Andersen.

A new volume of Andersen's poems, *Fantasies and Sketches*, came out the following month in January 1831, and did him no good at all. Even the supportive Ingemann commented on their melancholy nature and cautioned his young friend not to fall too heavily into the Byronic idiom, and Andersen, sensitive now about being called a fantasist, wrote back to protest that he had legitimate cause for unhappiness. Although the brief affair with Riborg had ended two months previously, he poured out all his woes afresh and ended, 'I wish I were dead! Dead!' Life, he said, was a long, miserable dream.

He was working on a play called *The Raven* and a libretto based on Scott's *The Bride of Lammermoor*, but his early popularity as a rising star had waned. *Letters From A Ghost* was attracting a gleeful readership, and Andersen was increasingly regarded – or so he suspected – as incompetent and pretentious. 'Everyone wanted to teach me,' he complained in *Mit livs eventyr*, 'and almost all of them said I was being spoiled by praise and so they at least would tell me the truth.' Edvard Collin was certainly determined to do so, and threatened at one point to walk out of an evening gathering if Andersen read so much as a single word. Depression grew, and when the spring came, Andersen was more than ready to accept Jonas Collin's advice that he should go away for a while and let things simmer down. On 16 May 1831, he got on the steamer and set off, inspired by Jette Wulff's journey the previous year and by Heine's account of travelling in the Harz mountains, to Germany.

Chapter 7
Letters Home

In a long letter dated 26 May 1831 to Mrs Laessøe, whose husband was also aboard the steamer to Lubeck, Andersen described how the passengers slept three to a divan in the saloon, head to toe, and how he had been grumbled at for being so inconveniently long. Partly perhaps because of this uncomfortable night, he was seized on the following day by an agonising attack of toothache. This recurrent affliction seemed particularly likely to strike when he was pent-up and anxious, and on the journey to Hamburg, he noted in his diary that he had to get out of the carriage at every inn to ask for some alcohol liniment to use as a compress. He finally bought a small bottle of it with some cotton wool, which 'helped somewhat'.

The coach arrived in Hamburg at five in the morning and Andersen, still suffering, did some dawn sightseeing, but was in too much pain to attend a theatre performance that evening, and went to bed at nine o'clock. The last story he ever wrote, 'Auntie Toothache', looked back across thirty-five years to borrow the exact words which he wrote in his diary that day:

> The nerves are in fact delicate tangents that imperceptible movements of air play upon, and that's why those teeth are tormenting me – first piano, then crescendo, all the melodies of pain at every shift in the weather.

He managed all the same to be up at dawn the next morning to write letters, and one of these was to Edvard Collin, with a request which had been preying on Andersen's mind since the beginning of their friendship. Tentatively and in terror ('Oh, please do not be angry with me – ') he asked Edvard to say '*du*' to him. Like most European languages, Danish has the familiar form, used with children and close friends, and the more polite plural. In today's Denmark, people will happily say, 'we are all *du*s here', meaning that the neighbourhood is a friendly one, and the formal address is kept only for courteous address between people who do not know each other well, but in the nineteenth century, a mutual agreement to say '*du*' was a step of some significance, often celebrated by the '*drikke dus*' ceremony of linking arms and drinking to the newly sealed friendship. Edvard had always maintained the formal address, despite occasional hints in Andersen's letters that this was irksome, and now, from the safe distance of another country, the traveller plucked up all his courage:

> Face to face, I could never have asked you, it's only possible now that I'm abroad. If you have any objections, then please never mention the matter and I of course will never ask you again . . . Are you angry with me? – You have no idea how my heart is beating as I write this, even though you yourself are not here.

Andersen had used '*du*' in his letters to Emil Hundrup, the school friend from Slagelse, but Edvard, although three years younger than himself, had never entered into this boyhood familiarity. Andersen had come into the Collin household as a poverty-stricken stranger in need of help, and for a long time, Edvard had maintained a certain distance. It was precisely this distance which Andersen now challenged, risking humiliation in a dangerous test of their friendship. The letter written and posted, he moved on, travelling across Luneberg Heath to Brunswick, a journey of thirty-six hours in a jolting coach with five other people which left him, he told Mrs Laessøe, feeling 'cooked and beaten'. Roads were still little more than cart-tracks and, after an alarming expedition down a coalmine when he feared losing touch with the guide and his candle, he was glad to set off on a walking tour of the Harz mountains, free of claustrophobic coachtravel. He walked forty-eight miles to Eisleben, Luther's birthplace, and then went on by mail coach to Leipzig.

On this trip Andersen was well supplied with the necessary letters of introduction. In Leipzig he stayed with a publisher, Heinrich Brockhaus, and there found another Danish visitor, Oehlenschläger's daughter, Lotte. With her, he visited Gellert's grave and, glancing round the flowered and beribboned cemetery, spotted one tombstone which had been decorated with sliced lemons. It looked, he said, 'like a compost heap'. He was beginning to enjoy himself, and wrote in his diary on 31 May: 'Oh, to travel, to travel, if only one could spend a lifetime flitting from one place to another! I really feel as if the world is my home . . . '

He had hoped to find a letter from Edvard waiting for him in Dresden, but there was none. However, he met up with the Norwegian painter, Johan Christian Dahl, with whom Jette Wulff had studied during her German tour the previous year, and through Ingemann's introduction, encountered one of Europe's leading poets, Ludwig Tieck. It was an emotional meeting which confirmed Andersen's conviction that he was of the brotherhood of great poets, and on departure, leaving Dresden after a three-day walking tour of Saxon Switzerland, he was deeply touched by a final visit to the old man:

> At three o'clock I went to see Tieck, he wrote a few farewell words, pressed me to his heart and kissed my cheek. I couldn't help weeping, even at the door he clasped me to his breast and told me to go with courage along the way to which I had been born.

In this north-eastern German town, Andersen had for the first time encountered the panoply and mystery of Catholicism. It ran completely counter to his mother's devout Lutheran belief, but witnessing the celebration of Corpus Christi moved him profoundly:

> The church was big and bright, with several chapels where people were kneeling. There was beautiful music, and the *castrati* sang like young girls. It had a strange effect on me. – In the aisles there were attendants in yellow robes and with big silver staves; in front of the altar stood three priests in white silk embroidered with gold and flowers. Choirboys in red robes covered by a fine, white tunic held candles and swung censers in many strange rituals.

The paradox of sexless motherhood which lies at the heart of catholic Christianity touched Andersen closely, for this same impossible ideal underlay all his ideas of female beauty and virtue. When he went with Dahl to the Art Gallery, he saw Raphael's Sistine Madonna, and commented, 'It is a childlike, ethereal face; it is to be worshipped, not loved!'

On his last day in Dresden, he wrote to Christian Voigt, for whom he had maintained an affectionate liking, and said firmly that he did not love Riborg any more, underlining the words, '<u>that is certain</u>'. It was less than a year since he had met her, but he suffered now, he claimed, from the emptiness of knowing he no longer loved. 'Oh, God! Christian! I hope you will never feel what I am feeling now.'

In Berlin he found the longed-for letter from Edvard. Only after several paragraphs on other matters did it mention the '*du*' question – and the answer was a flat refusal. Despite his firmness, Edvard floundered a little, knowing quite well that Andersen was aware that he was on '*du*' terms with other young men:

> If at a merry party among students etc someone suggests to me that we should say du to each other then I agree, partly through lack of more mature reflection, partly to avoid insulting the person concerned who thinks that this will establish a more friendly relationship.

Careless agreements of this kind, Edvard insisted, meant nothing:

> But when I have known for a long time someone I respect and like and he invites me to say *du*, then this unpleasant and inexplicable feeling arises in me.

He cited the poet Baggesen, who almost wrecked a well-established friendship through precisely that suggestion then, gathering courage, came closer to the point:

> And why should we make this change in our relationship? Is it in order to give others an outward sign of how we relate to each other? But that would be superfluous and of no consequence to either of us. And isn't our relationship very pleasant and useful to both of us as it is? Why then restart it in a new fashion, a fashion which, I feel, is of no importance in itself but for which I have, as I have told you, a dislike; I admit to being a curious person in this respect.

In his book, *H.C.Andersen and the Collin Family*, Edvard made it very clear that his refusal to comply with his friend's request sprang from an awareness that Andersen wanted a more passionate relationship than Edvard could contemplate. 'He dreamed of finding in me a "romantic friend"; but I would be no good at that at all.' Andersen was too firmly embedded within the Collin family structure for Edvard to break loose from him altogether, and as Jonas Collin grew older it was Edvard who took on the responsibility of guiding and advising their protégé but he strove constantly to keep Andersen within the bounds of decent convention, knowing the gulf of social disaster which yawned should their relationship become so close as to cause scandalous gossip. Much was permissible in those unsuspecting days, and men could unconcernedly embrace or walk arm-in-arm along a public street, but Andersen's impulsive, passionate nature rang warning bells in Edvard's mind. He ended his letter with a step back from the quagmire of feeling which Andersen offered:

> Let us speak no more of it. I hope we will both forget this mutual exchange. When you return I shall be in Jutland, so we will not see each other until the winter. There could never be any question of my being angry at your request. I shall not misunderstand you, and I hope you will not misunderstand me, either.

Andersen's first response, written from Berlin, was later described by Edvard as 'friendly', but in fact it was a stunned and terrified grovel:

> I love you like a brother, thank you for every line. No, I will not misunderstand you, I am incapable of being sad, for you open your heart to me so kindly. If only I had your character, your whole personality! Oh! I am acutely aware of how far below you I am in many ways, but please remain always what you are now, my true, perhaps my most sincere friend, I really need it.

Significantly, it was only at this point, in the fear that his ardour had driven Edvard away, that Andersen chose to reveal his love for Riborg Voigt. In view of his recent assurance to Christian that the affair was conclusively over, his account of it to Edvard bore a strong smack of reassurance. He played it like a long-held trump card, as if to prove to Edvard that there was nothing to be afraid of and that he, Andersen, took a normal, healthy interest in women:

> Last summer I got to know a wealthy, beautiful, lively girl who feels the same for me as I do for her; she was engaged and certain considerations forced her to marry a man who took her only for her fortune; she was married shortly before I went away; all I have from her are a few words in which she asks me, as a sister, to forget

everything. That was the reason why I had to go away, oh! I have been crying like a child. It was absurd of me, poor as I am, to fall in love; it is true that she had fortune enough for both of us, but then people would have said that it was a speculation on my part, and that would have hurt me deeply.

This fictionalised account must have caused some amusement in the Collin household, where the truth of the affair was already well known, Andersen having unburdened himself at the time to Louise, Edvard's younger sister, but it must have proved to Edvard just how dangerous Andersen was as a man whose turbulent feelings were far more real to him than the objective reality he shared with others.

In the first shocked days which followed Edvard's letter, Andersen doggedly continued his rounds of the famous. Through H.C. Ørsted, he was introduced to Adalbert von Chamisso, a polymath who was both scientist and writer, a member of the legendary group centred round Madame de Stael and a round-the-world traveller with a Russian biological expedition. When Andersen met him, Chamisso was keeper of Berlin's botanical gardens, but his fame rested mainly on his book, *Peter Schlemihl's Strange Story*, of a man who lost his shadow. It was an image that fitted exactly with Andersen's bereft state of mind, and he used it both as the title of the travel book he wrote on return, *Shadow Pictures*, and as the basis of the terrible tale of vengeance he wrote years later, 'The Shadow'. Chamisso himself was a strange figure in a long, grey-brown dressing-gown and with straggling grey hair, who said gloomily that these were not the times for a poet to be read, for the world wanted action – but he translated several of Andersen's poems into German and, being friendly with Ingemann and Oehlenschläger, continued to take a helpful interest in their young friend's work for many years.

Andersen was back in Copenhagen on 24 June after his month away, and at once set about writing up his travels. Reitzel paid him 150 rixdollars for the book, its full title being *Shadow Pictures of a Journey* to *the Harz Mountains, Switzerland and Germany in the Year 1831*, thus enabling Andersen almost to recoup the 160 rixdollars which the trip had cost him. The style, with its mixture of prose and verse, reportage and fancy, was a rather blatant imitation of Heine's *Reisebilder* (*Travel Pictures*) and Andersen permitted himself a last look at the Riborg Voigt affair with a sentimental tale about a bride who, at her wedding, looks in vain for the man she had really loved.

Edvard was still away in Jutland, but Andersen wrote him letter after letter, nagging at the pain of the '*du*' refusal and trying to prod his friend into an abandoning of his cool, detached attitude. In August he wrote, 'I long to speak to you from the heart and in friendship, alone', but complained that Edvard was sometimes 'so terribly sensible, repelling me like a shuttlecock from the racquet'. Too distraught to work well, he again took up *The Dwarf of Christian II* and wrote a vaudeville, *The Ship*, in the Heiberg manner which had a brief run at the Royal Theatre, but ideas flitted through his mind with febrile speed, none of them lodging there to develop properly. He wrote to Jette Hanck with the notion of publishing a book entitled *Ideas For Those Who Have None Themselves: A Needful Resource Book For These Lean Times*, but this, too, came to nothing. *Shadow Pictures*, which had appeared on 19 September, had been reasonably well received, but it did little to relieve a general sense of being bogged down.

Edvard remained the focus of Andersen's attention, and through him, the Collin family. There is a very clear implication that Andersen wanted a secure position within this clan which had nearly, but not quite, adopted him as a son. In his letter of 20 August to Edvard he spoke of Ingeborg Drewsen's year-old son, Viggo, in appealing terms. 'I love the child as if he were my own,' he wrote, perhaps seeing Edvard's little nephew as a part of the warmth and acceptance which he so desperately needed. 'He is the most delightful boy I know.'

On Edvard's birthday, 2 November 1831, Andersen could not contain his ardour and his resentment:

> You wrote to me, when I became too intimate with you, to say that you felt an inexplicable coldness towards people who wanted to say '*du*' to you. You know it was something which burst from my heart, a long-nursed wish, and I hope that my having expressed it in words has not caused you to feel that you cannot meet me in the way I would like you to?

Edvard remained compassionate but unmoved. That he had a liking for Andersen is beyond doubt, for he was consistently friendly and helpful, but he could not and would not encourage the tempestuous poet to believe that any closer relationship was possible.

Andersen published another book of verse in December, *Vignettes of*

Danish Poets and, still pestered by his mother for money, wrote to Mrs Iversen's daughters to tell them he had made arrangements for his mother to get meals from a local eating-house. He warned them that she would probably object to this arrangement and demand the money instead, and asked the girls to do what they could to make her accept his provisions. It did little good, for Anne Marie sent him a letter only a week later to say she needed money.

In the winter of early 1832, Andersen began to hanker for a longer period of travel, but had to accept that there was no hope. He was barely scraping a living from his writing and still went like a stray cat from house to house for meals, and he seemed incapable of writing anything that would really strike the public as notable. Edvard continued to torment his thoughts, and he continued to write him passionate letters. Looking back at that period in *Mit livs eventyr*, Andersen is clear about their respective characters:

> . . . gently and with all my heart I leaned towards him. He was the counterpart of the almost feminine features which were to be found in me. He was the sober-minded and practical one of the two and although younger in years he was the older as far as understanding was concerned; he was the leader, the one who took decisions, as if without question. Often indeed I misunderstood him and felt upset and cowed.

The theatre, which paid by the performance, was the best hope of making any money, and on 3 May, Andersen's operetta based on *The Bride of Lammermoor* had a five-nights' run at the Royal. Oehlenschläger said a little sniffily that this musical play was an easy form of work, bolstered on one side by Scott and on the other by the composer, and Andersen burst into tears and had to be calmed and consoled. Weyse, who had been his very first beneficiary, was interested in working on an adaptation of *Kenilworth*, but when this leaked out, a newspaper critic accused Andersen of tearing to shreds one great work after another, and he abandoned the idea.

On 22 June Andersen set off on a summer tour of Denmark, staying with friends in Sorø, Odense and Nørager Manor. While with Guldberg, now a General, he went to see Anne Marie, who was full of the story of how Crown Prince Christian Frederik had sought her out during a visit to Doctors Boder, to tell her that her son brought her great honour.

Andersen at this time had not published anything to put him at the forefront of Danish literature, and this tends to set the royal visit on a domestic level rather than an official one. Anne Marie, as previous episodes had shown, was obviously on fairly familiar terms with at least the servant hierarchy of the Court. Her excitement about the Crown Prince's visit was due to what he said, not to the fact that she had been spoken to at all by such an exalted personage, as it would have been to an outsider. Anne Marie was obviously to some extent an insider - but if indeed a child had been entrusted to her, there is no evidence that she knew his exact identity. A woman so addicted to gossip and alcohol would never have held such knowledge intact. As it was, the family mythology flirted with ideas of lost nobility, but it never went so far as to claim actual royalty. The Court managed its affairs adroitly, and whatever the truth, commoners such as Anne Marie were told no more than was necessary and convenient.

Andersen himself recorded the Crown Prince's visit with laconic satisfaction in the *Levnedsbog*, which he was writing at that time. The episode is run on straight from his indignant recall of the abortive conversation between him and Christian Frederik and the advice he was given 'as a poor child'. Reference to his lowly origins always angered him, although the theme of a triumphant rise from obscurity became a convenient self-description behind which he hid the more complex secrets of his life.

The summer tour continued – and so did Andersen's letters to Edvard, nagging and wheedling at his friend for a sign that the social difference between them did not matter. He snatched delightedly at Edvard's assurance that 'we at home long for you at least as much as you long for us', but still could not feel quite reassured. He wrote back to say that he still felt 'a stranger', no matter how much kindness he was shown. 'I regard your home almost as mine,' he ventured, then added, 'that's all right, isn't it?' He went on to push further at the barrier between them. 'How I wish you were my brother in the blood as you are in my heart and soul, then perhaps you would be able to understand my love for you!' He went on to object to the stolid, moralising tone which Edvard so often adopted:

> I swear to you, it makes me ill, it really does make me ill. Please be my
> dear and kind Edvard as you can be from time to time! That I attach

such great importance to your every word is simply because I love you so sincerely.

Edvard's response came very close to identifying exactly what it was about Andersen which he found unacceptable:

> Be assured that I did not misunderstand you when I read your letter, for I know you well, indeed, perhaps better than myself – and from your subsequent words asking me to be your dear and kind Edvard I knew at once that I had not misinterpreted you.

An unanswerable question hangs in the air as to whether at some time in the past the two young men had ventured into a homosexual encounter. Edvard's fear of being seen as too intimate with Andersen would then have more point, and so would the continued underlying affection in his responses to emotional demands which might repel a less sympathetic friend. There were good grounds for fear of any whispers about 'unnatural practices'. As late as 1905, Grand Duke Konstantin Romanov, of that ill-fated Russian dynasty related by marriage and blood to the Danish royal family, was blackmailed by a Captain Sosnitsky because of homosexual episodes in the Krasnoe Selo bath-house. Edvard's caution was essential for his future career, and his letter continued with a plea to keep the relationship between them cool and sensible. He undertook to remain 'a sincere and faithful friend, even though we do not address one another as "*du*" '. Among his more severe admonitions, this promise of continuing friendship was all that Andersen chose to see, and he replied in glad relief:

> Your letter made me extremely happy. I cannot love you more than I do, and yet I wish I could, for I see and I feel and I know that you love me too! Oh! My dear Edvard, my heart must always be open to you, for thus, and only thus, can true friendship exist.

Calming down a little, he continued this long letter with some talk about his latest literary idea, for a long verse play in the style of Oehlenschläger's famous *Aladdin*, to be called *Agnete and the Merman*. His autobiography came to an abrupt stop in mid-sentence in its account of the Riborg Voigt affair, for the simple reason that he at this point declared himself in love with Edvard's eighteen-year-old sister,

Louise. He gave her the manuscript of his *Levnedsbog* (as Hans Brix called it when he found and published it in 1926) so that she would know his whole story, and never claimed it back.

The Collin family was collectively horrified. If Andersen had thought that a safely heterosexual approach to a member of the clan would be reassuring, he was wrong. It was decided after the first two or three of his emotional letters to Louise that any further communications would first be read by Ingeborg Drewsen, Louise's elder sister, who, as a married woman, would judge whether they were suitable to pass on or not. Louise herself showed no sign whatever of returning Andersen's affections, for she was in love with a Mr W. Lind, to whom she became formally engaged at the end of the year. Andersen had again picked a girl who was unavailable – and close to the family as he was, he must have known this.

Louise's lack of response to the autobiographical pages he had given her irked him, and in a letter dated 27 October 1832 he complained that she had not said 'a kind word' to him about them:

> Why have you not spoken to me at all since I showed you my entire youth, not a single word about it? Is there something about me which makes me so repulsive, so unworthy of your friendship? – You and Edvard are the two persons in whom I have most confidence in your dear home, you don't mind my saying that, do you? There is nothing wrong in it. Oh, God! I have become so afraid to express any feeling, I am always scared that it will get me into trouble, that it will make me unhappy . . . I must go far away! If only it could happen next spring!

This was a reference to Jonas Collin's suggestion that he should apply for a travel bursary. Andersen's recently completed cycle of poems, *The Twelve Months of the Year* had, as protocol demanded, been dedicated to the king, thus automatically requiring its author to present the volume in person, accompanied by any request. Henrick Hertz, who had so wounded Andersen with his *Letters From a Ghost*, had already put in an application which everyone expected to be successful, and Jonas Collin, perhaps partly in the hope of detaching the young man from his family for a while, had advised Andersen to do likewise.

Meanwhile, Andersen's pursuit of Louise continued. He wrote her a poem in which he contrasted her blue eyes with Riborg's brown ones and beseeched her to take pity on his loneliness and lack of any proper home – and on encountering the family's resistance, lost his temper. In a letter dated only 'Sunday morning', his insecurity and resentment were nakedly revealed:

> Andersen is always the one who is wrong; for this he must also suffer the most in his loneliness, let that be his punishment! In some other world, in which things are clearer to us, I am sure he will abase himself even though he may have less need of his friends than he does in this one. Please accept his apologies for having occasionally thought of you as a sister and for forgetting that he himself is only
>
> H . C . A n d e r s e n

He had written a poem, 'Little Viggo', to Ingeborg Drewsen's small son during this time of frantic wooing of the Collins, and a three-act opera called *The Raven*, with music by J.P.E. Hartmann, had appeared briefly at the Royal Theatre, but the travel bursary remained the only real hope during a time of increasing confusion when nothing seemed successful.

On 7 December 1832, Andersen made his application to King Frederik VI. It was an unnerving occasion. The king, who had reigned since 1808, was not the father of Crown Prince Christian Frederik, and Andersen, with no childhood memories of this man as he had of little Fritz and his parents, was plainly uneasy in his presence. Like everyone else, he knew the monarch to be a bitter, suspicious man, the product of a cruel childhood dominated by Juliane Marie, his father's second wife, who disliked and maltreated him. Crippled by rickets, he was mistrustful of humanity and deeply frightened of the revolutionary surge that was extending from France across Europe. Writers were, in his view, a dangerous lot, and he had banished P.A. Heiberg from Denmark because of his satirical popular songs that had the monarchy as their butt.

The lanky young man who now stood before him with a book in his big bony hands was known to have been befriended by Heiberg's son Johan, a man of equally irreverent outlook, and the king listened irritably as Andersen stammered through an explanation that he was presenting a cycle of poems. 'A cycle, a cycle – ' Frederik interrupted testily, 'what do you mean?' Andersen managed to explain that *The Twelve Months of the Year* was about the cycle of months, and struggled through his prepared statement that he had been living on his writing with no assistance since having taken his *examen artium*. The king then gave him a wintry smile and said he might present his petition, and doing so reduced Andersen to tears of embarrassment. He blurted out that it seemed awful to bring the petition along with the book, which ought to have been a present in its own right, 'but I was told I had to and that was the way to do it'.

There is no suggestion here that Andersen received any special favour in the granting of his application. His petition had been prepared with seamless perfection by Jonas Collin (who as secretary of the fund probably already knew the outcome) and was supported by testimonials from, among others, Ørsted, Oehlenschläger and Heiberg. Frederik was not likely to be sympathetic to the young man, even if he knew that he was the bastard offshoot of his second cousin. The monarch himself, following the deaths of all his infant sons and a gynaecological injury to his wife which made further childbirth impossible, had taken a mistress, Frederikke Rafsted, by whom he had four children, and to him, Andersen's much lower status, half-royal or not, merited no unusual consideration.

There was a four months' wait for the result of the petition, and Andersen's confidence dwindled to a low ebb. Louise Collin announced her engagement to Mr Lind on the first day of January 1833 – and a few weeks later, Edvard succeeded his father as secretary to the fund *ad usos publicos*, to which Andersen was a supplicant.

Nothing could have shown up more sharply the social gulf which stood between the two young men, and Andersen was thrown into fresh misery. Oehlenschläger, aware of the emotional demands which the young man was making on the Collin family, had already rebuked him for being insufficiently grateful to Jonas Collin for all he had done, and this had provoked an agonised letter to Edvard:

> I feel so slavishly humiliated that I cannot speak to you properly face to face – I cannot tell you of my grief. Oh, God! – Edvard – you are far too highly placed to let me dare cling to you – the relationship which has arisen between us makes me infinitely sad, I feel only too well the truth of Oehlenschläger's words about my subordinate position, and I see clearly now how right you were not to give in to my childish demand that we should say '*du*' to each other, the way friends usually do. It has often made me cry, I have been more grieved than

you think, but I can see now that it would not have been appropriate.

After this brave statement his courage gave out. The longed-for trip to Italy would not happen, his poetic career was over, he longed for death and 'the end of everything'. In a more formal letter dated 7 March, he addressed his now rather eminent friend with a formal, 'Dear Collin', though he soon collapsed again into self-pity:

> I realise now that I am not what you need and have every right to ask for; every day you remove yourself further and further from me – at this time when so much affects my life and disturbs my soul, when I really need a friend, you hardly speak to me. I feel there is something beggarly, something degrading, in this constant demand for pity, but my pride is weakened by my love for you. I am so unutterably fond of you, and it fills me with despair that you cannot, will not be the friend to me that I would be to you were our situations reversed. – Is it possible that your new office will affect your life so much as to make you indifferent to the most sincere affection? – What have I done, then? What is it in my character that you dislike?

In fact, Edvard's increasing distance had nothing to do with anything Andersen had or had not done. He was seeing a lot of a young woman called Henriette Thyberg, and shortly after his promotion, he announced their engagement.

Andersen seems to have been unable to react. His friend had crossed an unimaginable divide, but its implications seem to have left him numbed, concerned only with the increasingly difficult state of his own life. With Edvard's firm shutting of the door on his entreaties to be loved, nothing remained but the quest for fame and the status of the great *digter* was proving difficult to sustain. From being a promising newcomer, Andersen was now, at nearly twenty-eight years old, in danger of appearing to be a peevish self-promoter whose work fell far short of his pretensions. He himself could only see that he was not appreciated, and his resentful anger led him into errors of judgement which made things worse. He published a piece called 'Chatter, Chatter', lampooning the social gatherings at which malicious smalltalk destroyed reputations, with the result that every one of his hostesses imagined herself to be the subject of his attack and was deeply offended.

In a more volatile and emotionally uninhibited country, Andersen might have caused less disapproval, but Denmark's virtues were those of quiet endurance and getting on with the job, and self-promotion was a suspect quality. Years after Andersen's death, Axel Sandemose put his finger on the point in his famous satire of 1933, *En flygtning krydser sit spor*, (*A Refugee Crosses his Tracks*), in which the laws of a fictional village called Jante are set out:

> You shall not believe that you are somebody.
> You shall not believe you are as great as us:
> You shall not believe you are cleverer than us . . .

and so forth. Andersen managed to break every one of these laws, and although he was not under such constant attack as his morbid imagination suggested, he made himself difficult to like, and when he at last heard on13 March that his petition had been granted, it came as a huge relief. With six hundred rixdollars annually for the next two years, he could leave the whole problem behind, and head for Rome.

Chapter 8
Rome

Andersen spent the month before his departure rushing about in pursuit of visas and letters of introduction, and at a series of farewell dinners asked all his friends to inscribe something in the album he carried on his travels. Among the flowery quips and verses of others, Ørsted inscribed three meaty equations:

> Reason in reason = the truth.
> Reason in the will = the good.
> Reason in the imagination = the beautiful.

Heiberg, however, was characteristically mischievous, and wrote, 'Do not travel so far that you forget Molbech's dictionary' – thus flicking at his young friend both for his awful spelling and for his loathing of the critic, Molbech, who had so often been disparaging about his plays.

On 22 April 1833, Andersen set out on his long journey. The Collin family came down to the quay in Copenhagen to see him off, and he wrote in his diary that he saw tears in Louise's eyes and that Ingeborg, too, was sad to see him go. 'They do like me after all! Those dear, very dear people.'

When the ship was at sea the next morning, the captain handed Andersen first a letter of good wishes from the faithful Jette Wulff and then one from Edvard Collin. Perhaps in the security of knowing that his friend would be safely out of the country for at least a year, Edvard was unusually affectionate:

> I shall miss you terribly, I shall miss your usual visits to my room to talk to me; I shall miss you on Tuesdays at your place at the table, and yet, you will miss us even more, I know, for you are alone.

The letter reduced Andersen to tears and he wrote an emotional reply at once, apologising for having thought Edvard unfriendly of late. 'I understand you better now, my dear, dear friend!'

Once into Germany, the journey settled into its leisured, uncomfortable pace. It poured with rain until they reached Hanover, and there it was 'villainously cold' and an epidemic of influenza was raging. In Cassel Andersen visited the composer, Ludwig Spohr, then went on to Frankfurt, in those days a huddle of ancient streets which he described as 'cosy'. He walked through the old town to the Jewish quarter, where he was fascinated to learn that the mother of Baron Rothschild still lived in the old house in a narrow alley, being convinced that to leave it would destroy the luck which had brought her sons good fortune. One of these sons lived nearby in a grand house with liveried footmen at the door, in strong contrast to the crowded streets which 'looked dark but not dirty, Jewish heads peeping out everywhere, and old women sitting in front rooms; trading was going on'.

At the Franco-German border, Andersen was met by the full force of French bureaucracy. Writing to a friend, Ludwig Müller, he said:

> There was so much bother with our passports, so many examinations and scrutinies, that I was almost fed up with the whole journey. The portmanteaux were opened about half a dozen times, and in every town we were surrounded by police.

The carriage was heavily laden, with 'fifteen people inside, and three or four outside, not to mention all the luggage', and the horses suddenly started to fight among themselves while going through a small town in the middle of the night. They kicked and bit at each other, then bolted. The ladies screamed and prayed, and Andersen said he simply hoped to die quickly of a broken neck rather than endure anything more lingering.

The horses having been thrashed into submission the journey went on, the carriage stopping every thirty miles or so to change horses and allow the passengers to seek some refreshment. In Verdun, Andersen wrote, 'we all got into a large kitchen, where we had some milk with a drop of coffee in it, which the French call café' – and on Friday, 10 May, they arrived in Paris. The journey from Mainz had taken five days and nights, and the exhausted passengers, after some trekking about in search of an inn, went early to bed.

Andersen stayed in Paris for three months, doing the rounds of his various contacts. Weyse had entrusted him with a composition to give to Cherubini, whom Andersen found, according to his diary, sitting at the piano with a cat on his shoulder. The later account in *Mit livs eventyr* doubles this to two cats, one on either shoulder – but whatever the feline situation, Cherubini was less than welcoming. He had never heard of Weyse and never bothered to acknowledge his gift.

There was a well-established group of Danish ex-pats in the French capital, and Andersen soon found friends with whom he plunged into sightseeing. In the Petit Trianon, he gazed with deep respect at the bed chamber once occupied by Napoleon, who had been such a legendary part of Andersen's childhood. His diary for that day is awestruck:

> I placed my hand on the steps and on his pillow. Saw myself in the mirror which must so often have reflected his face. How insignificant I looked! If others hadn't been there I would have knelt down.

A statue of the little Emperor was unveiled in July while Andersen was still in the city, and he heard guns fired from every quarter in commemoration of the Revolution. Although Paris excited his admiration, some aspects of it were hard to cope with, as he revealed in a letter to Christian Voigt:

> Paris is the most lecherous city under the sun. I don't think there is one innocent person there, things go on in an incredible way; openly in the street, in broad daylight and in a most respectable area, I have been offered "a lovely girl of sixteen" . . . Everywhere there are bawdy pictures, everywhere lasciviousness is considered no more than a need of nature, etc., so that one's modesty is almost deadened. Nevertheless I can say quite honestly that I am still innocent, though anyone who knows Paris would hardly believe it.

Since the farewell letter on the boat, there had been no communication from Edvard, and after nearly two months, Andersen wrote in reproach. 'Your silence has woken in me a strange feeling which I have never known before; it is a kind of anger verging on love and sadness.' This letter of 11 June went on to complain bitterly that Edvard had a family and a fiancée while he, Andersen, had 'No-one, absolutely no-one'. He wrote to Jonas to ask for an explanation of his son's long silence, and received a slightly reproving answer, assuring him that Edvard would prove himself a true friend when practical help was needed. If Andersen really thought the Collin family so inconsistent in its affections, Jonas went on, then he himself would have a right to be angry.

The silence continued, and on, 26 June Andersen wrote in despair to Christian Voigt:

> You think of me! You alone of all of them, faithful soul! I have been away from Denmark for two months; but have not received a single letter, except one which was waiting for me from Jette Wulff. Think what it is to be so far away in a foreign land and forgotten by all whom you love! Edvard has not sent me a word – no-one, no-one but you.

When a package finally arrived from Copenhagen, it turned out to be an anonymously sent copy of a Copenhagen newspaper containing a satirical poem about himself. Titled 'A Farewell to Andersen', it was a mocking lament that the young poet should have fled the country before learning how to write Danish properly, and that he had deprived himself of the pleasure of reading aloud to his reluctant listeners. To add to the insult, the package had been unstamped and had cost Andersen quite a lot to receive. The most distressing thought of all was that the sender must know him quite well to be aware of his poste restante address.

While in Paris, Andersen had started work on *Agnete and the Merman*, the verse play he had mentioned to Edvard, but it was going slowly. Anger and loneliness made concentration difficult, and social visits were a more attractive alternative. He went to see Heiberg's almost-blind old father, Peter Andreas who had never returned to Denmark since his banishment, and agonised over whether or not to make contact with that other and more famous exile, Heinrich Heine. Ever uneasy in the dangerous world of politics, Andersen tried hopelessly to steer a neutral course which would offend nobody, and thus, despite his fervent admiration of Heine's poetry, he was frightened of being associated with the great writer's revolutionary and unconventional lifestyle. Heine had been in Paris for two years by the time Andersen got there, having left Germany and its censorship so that he could continue to write as what he called 'a soldier of humanity'. The *Bund* had in 1832 issued a decree forbidding the publication of his work and that of his circle, and the French government had not yet accepted Heine as a political refugee worthy of support. A Jew turned Christian for purposes of expediency, he was living openly with Eugenie Mirat, a Parisian *grisette*, and this probably shocked Andersen's respectable acquaintances far more than any question of politics. The motherly Mrs Laessøe in particular was a stickler for the conventions, and to her Andersen wrote, 'I don't like Heine as a person; I have no faith in him whatever; I don't think he is any good!' Even to Christian Voigt, he wrote that Heine was 'a man one should beware of.'

Heine, hearing that the Danish writer was in Paris, called at Andersen's hotel in his absence and, having had no response, approached him in the literary club, Europe Litteraire with a warm handshake and a remark that Germans and Danes should be friends. Andersen excused his evasiveness by saying he had been afraid of finding himself the subject of Heine's biting wit. In fact the two men got on well. Heine wanted information on Baggesen and Oehlenschläger for a book he was writing, and before Andersen left Paris, he went to see Heine again, and was pleased to have a few words in German written in his album. In one of his many unanswered letters to Edvard written on 29 June, he demanded, 'What is the matter with Oehlenschläger, that he says a Jew cannot be a poet? Lord God, that great man can talk some rubbish . . .'

Andersen was writing frequently to Ludwig Müller, and when afflicted with the digestive upset 'from which all foreigners suffer' had, in the conviction that he was going to die, asked Müller to make sure that Edvard published posthumously the pages of autobiography entrusted originally to Louise. When a letter at last arrived from Edvard early in July, it made a somewhat irritable mention of this association with Müller, but the reason for Edvard's annoyance had more to do with the content of Andersen's previous letters than any mere jealousy.

Being convinced that *Agnete and the Merman* would sell well, Andersen had assumed that Reitzel would pay a good advance for it, and had rather airily asked Edvard to send him a considerable amount of money which he thought he could get from the publisher. It was of course an impossible request, and its somewhat peremptory wording was in strong contrast to the warm letters to Müller.

Andersen was instantly contrite, though more at the thought that Edvard might be jealous than through any real understanding that he had caused offence. Edvard accepted the apology and wrote back with stoicism:

I have known you as a young student, I have followed you on your course of education, and finally, I have come to see your true poetic talent, the uncorrupted, natural heart. I have learned to respect the former and love the latter. Here is my hand, Andersen, we are old friends.

'Edvard, you are infinitely dear to me!' Andersen wrote back. 'Your Jette can, in her own way, be no fonder of you than I am. You are always in my thoughts, and I know you are and will always remain faithful to me.' In the fresh confidence sparked by this warm exchange, he got on with the writing of *Agnete* and posted the first half of it to Edvard on 14 August, his last day in Paris. Pausing only for a visit to the slightly reluctant Victor Hugo, who interviewed him in dressing gown and slippers, he set out for Switzerland, arriving in Geneva five days later.

After a detour through Lausanne and Vevey to see the Castle of Chillon with its Byronic associations, Andersen went on through the Jura to Le Locle, a little town near Neuchatel, where he stayed with relatives of his friends in Copenhagen, the Jürgensens. For the next three weeks he was treated as a welcome guest by this family, the Houriets, and because they were eager for news of the sister who had married a Dane, Andersen was forced to get to grips with French, a necessity which had hardly cropped up in Paris with its resident Scandinavian community.

In his upstairs room with its little window which looked out onto the slope of the hill and the tall pine trees, he settled down to the second half of *Agnete,* in high hopes that this would be the work to silence all opposition. The story came directly from an old folk legend about a girl who marries a merman and goes to live with him under the sea. Having borne him seven sons, she one day hears the church bells ringing in her village and asks permission to go back to see her family. Her husband agrees, on condition that she speaks no word about her underwater life – but the girl pours out the story to her mother, and the broken-hearted merman cannot reclaim her, for the magic has been destroyed.

The foreshadowing of 'The Little Mermaid' is obvious, but Andersen had not yet found his sureness of touch. He was too taken up with enhancing his own reputation to have a properly scrupulous eye to the quality of his work, and poured into the verse whatever observations and convictions happened to strike him, regardless of whether the slender tale could bear so much verbiage. A collection of his poems, one hundred and fifty-eight in all, appeared at this time, boosting his confidence, and although he was a little dashed to see his 'The Dying Child' attributed to Oehlenschläger in a German newspaper, this merely confirmed his conviction that he must at all costs consolidate his reputation. In the ludicrously short time of two weeks, he dashed off the second half of *Agnete and the Merman*, and posted it to Edvard. He also sent a copy to Mrs Laessøe, as he had done with the first half, accompanied by an optimistic letter:

I have been in a sort of ecstasy for some days, and I have now finished 'Agnete' – I am satisfied. The end will please you more than the opening part (with which you are familiar). I don't know whether it is this ecstasy or the cold weather which has influenced me; but I am strongly excited, there is fever in my blood, and I cannot sleep. I am leaving in about eight days. This letter brings you my 'Agnete'. Please accept in a friendly spirit this Danish child which was born on the border of France and Switzerland, in the midst of northern scenery, yet on the edges of the flowery south. I shall finish this letter when I leave Le Locle.

He did so, and returned to the theme of *Agnete*. 'Oh, how I am longing to know how people at home like her!' He quoted a Danish journal which had referred to him as 'a poet who had once shown some promise':

Those words have rankled like poison in my heart; may 'Agnete' only get praise and sunshine enough to disperse what is killing me. I hope she may be grammatical enough! Let that be as it may. I did not have Else the schoolmistress in my mind, but only Aphrodite, when I raised my 'Agnete' from the waves.

He included with the piece a long, fulsome introduction, full of unwise reproaches and instructions to all Danes to give *Agnete* a warm welcome.

This done, he said goodbye to the Houriet family with its children who shouted at him as if he was deaf and the two 'magnificent old aunts' who had knitted him woollen mittens to protect his hands against the cold in the Simplon Pass, and set off for

Brig and the way south.

Throughout his travels, Andersen carried a small sketchbook, and the drawings he made, though primitive in their grasp of perspective, are sharply evocative. He worked in pencil, sometimes going over the sketches in sepia ink to improve their durability, and his drawing of the gateway at Brig, like the one of the view from his room in Le Locle, is full of atmosphere. Having no pretensions as works of art, these little pictures retain an honesty and charm which is notably lacking in Andersen's early literary work.

The woolly mittens came into their own as the over-full coach left Brig at two in the morning and made its slow way through the Alps. The Simplon was, Andersen recorded in his diary, 'like driving through the earth's backbone'. In the inn where they stopped, the warmth of the tiled stove was welcome, though venturing out to the privy meant braving the cold and the bitter wind again. In that small and smelly place, Andersen noticed two cupboards, and opening one of them, found jars of preserves. 'I thought I was back with the Meislings!' he commented.

In twelve hours, they came to Domodossala, where Andersen got out of the coach to buy a handful of grapes, and then went on to Baveno. At six the next morning, he jumped out of bed to join the other passengers in a steamer trip across Lake Maggiore to the Isola Bella, but he had overslept and had to hire a small boat to ferry him out to the ship. 'Eight francs!' he recorded, horrified. The stay in Paris had eaten up a lot of his money, and he worried constantly about expenses.

The first sight of night-time Milan did not appeal to Andersen because of its dark, narrow streets, but Italy itself already enchanted him. As he wrote to Jette Wulff, 'France and Germany do not count for much! No, behind the Alps is the Garden of Eden with marble gods, music, and God's clear sky.' His rapturous diary entries gave way after the weekend of 21–22 September to some brooding reflections prompted by the knowledge that Henrik Hertz, whose travel grant had been considerably larger than Andersen's, was following the same route and had now arrived in Milan. Hertz had also been in Paris in June, but Andersen had managed not to meet him. Now, he mused that poetry was 'the gold in the mountain', but some clever craftsmen knew how to fashion it out of lesser stuff:

Letters of a Ghost is that sort of goblet; it is polished to shine like silver and reflect the flaws of everything it is held up to. It is a nice piece of work, only not of gold, though that sort of thing has its uses. Hertz is, so to speak, a kind of poetical tinsmith, a tinker.

Carsten Hauch, Andersen went on, worked in mere copper, and as to Molbech – he used mere clay, and fashioned it into chamber pots, the contents of which he emptied onto other people's heads.

Andersen's truculent mood deepened the next day, for a letter from Edvard, who had only just received the first part of *Agnete*, was brutally candid about its shortcomings. The piece was, he said, derivative and essentially trivial, with long bombastic passages that were hackneyed and lacked any originality. Andersen's diary entry made no reference to the damning criticism; it was concerned only with Edvard's attitude:

> I don't want to go on being the one who always gives in, to be treated like a child by someone younger than myself; even if he is a friend! The tone Edvard uses demands to be opposed, even though I love him dearly!

His reply to the letter did not attempt to defend *Agnete*. Angry and petulant, he referred again to the open wound of the '*du*' question, and while admitting that criticisms were doubtless made with his welfare in mind, he could not bear such painful attacks on his self-esteem. 'Praise, infinite praise, as I have said so often, will have the most beneficial effect on me.' His refusal to accept that *Agnete* might have its faults was total, and he took refuge in the thought that Edvard had not yet received the second half of the work, and that Reitzel might not share his low opinion of it.

That evening, interrupting Andersen's letter to Edvard, two fellow-Danes arrived at his lodgings, and his resentment was set aside while he, with the newcomers Dinesen and Neergaard, spent the next two days sightseeing and visiting the theatre. He posted his reply to Edvard on Wednesday, 25 September, and his diary sounded carefree again. 'Today we met our first monk in a brown cowl with bare feet; he was hardly twenty years old and beautiful.' By the end of the week, he was moving on towards Rome. From Genoa he wrote to Jette Wulff about his two-and-a-half days of coach travel across the Po valley, remarking that:

everything is dirty to a degree you cannot possibly imagine; we have had to threaten to call the police, had to guard our luggage, have seen robbers dragged away by soldiers.

There was a touch of relish in such reports, but in Genoa, Andersen was genuinely unnerved by a visit to the Arsenal, a particularly appalling penal institution run by the Navy. In *Mit livs eventyr* he still sounded horrified by seeing the prisoners chained in pairs like galley slaves when they worked during the day, and more so by the fact that they slept shackled to iron rings in the wall beside the rough bunks:

> Even in the sick-room a few lay in chains. Three of them, with yellow-brown faces and glazed eyes, were on the point of death, and I was deeply affected by them. The others noticed this, for one of the criminals there stared at me with an evil look in his eyes. I knew what he meant; I had come merely out of curiosity, to stare at their sufferings . . .

Zigzagging back across Italy, there was no improvement in the travel conditions:

> We were continually cheated at the inns, for ever asked to show passports (they had been inspected and endorsed more than ten times in a few days), and our coach driver did not know the way and took the wrong road, so that instead of arriving in Pisa in daylight, we did not reach it until the middle of the night.

The gate was shut, but after yet another passport inspection, they were allowed into the town and given a flaming brand for the coachman to hold above his head to cast some light in the pitch-black streets. The next day, Andersen ventured up the Leaning Tower, and found it an alarming experience:

> At the top there are no railings. The sea wind is spoiling the side facing the sea; the iron is rusting away and the stones are becoming loose; the whole construction is a dirty yellow colour.

All in all, he did not like Pisa. He went to the Synagogue, reputed to be the most beautiful in Europe, and said it looked like a Stock

Exchange. He was glad to leave 'the filthy town' and go on to Florence and its art galleries, where he filled his diary with descriptions.

The last leg of his journey, the six-day trip from Florence to Rome was, Andersen said, 'wretched'. It was now October, but still unseasonably warm, and after dark, because the passengers rashly left the carriage windows open for the sake of air, they were so badly bitten by mosquitoes that 'we swelled up and bled; one of my hands alone had no less than fifty-seven bites and the poor horses looked like carrion.' The inns proved to be dreadful, dirty and unwelcoming, and one particular landlady in a filthy blouse 'spat every time she brought us a fresh course'. Bedbugs made the nights a misery, and at last the travellers retreated to the stables for a few hours of sleep. When the heavy coach at last rolled into Rome on 18 October, there was little sense of a pilgrimage accomplished; Andersen merely remarked, 'Thank goodness – now perhaps we can get something to eat.'

Within a few days, he had settled into the Scandinavian community which centred round the Danish sculptor, Bertel Thorvaldsen. This extraordinary man had been in Rome ever since his first arrival on a travel grant in 1797, having found Italy far more to his taste than Denmark. Known appropriately as 'Thor', he was as godlike in appearance as the old Norse deity, broad and strong, with curling chestnut hair and eyes as blue as the Italian skies, and he could out-work, out-drink and out-gamble anyone in the city. Since winning the Danish Academy's silver medal at the age of eighteen he had paid scant attention to his native country, though a visit to Copenhagen in 1820 had landed him a commission to produce statues of Christ and the twelve disciples for the church of Our Lady. At the time of Andersen's arrival, he seemed in no hurry to complete this enormous task, for he was running a large-scale atelier which employed several assistants and turned out a stream of profitable work.

To the young Danes who used his studio as their meeting-place and spiritual home, Thorvaldsen was both amazing and exasperating. They learned to let him win at Lotto rather than endure his rages if he lost, and accepted that he would never set up house with his fiery mistress, Anna Maria Magnani, by whom he had two children, but his warmth and humour and the vastness of his artistic output, both in size and quantity, entranced them. Andersen found himself accepted in this bohemian community, and at the Caffe Greco in the Via Condotti, a favourite haunt of the Danish ex-pats, met several young men who would become close friends. Ludvig Bødtcher, chubby-faced and bespectacled, purported to be a poet though he had published nothing in his nine years of living in Rome, but Albert Küchler, a painter, was busy and active. He took a great liking to Andersen and painted and drew him several times, always rendering him with a brooding quality of strange spirituality.

Rome itself proved extraordinary. On his very first day there, Andersen witnessed the weird ceremony of the reburial of Raphael. It had long been rumoured that a skull kept at the Academia was that of the great painter, whose presumably headless body reposed in the Pantheon, but when the coffin was opened, the skeleton inside it was found to be complete. Now, with as much pomp as possible considering the slightly ludicrous circumstances, Raphael was to be re-interred. Andersen's new-found friends procured him a ticket for this event, and they all went along to watch while a record of the findings was placed in the coffin while 'an invisible choir sang beautifully'. The gold cloth was replaced, and Andersen's diary entry went on to note how, when the coffin was tilted to lower it through the narrow entrance to its resting-place, all the bones fell to one end. 'We could hear how they rattled.' Thorvaldsen was among the important personages present, each one holding a lit candle.

Andersen was immensely happy. He joined in the café society and in the expeditions on donkey-back to explore and sketch the surrounding countryside. 'Rome has opened my eyes to beauty,' he wrote to Jette Wulff.

His diary during that autumn contained casual references to visiting 'the princess'. This was Charlotte Frederikke of Mecklenburg-Schwerin, wife of the Crown Prince Christian Frederick. Her son, 'Fritz', who would rule as Frederik VIII, and with whom Andersen had played as a child in Odense Castle, had been born in the year of her marriage, 1808, but it seems that she was not happy. On Sunday 20 October, Andersen recorded that Charlotte 'regretted being forced to live in Piacenza, said that she never wanted to return to Denmark, asked me to spend the evening with her whenever I didn't have anything better to do.'

Three days later, he saw her again, though this time in the company of other young men:

We spent the evening with the princess, who did not seem very aesthetically inclined. She started off by asking me whether I would get on with my reading straight away since she had to leave at seven o'clock. It lasted until 8.30.

The contrast between the informality of the first occasion and the stiffness of the second is very marked.

On 21 November, Henrik Hertz finally arrived in Rome, and Andersen's fears proved groundless. Hertz was a tubby, cheerful young man, grateful for Andersen's help in finding him a room, and from being an unknown potential enemy, he quickly became a friend. Edvard, meanwhile, struggling with the problems of *Agnete* while Andersen's letters brought rapturous reports of what a good time he was having in Rome, lapsed into a further silence.

Despite the company of his new friends, Andersen was concerned. Nobody could take the place of Edvard, and on 16 December, his diary contained a typical mixture of practicality and yearning, followed by an entry later on the same day, after the post had arrived:

> Today I bought myself a brazier. It is standing on one side of me, and the sun is shining from the other. It makes me feel better, but I am somewhat debilitated. If only there should be a letter for me today! – (later) There was a letter from Collin senior; it reported my mother's death. My first reaction was: Thanks be to God! Now there is an end to her sufferings, which I haven't been able to alleviate. But even so, I cannot get used to the idea that I am so utterly alone without a single person who must love me because of the bond of blood!

In the same letter, Jonas had warned him that *Agnete* was not very good. 'I hope it will not meet with over-severe criticism, for the form, my dear Andersen, the form, to which you do not pay sufficient attention, leaves much to be desired.' In the same fateful post-bag there had been a letter from Heiberg with a severe criticism of two libretti which Andersen had left for his consideration. 'I am just an improviser,' Andersen's diary went on. It was a term which stuck in his mind, for he was to use it in the novel he wrote about his experiences in Italy. He added stoically, 'People are concerned about the criticism of my Agnete and Reitzel won't dare risk a hundred rixdollars on it. So I'll just have to publish it myself!' That task, needless to say, fell on Edvard.

Hertz offered condolences on the death of Andersen's mother and advised him not to let it get him down, but it was a letter from Mrs Laessøe which gave him the assurance he really wanted:

> To say that there is no-one here who loves you is not true, for I love you as a mother loves her child. I cannot help counting you as one of my sons. You'll have to put up with that!

Thorvaldsen, too, gave him comfort, and within a remarkably short time, Andersen's diary was back to its notes about art galleries and social events.

He spent a riotous Christmas with the Scandinavian ex-pats in the grounds of the Villa Borghese, where a great celebratory dinner was held. Andersen arranged flower garlands all round the festive table and gave each plate a wreath of ivy. 'A big orange tree with the fruit still on it was our Christmas tree,' he remembered in *My Life's Fairytale* and he had been 'the lucky one who won the best prize, a silver mug inscribed, "Christmas Eve in Rome 1833".' His diary entries written at the time, however, indicate that things got somewhat out of hand. There was, he said, 'some trouble between the Swedes and the Danes . . . Sonne, Petzholdt and several others were terribly drunk. Stammann was much too familiar with Mrs Jensen.'

On Boxing Day, Andersen sounded distinctly dyspeptic. 'Hanging around a lot with one's countrymen is not a good thing,' he remarked in his diary. 'They aren't interested in each other, either – it's the tavern and the meals that bring them together.' He took himself off to see Charlotte Frederikke:

> Today I made a visit to the princess. She was very amiable. (It was the first time I had been there since reading from my *Agnete*.) She very much regretted that she had not been able to participate in the Christmas tree party, but as a Catholic she had to observe the customs, specially since the Pope had mentioned that he would not be pleased.

After leaving the princess, Andersen returned to his friends, and was swept into an outing in three coaches along the banks of the Tiber. To his great annoyance, he as a gentleman was required to pay for Mrs Jensen. This was not at all to his taste, and he looked with new speculation at the young men who surrounded him, hoping perhaps for a warmer relationship to develop. 'The association with Hertz could perhaps be of the greatest benefit to me, but – no! No!'

The following day, Andersen started work on the novel he would call *The Improvisatore* — the English translation of the title kept to the Italian form of the word – but on Monday, 6 January 1834, a letter arrived from Edvard which put all thoughts of work out of his head. It began inoffensively enough with a compassionate breaking of the news of Andersen's mother's death, evidently unaware that Jonas had already done this, then moved into a sustained and furious outburst about *Agnete*. Having been struggling with the task of editing and publishing the complete manuscript, Edvard was at explosion point. Exasperated by the airy ease with which his friend appeared to think he could turn out popular books, he pointed out some unpleasant truths; beginning with the over-production which was making Andersen a laughing-stock:

> While one work is being printed you are half way through writing the next; due to this insane, deplorable productivity you reduce the value of your works to such an extent that in the end no bookseller wants them, even to give away as presents.

He went on to reprove Andersen for his intention to write a book about his journey to Rome, pointing out that a thousand people had done the same thing and that it was pure egotism to imagine that anyone would be interested in yet another account. Spiking his friend's guns, he went on:

> If I know you, Andersen, you'll reply quite smoothly and with unruffled confidence, "Ah, but when people read my Agnete they'll change their minds, and then you'll see how my journey has improved everything, made me more mature, etc."

Reading the proofs of *Agnete*, Edvard said, had made him almost weep with exasperation because of its 'desperately deformed' writing. Lest Andersen should think he was being unreasonably severe, he had gone to the lengths of calling in another opinion:

> I confided my distress concerning your proofs to a man who takes

great interest in you, and whom you respect highly, and to whose judgement you attach great importance, and I asked him to go through the manuscript, so that Agnete could appear before the public in reasonably decent shape.

He went on to quote in full the report written by the unnamed consultant, whom Andersen later found out to be J.M. Thiele, the man who had written such an evocative sketch of the gawky fifteen-year-old who had come to his office in thanks for financial help. Thiele, now President of the Royal Academy of Arts, was forthright in his opinion, and his evident anxiety on Andersen's behalf made his criticism impossible to ignore:

> It had been my intention to spend this evening reading Andersen's Agnete; but I cannot endure it! I find it painful to read such a mediocre product of his, and I must ask you to excuse me, for I cannot while reading it think of correcting small mistakes, since what I have read so far very rarely offers a single bright spot. If we have the welfare of our absent friend at heart, then we really ought to prevent it from being published at all; this in my opinion would be a true act of friendship towards him. Unfortunately Oehlenschläger once sent home from Paris works of great merit, which is probably why this has been scribbled down in such a hurry. I return the manuscript to you and wash my hands of it – you ought to do the same thing! In time we may regret having acted as godfathers to this baby.

Edvard, who had against his own better judgement seen the book through to publication, added several more bitter paragraphs then advised his friend, 'for God's sake' to stop writing and simply enjoy the experience of being abroad.

Andersen was thrown into hysterical misery. 'I was so overwhelmed that I was left numb,' he wrote in his diary that day, 'my belief in God and my fellow man destroyed. The letter drove me to despair. Bødtcher tried to comfort me. How could he?' To make things worse, Edvard had enclosed a clipping of a scathing criticism of Andersen's poetry in a leading Danish magazine, written by his old enemy Molbech.

Edvard in his later book goes into some detail on the *Agnete* affair claiming that it was Thiele's report which finally caused him to lose patience. At Andersen's request, he had shown the second half of *Agnete* to Mrs Laessøe, who had sighed that she wished she could have said she read it with pleasure. As it was, she found most of the work 'a morass without a gleam of sunlight'. Andersen had also asked Edvard to show the manuscript to Jette Wulff, but he did not do this. Jette, who had read the first part, was furious, and described Edvard in a letter to Andersen as 'a despot'. He had been holding forth, she said, about how damaging it was for Andersen to be so dependent on receiving letters from home, and added, 'but you will keep on writing them, won't you?' She herself was planning a trip to Italy the following year, and was eager for descriptions of her 'longed-for paradise'.

About the part of *Agnete* she had read, even the encouraging Jette was cautious. It was, she said, charming in places but, like any work of art, had 'light and shade'. She suggested that one of the characters embodied the author's own sufferings, and rushed to add, 'Dear Andersen, are you angry? Forgive me, won't you?' Such sensitivity was typical of her amusing and yet tender letters, and raises the poignant possibility that JetteWulff, with her bent, misshapen body, might herself have been in love with a man who never suspected it, and certainly could not return it. She was adamant that she would not ask Edvard to show her the second half of *Agnete*. 'I will not ask for what should be mine by right.'

Andersen poured out his anguish to his friends in Rome. Hertz, ironically enough, advised him not to take adverse criticism too seriously, and for the first time, mentioned his own tilt at Andersen in *Letters of a Ghost*, assuring him that such little public spats were if anything beneficial to an artist's career. And Molbech, he said, was simply someone who pontificated on taste while having none himself. The next day, convinced by now that he was seriously ill, Andersen staggered round to Thorvaldsen's studio, and although the sculptor's hands were covered with clay, he embraced the distraught young man and said, 'For God's sake don't let such things bother you; the less a person understands about art, the more likely he is to pass judgement on it.' He made Andersen a present of thirty pages of his sketches and told him to take the world's injustices lightly.

It was all very well for Thorvaldsen to give advice. A man of such confidence and charisma, for all his kindness, could not imagine the abyss of uncertainty which made Andersen so vulnerable. Edvard's thunderbolt had come as a shattering destruction of the happiness he had begun to enjoy in Rome, and both his future as a writer and his trust in his beloved friend now seemed unbearably fragile. If Edvard expected the announcement of his engagement to bring Andersen to his senses and stop the constant pressure for a closer relationship, he was to be disappointed. Nobody among Andersen's new friends in Rome could replace Edvard in his affections, though Albert Küchler, who later became a Franciscan monk, seems to have stood in a somewhat ambivalent relationship which excited a mixture of emotions in Andersen. *The Improvisatore* features an artist very similar to Küchler, and details an episode which is extremely close to what happened on the very day when Edvard's fateful letter arrived. Andersen's diary records that he had gone as usual to Küchler's studio to sit for his portrait:

> While I was there a young model of about sixteen years of age came in with her mother. Küchler said he wanted to see what her breasts looked like; the girl seemed a little shy because I was there, but her mother said, 'Oh, nonsense!' and loosened her daughter's dress, pulling it and her shift right down to her waist. There she stood, half naked, with somewhat dark skin, arms a bit too scrawny, but beautiful, round breasts. As the mother exposed her, I could feel my whole body tremble. Küchler saw that I went pale and asked if there was anything wrong with me.

Whether his trembling was due to a rush of desire or to revulsion is difficult to determine, as is the intention of Küchler's kindly – or malicious – question, but from the time of Edvard's letter about *Agnete*, Andersen's diary ceased to concern itself with the joys and strangenesses of Rome. Almost daily, he wrote of his angry conviction that Edvard and his family had now become enemies, though at the same time he longed for the more friendly letter which Edvard had promised in his closing paragraph. On 25 January, after two weeks of fruitless waiting, he wrote, 'Still no letter today. I walked through the streets, almost out of my mind, poison and hatred filling my veins. I could have torn my enemies to pieces.' Six days later, having still received no letter, he was even more distraught:

> Since I lived at the Meislings' I have not experienced such a destructive feeling every morning as now. Then, I was broken-

hearted, but now it is rage and misery. My God! Edvard, what a brute you are – and the others as well! You are killing me!

The non-response was partly his own fault, for in the heat of his rage he had written such a furious letter that he had not dared to send it to Edvard himself, but instead had posted it to his father, Jonas Collin, enclosing a note to say that it could be handed to Edvard if Jonas so chose. Jonas had very sensibly burned it, but Andersen was left in limbo, paralysed by the fear that Edvard would never speak to him again. He was completely unable to write, and Rome was now overlaid with such unhappy associations that its charms had evaporated. On 5 February, he noted:

My spirits are low, I'm longing to go on travelling, always to travel further on! – Imagination, idealism, everything I used to possess seems to have been killed in me by recent events. I can do nothing and – therefore unhappy.

The Roman carnival, which began at just this time, broke into his melancholy and forced him to enjoy himself. In a letter to Jette Wulff, he described the confetti mock-battles which took place in the streets – 'the ladies emptied whole basketfuls over us' – and admitted that he was robbed of his purse by a thief who threw confetti in his eyes, and there is every sign that he entered into the thing with gusto. 'Hertz had to take refuge in a shoemaker's shop, and having run out of confetti, he threatened to throw boots at me instead.'

On 12 February 1834, when the carnival had ended, Andersen, with Hertz and a couple of other friends, left Rome and headed south on the four-day trek to Naples.

In Naples, despite his troubles, Andersen could no longer be miserable. It was, as he said in his diary, paradise. Sitting in his hotel room with a bottle of Lachrimae Christi that had 'a smell of Vesuvius in it', he wrote to Jette Wulff in high good humour:

> SKAAL! My dear sister! Listen, now they're singing serenades in the street, and playing the guitar. Oh, this really is too good! My soul is full of love, for a long time I haven't been as happy as I am now. My distress is crushing when I suffer, but my joy when I am happy is also unspeakable. I shall never be contented in the cold land to which I am forced to belong. But thank God that I at least have seen and felt heaven; I shall dream about it, I shall sing about it.

As if to crown Andersen's delight, Vesuvius began a dramatic eruption just after he arrived. He heard it while sitting in his room, 'a strange sound in the air, like when several doors are slammed all at once, but with a supernatural power'. He ran out, and there saw that 'one side of the mountain was a river of fire flowing downward, and the crater was burning like a bonfire'.

A psychological dam seemed to have burst as well, for a few days later, on 20 February, letters arrived from both Jonas and Edvard Collin. Jonas was diplomatic as always, stating that he had burned Andersen's offensive letter to Edvard lest it should cause 'a result which would grieve me sorely – namely, a break between you and him'. He counselled tolerance and added that Edvard 'really is extremely fond of you, and he is your warmest defender whenever it is needed'.

Edvard was still a little prickly, irritated by Andersen's bland assumption that *Agnete* would make him a profit of 200 rixdollars when the book had caused so much trouble and had left Edvard with the task of trying to cover its printing costs. He had not been annoyed in what he had said, he pointed out, but merely honest. This, of course, was not at all what Andersen wanted to hear, and he wrote back in stiff and formal terms, thanking his friend for the hard work he had put in. To Jonas, however, he was more relaxed:

> All the bitterness will be forgotten, and I know I will love Edvard as before; I only want to see the good, the many good sides of him. I just wish I didn't have to feel obliged to him all the time, it damages our friendship, it puts a gulf between our hearts.

With the immediate crisis over, Andersen turned in relief to the delectable world offered by Naples and its surrounding landscape. With Hertz and three others, Berg, Zeuthen and Lennel, he set out to take a closer look at Vesuvius. Crammed into a one-horse carriage, the five of them drove to Herculanum, and after exploring there, tackled the volcano itself, mounted for the first part of the ascent on 'miserable mules'. It was a very long way, but Andersen was enchanted by the view which lay spread before him as the sun began to set, remembering in *Mit livs eventyr* how;

> the sky was a glimmering gold that shaded over into ethereal blue. The sea was indigo and the islands were lying in it like pale blue clouds. It was a magic world ... '

When the mules could go no further, the young men continued on foot, sinking over their knees into ash. Tubby little Hertz was struggling to keep up, and threatened to go back if the others didn't wait for him. Andersen and Berg took him by an arm each, and Andersen 'sang loudly to show how little it was tiring me'. At well over six feet tall, he had a significant advantage.

After an hour, they reached 'the cauldron'. It was dark by this time, and their progress sounds distinctly hazardous:

> In order to see the new lavaflow we had to cross one that had been flowing the previous night; only the outermost crust was black and hard, and red fire was burning in the cracks. We stepped out onto it; it burned the soles of our shoes. If the crust had broken, we would have fallen into a sea of fire. Then we saw the monstrous stream of fire pouring slowly, thick and red like porridge, down the mountain.

Andersen, so terrified of rough seas, fierce dogs and loneliness, seemed quite unafraid of the volcano:

> The descent was great fun. We charged off, had to brake with our heels, fell from time to time in the soft ash. That airborne coming down lasted ten minutes . . .

The mules were waiting where they had been left, but the tired animals made heavy weather of the return:

> Berg fell off. The mule stepped on him; it looked awful. When mine stumbled, I nearly ruptured myself on the pommel of the saddle. The lava looked like colossal, fallen stars.

Late at night, there was no coach to be hired from the sleeping village, so the five young men set out for Naples on foot. The city gates were closed, and Andersen noted with some pride that his explanation in Italian was understood and accepted.

The next morning, he was up earlier than his exhausted companions, though admitting that the mule ride had left him with a severely bruised backside. Hertz, who had fallen on the mountain and hurt his leg, affectionately called him 'a big giraffe'. A warm friendship had developed between the two, and they talked a lot, according to Andersen's diary, about the sensual feelings prompted by Naples and the south. Hertz evidently did not believe in chastity, as his companion had discovered on 19 February:

> God only knows what Hertz was up to when I got home! The room was locked, and when I knocked on the door he came out and, speaking to me with the door closed behind him, apologised for the fact that I couldn't come in. He appeared to me to be flustered.

Andersen himself had been the butt of some teasing about his virginal prudishness, and the uninhibited sexuality of Naples was a constant torment to him. Since his first arrival, he had, like all visitors, been pestered by prostitutes and pimps – often boys of no more than ten or eleven years old – offering indiscriminately a *ragazzo* or *ragazza*. He was not unaffected by these invitations, as his diary entries frequently show. 'My blood is churning,' he wrote on 23 February:

> Huge sensuality and struggle with myself. If it really is a sin to satisfy
> this powerful urge, then let me fight it. I am still innocent, but my
> blood is burning. In my dreams I am boiling inside. The south will
> have its way! I am half sick. – Happy is the man who is married,
> engaged to be married! Oh, if only I were bound by strong bonds!

Three days later, he was sorely tempted:

> Spent the whole afternoon strolling along Toledo Street, looking at
> the motley crowds and being pursued by pimps. The boy in the white
> hat, who keeps trying to seduce me, couldn't praise his *donna*
> enough. "Oh, *multa bella!*" he said. She was only thirteen years old and
> had just this month given herself over to carnal pleasure. Finally I got
> tired of him and turned onto a side street; he suddenly darted ahead
> of me because that happened to be the very street she lived in. He
> showed me the house, begged me to take just one look at her and said
> I wouldn't be able to resist. "Exactly"! I thought, and said, "No! No!
> No!" as I walked to the next street.

As always, it was the very young who most closely threatened
Andersen's self-imposed celibacy. Mature women continued to repel
him, but the semi-religious idea of a pure love which at the same time
provided a sexual outlet was a dream which centred round the barely
pubescent girl, still free of female carnality. It was a dream hedged
about with taboo, as he was well aware, and he stated his dilemma at
the end of his diary entry about the boy with the white hat. 'I don't
regard this gratification as a sin, but I find it disgusting and dangerous
to do it with such creatures, and with an innocent, an unforgivable
offence.' There was no room between these options for the
combination of opposites which he sought in his ideal of sexual purity.

That the solution to his dilemma could have lain in a homosexual
relationship does not seem to have occurred to Andersen – or, if it did,
he suppressed it as unthinkable. It is clearly evident that he was deeply
in love with Edvard, and had lost him to the legal demands of correct
and conventional marriage, but these were demands which he did not
query. His musings about gratification ended with the words, 'I am at
the point of saying with Hertz; happy the man who is married and

doesn't commit lechery.'

Andersen could not even begin to accept that marriage exists at its most basic level to give legality to sexual love and continued to torment himself with his contradictory ideals. During his last days in Naples, he came close to finding the perfect embodiment of them. He and his friends, having recovered from the trip to Vesuvius, set out again, this time to Pompeii and Peastum, with a visit to the Blue Grotto. Among the classical ruins, there sat a beggar girl who was Andersen's idea of perfection. He used her as the mystic heroine of *The Improvisatore*, described in virtually the same words which appear in *Mit livs eventyr*:

> I saw a poor, blind girl, dressed in rags, but a picture of great beauty, a statue come to life, but still almost a child; she was fixing some blue violets in her jet black hair; that was the only decoration she bore. She made an impression on me as though she were a revelation from the world of beauty. I could not give her money and stood gazing at her with some strange sort of respect, as though she were the very goddess from the temple on the steps of which she was sitting among the wild figs.

Time and money were running out. Although his travel grant had been for two years, Andersen had been away for barely twelve months and would now have to return to Denmark and take up his troubled career. In an ongoing letter which he began to Mrs Laessøe on 18 March 1834, he described his final days in the 'paradise' of Naples, crowned by hearing the famous Madame Malibran sing in three operas, and admitted that return to Copenhagen was like a submission to 'the iron ring to be fastened to my foot'. Two days later, he left Naples and started on the long journey home.

He spent Easter in Rome, and his letter to Mrs Laessøe revealed a deep disgust at seeing the ritual baptism of a Jew in St Peters, noting that:

> this time they had only been able to procure an ugly little boy with a scurvy head, who looked awful as the water was sprinkled over him. His boots and stockings were dirty, but over all the dirt was a glittering white silk robe given by the church.

At the same time, Andersen, perhaps additionally influenced by

Princess Charlotte's faith, could not help being moved once more by the panoply of Catholicism. 'For sensuous beings a sensuous worship of God is necessary,' he wrote.

More personally, he took up Mrs Laessøe on her advice that he should set aside his grumbling when he came home, and settle down to his work. He reiterated his deep resentment of the criticism from Molbech and from Edvard:

> I have written nothing here, they have broken the pinions of the bird. You say I could make a living; would that it were so. But there are many dogs after that bone. I will have to bury the poet they have murdered. God gave me the spiritual diploma of nobility, which they have torn to shreds. I am a poet, but I can relinquish my nobility and disappear into the crowd. I'm not writing this in a dark moment – I am perfectly calm, as happy as it is possible for me to be, and my only wish is never to produce any new work. My delight, my courage, my whole soul hung by only one thread, and it has been severed by my friend. The operation is over, the patient is well.

In the same passage he lamented his enforced departure from his beloved Italy, and returned to the enigma of his own self:

> Ørsted says that his and my aesthetic religion are widely different; I seek all the discords of the world, while he insists that a poet must seek the harmonies; but I believe I am myself the discord in this world. Too many bitter tears have fallen on the chords of my love to produce harmony, and I shall not attain that which I aimed for. You may not understand me, but I dare not speak plainer.

Here, surely, he came close to admitting the inner nature which he kept so carefully hidden. His declared affairs with Riborg Voigt and Louise Collin had been spoken of extremely plainly and at great length to anyone who would listen, but the love he could not attain could only have been that of Edvard.

Andersen was still terribly afraid that their friendship was over. Following the angry exchange about *Agnete* and his own stiff response to Edvard's stiff apology, there had been no more correspondence. In Naples, he had been too happy to worry much about the absence of letters from Edvard, but as he journeyed north, dread began to overwhelm him. In Venice he stared gloomily across the lagoon and declared that the place looked like a dead swan floating on a pond, and in Munich, where he spent the whole of May, agonising toothache returned to torment him. 'Oh, I wish I were dead,' he wrote in his diary on 14 May. 'Life holds no joy for me.' He spent his time reading the books of other writers who had been to Italy, and went with no great enthusiasm to art galleries and the theatre, but could find no peace of mind. His lingering in the city was probably in the hope of a letter to the Munich poste restante address, and he was rewarded on 25 May when he heard at last from Edvard, who contended with some justice that it was Andersen's wounded pride which had caused the long break in their correspondence.

That day, Andersen wrote with resentment in his diary that Edvard addressed him like a lord to his humble servant and yet when he wrote back it was to try and ingratiate himself afresh:

> Your heart may be able to do without me, mine cannot do without you, and yet I may lose you. I am seized by a strange fear, a fear which tells me how infinitely dear you are to me, and how unhappy you can make me.

This reply posted, Andersen moved on, still grieving for his lost Italy. In Innsbruck he went for a mountain walk with a young Scot who was desperately homesick for his native Highlands, and admitted in a letter to Jette Wulff that he could feel no such nostalgia for his own homeland:

> I am longing for my home where the oranges grow, where the endless blue sea stretches out with its swimming islands, Vesuvius with its red lava, and the whole life there. Oh! If only I had died in Naples, if only I could live there always!

Via Salzburg and Vienna he came to 'that German Sodoma, Berlin', where he went to see Chamisso, then shifted north again. From a Bohemian town called Kolin he wrote again to Edvard, pleased that the name of the place sounded like Collin. As if afraid that Edvard would have found his previous letter too emotional, he claimed brashly to have picked up enough Czech to shout through the carriage window, '*Krasna jeftsja, dia si miloju*' (his diary's phonetic representation of what

he heard), meaning 'Pretty girl, I love you.' He had felt pleased, he
said, at having had the courage to say this to 'a female creature'. Then
he abandoned his pretence:

> We will soon meet again. I wonder whether you look older? I wonder
> whether – now, please forgive me! – whether you will delight me even
> more than before? I don't think I am as passionate and soft as I used
> to be, that was a mistake and has been corrected, I wonder whether
> you will like me better?

That Andersen had not overcome his distaste for the 'female
creature' was demonstrated by a curious incident that took place on
the way to Prague. A young couple joined the coach, and the girl
chatted non-stop about her father's big house and great library while
she stroked what she referred to as 'the angelic little head' of her
sleeping companion. Andersen, well used to visiting the houses of the
European literati, made his way to the mansion the girl had
mentioned, encouraged by her assurance that it was a meeting-place
for all the poets in Prague, and was surprised, once admitted, to be
directed up a mean stairway to the attic. The door to a small, squalid
apartment was opened by an old man in a dressing gown and the
'great library' was revealed as a clothes basket full of old books.
Embarrassed, Andersen mentioned his travelling companions by
name, and was rewarded by a shriek of '*Mein Gott!*' from the adjoining
room:

> It was the young lady's voice. I looked towards the sound, and saw her
> in her negligée, with her travelling-dress of fine, black silk poised
> above her head as she tried to put it on, and in the bedroom her
> husband gave a sleepy yawn and lifted his 'angelic little head'. I stood
> in amazement; the lady came in with her dress unbuttoned at the
> back, and with an untied bonnet on her head, blushing deeply at the
> surprise. 'Von Andersen,' she said, and asked for forgiveness.

A more blasé traveller would tell such a story to get a laugh, but
Andersen was clearly shocked.

His dread deepened as he made his way home, 'towards my
Gethsemene', as he wrote to Jette Wulff, 'to Judas kisses and cups of
bitterness.' Needless to say, when he arrived at the Collin house on 3

August, Louise's birthday, he found the assembled family as pleasant and welcoming as ever, their urbanity undisturbed by any emotional turmoil.

There is a curious lack of any reference to Edvard in the weeks that followed. Andersen stayed for the first two weeks after his return with the Wulffs at their apartment in the Naval Academy, though Jette had set off on her own long visit to Italy. Following that, he went to the Ingemanns' at Sorø, and while there, wrote a cheerful letter to Mrs Iversen, detailing the important people he had met in Copenhagen since his arrival back in the city. 'The king was also very kind to me,' he added laconically, all resentments apparently forgotten.

In September, he moved into two rooms by the side of the Nyhavn Canal in what is now number 20, and settled down to work on *The Improvisatore.* He was penniless, but borrowed enough money to live on from the ever-patient Jonas Collin. His poverty worried him, and he applied for a post in the Royal Library, submitting a testimonial from H.C. Ørsted which merely supplied an added reason for a refusal on the grounds that he was 'too talented.' A libretto for an opera met with little success, and there was nothing for it but to concentrate on the novel. For three months Andersen worked in a fever of nostalgia for Italy, setting down the scenes and events which continued to live in his mind and linking them with a romantic, if unlikely plot. Reitzel had no more faith in this new book than in *Agnete* and would not offer an advance.

Edvard's gibe that nobody would want to read another travel book about the well-trodden path to Rome had found its mark, and so, despite Andersen's furious resistance, had his hard-hitting comments about over-production and low standards. In effect, Andersen had done exactly as Edvard had suggested, writing nothing for six months while he immersed himself in awareness of his surroundings, and his fresh beginning was cautious. For the first time, his writing showed some awareness of the potential reader's tastes, and self-indulgent bombast gave way to descriptive colour and a story which was, in Andersen's peculiar way, frankly erotic. His reading in Munich of Italian travel books by such famous writers as Goethe, Heine and Madame de Stael had provoked a sniffy comment about how 'empty' he found them, but he now had to ensure that his own book was full of interest. Familiar with Ingemann's Scott-inspired blood-and-thunder novels, he went all out for the rattling good yarn. The eponymous improviser is a thinly disguised Andersen, called Antonio, and much of the action concerns this character's passionate friendship with Bernado, a handsome young man who deserts him to become engaged to Annunciata, an opera singer. The story then lurches off into Antonio's vying with his friend for Annunciata's affections, a theme which was to crop up very frequently in Andersen's later stories. Having successfully lured the girl away, Antonio cannot take her from his friend – and neither can the author square up to depicting physical attraction between a man and a woman. Instead, through some mystical contortions of plot, Antonio ends up with Lara, a blind beggar-girl from Paestum, complete with violets in her hair, 'a child who wonderfully attracted me', as the first-person hero confesses, 'as only a child could.' This 'firm knot between the supernatural and the real' neatly side-steps any question of physical love, and the couple are united and produce a child from what appears to be disembodied spirituality.

At the end of the book, Andersen performs a post-modern jump, introducing himself into the narrative, accompanied by the very recognisable Henrik Hertz. He even dates the episode – 6 March 1834, the actual day of his visit to Paestum – as if to distance himself from any suspicion that the characters might embody their author's identity. Having described how the 'foreign gentleman, quite tall and somewhat pale, with strong features and dressed in a blue frock-coat' was delighted to meet Antonio and Lara's baby, held – as though to minimise the fact of physical parenthood with all its sexual overtones – in the arms of 'an elderly lady' rather than its father or mother, he then went on to hammer home this other reality. The foreigner, he states, was Danish, as was the 'grave little man' who accompanied him. 'They were countrymen of Federigo and the great Thorvaldsen.'

Here is another magical wave of the fan. Thorvaldsen was real enough, but Federigo appears in the book as a slightly enigmatic character, responsible for a sexual encounter during Antonio's early boyhood which is described with no sign of any authorial disapproval. It seems rather to have been the awakening of the young Antonio's passions, and Federigo appears at the end of the book to catch up the theme of 'the thread of happiness' established in the early episode.

Andersen was emphatic that the characters in *The Improvisatore* all came from life, and scholars have for some years suggested that he himself underwent a paedophiliac encounter as a boy, but the episode from the book must be left to speak for itself. Federigo, an artist, lures Antonio into a deep cave, unrolling a ball of string as they go. He kisses and caresses the boy, gives him money and threatens to beat him when he takes fright and starts to call for his mother; the candle goes out and the string which will guide them back to daylight is lost:

> After vainly searching, he threw himself on the ground, flung his arms round my neck and sighed "You poor child!" I wept bitterly then, believing I would never go home again. He clasped me so closely to him as he lay on the ground that my hand slid under him. Involuntarily I clutched at the sand, and found the string between my fingers. "Here it is!" I exclaimed. He seized my hand and became, as it were, frantic for joy, for our lives really did hang on this single thread.

On emerging from the cave, Federigo kisses the boy 'yet again' and gives him his silver watch:

> I quite forgot about what had happened, but once my mother heard about it, she could not forget it, and would not let Federigo take me out again.

It is impossible to be certain of the identity of the real-life Federigo, but a likely candidate must be Fedder Carstens, both for the similarity of name and for the fact that the affectionate schoolmaster disappeared so abruptly from Odense when Andersen had been in his care for a few months, apparently never to teach again.

Andersen as an adult had a strong dislike of underground places, as witness his fear of the candle going out when in the Dannemora mines. In *Mit livs eventyr*, casting his mind back to such places as the caves in the Harz, salt-works at Hallein and the catacombs of Rome and Malta, he said, 'There was no pleasure in any of these places; it was unpleasant, oppressive, a horrible nightmare. I prefer not to go under the earth until my dead body is laid to rest there.'

The cave episode in the novel, however, is given a religious twist which adroitly diverts the reader's suspicions. The pious Fra Martino points out that 'the thread of happiness' was found by the innocent child rather than the notoriously heretic Federigo (or perhaps by the Jewish real-life Fedder Carstens). From that point, the Antonio-narrative rushes straight on to his determination to become a priest 'because, with the exception of my mother, I could not endure women'.

With no pause, he is straight into a version of the Küchler episode in which a mother stripped her daughter for his inspection, but with the added horror that Antonio/Andersen is dragged into a close encounter. Federigo, the artist, uses a model called Mariuccia, who teases the young Antonio, calling him her little bridegroom who 'must and will give her a kiss'. The boy refuses, but, saying that he cries like a baby and behaves like a child that is still suckled, Mariuccia tries to put him to her breast:

> I rushed down the steps, but she ran after me and caught me, held me between her knees and pushed my head, which I turned away with disgust, ever closer and closer to her breast.

Antonio's mother laughs and encourages Mariuccia, 'while Federigo, unnoticed, stood at the door and painted the whole group'.

In the strongest possible contrast, the later development of *The Improvisatore*, dealing with Antonio and his beloved friend Bernado, evokes the prickling senses which any lover will recognise. After a long absence, Antonio catches sight of his friend in the colonnade flanking a ballroom, and is completely overcome:

> A thousand emotions agitated my heart: – he here? I so near him? I felt a trembling in all my limbs, and was obliged to sit down. The fragrant flowers, the subdued music, the twilight, even the soft, yielding sofa, all carried me into a kind of dream-world, and only in such a one could I hope to meet with Bernado.

Telling his friend that he wishes they could always be together, Antonio receives a dampening reply which could have come straight from Edvard:

> "That would ruin our friendship," he answered. "No, it would come to an end before we knew it. Friendship is like love, all the stronger for separation. I think sometimes how tiresome it must actually be to be married. To see one another for ever and ever, in the minutest of detail. Most married people are disgusting to one another; it is a sort

of propriety, a kind of good nature, which holds them together in the long run."

Through Antonio, Andersen explored a little further the feelings he had so tentatively expressed to Mrs Laessøe:

> There are conflicts, thoughts even, which the majority of mortals dare not express, because the Angel of Innocence in our breast regards them as sinful. They who can indulge the longings of their hearts may philosophise beautifully over what I say. Judge not, lest you be judged! I felt that within myself – in my own corrupt nature – there abode no good thing.

This passage follows close on one in which Antonio is teased by his friends, as Andersen was, about the 'goat's milk in my blood' which robs him of normal interest in young women. He has narrowly escaped seduction by Santa, in an episode taken straight from Mrs Meisling's invitation to feel how loose her dress is, saved only by a picture of the Virgin falling rather symbolically from the wall. From that point on, the book follows Andersen's own difficult path through contradictory ideals to an ending which, while conventionally happy, has parted from all recognisable reality.

Despite its implausible plot, *The Improvisatore* was set in such a detailed and convincing picture of Italy that it remains readable today. The loneliness which Andersen felt while travelling laid him open to a raw impressionability, and this resulted in writing which is full of colour and flavour, including all the small discomforts which bring home the real meaning of being away in some unfamiliar place.

The book was finished by the end of 1834, and by way of light relief, Andersen turned to the concoction of some stories, meant primarily for children. The very fact that he did not regard these as part of his ongoing pursuit of fame gave them the fresh, matter-of-fact quality for which he is still known, but at the time, his attention was still firmly fixed on the problems of the novel, of money, and of Edvard.

At the beginning of 1835, Andersen's financial situation was desperate. *The Improvisatore* was not yet out, and he owed Jonas Collin the money for its publication, plus his own living expenses since the return from Italy. The two-act musical play, *Little Kirsten,* which he had written in the autumn and submitted to the theatre had been damned by its commissioning reader, Molbech, ever the black dog on Andersen's back. In a derisory report on 30 January, he conceded that the piece suffered less than usual from 'the peculiar bad taste shown in the author's earlier works', but added that it had more 'vacuity, thinness and dramatic poverty'.

It was a justified criticism. Drama, so intimately bound up with Andersen's self-projecting ambition, was for that very reason his least successful genre. He wrote plays fast and carelessly, intoxicated by the conviction of his own talent, and never realised that the true writer's worst enemy is the desire to impress. To be 'natural' on purpose demands an immense amount of skill and hard work, and Andersen, always awkward with words and temperamentally disinclined towards critical self-scrutiny, seldom produced more than slipshod melodrama.

During the winter months, his depression deepened. Despite Edvard's engagement to Jette Thyberg, whom Andersen could not help liking for her good humour and friendliness, there was no slackening in the intensity of his attachment to his friend, although the efforts to control it were very evident. On 20 October, not long after his return from Italy, Andersen had written:

> I'm sorry I was a bit emotional the other day, in too loving a mood, you don't like that; but I was not feeling very well – I'll cool down presently.

A month later, having begun a letter in a business-like tone as if from author to slightly dilatory agent ('I am reminding you urgently to go and see Reitzel . . . ') he struggled to distance himself from the passion which he knew Edvard found embarrassing:

> In the evening, I get emotional; last night I wrote another poem to you, which you won't receive. Don't think it's 'the old emotionalism', it's not that I have an ideal Edvard, a friend of great kindness; I stretch out my arms towards him, but it isn't you at all. You have too many faults, failings and sharpnesses of tongue to allow me to dream of you.

Edvard, in what seems a rather desperate effort to provide a neutral basis, insisted on playing chess when he and Andersen met, provoking a comment at the end of the October letter:

> We haven't really talked in a friendly and sensible way one single time since I've been home; but that's because of your damned eagerness to play. Can nobody checkmate you?

That Jette Wulff was still in Italy added to Andersen's gloom, and on 16 March he wrote to her, lamenting that Denmark was still shrouded in rain, slush and fog, and that the only blue he had seen for five months was the colour of his own overcoat. In the same letter, he remarked that Ørsted had been impressed by the four little fairy tales he had shown him. These, he had predicted, would make Andersen immortal. Andersen himself disagreed. 'I do not think so,' his letter went on. 'He does not know Italy, and so cannot delight in the familiar atmosphere which the novel recreates for me.' He added that *The Improvisatore* was already, before its Danish publication, being translated into German, and that the publishers there wanted a different title. 'Can you suggest one? Which is better, *The Boy from the Roman Campagna* or *The Blue Grotto of Capri*?' In the end, the Germans settled for *Jugendleben und Träume eines Italienischen Dichters*, (*The Young Life and Dreams of an Italian Poet*) which hardly seems an improvement on the original.

The novel was published in April 1835, a few days after Andersen's thirtieth birthday, and although he always claimed that Danish critics treated him badly, the book was in fact a great success. Action-packed, erotic and colourful, it also broke new ground in its descriptions of the lives of common Italian people, and in the days when travel was the prerogative of the privileged classes, such insight won countless fascinated readers. Andersen, for all his letters of introduction and his seeking out of hospitality in the houses of the wealthy, had not as far as he knew been born into these circles. Whatever his true origins, he travelled with the open impressionability of an unsophisticated man. *The Improvisatore* would within a few years be translated into Swedish, English, Dutch, French and Czech as well as German – an unprecedented feat for a Danish author. Andersen sent a boxful of copies out to Frederik Petzholdt, one of his friends in Rome, with a letter (couched in '*du*' terms) pointing out that Petzholdt was immortalised in the Blue Grotto scene.

Edvard in his later book included this letter, commenting on the fact that its almost cockily jovial tone was in strong contrast to the ones Edvard himself was receiving, for Andersen's economic worries had grown 'to a disturbing degree'. Far more typical, Edvard contended, was the frantic appeal Andersen had sent to his father, Jonas Collin, on 14 May, barely a month after *The Improvisatore*'s appearance. This, almost suicidally depressed, complained of the 'injustice and petty judgement' which met all his best efforts and condemned him to live 'like the most wretched beggar'.

The letter was in fact a reluctant and agonised appeal to Collin for a further loan, though Andersen suggested that he could if all else failed take 'a poor teaching job' somewhere in the country and forget all his literary ambitions. Collin answered with a bare couple of lines, dry and practical. 'Calm down and get a good night's sleep. Tomorrow we'll talk and think about resources.'

The two leather-bound volumes of *The Improvisatore* had been dedicated to the Collin family, to whom the author brought 'with a filial and fraternal heart, this the best which I possess', and Jonas, who had never had any enthusiasm for his protégé's writing ambitions, again lent him money. Meanwhile, on 8 May 1835, the unbound paper-covered booklet containing the first four fairy tales had been launched, with as little ceremony as a child's paper boat in a gutter.

The first of all Andersen's stories was 'The Tinderbox', published together with 'Little Claus and Big Claus', The Princess and the Pea' (which in its less delicate Danish title was called 'The Princess On the Pea') and 'Little Ida's Flowers'. They came out to a baffled silence, and when a review finally appeared in *Dannora* it commented with disapproval on their lack of 'edifying effect', and doubted whether they could even be regarded as harmless. The reviewer was appalled by the casual way in which Big Claus kills his grandmother as if she were 'just a bull being knocked on the head', and 'The Princess and the Pea' was 'not only indelicate but quite unpardonable, since it may give a child the false impression that so august a lady must of necessity be terribly sensitive'. The notice ended in the hope that 'this talented author, with a higher mission to follow, will waste no more of his time in writing fairy tales for children'.

Infuriatingly to Andersen, *Dansk Litteraturtidende* objected to the stories because they failed to teach a moral lesson, and cited Molbech's homilies for the young as the standard to be aimed at. Their critic also commented that 'one must not put one's words together in the same disorderly fashion as one may do perfectly acceptably in oral speech.'

The point is a significant one, for it shows clearly that Andersen was a genuine pioneer in writing *for* children rather than *at* them. The tales were specified in their collective title as being '*Told for Children*' [my emphasis], and Andersen insisted in his later notes to the stories that their oral quality was deliberate:

> I wanted the style to be such that the reader felt the presence of the storyteller; therefore the spoken language had to be used. I wrote the tales for children, but older people ought to find them worth listening to.

Translated into English by worthy Victorians, little of his down-to-earth, laconic quality came over, and there must be many British readers of the older generation who have retained a sense of Andersen's stories as charged with a kind of poetic wistfulness, totally missing the black, casual humour which redeems them from sentimentality. More than a century after his death, translations have improved immensely, but the boat has long been missed in terms of his revolutionary use of demotic Danish. Just as Pushkin opened up the Russian literary scene to the language of the common people, so on a smaller scale did Andersen. The closing paragraphs of 'The Princess and the Pea' are miles away from the solemn moralisings of Molbech and his ilk:

> The king and the queen were delighted. If this girl could feel one little pea through twenty mattresses and twenty duvets, then she must be a real, proper princess. Nobody else would be so sensitive.

So the prince married her. And what happened to the pea? Oh, they put that in the royal museum. You can see it there to this day, if nobody's pinched it.

So there you are – that's the story!

Even some of Andersen's closest friends were a little shocked. Ingemann, who had always been so supportive, said they should never have been written. Carsten Hauch was cautiously approving though he frowned over the 'moral indifference' of 'The Tinder Box', and Heiberg, himself a pioneer in the use of the demotic, agreed with Ørsted that these were the best things Andersen had ever written.

The timing of the stories was perfect, for the ground had already been laid. In 1812 the Grimm brothers had published their first collection of German folk-tales transcribed (and often squeamishly sanitised) from oral sources, and nearer home, N.F.S. Grundtvig had reawakened interest in Scandinavian mythology. For him, the violent, mysterious beauty of early Nordic oral history represented the divine spark which is present in humanity. Born in 1783, he hated the eighteenth century for its cool, anti-emotional logic, and turned with religious passion away from the Enlightenment into the rich darkness of legendry. In 1820 he had published a first Danish translation of *Beowulf,* and shortly before Andersen's departure to Italy, he had issued a revised edition of his *Nordens Mythologi* which sought to bring the old myths into line with Christianity. Oehlenschläger's hugely successful reworking of the *Aladdin* myth had been a powerful influence on the young Andersen, and across the world, interest was awakening in the old tales of classical Greece and Rome. Nathaniel Hawthorne, just one year older than Andersen, was writing his *Twice-Told Tales* which would the following year top the American best-seller lists, and in Britain the traditional fairy tales began to be used as subjects for pantomime and, despite opposition from the moralists, were issued in book form.

Of the four stories in Andersen's first collection, only 'Little Ida's Flowers' was an original idea, the others being derived from old folk-tales known to him since childhood. The eponymous Ida was the daughter of Thiele, who had so devastatingly confirmed Edvard's low opinion of *Agnete* the previous year, and the plot of the story turns on the simple idea that the flowers are wilting because they were out at a dance all night. In this tale, too, Andersen introduced himself as a character in the story:

> The young man was sitting on the sofa. Ida was very fond of him
> because he knew the most marvellous stories and with a pair of
> scissors could cut out of paper the most wonderful pictures; flowers,
> hearts, little dancing ladies, and castles with doors that could open.

It was no vain boast. Andersen's paper-cuts were astonishingly
intricate, at their most elaborate a filigree of tiny detail though he
worked with a heavy, long-bladed pair of scissors. The decorative,
fanciful side of his nature came straight from the childhood spent in
devising miniature scenes and costumes for his toy theatre, but
Andersen was still disinclined to regard this as important. He was
already working on another novel, and on 28 August wrote to Edvard
to make it clear that it would refer to their relationship. One of the
characters, he explained, would have Edvard's personality and the
plot would lead to a reversal of social positions. '*I* will become the
nobleman and *you* will have the more humble position.'

This slightly vindictive intention was declared at the end of a letter
in which a continued nostalgia for Italy overflowed into an unbridled
declaration of love:

> I long for you; yes, at this moment I long for you as if you were a lovely
> Calabrian girl with dark eyes and a glance of passionate flame. I never
> had a brother, but if I had, I could not have loved him as I love you,
> and yet – you do not return it and this causes me pain – or maybe it is
> precisely what binds me to you. My soul is proud, no prince could be
> prouder; I have clung closely to you, with you I have – – – basta; that's
> a good Italian word which in Nyhavn would mean: shut up!

Unable to duck the fact that Edvard was engaged to be married,
Andersen began to see his fiancée, Jette Thyberg, as an additional
pathway to his beloved friend. From Odense during a two-month
summer tour in Denmark, he wrote with the request that Jette should
tell Edvard on his behalf, 'I love you!' – using the '*du*' form forbidden
to himself. He wrote also to Edvard's sister, Louise, and while saying he
would not talk about his feelings, could not help going on to discuss
Edvard, who was sometimes so affectionate and sometimes
unknowable and frightening. The desperate need to be accepted by

the whole Collin family came out in the same letter, dated 22 June, with a small spurt of jealousy. 'Why did Viggo say to his father rather than to me that he should say hello to the flowers in Jutland? Poets and flowers have far more to do with each other than politicians and flowers.'

As the success of *The Improvisatore* began to yield some profits, Andersen's financial situation eased, and by the end of the year he was beginning to enjoy what he himself admitted to be a 'pleasant existence'. In January 1836 he wrote to Jette Hanck in rare contentment:

> The publishers send me magazines, Reitzel sends me books and prints, and then I sit with my gaily coloured slippers, in my dressing gown, with my feet up on the table, enjoying a smoke. Then I think of the poor boy in Odense wearing his wooden shoes, and my heart melts and I bless the Lord. I think I have now reached my zenith. Later on it will go downward.

He enlarged on the same theme to Jette Wulff:

> My years of writing began with my return from abroad; I may have another four or maybe six years in which I will still be able to write well, and I must use them.

The second instalment of fairy stories, comprising 'Thumbelina', 'The Naughty Boy' and 'The Travelling Companion' had just appeared, in time for Christmas 1835, and this time, approval had been almost unanimous. These tales were much closer to Andersen's own strange feelings, and were consequently charged with a power which was impossible to ignore. His complex responses to sexuality and marriage found rich expression here, and these stories cast a fascinating light on what was going on in his mind as Edvard's marriage drew nearer.

Thumbelina, the tiny girl born through immaculate conception in the heart of a tulip, is stolen away by a toad who wants her as a wife for her hideous son. Escaping this fate, she is rescued by a field mouse from the winter cold, only to find the dark underground forces of sexuality reaching out for her again in the form of the mole, in whose underground home lies the apparently lifeless body of a swallow. This free-flying bird is an obvious metaphor for the poetic soul, and

Andersen had a special venom for those who belittled it:

> The mole kicked the bird with one of his short legs and said, 'It's stopped its chirping now. How dreadful to be born a bird. None of my children will be born birds, thank God! All they can do is chirp, then die of starvation when the winter comes.'

Warmed back to life by Thumbelina, the grateful bird takes her away on its back to Italy, where she makes a typically Andersenian marriage, to a tiny angel sitting in the middle of a flower. 'He was white and almost transparent as if he was made of glass.'

The author again enters the story as the swallow flies back to his window to tell the tale, establishing an innocent detachment. None of this, it is implied, came from Andersen's mind – he is not responsible. He simply wrote down what the bird told him.

To this day, his trick of distancing himself from the display he is deploying has bamboozled the critics. As John Goldthwaite puts it in *The Natural History of Make-Believe*, 'He lacked that essential ingredient in a storyteller – the humility to absent himself from the tale in order to do it full justice.' Goldthwaite concludes that Andersen's fairy stories have no value except 'as a cautionary fable on how not to write them'. To hold this view is to ignore or be unaware of the double-layered structure of Andersen's work, behind which he hides his secret and vulnerable self; it disregards, too, the traditional craft of the performing storyteller, present in the flesh even as he evokes a different world. Andersen came from a tradition of listening to such tales and being aware that at their ending, the teller had to return the listeners to their own reality with one of the phrases he so often uses – something along the lines of, 'So there you are – that was the story.'

That Andersen was a little more elaborate in turning the readers' attention back to the separate self of the storyteller does indeed seem an irritating trick now that we are quite happy to accept the implications of what he wrote, but in the mid-nineteenth century, there was much to hide. An evident loathing of women emerges in 'The Travelling Companion', where a bewitched princess is beaten so hard with birch-twigs as she flies through the night sky that 'blood dripped down on the earth, and the princess could hardly fly'. The hero, who in this case is not even the narrator but his side-kick, the travelling companion, advises on how to answer the trick questions and win the bride, and sets up a wedding-night in which the evil spirit of the princess-bride has to be driven out by half-drowning her in a tub of water. The travelling companion who has been responsible for all this moves on and the narrator is left doubly innocent, recording the events as if surprised to hear of them.

Even 'The Naughty Boy', a straight reworking of Anacreon's poem about Cupid, has something to conceal, for the first victim of Cupid's dart is a student who, not recognising the naughty boy in his academic cap and gown, takes his arm. The love affair between two young men is thrown in casually, subordinate to the main theme of Cupid's breaking of the poet's heart, but it is there. The layers are so lightly piled, the feathers so adroitly deployed, that nobody notices.

In April 1836, Andersen's second novel was published under the enigmatic title of *O.T.*. The initials have a double meaning; they stand both for the hero's name, Otto Thostrup and for the gaol in Odense, Odense Tughus. Contrary to Hans Christian Andersen's threats, Edvard appears in the book as Baron Vilhelm, to whom Otto is powerfully attracted, and this relationship is established before the rest of the action starts.

Like all Andersen's novels, *O.T.* is compounded of elements from his own life, in this case centring round the unknown and vaguely alarming figure of a lost elder sister. Otto Thostrup, brought up by his mother in some strange building which he takes to be a kind of factory, is haunted by the nightmare quality of this childhood. He falls in with a deeply sinister figure, 'German Heinrich', richly tattooed and claiming some knowledge of the boy's family. At Otto's own request, Heinrich tattooes the initials, O.T. on the skin of the boy's shoulder, and when Otto bears the pain of this without crying out, consents to tell him what he knows. The 'factory' was Odense Gaol, where Otto's mother was a prisoner, and the lost sister is Sidsel, an evil girl of whom Otto is terribly afraid.

This knotted situation is resolved by some ruthless authorial knife-work. Sidsel turns out to be not Otto's sister at all, but German Heinrich's daughter, and the pair of them are conveniently drowned in a storm. Otto's mother is innocent of the crime for which she was convicted, having taken the blame for her criminal husband, and when the missing sister is found, she is pure and ethereal, but dies before she can be reunited with her brother.

The book was popular with the public, not because of its somewhat implausible plot, but for its knowledgeable depiction of working-class life. Denmark had long been in the aristocratic tradition of regarding the arts as the prerogative of the cultured classes, but the country's early introduction of universal education, combined with a fast-growing democratic movement, was beginning to throw up a new school of social realism in writing, of which Andersen found himself a prominent member.

He was already at work on a third novel, *Only A Fiddler*, and in a letter to Ingemann confided that, in contrast to the carefully planned *O.T.*, this book was proceeding without any clear idea of what was to come next. In a rash statement which has been seized on gleefully by his detractors, he claimed an almost divine inspiration:

> I do not write a single word without it being *given* to me, almost forced upon me. It is as if the memory of an old tale has come to my mind and I have to tell it. If it weren't too profane to say so, I would maintain that I now know the meaning of the Biblical quotation, 'The entire Writ is inspired by God.'

In actual fact, the literary auto-pilot was set on such a well-worn course that nothing very original came of it. *Only A Fiddler* is essentially a novel of complaint about the lack of encouragement which forces a poor but musically talented boy back into obscurity while the beautiful Jewish girl who has been his childhood friend rises into the ranks of the nobility. Again, the insight into the lives of disadvantaged people is acute, and the book contains a mass of detail which it is tempting to take as autobiographical. The assumption that Andersen's father joined Napoleon's army as a paid substitute is based on the detailed description of that event given in the novel, and the whole childhood background is close to all the known facts. Once again, the novel impressed the public, and Andersen was now established as a contemporary Danish writer of considerable authority.

He himself was unable to build on this reputation as Charles Dickens was doing in Britain. Much to the irritation of Edvard, who had a much more objective view of Andersen's career than the writer himself, he continued to dabble in drama, turning out a double-bill operetta called *Parting and Meeting* which was briefly staged in April 1836, the same month as the publication of *O.T.*.

Four months later, on 10 August 1836, Edvard married his fiancée,

Jette Thyberg. Andersen took himself off to Odense, and from Svendborg wrote on 4 August to bid his friend goodbye as he stepped away on a journey where Andersen could not follow:

> You'll be a married man when my letter reaches you. I don't think I can come to the wedding, but whether or not I appear, I will be there in mind. I see the pair of you, serious and yet so happy. In my heart, I pray the good Lord to give you good fortune. Tears come to my eyes as I write this; as Moses did, I stand on the hill and gaze into the promised land into which I will never come.

He went on to regret that he would never know the blessings of a home with wife and children. Friendship, for him, would have to take the place of these things, and he implored Edvard to 'give me as much as you can, for you are the one I love most highly'. He claimed that he had loved Edvard 'as you love your Jette', then added that it was something he and Edvard had never talked about. 'It would have been better perhaps not to have written this letter' he admitted, but Edvard's wedding 'goes deep into my heart, awakes all my memories.' Italy, he claimed, was his bride, and he would return to the south.

Despite the success of the novels, Andersen did not have the money for such a journey, and he had no option but to accept the situation. He returned to Copenhagen a week after the wedding, on 18 August, but meanwhile wrote a cautious letter of welcome to Edvard's bride, whom he addressed as 'My dear Edvard's Jette'. It is a touching document, almost motherly in its tone, giving his successor 'some good advice as a bride':

> Don't let him have all the power, don't let him assume the right to be irritable, don't give in to him in everything. There is good nature in him, he has heart as well as mind – yes, you have given him yours so he had at least an equal exchange, but he must keep in step and behave properly. Soon I'll come and see the little household, the lovely young bride, rejoicing in your happiness and never losing friendship,
> Your faithful
> Andersen.

Jette Collin, lively, dark-haired, highly intelligent and with a pretty face which seemed always ready to break into a smile, seems to have understood the bizarre situation very well. She had come into a position which might well have caused her husband's passionate friend to resent and dislike her, and yet she managed to reassure Andersen and gain his trust and liking. She had none of the despotism which Jette Wulff had identified in Edvard, and she had the huge advantage in Andersen's eyes of being without any part in the moral debt which he felt he owed the family. For all that, the fact of Edvard's marriage was a deeply painful one, and the inadmissable resentment began to make itself felt in the form of a story which, Andersen said, 'intruded and would not go away.' As he worked on the formless meanderings of *Only A Fiddler*, the theme of *Agnete and the Merman*, together with the breakdown of his friendship with Edvard which it had caused, was back in his mind with renewed strength.

'The Little Mermaid', as the small bronze statue in Copenhagen harbour testifies, is a classic story, the one for which, together with 'The Ugly Duckling', Andersen is best known – and yet, few people, if asked, will remember more than the mermaid's falling in love with a human prince and the agony she went through as the sea-witch gave her the power to split her tail into human legs, and cut out her tongue in payment. What happened next, and how the story ends, can easily slip into obscurity. More attentive reading reveals the tale to be centrally about the rejected lover who has to come to terms with the marriage of the loved one with a female of his own kind.

Once it is accepted that Andersen could and did write through a persona very different from his six-foot male self – a fir tree, a nightingale, a daisy – there would be no difficulty in seeing that the mermaid, a 'different' creature who is not of the normal human world, is here his chosen self-representation. Falling in love with the prince, her only chance of saving herself from death as the penalty for having become human is to kill him as he lies asleep with his young bride. The sea-witch has given her a sharp knife to use for this deed, but as the mermaid looks at the prince's sleeping face, she cannot take the chance she has been offered, for she loves him too much. She flings the knife into the sea and feels herself dissolving into death, though the spirits of the air save her eternal spirit as a reward for her goodness.

For over a century, critics have assumed – as they were meant to – that the story centres on the question of pure moral goodness. Goldthwaite complains that Andersen's characters have a habit of dying 'for some higher cause than our base instincts could ever comprehend'; but in fact they usually die for love. Once it is accepted that the little mermaid could represent the soul of a tall, craggy man, the metaphor for his own doomed love becomes blindingly obvious. Andersen knew that Edvard could not join him in his own world, but the effort to make himself acceptable to Edvard's 'normality' demanded a gross distortion of his real nature. Like the mermaid, he could not talk about this, and like her, he could not wish harm to his beloved and the innocent girl he had married.

In Andersen's own time, such extended metaphors were taken at face value. If stories had an implied meaning, it was expected that the author would make this clear as Aesop had done in his fables, adding the 'Moral' which explained the story's thrust. It was a convention which gave Andersen the cover he needed, but in today's more perceptive understanding, it should be possible to see that his anger and sadness had deeper roots than his much-vaunted ambition.

'The Little Mermaid' was published in April 1837 with just one other story, 'The Emperor's New Clothes'. Andersen's notes credit the source of this tale to Prince Don Juan Manuel of Spain, born in 1277, but it has an obvious relevance to Andersen's own deeply hidden fear of being revealed. More easily accessible is the author's tilting at those who admire status for its own sake. This may seem to come strangely from a man who was so desperate to court the favours of the nobility, and yet the story's closing words contain a hint of fellow-feeling for the emperor himself, who saw through the motives of his sycophantic courtiers. Being inwardly certain that the child who has shouted the truth is right, he shivers at the horror of the situation, knowing that he is indeed naked:

> "I must bear it until the procession is over," he thought. And he walked even more proudly, and the two gentlemen of the imperial bedchamber went on carrying the train that wasn't there.

This was a story which Andersen delighted in reading aloud in the houses of the great and even to kings in their palaces, particularly, as his diary shows, when he was feeling at all put upon or under-appreciated, but the very convention which he mocked held safe enough to prevent any challenge.

All kinds of small events were beginning to act as a source of material for further tales. H.C. Ørsted's enthusiasm for the future of modern science led to an argument one evening at a party, when a certain Councillor Knap contended hotly that any time in the past was better than the decadent present. Andersen, very much on Ørsted's side, wrote a long story called 'The Magic Galoshes', in which these overshoes take the wearer back through time to various states of disadvantage. The tale contains a sharp portrait of Andersen himself on his travels:

> He was in a stagecoach with eight other passengers. He sat squeezed in the middle. He had a headache and a crick in his neck. All the blood seemed to have gone to his legs; whatever the cause, his feet were swollen and his boots pinched.
>
> He wavered between the waking state and dozing. In his right-hand pocket he had some letters of credit; in his left, his passport; and on a string round his neck hung a leather purse which contained a few louis d'or. Every time he fell asleep, he dreamed that one of his valuables had been lost; then he would wake with a start and move his hand in a triangle from left to right and to centre, to make sure that everything was there. The umbrellas, canes and hats hanging from the net above his head made it difficult for him to see out of the window. "Travelling would be fine if only we didn't have a body," sighed the student. "If one's spirit were free to go by itself."

Andersen much preferred the modern blessing of the train, and would almost certainly have embraced the comforts of the executive jet, had it been available.

Quite soon after Edvard's wedding, on 27 August, Andersen wrote an impatient letter to Jonas Collin, insisting that his future as a writer depended on being able to travel and complaining that a request to Edvard – now secretary of the public fund – for a further travel grant had been ignored. In fact, he had received a grant too recently to be eligible for another, and Edvard was powerless to do anything about it, but Andersen was desperate to get back to Italy, and wrote to Ørsted urging him to use his influence:

> The usual way into the *fund ad usus publico* is unavailable; but a man in whom the king has confidence, a man whose aesthetic opinion is

valued, could perhaps put to the king what I have told you in this letter. You are the only one who can do it.

Andersen showed little sign of appreciating just how eminent the physicist was. Ørsted had become a leading figure in the world of science and at the time of Andersen's somewhat peremptory request, was about to attend a September international conference in Southampton. John Herschel was to say of him there that he 'wielded an intense power, capable of altering the whole state of science, and almost convulsing the knowledge of the world'. Although Ørsted, for all his fame, was a modest man and a generous teacher, the first to open his lectures to common men and even women (an unheard-of innovation) he could not at such a busy time attend to his young friend's request, which was in any case completely against the rules. Andersen had to accept that he was stuck in Denmark.

He sat for his portrait to C.A. Jensen that summer, looking gloomy and Byronic, and was irritated to find by Christmas time that the artist was selling engraved reproductions of the picture at a steady profit. *Only a Fiddler* was finished by the summer and went off to the printers, and new stories were being written at a steady rate, but Edvard was now married and there was no escape from that fact, to Italy or anywhere else.

Chapter 11
Ambition

Andersen was cheered up a little by a meeting with the French author, Xavier Marmier, in the autumn of 1836. Marmier was full of enthusiasm for the Dane's work and proposed to write a biographical sketch for publication in France. This country had never shown much interest in Andersen's work, so the suggestion was a welcome one, but overall, the time was one of flatness and despondency. Edvard's refusal to pull strings for him with the public fund still rankled, and so did the Collin family's continued disinclination to take him seriously as a writer. It did not help, of course, that his own sufferings and yearnings were so transparent in his work to those who knew him well, and that Edvard had appeared in the novels in such thin disguise, but Andersen showed no sign of seeing this. With Edvard decisively out of reach, there was nothing now to aim at except fame. Love and acceptance seem to have been bound up in his mind with the achieving of respect, and he wrote unguardedly to Mrs Iversen in January 1837, revealing a desperate seeking of status which sounds almost pathological:

> The poor washerwoman's son who ran about with wooden shoes on his feet in the streets of Odense has got so far that he is now treated like a son in the house of one of Denmark's most highly respected men, and has friends among worthy and brilliant people. I <u>must</u> be mentioned among the <u>good</u> writers of my age; but I want more than that! May God give me strength towards it; I want to be ranked among the <u>foremost</u> of Denmark's writers, I want to be mentioned in the same breath as Holberg and Oehlenschläger.

Later in the year he explained the reason for his ambition in a letter to Mrs Iversen's grand-daughter, Jette Hanck:

> I covet honour and glory in the same way as the miser covets gold; both are probably empty, but one has to have something to strive for in this world, otherwise one would collapse and rot.

Meanwhile, the need to travel still had him in its grasp. On 20 June, at his own expense, he set out on a month's trip to Stockholm, though agonising in his diary about the 'calculation upon calculation' he had to make in order to ensure that his money would last out. Although a young writer who was able to afford a month's holiday could not really be called poverty-stricken, Andersen, in common with many people who have come from a background of harsh struggle, could never quite believe that there was no longer any real need for anxiety.

In *Mit livs eventyr,* he gives the impression that he did not expect much from his Swedish trip, but in fact it turned out to be a pleasant experience. He found that he could understand the language without much difficulty, and that Swedes could grasp what he meant in his native Danish, and his inherited prejudice began to fall away. As his autobiography explains, earlier wars had left a mutual suspicion:

> in winter when ice linked the two countries together and the Swedes came over to us by sleigh the street lads in Copenhagen always shouted rude and offensive things after them; very little was known about Swedish literature, and few Danes realised that with just a little practice we could read and understand the Swedish language.

An unexpected bonus on his summer journey was to find that he was sharing the canal boat with the Swedish novelist, Frederika Bremer, whom he described respectfully as 'a noble woman'. Bremer's impression of Andersen was less effusive. He was, she said, 'of somewhat peculiar appearance, but simple, with a sensitive and warm heart, kind, pious like a child, and the author of some good books'.

In Stockholm, another Swedish writer, C.F. Dahlgren, gave a far more evocative description of the Dane in a letter to a friend:

> I always called him the Crane, for I have never seen any human being more akin to the appearance of that bird than him. Imagine a tall person, even taller than myself, with long, thin legs and a long, thin neck, topped by a head like a knob; imagine this figure with a stooping, protruding back and a gait which was never a walk but a hopping along almost like a monkey or like a tripping crane; and finally, imagine his long arms hanging down like a couple of dangling straps at his sides, and an ugly face . . . Big lips, light blue eyes, dark hair and long teeth, like tusks.

Dahlgren, despite this uncharitable picture, was a priest, well known –
or so Andersen claimed – for his humorous writing, and he composed
a song for the crane-like visitor, and gave it to him.

Through an introduction from Ørsted, Andersen was made
welcome in Swedish literary society, and Professor Rudberg took him
up the Mound in Uppsala where 'we drank the health of the North in
champagne from the great silver horn which King Carl Johan had
presented'. In his diary, Andersen also noted that when he 'sang out
the name of the woman I love, the cold northerly wind carried it away'.

This time, it was Ørsted's sixteen-year-old daughter, Sophie, who
had taken his fancy. Andersen had known her since babyhood and had
thought of her simply as one of a family of seven children but Sophie at
this time had announced an interest in Fritz Dahlstrøm, to whom she
became engaged in December of the same year. Here was another girl
who, safely out of reach, could be romantically worshipped.
Andersen's letter to Jette Hanck makes it clear that he had no real
expectations of being take seriously by Sophie, and there is no
evidence that he ever declared his feelings except to others:

> There is a young girl who is beautiful, spirited, kind and charming,
> she belongs to one of the most distinguished families in Copenhagen,
> distinguished in spirit, that is; but I have no fortune and – I shall not
> fall in love.

In order to marry, he went on, he would need an income of two
thousand rixdollars a year. To Christian Wulff, he set the figure at three
thousand. Considering that his travel grant had been six hundred
annually, this was perhaps a little high, but his excuses for lack of
interest in the opposite sex were always at the ready. At thirty-two, he
told Ingemann he was too old to consider marriage, and several times
he had lamented that he was too ugly. In his diary, however, he
remarked, as he did to Jette Hanck, that he would never be engaged,
and added that 'it would be a great misfortune if it ever happened.
God has arranged everything for the best.'

Back in Copenhagen, people had warmed to 'The Little Mermaid'
and were looking at Andersen's fairy tales with new respect. He went to
Odense for a summer visit and there had a meal at the house of Mrs
Laessøe's brother, Joseph Abrahamson, during the course of which so
many toasts were drunk to the success of the author and his books that

Andersen remarked in a letter to Edvard, 'It's just as well I've only written three, or I'd have been under the table!'

Only a Fiddler came out on 22 November 1837. By today's standards, it is barely readable but for the light it throws on Andersen's childhood, being diffuse, sentimental and lacking in any real urgency, but in its own time it was popular for its sociological slant and for the psychological insights into its non-successful hero. Ignaz Castelli, a poet whom Andersen had met in Italy, wrote to him to point out that the book was 'really a compilation of incidents from your own life', and this was nothing new. Of *The Improvisatore*, Andersen himself had said that every single character was known to him in real life, and he made no apology for this. *Only A Fiddler*, with its tale of the lowly village musician who perishes for lack of opportunity and encouragement, contained derisory portraits of the Meislings and of Christian Molbech, and Edvard appears as the nobleman who gives lofty advice to the struggling boy, but its real purpose was to stress that genius must be cherished if it is to blossom.

Despite his increasing success, Andersen still felt himself under-appreciated, as his autobiography makes so abundantly clear. He had began to resent the fact that whereas many well-established authors received what was in effect a state salary in the form of an annual stipend, he did not – but shortly before the Christmas of 1837, he had a stroke of luck. A Holstein nobleman, Count Rantzau-Breitenburg, wrote to him in praise of *The Improvisatore* and Andersen, who never failed to follow up any promising lead, promptly sent him a signed copy of *O.T.*. Rantzau wrote back to ask if he might call. The idea of entertaining a nobleman in his two small rooms in Nyhavn perhaps did not appeal to Andersen, for he went round to Rantzau's house at once. The aristocrat, who was a member of the Danish cabinet, touched delicately on the subject of writers' financial difficulties and thus gave Andersen the opening he had been hoping for. His subsequent letter to Rantzau is a masterpiece of graceful self-presentation, stating his working method to be dependent on the stimulus of travel, but it moves in for the kill with steely determination. Begging Rantzau to present a petition to the king on his behalf, Andersen wrote, 'Do not refuse me. A refusal, however pleasantly worded, would destroy every hope in this direction. I should then be able to do nothing more, and my work would be at an end.'

Rantzau complied with this request at once, presenting a petition to

King Frederik VI in January 1838, and in May, Andersen was awarded an annual stipend of four hundred rixdollars. There is something almost suspiciously neat and fortuitous about Rantzau's intervention, as if he had been set up to implement a decision already taken at high level. In the small social world of the nobility, this would have been a simple matter to arrange. As Andersen's fame began to grow, his constant complaints about the meanness of the royal authorities was beginning to be embarrassing, but it was unthinkable for a direct approach to be made to him. The fund *ad usos publicos* could not be seen as open to moral blackmail.

Andersen himself was untroubled by any concern about the underlying circumstances, regarding his newly won state salary as a personal triumph. As he wrote jubilantly to Ingemann, 'Now I've a little bread-tree in my poet's garden, I won't have to sing at every door any longer for every crumb!' Four hundred rixdollars was not a fortune, but before the money had even been paid, Andersen rushed out to buy new clothes. In a letter to Jette Hanck, he claimed that his friends now considered him 'marvellously foppish, the greatest dandy!' He detailed the velvet-lined overcoat worth sixty rixdollars and the hat 'like an umbrella' with uninhibited glee, but admitted that Jette Wulff had not been impressed. ' "Before, you were wonderfully original, but now you look like a gentleman-in-waiting, a lieutenant, ugh! a refined member of the upper classes." '

Edvard's elder sister, Ingeborg Drewsen, was equally sardonic:

> Our friend is becoming handsome in his old age, but he is still the same silly old fool. Is he supposed to be a célèbre poète? Well, if you knew him as we do . . .

Andersen quoted her words without real resentment in his letter to Jette Hanck. Ingeborg, of all the Collin clan, was the one whose teasing he knew to be truly affectionate at heart.

Despite his new-found source of income, Andersen did not go abroad that summer, but contented himself with another leisured journey round Denmark, staying at the manor-houses of his wealthy friends. Jette Wulff and her brother Christian joined him as fellow-guests at Nysø, the home of Baroness Stampe.

In the autumn, Andersen found himself the subject of an extraordinary attack by a then unknown young student of theology called Søren Kierkegaard, whose first book was published on 8 September 1838. It consisted of a sustained attack on *Only A Fiddler,* and was called *From the Papers of a Person Still Alive, Published Against his Will,* with the sub-title, *On Andersen as a Novelist.* Kierkegaard had evidently been outraged by Andersen's contention in *Only A Fiddler* that creative ability must be nurtured and encouraged or else it will fail. Kierkegaard's masochistic pleasure in opposition was already underpinning his whole thinking, and he found it contemptible that an author should seek easy approval. He himself remarked in his journals that 'the worst pain is to find oneself the object of sympathy' and added later that 'my sorrow is my castle', and so any plea for encouragement disgusted him. Andersen, he remarked in the book, was 'not a struggling genius but a sniveller' who succumbed at the touch of a little adversity.

Kierkegaard's book developed its argument in such obscure Hegelian terms that very few people understood what he meant, and it was lightly said in Copenhagen that only two men had ever read the book – Kierkegaard and Andersen. For this reason the attack lacked any real force, and Andersen himself, though predictably upset, was taken up by a far more traumatic event which occurred on the very day when he read the reports of Kierkegaard's book. Jette Wulff's father, Admiral (as he now was) P.F. Wulff, had heard through a third party of a slanderous remark which Andersen was alleged to have made, and without checking the veracity of the rumour, wrote Andersen a furious letter, breaking off any further relationships. The Wulffs were such old and supportive friends that this came as a terrible shock, and Andersen was so distraught that he noted in his pocket almanac that 'Edvard gave me a sedative'. The edict held for three weeks, and then Admiral Wulff learned that he had been mistaken, and wrote a humble letter of apology.

On 17 September 1838, while Andersen was still agonising over the Wulffs, Bertel Thorvaldsen came back from Rome. It was a huge occasion that threw all Copenhagen into excitement, for his return was that of the conquering hero. He came with the twelve huge marble sculptures of the apostles and the figure of Christ, commissioned so long ago for the Church of Our Lady, though he had with a fine disregard for convention made them far too big to fit into the niches for which they were intended. The outside walls of the museum which now houses his life's output is decorated with friezes which show the unloading of this precious cargo and its manhandling through the streets, men and horses straining at the vast burdens, while the sculptor himself steps ashore with godlike magnificence.

The whole event had been stage-managed with great skill by Thorvaldsen himself. He had only been willing to return from his beloved Italy on condition that Copenhagen should build a large museum in a prominent place, dedicated to his works, and when the city fathers had begun to murmur at the prohibitive cost, he had let it be known that Rome was eager to take over the project. The strategy, though baseless, had worked brilliantly, and now the bands played and a flotilla of beflagged and flower-decorated boats set off across Copenhagen harbour to meet his returning ship. Among them was a small boatload of writers, also to be depicted on the museum walls. Heiberg had decided who should be in the company, but he and Oehlenschläger got themselves ferried out to the ship ahead of the others, without declaring this intention, and it was Andersen who, according to his own account, suggested to the assembled literati that they should wait no longer. A rainbow arched across the sky as the great man came ashore, and this was widely regarded as a sign of divine favour.

The whole city was in a fever of Thorvaldsen-worship. He was given the freedom of Copenhagen – the first man to receive such an honour – and the feasting and banqueting went on for days. The sculptor, having no home of his own to return to, took up residence at Nysø, the manor-house of Baroness Stampe which Andersen had visited with Jette and Christian Wulff during the summer, and there Andersen went to see him on the morning after his return. He was greeted 'with a kiss' as he told Jonas Collin in a triumphant letter, and he at once moved in to stay at the manor for several weeks. Baroness Stampe was delighted to see her home become the Bohemian centre which Thorvaldsen managed to create around him wherever he went, and built a studio for the sculptor in the grounds where he could continue to work.

Despite his hero-worship, Andersen began to show signs of growing bored with the great man's foibles, specially when it came to the endless games of Lotto which he had to be allowed to win, and recorded in his autobiography that he would on occasion take himself off into the grounds for a walk among the trees despite shouts for him to return to the game.

Sad news brought Andersen down to earth later that autumn. One of his closest friends in Rome, Fritz Petzholdt, had been murdered during a trip to Greece. This tragedy struck very close to the Collin family, for Petzholdt's sister, Augusta, was married to Gottlieb Collin, Edvard's elder brother. Andersen, while mourning his friend as 'a natural talent, a great landscape painter' could not refrain from adding in some astonishment that Fritz had left a fortune of 80,000 rixdollars.

On 4 November, a Norwegian violinist called Ole Bull played in Copenhagen, and Andersen was deeply impressed by the power and passion of his music. He learned, too, that Bull, like himself, came from humble beginnings, and rushed round to his publisher, Reitzel, to procure a copy of *Only A Fiddler,* which he inscribed and pressed into Bull's hands. Whether the irony of the title amused the violinist is not known, but it was to be the first of several encounters, not all of them so cordial.

Andersen moved out of his Nyhavn rooms on 4 December, and took up residence at the Hotel du Nord, on the corner of Vingaardsstraede, declaring himself well pleased with this new comfort. In unusually good humour that winter, he risked a cheeky test of his own popularity. Early in 1839, he wrote an anonymous criticism of himself and read this, straight-faced, to his friends. The 'good-natured, childlike, vain Andersen', it said, had no true originality, and his novels were 'nothing more than a poetic embellishment of experienced facts'. He revealed the trick in a letter to the ever-trustworthy Jette Wulff, but everyone else took it to be a genuine piece culled from some literary periodical, and they discussed it seriously. Ørsted thought the criticisms were unnecessarily harsh, though the piece as a whole was lucid and perceptive, but the Collin family confirmed all Andersen's worst suspicions by agreeing with every word of it. When told of the deception they were astonished that their emotional friend had proved himself capable of such a dispassionate look at his own personality, and Andersen's ruse perhaps did more to improve his standing in their eyes than any amount of published work. Ørsted was immensely tickled by the whole thing, and said Andersen was a true humorist.

That summer, Andersen went again to Sweden, and this time met on the boat a much less welcome fellow-traveller than Frederika Bremer. His old enemy, Christian Molbech, appeared beside him on the deck and asked conventionally whether he, too, was going to Sweden, but when Andersen volunteered that he would be staying with Baron Wrangel, Molbech snapped, 'I don't want to know who you're going to visit.' The conversation seems to have got no further.

Among the Swedish nobility, Andersen met a Count Barck and his two pretty daughters, Mathilda and Louise, and threw out hints once more that he might be in love, though in a letter to Jette Wulff he made the usual disclaimers. 'Alas! My old heart – if only I had enough money I would fall in love in my old age.' He was still only thirty-four.

On return, he wrote up his two Swedish journeys into *Picture Book Without Pictures*, a mingling of travel experiences with myth and story, and in this he conflated the figures of Sophie Ørsted and Mathilda Barck into a single romantic entity whose name is breathed after the draining of a silver mead-horn, heard only by the moon. The book was in print by December of the same year.

It was a time of tremendous productivity for Andersen, with a vaudeville which ran for several days in June and a further instalment of stories published in August which included 'The Flying Trunk' and 'The Storks'. Through the autumn he worked on a play, *The Mulatto*, and despite the usual objections from Molbech, it was accepted by the theatre directors and scheduled to open on 3 December 1839. On this very day, however, King Frederik VI died, and the theatre was closing for a period of mourning.

The death of the old monarch marked a change in Andersen's relationship with the Court. He had known the Crown Prince, now to be crowned as Christian VIII, since childhood, and was on easy terms with him. Just a few days before Frederik VI died, Andersen had been at the palace, reading his new play to the man who could, unknown to him, have been his father, and he now dedicated the play, *The Mulatto*, to Christian VIII. His diary entries from this time onwards make it clear that his access to Denmark's new ruler was easy and informal. Though filled with the respect which even members of the royal family felt for the ruling monarch, Andersen was not afraid of this new king as he had been of the old one.

The Mulatto was staged two months later, and met with a startling success. In a few weeks, it had netted its author more than eight hundred rixdollars – double his annual stipend – as well as providing a further income from its publication in book form. But there was just one snag. Andersen had neglected to mention that the plot of his play had been derived from a French short story, 'Les Epaves', by Fanny Reybaud. When this came to light, there were angry mutterings about plagiarism, and Heiberg, as artistic director of the theatre, felt that he had been duped into accepting the play on false pretences. His attitude to Andersen developed a frostiness from which it never quite recovered, and the whole thing turned into something of a literary scandal. Andersen himself, choosing not to notice what a brick he had dropped, simply went back to Sweden, where his reputation was unblemished. *Picture Book Without Pictures* had been a huge success in its Swedish translation, and the triumphal tour he took that summer culminated in a banquet given in his honour by the students of the University of Lund, the first time that a Danish writer had been so feted.

Such cossetting in Sweden did not endear Andersen to his fellow Danes, particularly following the scandal about *The Mulatto,* and he came back to Copenhagen to find himself the butt of some satirical comment. Heiberg remarked sarcastically that he'd better take Andersen with him next time he went to Sweden so that he, too, would come in for plaudits – and Andersen made completely the wrong response. Instead of assuring Heiberg that he was far more famous in his own right than Andersen – which was the truth – he blundered into saying that if Heiberg wanted homage in Sweden, he'd better take his wife with him.

The beautiful Johanne Heiberg was indeed Denmark's leading actress, but Andersen's remark was unbelievably clumsy, and he paid for it. Having rushed to write another play, *The Moorish Girl,* this time entirely of his own invention, he asked Mrs Heiberg to play the lead part – and she flatly refused. Her judgement that the role lacked real dramatic content was justified but it threw Andersen into a fury of resentment. All else apart, the play would be paid for at a lower rate if it could not boast a star-quality actress in the leading role, and Andersen had counted on good earnings to fund a further long trip abroad. At that time, as he explains in *My Life's Fairytale,* productions were paid for on a simple piece-rate basis, by the quarter-hour:

> At the first performance, the stage-manager stood with a watch in his hand and wrote down how many quarters of an hour it took; these were added together, and the fee was paid according to the total.

Andersen, as always when upset, complained loudly to all his friends about the way he had been treated, thus blowing the affair into a publicly aired grievance which rebounded on him very badly. Heiberg was a powerful and much-respected man, and nobody was prepared to side with a notoriously self-seeking young writer who seemed to be suffering from a bad case of swelled head. In a culminating folly, Andersen wrote a resentful and self-pitying preface to the play which caused malicious glee when it became known in theatrical circles. His alarmed friends urged him to go abroad, regardless of whether he had as much money as he had wanted, and Andersen, though still truculent and regarding himself as the injured party, agreed. A farewell dinner was held for him on 30 October by a group which included Ørsted, Jonas Collin and Heiberg's main literary opponent, Adam Oehlenschläger, and the next day, Andersen boarded the steamer for Kiel, seen off by the Collin family.

'Edvard C. was the last person of whom I took leave,' he wrote in his diary on Saturday 31 October 1840; 'he pressed a kiss onto my mouth! Oh, it was as if my heart would burst!' He would not be back in Denmark for nearly nine months.

Andersen's journey of 1840 was to be an ambitious one. This time, he had set his sights beyond Rome or Naples, determined to follow in Byron's footsteps to Greece and, if possible, Turkey. Lamartine's *Journey To the Orient* had fired his professional envy – and besides, he was more than usually exasperated with his own country, and was bent on escape. Despite Mrs Heiberg's refusal to take part in *The Moorish Girl*, he calculated that when it was eventually staged it would earn him something between eight hundred and a thousand rixdollars, and this, added to his savings, would enable him to stay abroad for the best part of a year.

He had become a careful and meticulous traveller. 'Reason, not poetry, is the essential thing on a journey,' he had written from Italy in 1833. 'I have really had to have my wits about me, and thank goodness I have not forgotten the least little thing the whole of the way.' Visits, too, were planned as an integral part of the itinerary, and his first port of call was the Holstein castle of Count Rantzau-Breitenburg, whose influence had procured Andersen's annual stipend. From there, he went on to Hamburg and met up with the German author Karl Gutzkow, who was involved in the radical Young Germany movement, one of the many rebellious groups now springing up all over Europe. He described Gutzkow as 'warm and friendly' despite having been warned that he was a cold, distant character, but changed his opinion later. Although he was staying in an hotel in Hamburg, his social life was busy, and he went from the extremes of a 'boring' visit to a much-enjoyed one in the company of the Danish ambassador to Count Holck's, where they were served oysters and champagne.

That same evening, Friday, 6 November, he was given a ticket to hear the Austro-Hungarian Franz Liszt play. This was his first sight of the famous pianist and composer, and he refused to be impressed. Andersen was always ready to admire older men of established reputation, but Liszt was six years younger than himself, and the gala atmosphere clearly brought out a touch of jealousy in the writer:

With the ladies, I went in through a back door of the Stadt London to a magnificent hall which had been full of people for an hour. A Jewish girl, fat and bedizened, lay on a sofa – she looked like a walrus with a fan. The merchants from Hamburg seemed to hear the clink of gold pieces in the music, and that's why there was a smile about their lips as they sat there. I was seeing Liszt face to face! Great men are very like mountains! They look best from a distance – that's when they retain some charisma. He looked as if he'd been in the Orthopaedic Institute to be straightened out. There was something so spiderlike, so demonic about him! As he sat at the piano, his face pale and full of violent passion, he seemed to me like a devil trying to play his soul free! Every note poured from his heart and soul – he looked to me to be on the rack.

Andersen was dismissive of the wreaths which were thrown on to the stage at the end of the concert. 'The bathing attendant at the hotel had bought most of them and arranged for people to toss them up . . . ' With no apparent awareness that his stricture might apply to himself, he added, 'We Copenhageners are good at seeing things in their worst light.' On the way home, he posted a letter to Gottlieb Collin, Edvard's elder brother, containing a song written for their sister, Louise, for her forthcoming wedding.

The following day, he crossed the Elbe on a steamship and set out across the dreaded Luneburg Heath in a dilapidated coach, the journey made worse by the fact that he 'had to ride backwards', which he always disliked. Anxieties were beginning to set in. He worried that he would not have enough money to complete the trip and, as so often when under stress, began to suffer from toothache, and complained of a nodule on his gum, afraid that it would develop into an infection. In fact, the road had been improved a lot since his previous visit, and in Magdeburg, he was immensely cheered by the novel experience of riding in a railway train. The line to Leipzig – the first in Europe – had only recently been opened, and when Andersen caught a glimpse of the steam engine on the day before his journey in the train, he described it as looking 'like a rocket whizzing along the ground'. The ride itself enchanted him:

There is something quite magical about it. I felt like a magician who has hitched a dragon to his coach and now sweeps past mere mortals who, as I looked at the road alongside, were crawling along in their vehicles like snails. When the steam is let out, it sounds like a demon groaning. The signal whistle is frightful – it sounds like a stuck pig.

His fellow-passengers in any mode of transport were always a problem to Andersen, and his diary entries make it evident that he had not lost his childhood fear of the common mass of humanity which might so easily prove itself dangerous and cruel. He has been much criticised for the sycophancy which led him to seek the houses of the great, but it is also true that he felt safe among people whose courtesy, at least to his face, was absolutely assured. In the train to Leipzig, he found himself alone in the compartment with one other man, and started to worry that he 'might be crazy and have a fit. I got all worked up about it.' When four more passengers got in, things were not much improved, for 'one of them was very talkative and had a voice like a woman with a frog in her throat'. While theoretically in favour of democracy, Andersen could never quite bring himself to trust the common people.

He spent a busy time in Leipzig, and among other engagements, called on Felix Mendelssohn-Bartholdy. The composer was friendly with Ingeborg Drewsen, Edvard's elder sister, but Andersen had no letter of introduction, and simply walked into the concert hall where Mendelssohn was rehearsing an orchestra in Beethoven's Seventh Symphony. It was not the smoothest of meetings, but when Mendelssohn realised who the intruder was, his annoyance evaporated, and the two men took a liking to each other. That first meeting was a brief one, for Andersen had to join the coach to go on to Munich.

Pausing in Augsburg, he was greatly impressed by seeing a daguerreotype for the first time. Louis Daguerre had invented this early photographic process in 1826, but was still working on ways to improve it, and Andersen was fascinated by the fine detail which could be obtained by the action of iodine vapour on a silver-coated copper plate. He had heard from Ørsted about the technique, and had written to Jette Hanck in enthusiasm for the idea of a faithful reproduction through the use of light itself, but now that he saw proof of it for himself, he was astonished. The hair was beautiful, he remarked in his diary, and 'the eyes quite distinct, including the bright point of light in the pupils.'

In Munich he had a bizarre encounter with a bookseller who insisted that a German translation of *The Improvisatore, Part 1,* was the entire book. 'Didn't it seem to end rather abruptly?' Andersen asked him. The man agreed that it did, but said it was like the new French novels which ended 'in a sophisticated way'. Continuing to insist that it was the whole book, he added, 'I tell you, I've read it.' 'But I wrote it,' said Andersen.

He spent most of his time in Munich with Hans Peter Holst, a Danish poet six years younger than himself but enjoying great popularity in his own country. He was, as Andersen put it a little bitterly, 'the lucky poet of the moment', having received a handsome travel grant. The hated Molbech had once held Holst up as the example Andersen should aim at, and an element of professional rivalry made it difficult for the two men to get on well. This was unfortunate, for the plan had been for Holst to link up with Andersen in Munich and accompany him on the rest of the journey to the eventual destination of Constantinople (now Istanbul). Andersen, with his dread of loneliness, had been looking forward to this companionship, but in *Mit livs eventyr* he is frank about his failure to fit in with the Munich expat community. The café which they frequented was, he said, a Bavarian copy of life in Rome:

> but it was beer and not wine which sparkled there; nor did I feel at home in all this merriment, and not one among my countrymen really appealed to me; and as far as my qualities as a poet were concerned, they judge by Copenhagen standards. . . . They were more friendly towards Holst, and so I went about mostly on my own, sometimes full of gaiety but more often doubting my own abilities. I had a perverse talent for dwelling on the gloomier aspects of life, re-experiencing bitter memories; I was an expert at torturing myself.

Such admissions are easy to make in retrospect, but in 1840, waiting in Munich for Holst to decide whether or not he was going to come to Turkey, Andersen's depression was profound. He wrote to Jonas Collin in a mood of homesickness which only made his self-banishment more bitter, blaming his unhappiness on the failure of Copenhagen society to understand and appreciate him. Driven to a bleak introspection, he confessed, too, that there was 'much that may lie hidden in one's soul, impossible to express even to oneself'.

As the days shortened towards winter, Andersen's patience began to wear thin. Holst was sitting for his portrait and claimed that the painter still needed him in Munich, and he would give no promise of when, or even if, he would consider setting out for Turkey. At last Andersen could wait no longer, and on 2 December he left Munich on his own and embarked in low spirits on the journey through the Brenner to Italy. On the long, cold coach journeys that took him through Verona and Bologna to Florence and then southward again, there was no recapture of his previous joy in Italy, and he described the muddy winter landscape as 'a pig-sty'. His fellow-passengers continued to irk him, and he was unlucky enough to encounter a truly terrible specimen of the Englishman abroad. He described him in a letter to Jette Hanck:

> He always took the best seat in the carriage, was constantly awkward and inconvenient, took the food from our plates if he spotted a tasty morsel we'd been given, plundered the kitchen in every inn so there was always a row, and demanded a subservience which out of foolish kind-heartedness I gave him for the first two days, though after that I sent him about his business.

Andersen arrived in Rome on 19 December, but it was not the city he had known before. Thorvaldsen had gone back to Denmark, and although his atelier was still there, now run by one of his students, the charismatic presence was lost and Andersen's friends were dispersed. Petzholdt was dead, the genial Hertz had moved on, and Küchler, though still in Rome, had joined the Franciscan order as a monk. The weather was bitterly cold, and Andersen wandered the streets, lonely and disappointed by the let-down from Holst. He spent a wretched Christmas in a two-roomed apartment in the Via Purificazione, still hoping that Holst would come and join him. Frost gave way to rain, and Rome ran with flood water. Writing about it afterwards in *Mit livs eventyr*, Andersen remembered every grim detail:

> The earth trembled, and the Tiber ran through the streets; people sailed about in boats, and the fever took a heavy toll. Within the space of a few days the Prince of Borghese lost his wife and three sons; there was sleet and a cold wind, and it was not at all pleasant. In the

evenings I usually sat in my large drawing-room with its draughty windows and doors; the thin bits of wood in the hearth flamed up, and the heat from them burned me on one side, while the other was chilled by the cold air; I sat wrapped in my cape and with my boots on indoors, and to make things worse, for weeks on end I had a most violent toothache . . .

Dentistry was an undeveloped art in the mid-nineteenth century. Before the advent of electricity, the dental drill was a slow and crude affair, and although fillings were undertaken, using whatever paste or filling material the operator favoured, the public still tended to regard extraction as the only cure for dental pain. Andersen, marooned in a foreign country, seems to have made no effort to seek any help for his torment, regarding it more as a kind of recurrent migraine than the result of decay. To some extent, he may have been right, for his attacks of toothache were closely related to periods of particular strain or unhappiness.

During the cold Roman winter of early 1841, Edvard's harsh response to *Agnete* was again in Andersen's mind, and he wrote a sombre poem in a limping three-line form, the middle verse of which ran:

> The friend I left when I came to Rome
> Sent me the poison he gathered at home
> And bade me drink it to make me strong.

It ended with a reiteration of his constant theme:

> The critics derided what came from my soul
> And laughed at my verses; they said that I stole
> From Heinrich Heine the words of my song.

His diary for 16 January spoke of deep misery:

How lonely I am! At home by 5.30 every evening. I am tired of reading and constantly glancing at the clock to see if it isn't past nine yet, so that I can go to bed and sleep my way to another day! I'm not afraid of being attacked any more. Sometimes I even think it might be a good thing if I was killed. I can see it plainly enough. I have nothing left to live for.

A main cause of his extreme despondency was the letter he had received from Jonas Collin on 8 January, breaking the news that *The Moorish Girl*, which had opened at the Royal Theatre on 18 December, had been taken off after only three poorly attended performances. At the very best, all Andersen could hope for was three hundred rixdollars, and probably not even that. The continuation of his journey looked impossible, and he was now stranded in Rome, virtually penniless. A final drop of bitterness was added by Edvard, who wrote one of his most dispassionate letters, advising Andersen not to worry about the failure of *The Moorish Girl*. Nobody in Copenhagen would notice, he said, because they were all talking about Heiberg's new book of satirical poems. This news, far from comforting Andersen, merely convinced him that his play had been dropped as an act of malice on Heiberg's part, and his suspicions seemed confirmed when Mrs Laessøe wrote with further details. Heiberg's *New Poems*, which in fact were verse sketches, contained one, 'A Soul After Death', which was an elaborate joke at Andersen's expense.

The arrival of Mrs Laessøe's letter on 22 January threw Andersen into a near-suicidal mixture of grief and fury. He railed in his diary about the so-called friends who sent him 'these drops of poison' and doubted whether even God could be relied on. Had he known the actual content of Heiberg's skit, he might have been less upset, for it merely depicted a hell in which Copenhagen's citizens were subjected to endless performances of *The Mulatto* and *The Moorish Girl* – the sort of light quip which is meant to amuse rather than wound. Heiberg, knowing that Andersen was heading for Constantinople, added a fantasy in which the bemused members of a sultan's harem are subjected to a reading of *The Mulatto* by the Grand Eunuch. Whether this was a deliberate sexual innuendo is impossible to tell, but there is no doubt that he was getting his own back for Andersen's general conceitedness.

Holst had still not sent any word of intention to come to Rome, and Andersen wandered through the streets in misery. He had sent an urgent appeal to the Danish king, asking for help from the public fund, but was meanwhile marooned and unable to make any plans. His mind continued to run on Edvard's coldness, as his diary entry for 3 February shows. 'I went into a church in the Corso where a baby was christened Eduardo. My Eduardo might think of me if I received my christening; three spadefuls of earth on my coffin.' Despite these outbursts, he went on being interested in his surroundings, and the bulk of his diary notes constitutes a sharp commentary on the life that surrounded him. He was particularly diverted by the annual blessing of the donkeys at S. Antonio's church:

> An old woman was leading a tiny donkey with a ribbon on its tail and a tinsel pig fastened to each shoulder; she took it right up to the door and curtseyed low and made the sign of the cross as she and the donkey received the holy water. Some boys teased the little donkey as she was leaving, so the soldiers had to help her.

Holst arrived from Munich just in time to prevent Andersen from sending an explosive rhymed riposte to Heiberg. Although the writing of this had made its author feel 'more lively and satisfied all day', it would have been socially disastrous. The common sense and company provided by Holst and his friend Conrad Rothe came as a relief, but physically Andersen was in a bad way. His toothache had persisted for several weeks, giving rise to a fever which he could not shake off, and when he and his fellow-Danes arrived in Naples on 28 February after a three-day journey, a doctor was called and he was bled. Curiously enough, this medieval treatment worked very well, and he soon declared himself feeling much better.

Holst, for all his practicality, was not the most sympathetic of travelling companions. A letter to a friend revealed scant patience with Andersen's activities abroad:

> Heaven only knows what he will do in Greece and Constantinople, for he spends his time in the most ridiculous way. He sees nothing, he enjoys nothing, he delights in nothing – he does nothing but write. When I see him in museums, his pencil going all the time to write down the keeper's information about statues and paintings rather than looking at them and enjoying their beauty, he reminds me of the executor of a will going through the property of the deceased and itemising every one with meticulous care, constantly afraid he may have forgotten something.

In *Mit livs eventyr*, Andersen described travel as 'a refreshing bath for the spirit', and yet there was some truth in Holst's comment. Andersen himself confessed that when abroad, he felt he had to be 'on the go from morning to evening'. He refuted Holst's accusation of unperceptiveness however, insisting that his main purpose was to 'see and see again. Something is seething and fermenting inside me, and once I am back in the good old town of Copenhagen and given physical and mental cold poultices, then the blossoms will spring forth.' For him, travel was not undertaken purely for pleasure. As he had written to Mrs Laessøe from Odense nine years previously, 'I can never enjoy the present, my life is in the past and in the future, and immediate reality contains too little for the real man.' Experience was not enough; he had to feel, evidently, that he was making something of it.

In early March, Andersen heard from King Christian VIII that he had been granted six hundred rixdollars to enable him to complete his journey. It was not as much as he had hoped for, but at least it broke the deadlock. After a few more days in Naples, Holst decided against accompanying him, so Andersen said goodbye to his companions and set off alone on 15 March, taking the steamer *Leonidas* to Malta. His aim was Greece, however, and the next ship took him to Syros, together with some colourful passengers. Andersen was struck by a Persian who 'played with his great sabre, stroked his pistols or twisted the silver rings in his dark brown ears.'

In *A Poet's Bazaar*, the book Andersen wrote as a record of his journey, he touches on the loneliness which assailed him so often when travelling. It was not a sense of unfamiliarity, for, as he puts it, 'He who has a proper home can feel homesick; he who has no home feels himself equally at home everywhere.' His diary for Sunday 21 March has in its very brevity of expression a strong sense of his constant need for companionship:

> Wandered around in the town alone; small, narrow streets; sails stretched out over them; the houses only one or, at most, two storeys high. Went up to the church; small, with frescoes. In the café – the only privy, a rock by the shore. Went to a barber and sat there with the other Greeks on the bench along the wall and was shaved. Found my fellow travellers in the Hotel de la Grèce, where pepper plants were growing in boxes on the wooden balcony.

The relaxed run of those last words after the tight note-form of most of the entry speaks poignantly of relief.

On Syros, Andersen learned that the ship which normally went to Piraeus had broken down; he could wait a week for the Austrian steamer or else join the French warship *Lycurgus* that day – the only snag being that she had come from plague-stricken Alexandria and was under quarantine. He opted for the plague-ship, lying in the bay under its green flag, and sitting on the plinth of a cannon as they sailed that evening, recognised again the Persian, who 'touched his turban with chestnut brown fingers'. They offered each other fruit. 'I thought I must say something' Andersen wrote in *A Poet's Bazaar*, 'if only a flow of words of a language that was related to his.' He pointed to the stars and recited in schoolboy Hebrew the first words of the Book of Genesis. The Persian smiled and made a similar effort. In English, he said, 'Yes, Sir, verily, verily!' That was the limit of their conversation but, Andersen remarked, 'What good friends we were!'

The ship lay at anchor in Piraeus, waiting for the period of quarantine to elapse, but after two days, the passengers were rowed ashore and Andersen shared a carriage with four Americans and a Russian to Athens. The road was, he said, 'very dusty – but at least it was classical dust.'

He found a well-established Danish expat community in Athens and at last began to enjoy himself. In the large and splendid café used by the Scandinavians as their meeting-place there were French and German newspapers, and Italian opera was being performed at the theatre; this, for Andersen, was cosmopolitan travel at its best.

Despite this, he was acutely aware of the devastation which had befallen Greece during the centuries of Turkish occupation. It was only eleven years since the Treaty of Adrianople had declared Greek independence, following a rebellion which had started in 1821, and the public imagination in Europe was still fired by Byron's expedition and his death in 1827. It was only then that Britain, France and Russia had combined naval forces to destroy the Turkish fleet, and in 1841, Andersen found Athens to be the remains of a battlefield. He walked up to the Acropolis and was dismayed, for it was 'wretched to a degree I have never seen before'. The Parthenon had been 'the target for cannon balls and bombs', and human bones lay among the weeds that grew between the ruins of both classical antiquity and the mud huts in which people had lived. The Temple of Erechtheus with its caryatids stood in a pit of rubbish, and the skeleton of a donkey lay in front of the excavated marble steps. 'A tumble-down brick column filled the place of one caryatid which Elgin had stolen for the British Museum,' Andersen noted. Greeks were working patiently among the ruins on the colossal task of reconstruction which lay before them, a scene depicted in a painting by Martinus Rørbye, an old acquaintance, who later produced a notable portrait of Andersen.

During the month he spent in Athens, Andersen became very well aware of the turbulent political history which had brought the country to such devastation. Listening to folk musicians who sang a Greek lament, he was deeply moved. 'The tone was both gentle and elegiac, as if fear constrained their voices; but sometimes the hurt and pain swelled up into a wild cry, as if the whole people wept.' He was horrified by the Turkish desecration of the Orthodox churches, recording the bullet-riddled mosaics of Christ and the icons defaced with obscene graffiti and noting the skulls and bones which lay under the nettles growing beside the ruined high altar.

For all the glories of Easter in Rome, Andersen observed perceptively that 'in Greece it is a festival which flows from the hearts and minds of the people'. The intensity of the ceremony which followed a long fast touched his theatrical soul deeply. A coffin filled with fresh roses to symbolise the dead Christ was carried in slow procession through the streets in the late evening, where at every balcony and in every window people stood holding lighted candles and the church bells rang a single repeated note. Then at midnight came the great cry of 'Christ is Risen!' Cannon were fired, rockets flared, bonfires were lit and the smell of roasting lamb filled the streets as people danced and kissed and repeated the affirmation, as they do to this very day. Carried away with the emotion of it all, Andersen wrote one of his most passionate stories, 'The Pact of Friendship', and included it in *A Poet's Bazaar.*

The pact which forms the subject of the tale is between the shepherd-boy narrator and his beloved friend, Aphtanides, who go through the ceremony of swearing brotherhood. The occasion is described in reverent detail:

> I wore my best clothes. My red blouse fitted me tightly round my waist. Silver was woven into the tassel of my fez. In my belt were stuck not only a knife but a pistol as well. Aphtanides wore the blue uniform of

a Greek sailor; on a silver chain round his neck he wore a medallion of the Holy Virgin. His scarf was as costly as only the richest men wear. Everyone could see that we were dressed for a special occasion. We walked into the little church. The evening sun shone through the door, and the many-coloured pictures and the silver lamp reflected its light.

We kneeled down in front of the altar.

Anastasia, the boy's adopted sister, assists at the ceremony – but when Aphtanides goes back to the sea the next day, he tells his sworn brother that he is in love with Anastasia. The shepherd-boy then reveals that he, too, loves her.

Once again, Andersen is writing of a triangle in which love between two young men is disrupted by the arrival of a woman. In this case, the shepherd-boy's winning of Anastasia is depicted with no joy – quite the reverse, for as she kisses him, the lamp falls from her hand and the room is plunged into a darkness as sombre as 'the heart of my poor brother Aphtanides'. The story then ends with the bald and joyless statement, 'A few days later Anastasia became my wife.'

Greece, with its classical tradition of homoeroticism, fitted easily into Andersen's dreams of the lost Edvard, but the theme of the fatal kiss and its results had appeared in a story Andersen published in 1840. 'The Garden of Eden' is a Biblical re-telling mingled with a fairy-tale in which the prince disobeys orders and kisses the princess. At once, the idyll is destroyed in a storm of wind and rain, causing the prince to realise that he has 'sinned as Adam did', betraying a God-given state of chastity for the evil trap of the female. The author's distaste ran very deep.

As a leading member of the Danish community, if for no other reason, Andersen was introduced to King Otto of Greece, a Bavarian son of a previous king chosen for office after the first Greek president, Capo D'Istrias, had been assassinated in 1831. He was amused to learn that on their majesties' arrival, the queen had been presented with a bouquet of potato flowers, that plant being a newly arrived wonder in the land.

On 20 April, Andersen left Athens, embarking at Piraeus on the French steamer *Eurotas*, bound for Smyrna. 'I was now alone,' he noted bleakly, bereft of his Scandinavian friends. It was an appalling crossing:

The sea rose higher and higher; it was as if the storm came out of the hills on Tenos. The open sea lay before us – foam black and white! Waves were already breaking over the ship. The wretched deck passengers huddled up by the funnel . . . Greek women clung to each other and howled. On the deck children lay as if half dead, and the sea smashed over the ship so that everyone was soaked.

Andersen retreated to his cabin and prayed, and confessed later in a letter to Jette Wulff that he had fully expected to drown.

In Smyrna, the ills of solitude began to assail him again. He worried that his money might run out, complained of a sore throat and also of a recurrent pain in his penis, terrified that he might have caught a disease from the ship's toilet. 'Heaven knows, it isn't my fault,' he added. From there, he went on to Constantinople, and took a room in Pera, the European section of the city. Here, he was befriended by Adheras, 'a young, blond, Russian fellow' and again contacted the resident Danish community.

Sexual arousal started to play a big part in his diary entries, particularly after his meetings with the Russian, and on 1 May, he wrote, 'Sensuality is a thrilling tingling through the nerves as you release a drop of your vitality'. On the next day, he added, 'An Asiatic sensuality is torturing me here. Oh, how I'm burning with longing!'

Turkey was exotic and alarming. In Scutari Andersen had seen a dance of dervishes, some of them mutilated, in a galleried hall 'heavily grated to keep women out', and found the performance so violent and outlandish that he was glad to get back to the company of Europeans. In Pera, though, he saw whirling dervishes whose dance seemed to him more like a kind of ballet, portraying the circling of the planets. His sketch of these figures with their tall hats, outstretched arms and full-skirted coats is rough but oddly evocative.

As Andersen's funds dwindled, it was time to think of the return journey. He had planned to go back by way of the Black Sea and the Danube, only recently navigable since the introduction of steam-powered ships, but now heard that the Bulgarians and Romanians were in revolt and that several thousand Christians had been murdered. His fellow-travellers at the hotel went for the safer option of returning through Greece and Italy, but Andersen was reluctant to abandon the itinerary he had set for himself. He seemed a little surprised by his own obstinate courage. As he wrote in *Mit livs eventyr*:

> I am not one of the brave, people have often told me, and I believe
> them; but I really think it's only small dangers that frighten me: big
> ones, on the other hand, specially when there's something tangible to
> be gained, bring out all my determination, which has become
> stronger year by year; I tremble and feel terrified, but I do what I
> think is right.

Baron von Stürmer, the Austrian minister in Constantinople, in
whose house Andersen was now staying, reassured him. A Russian
courier had arrived safely the previous evening, having come by the
Danube route – and in any case, two Austrian officers whom Andersen
had met, Colonel Philippovitch and Major Trattner, would be
travelling on the same journey as Andersen and expected official
protection.

The decision made, Andersen spent his last evening in Turkey with
the Russian Adheras, looking at the 'fairy-tale' city, which was
illuminated to celebrate the birthday of the Prophet:

> We took some paper lanterns and went for a walk in the moonlight...
> in the quiet evening we walked beneath the cypresses. At 9 o'clock
> cannon shots from all the ships and from the coast, so that the
> windows rattled. Shot after shot.

A letter of rare admiration came from Edvard. 'You are a devil of a
chap for travelling,' he wrote; 'the way you have managed on this trip is
something which few could aspire to, and if you are not brave at least
you have a strong will, and that is just as good.' With cheerful self-
mockery, he added, 'This testimonial is given by the undersigned,
who is not in the habit of flattering you.'

As a family, the Collins found Andersen's footloose habits
incomprehensible. Ingeborg, whose tenacity had brought her through
seven weeks of smallpox a few years previously, had been crisply
impatient with his despairing letters from Rome during the winter.
'Heaven knows why you don't stay at home to see the many lovely
things we have here!' she had remarked. 'What is the pleasure in being
cold in Rome? It would be better to be cold in Copenhagen.' His

complaints about the money situation had received short shrift from Jonas during the same period. 'Your trip to Greece will probably come to nothing, and I do not regret this, for goodness knows what you want to go there for.' After such disparagement, Edvard's letter must have been doubly welcome.

With his usual anxiety that his passport hadn't been stamped properly, Andersen boarded the steamship *Ferdinando*, which sailed on the high tide at 4.30 am. He woke as he felt the lift and swell of the open sea, and went up on deck to find everything shrouded in thick fog. The captain dropped anchor several times, fearful of the treacherous sandbanks where several steamers had gone aground, but by ten o'clock the next morning they were in Constanta, and the passengers went ashore for a stroll. It was, Andersen thought, a bleak place, barely yet recovered from having been destroyed by the Russians in 1809. His depression was compounded by finding a dead stork at the water's edge. The stork is a powerful Danish symbol of good luck, eagerly watched for each year as it returns to build its untidy nest above the roofs of the favoured, and to find this sodden traveller which would not complete its journey filled Andersen with superstitious gloom.

The lifting of the fog and a good dinner on board in the company of the Austrian officers cheered him up, and the three were joined by an Englishman, William Ainsworth. To Andersen's delight, he turned out to be a cousin of the novelist, W. Harrison Ainsworth, currently editor of *Bentley's Miscellany*, and a good friend of Charles Dickens.

Routine quarantine was enforced at the Hungarian border, and so the passengers were taken for ten days into a quarantine camp at Orsova. Sharing two small rooms with Ainsworth, Andersen endured his first days of imprisonment without much complaint, but the heat, airlessness and tedium soon became hard to bear. In a footnote to *A Poet's Bazaar*, he allowed himself a quip at Heiberg's expense, mentioning a dream of hell in which the condemned rose in protest at a proposal to stage Heiberg's new drama, *Fata Morgana*. Characteristically, he disclaimed responsibility for the thought – after all, it was only a dream.

Once released, Andersen went on up the Danube, and in Vienna, looked hopefully for letters. Despite his punctilious instructions about poste-restante addresses, there was only one, from the faithful Jette Wulff. He was plunged into instant despondency, and on 4 June noted, 'All the unpleasantness of home came back to me; I could sense the

German-Danish atmosphere – I wish I had died in the Orient.' He had said the same thing on returning from Naples, and for the same reason; his home town filled him with dread that the public, the critics and, most of all, the Collin family, would give him no welcome.

He lingered in Vienna for three weeks, going to the opera and looking up old acquaintances, then began the last stage homeward. Letters from the Collins awaited him in Dresden, delighting him so much that all complaint was forgotten and the evening 'turned out to be the happiest of my trip'. From Leipzig he wrote to Ingeborg Drewsen's husband, Adolph, boasting a little about the number of calling-cards he had received 'from all the noted artists'. Here, he was dined and feted, shared a box at the opera with Goethe's daughter-in-law and again visited Mendelssohn before going on through Hamburg and Kiel to his native Funen. To his irritation, the Danish authorities subjected him to five inspections of his baggage as he made his way to Copenhagen, and when a woman asked him if he had ever seen anything lovelier than the Danish landscape on his travels he said flatly that he had, on many occasions. She retorted that he was not a patriot.

In Odense, St Canute's Fair was on, and an ex-neighbour remarked that it was very sensible of him to arrange his travels so that he could attend it. 'I always said you liked Odense,' she said. Andersen was left speechless – but he was touched to see an old couple, Pastor Bastholm and his wife, walking through the cornfield. He had known them in the dark days of school at Slagelse, but now he saw them with a traveller's clarity, imbued with a quality he could not name. It was, he said, 'strange'.

The diary Andersen had kept throughout his eastern travels ended on 17 July 1841, the day he arrived at the manor of Glorup. Having no home of his own other than a couple of rented rooms which he did not keep on during his long journeys, he was apt to alight wherever he was assured of hospitality and a welcome, and Glorup, the country estate of Count Moltke-Hvitfeldt, whose family had long been closely involved with the royal court, was a favourite place. A lithograph of the time shows the gracious house standing behind a sweep of lawn that slopes down to an ornamental lake with an island in the middle. A pair of swans glide and a formal fountain plays, and the perfection is undisturbed by any human being. For the five days of his stay, Andersen was given 'two cosy rooms' and left to do exactly as he liked. A letter to Edvard outlined the daily routine:

> Every morning I make a dutiful but short visit to the old Count, and half an hour later he comes up to my room to return the visit; the only variation in all this is that sometimes he comes first and I last. Then I see nobody until four o'clock, and throughout that time I sit quietly, read and write or stroll up and down the two old avenues in the garden; my days are as long and steady and uneventful as the days in a monastery.

Back in Copenhagen, he quickly completed *A Poet's Bazaar,* which appeared on 30 April 1842. Even today, it is a highly readable travel book, crammed with small events and enlivened with stories and shrewd reflections. Andersen is constantly immediate, recording how the carriage going across the Brenner was filled with hay to keep the passengers' feet warm, and how in northern Italy the driver went to sleep for some hours, and the horses kept going of their own accord, passing the first three inns. He noted that the towns of Buda and Pest were joined by a bridge of boats across the Danube, a structure which rocked alarmingly as the wagons drove over, and he included a tale

called 'The Bronze Boar', in which a Roman fountain figure comes
alive when kissed by a 'handsome, half-naked boy, his fresh young
mouth against its snout'. The boar saves the lad from the parental
beating he will get for having failed to beg enough money – a clear
harking-back to Andersen's mother's story of her own childhood.

The book was instantly popular abroad, but Danish critics were
lukewarm, largely because Andersen had dedicated each section to a
different notable person, thus producing an overload of ingratiation
which verged on the ludicrous. He included Count Rantzau-
Breitenburg, Oehlenschläger, Baron von Stürmer (with whom he had
stayed in Constantinople), Liszt, the concert pianist Sigismund
Thalberg, Frederika Bremer, Ingeborg Drewsen, the Danish Minister
in Athens and a Greek professor of archaeology.

His most fulsome dedication, however, was reserved for Johanne
Luise Heiberg, who had the Christmas volume of new fairy tales all to
herself. 'Fairies have always been said to exist only in fairy-tales,' he
wrote, 'but then you came, and made it evident that one can exist in
reality.' This blatant attempt to get his stripes back after the falling-out
over *The Moorish Girl* must have amused the Heibergs, and yet
Andersen's undisguised openness made him impossible to dislike. His
self-portrayal as a fame-seeking poet has earned him many enemies
both during and after his lifetime but, all questions of a deeper truth
apart, who can be sure that his pursuit of popularity was unnecessary?
Popular writers of today seldom leap into prominence without the
help of a publicity industry which in Andersen's day existed in the
form of an inner circle centred on the aristocratic and the very rich.
Had he not prodded relentlessly at this coterie, he might well have
remained unrecognised.

The Heibergs themselves, though central figures of the Danish
theatre, were by no means pillars of the establishment, and probably
had more sympathy for Andersen than he recognised. Johan Ludwig,
child of a revolutionary poet and his beautiful, badly treated young
wife, Thomasine, had been given to foster parents when the stormy
marriage broke up, and Johanne Luise had been the obscure little
Jewish girl whom Andersen had first met in 1821 when he was a troll
and she a cupid in the ballet *Armida*. Intellectually, they ran rings
round the blundering Andersen, but his tacit apology was accepted,
and so, a few months later, was his one-act operetta, *The Bird in the Pear
Tree*, which ran at the Royal Theatre for a few days. Heiberg's press

notice was wearily tolerant, remarking that:

> even if it does no good, neither does it do any harm; it is too small, too insignificant and too innocent for that. It is the stop-gap which the theatre often requires, and as such it can perhaps amuse many and will cause nobody any offence. It is, in fact, not quite devoid of odd traces of naïve and lyrical beauty.

From Heiberg, this was an accolade, but Andersen saw it merely as patronising, as his autobiography makes clear.

1842 had from the beginning been a difficult year. On 2 February, Admiral Peter Wulff died in a cab on the way home from the theatre. Despite the short-lived misunderstanding which had caused Andersen such distress in 1838, Wulff had been one of his most steady and encouraging supporters, always ready to laugh at the young man's funny anecdotes. These could be so hilariously bizarre that Wulff had once torn his own hair, declaring, 'It's a lie, it's a bloody lie, such things don't happen to any of us.' Now he was gone – and six days after that, an even more disquieting thing happened. Andersen received a letter from his half-sister, Karen.

He had heard no news of her since his schooldays in Slagelse, when the threat of her appearance had so alarmed him, but now that his name was becoming publicly known, this ghost of his early childhood had tracked him down. Andersen was thrown into a frantic state of mind. 'Feverish,' he noted. 'A terrible night, sensuous thoughts and despair mockingly filled my mind.' That his sister was bound up with eroticism is curious, and underlines the sexual horror which could not be dissociated from his feelings about the women in his family. He knew Karen to be illegitimate, and had witnessed the furtiveness and shame which his mother had suffered as a result. He had seen, too, his aunt's profitable trading in prostitution – but by contrast, his father's pure-minded love of books and the theatre had disintegrated into sickness and death. Carnality had seemed to triumph over beauty and purity, and now, in the person of Karen, it was grinning triumphantly at him, about to expose to the whole world just how shallow his claim to poetry and fame really were.

In the morning, Andersen fled to pour out the whole tale to Jonas Collin. It was the first his benefactor had heard of Karen's existence, significantly enough, and Collin at once set about disentangling the facts from Andersen's garbled story. His son-in-law, Adolph Drewsen, was a police court magistrate, well equipped to establish the truth, and within three days, he had established that Karen was now known as Mrs Peder Kaufmann. A little reassured, and no doubt guided by Collin, Andersen wrote a suitably urbane letter, not to his half-sister herself, but to her husband, asking him to call.

Kaufmann turned up promptly the following day, looking, as Andersen noted in the small almanac he kept at the time, 'honest and decent'. He asked for money, and Andersen gave him four rixdollars. It was not the end of the affair, for Kaufmann continued to request financial help from time to time, though Andersen handed out smaller and smaller sums − but at least the spectre of Karen had dwindled into an almost acceptable reality. He still could not bring himself to confront her in person, but his panic receded.

A few weeks later, on 29 March, August Bournonville's new ballet, *Napoli*, received its première, and Andersen was enraptured. Bournonville, best known in Britain as the choreographer of *La Sylphide*, had in his turn been on the grand Italian tour and, like Andersen, had been enthralled by the Blue Grotto, using it as a magnificent backdrop to the second act of his ballet. The ballet-master was a controversial figure, having a year previously committed an unheard-of *faux pas*. In the middle of his production, *The Toreador*, enraged by a caucus of cat-callers and whistlers who were friends of the ballerina, Lucile Grahn, with whom he had quarrelled, he strode out onto the stage and appealed directly to King Christian VIII in the Royal Box for advice on what to do. The king, furious at being dragged into a personal vendetta, had answered drily, 'Proceed' − but the resulting fracas had been such that Bournonville had thought it best to disappear from the country for a few months. His trip to Italy had been the result.

For all his royalism, and his personal liking for the king, Andersen had been fervently on Bournonville's side, as had Thorvaldsen, and this first production since the ballet-master's return was an emotional one. Andersen went round to the Bournonvilles' house after the show, and the two men drank a pledge to use the '*du*' form with each other. Bournonville, who had fathered a baby daughter during his student days in Paris and who was now married to a dancer, Helene Håkansson, by whom he had a large family, evidently found nothing compromising in this ceremony. He, being both bohemian and robustly heterosexual, could accept Andersen without embarrassment.

Edvard Collin and his wife, Jette, also had a small daughter, and a baby boy, young Jonas, had been born to them in 1840. Andersen had long ago accepted that there were no grounds for any continued romantic feelings towards his friend, but nobody had taken Edvard's place, and he was still restless and unhappy. Critical acceptance continued to elude him, and *A Poet's Bazaar* was attacked by Meier Aaron Goldschmidt in his satirical journal, *The Corsair*, on the grounds that it showed no awareness of the political tensions in Europe. While full of evocative descriptions of places, Goldschmidt complained, it said nothing about people.

Such a critical stance is of dubious validity at the best of times, and Goldschmidt, a political commentator above all else, overlooked the many sensitive human observations in Andersen's book – and yet, in the ferment of the early 1840s, his impatience is understandable. The Carlsbad Decrees of 1835 had effectively killed free speech in Germany; the poet Fritz Reuter had been in prison for nine years, Heine, among many others, was in exile, and it was rumoured that the *Rheinische Zeitung*, edited by a young man called Karl Marx, was about to be closed down. How could Andersen ignore such things?

In *Mit livs eventyr*, Andersen gives a firm answer. While respecting the convictions of those who strive to improve the common good, he himself cannot see people as components in the political chess game. 'Politics is not for me to dabble in; I have nothing to do there. God has given me a different task; I know this and have always known it.'

With a little more perception, Goldschmidt might have spotted that Andersen's stories, for all their pretty trappings of roses and nightingales, often contained a bitter attack on the perverted standards of the wealthy. 'The Emperor's New Clothes' is an obvious example, but the more recent volume dedicated to Mrs Heiberg had included 'The Princess and the Swineherd', a scathing tale of the aristocratic woman who will trade kisses for a mechanical toy bird while despising the real thing.

In the summer of 1842, Andersen moved from one manor-house to another as the guest of his various high-born friends. On 12 July, he received from the king a ruby ring set with thirty small diamonds. It seems odd that such a notable gift should have been bestowed for no particular reason. No birthday was being celebrated, no rite of passage marked – or was it? Supporters of the royal birth theory claim that it was during this summer that Andersen was at last told the secret of his ancestry.

Should this be true, it begs the question of why such a revelation should be made at this particular time. One answer, at least, seems obvious. Andersen's recent stories, notably 'The Emperor's New Clothes' and 'The Princess and the Swineherd', had started to express a satirical disrespect for the court and all its doings – and the monarchy was in too shaky a situation to stand much satire. Its absolute power was failing (though Christian, alone among the European rulers, had the good sense to see that controlled liberalisation was the way forward) and Denmark was threatened with the loss of its southern duchies, Schleswig and Holstein, because of their allegiance to Germany rather than to the Danish crown. Andersen, rapidly becoming Denmark's most popular writer, was a loose cannon which urgently needed to be chained down. Disapproval of his fun-poking would only play into his hands and make the court look even more ridiculous; the only possible tactic was to bring him into the fold.

Nobody can be sure of what was said to Andersen at that time, but two things are significant. No more satirical stories were written – rather regrettably, that vein of political levity never appeared again – and Andersen in those same months began to grapple with the construction of what became his most famous story, 'The Ugly Duckling'. This, as countless people know even if they have not read the tale, is about a duckling's arrival as one of 'those royal birds', the swans, after a lifetime of persecution and misery, and in it, Andersen states:

> It does not matter that one has been born in the henyard so long as one has lain in a swan's egg.

The sentence stands alone, as a separate paragraph.

He kept a diary only from 30 June to 30 August in that year, but details his visits to Bregentved, Glorup and Gisselfeld where he met the ducal family of Augustenborg. He mentions, too, the slow evolution of the story, sparked off by a walk round the ornamental lake at Bregentved. Its title shifted from 'The Story of a Duck' to 'The Cygnet', and devising the contents gave him endless trouble.

There was no sign of exhilaration. At Gisselfeld, Andersen was deeply depressed, and remarked that work on the story 'helped my sunken spirits'. Whatever the meaning of the gift of the ring, it brought him no lasting happiness. This is hardly surprising, for even if he had learned of a royal connection, he would also have been told that it could never be revealed. His wings might be white and shining, but they had been clipped.

Anyone who takes the trouble to read 'The Ugly Duckling' as Andersen wrote it may well be struck by the multilayered allusions which lie within its apparently simple story. It is a far more subtle tale than the saccharine caperings of the Danny Kaye film implied, and new interpretations of its symbolism are being made all the time. In 1995, Will Roscoe asserted in *Queer Spirits*, an American study of gay men's mythology, that the story was a clear analogy of the repressed homosexual who was at last able to 'come out' in his white-feathered glory, and it is not hard to find supportive evidence for this theory in Andersen's own words. Although he constructed the story with great care so that it might appear to be no more than a rags-to-riches fable of personal success, it works equally coherently as a search for sexual identity. When the cygnet, driven out of the poultry-yard by the other birds because he is 'different', meets up with two wild ganders, specifically stated by Andersen to be male, with whom he strikes up a friendship, the association is brought to a swift end by a couple of hunters' bullets. Although the author had covered his tracks by making the ganders a laddish pair with an eye to the maiden geese who swam on a distant swamp, he still made the point that association with one's own kind is not allowed.

Speculation on Andersen's latent homosexuality is far from new. As early as 1901, a German study called *H.C. Andersen – Beweis seiner Homosexualitat* (*Evidence of his Homosexuality*) was published by a certain Albert Hansen, and this formed the basis for a book by Professor Hjalmar Helweg, *H.C. Andersen – En psykiatrisk Studie.* Hansen, a Dane whose real name was Carl Hansen Fahlberg, quoted the even earlier work of Magnus Hirschfeld, born in 1868, who had preceded Kinsey in attempting a survey of men's sexual orientation and held that Andersen was bisexual. Both men paid dearly for their airing of this taboo subject. In 1934, Nazi students stormed Hirschfeld's institute and burned his books, and Hansen, a high-ranking lawyer, had in 1906 been arrested by his own colleagues. He was never convicted of any offence, but spent a long time in custody before the trial which freed him, suffering a nervous breakdown as a result. He later committed suicide.

None of this received much general attention in Denmark until Aksel Dreslov published his study of the two men, *H.C. Andersen og 'denne Albert Hansen'* (*and this Albert Hansen*) in 1977, and even then, it made little impact. Elias Bredsdorff's biography of Andersen was published two years before the appearance of Dreslov's book and shrugged off any question of homosexuality for lack of proof – and the English edition published in 1993 remained unamended.

Danish academics at the present time accept that sexual ambivalence played a strong part in Andersen's life, but there has been little attempt to study the detailed way in which a repressed homosexual love finds its way into the fairy tales and stories. This is a continuing result of Andersen's complex and deliberate cover-up, which remains effective to this day. He clothed his feelings in a symbolism so beguiling and innocent-seeming that it takes real effort to break through the prettiness of his nightingales and daisies and perceive that he spoke constantly of a painful exclusion from the world which others regarded as normal.

In the mid-nineteenth century, readers were not armed with a post-Freudian skill in deciphering psychological codes. A fir tree spoke as a fir tree, a darning needle as a darning needle; Andersen's stories were easy to take at face value. Even now, his quality of narrative sweeps the reader or listener along like a leaf on the stream, unaware that the poignant atmosphere of his work comes from the depths which lie below. All poets, whether working in verse or prose, have the power to short-circuit the reader's rationality and touch his or her central being with writing that makes a direct emotional connection, and to find out how the trick is done defies analysis. In Andersen's case, the sleight-of-hand is doubly mysterious, for it is not the choice of words which achieves the magic effect, but rather the simple presentation of the story's events. His many redrafts and deletions show that he took great care over the construction of the metaphorical mini-world he was putting together, and so seamless was it in each case that it left the underlying motive deeply secret, perhaps to himself as well as the reader. That his stories work so well in often poor translation only goes to prove their durability and coherence. Danish, because of its very simple grammatical structure and its relatively small vocabulary, is rich in a kind of laconic implication which is very difficult to render in another language, and although Andersen's stories often lose this quality of wry amusement in translation, their sense of personal reality transcends all that, exotic and unlikely as it often is. These tales are classic not because of their charm but because they were built as tough, assault-proof vehicles, both containing and hiding a vulnerable truth.

On 29 August of that same summer, Andersen went with the Hauchs to Roskilde, where he visited the composer, Christophe Weyse, now a very old man. It had been Weyse who had organised a whip-round for the gauche boy who had burst in upon a dinner party back in 1819, and Andersen was glad to have paid him this last visit, for Weyse died a few weeks later, on 8 October. At the funeral, Andersen was concerned that the corpse did not seem to be quite cold. Horrified by the thought that his old friend should wake to find himself in his grave, he entreated a doctor to sever Weyse's arteries. Oehlenschläger, overhearing this request, was shocked and said so, but Andersen rounded on him, protesting that he himself would want to be absolutely certain of his own death when the time came. Being apparently dead but still conscious was a recurring nightmare to him throughout his life, and speaks very clearly of his horror of being powerless in the hands of others.

A few weeks previously, on 30 September, Andersen's half-sister, Karen, had herself come to see him. After all the dread and panic, the occasion was something of an anticlimax. He noted only that she 'looked quite well-dressed and young. I gave her 1 rixdollar.' He never saw her again. Kaufmann turned up one more time, on 25 November, when Andersen gave him four marks – no more than a few coppers – then the pair of them disappeared into their unknown background.

By the end of the year Andersen was restless again, and on 30 January 1843 he set off on another of his slow and meandering trips, this time heading for Paris. He spent two weeks with Count Rantzau-Breitenburg where he started work on a dramatic poem called *Ahasuerus*, then went on to Hamburg, a town so devastated by a recent fire that most buildings 'still lay in ruins with charred beams and crumbling towers'. Travellers were having difficulty in finding a bed for the night or indeed in finding an inn that was still standing, but Andersen was welcomed into the home of Count Holck, the Danish postmaster. He also met Otto Speckter, who was just beginning a set of illustrations to a German edition of the fairy tales.

There was still no railway across the Lüneberg Heath, so Andersen travelled on by mail coach through Osnabrück to Dusseldorf, arriving on the last day of the carnival and amused to see 'in German guise what I had already seen in Roman dress'. He went by train to Brussels and enjoyed Donizetti's opera, *La Favourita,* though the Art Gallery was not at all to his taste, containing as it did a lot of 'Rubens' fat, blonde women'. On 8 March he arrived in Paris, where he stayed for two months. In the Café du Danemark, he found among other Scandinavian expats Edvard's younger brother, Theodor, a medical man who would later become Andersen's personal doctor.

The brief biographical sketch written by Xavier Marmier which had preceded Andersen on his journey to the East and done much to ease his passage there was similarly useful in France, and Marmier himself, a Parisian who spoke passable Danish, was an immensely obliging guide. The Frenchman had no great opinion of Andersen's fairy stories, curiously enough, contending that their humour was a style which did not suit the writer, who 'cannot have been at ease behind this borrowed mask'. Neither was he impressed by the poetry, which he found weak; it was Andersen as a man who so fascinated Marmier, the true story of his rise from obscurity having far more appeal than any of his fictions – but whatever its cause, his enthusiasm for the Dane had great practical uses. Through Marmier, Andersen met several of the French leading literati, among them Lamartine, who invited him to his very grand house on 1 May. Andersen's diary for that day sounds deeply impressed:

> Many liveried footmen received us, we went through large rooms into one adorned with splendid paintings, including a life-sized one of Lamartine. He received us very kindly; there were several Members of the Chamber of Deputies; Madame Lamartine, who is not beautiful, looks very intelligent; I spoke a good deal.

He might have added, 'in French', for to express himself in that language was a challenge, and he was eager to talk to the great man (whom he called 'the prince of them all') about eastern travel. Lamartine's *Souvenirs d'un voyage en orient,* published in 1835, had been the cause of Andersen's determination to reach Constantinople, and he admired the Royalist French poet passionately. On parting, Lamartine promised to send his Danish colleague a poem, and did so two days later, on 3 May:

Cachez-vous quelquefois dans les pages d'un livre
Une fleur du matin ceuillie aux rameaux verts
Quand vous rouvrez la page après de longs hyvers,
Aussi pur qu'au printemps son parfum vous ennyvre;
Après les jours bornés qu'ici mon nom doit vivre
Qu'un heureux souvenir sorte encore de ces vers!

The neat rhyme-scheme demands a verse translation:

Some time, hide a flower in a book's deep fold,
A blossom morning-gathered from a green-leaved tree
And after those long years in which the winters flee
Be drunk again upon the fresh spring scent of old;
Hard upon the dull days which now my spirit hold
Leaps from these lines once more a happy memory!

Andersen also went to see Alexandre Dumas, and found him in circumstances very different from Lamartine's splendour. Wearing a blue-striped shirt and baggy trousers, he greeted his visitor in a room cluttered with papers and containing the unmade bed from which he had just risen. He introduced Andersen to his family of children and to his wife, of whom the sculptor David said unkindly that she had 'nothing upstairs', and regretted that his eighteen-year-old son, Alexandre *fils* had no son of his own. 'When I was eighteen, I already had him,' Dumas *père* pointed out. On a second visit, Andersen found the great writer actually in bed, busy with the final scene of a play, and was asked to wait while the closing lines were scribbled down. '*Voila!*' Dumas then cried, and jumped out of bed. For all his eccentricities, he was a well-accepted figure of French society, and a few evenings later, introduced Andersen to Elizabeth Felix Rachel, known simply as Rachel, the young actress who was taking Europe by storm. Although only twenty-two years old, her current performance in the title role of Racine's *Phedre* was the talk of Paris, and Andersen, still as stage-struck as ever, was quivering with excitement at the thought of meeting this goddess. Invited to a soirée at her house, he wrote to Jette Wulff in glowing terms about the occasion:

There was a splendour, a wealth in those rooms – scarlet walls, carpets of the same colour, costly curtains and tasteful furniture. I and an elderly gentleman were the first to arrive; she asked me to sit next to her on the sofa, just in front of the fireplace; she was dressed in black and extremely graceful.

Andersen was less rapturous about an invitation to visit Heine, but when he did call at the great writer's house a few days later, he was warmly received. Heine told him how he considered himself more French than German, specially since he had on the eve of a potentially fatal duel married his mistress, Eugenie Mirat, rather than risk leaving her destitute. He went on to express great interest in Scandinavia, which he regarded as a treasure-house of ancient poetry, and regretted that he felt too old to begin learning Danish. They met twice more, and on one of these occasions, Andersen was prevailed on to tell some of his own stories. Heine remarked that he was a natural raconteur. 'So was Goethe,' he added, 'but I'm not.'

Andersen's diary contained a note that he didn't trust Heine's face. He perhaps sensed that Heine, for all his cordiality, had some reservations about his Danish visitor, as a letter to a friend written shortly afterwards made very clear:

> He is a tall thin man with hollow sunken cheeks and his manner shows the sort of fawning servility which princes like. That is why princes have given Andersen such a brilliant reception. He is a perfect example of the type of poet they like to see. When he visited me he had adorned himself with a large tie-pin; when I asked him what it was that he had on his chest, he replied with great unction, 'This is a gift graciously bestowed on me by the Electress of Hesse.' In other respects, Andersen is a very admirable character.

Political differences apart, the two men had much in common. They shared a bitter resentment about lack of appreciation from their respective countries, and grumbled pleasurably about the shortcomings of translators. Kruse's German translation of *The Improvisatore* was very poor, Heine said – but then, the wretched man had just died in hospital, 'so sick of everything that he didn't even have an appetite for men any more!' Apart from the exclamation mark, Andersen added no comment when he inscribed this in his diary.

He paid two visits to Alfred de Vigny and was presented with the French poet's complete works, and also met Balzac at a soirée given by

Countess Pfaffins, referring to him as 'a broad-shouldered little clod.' His account of the occasion, in a letter to Ingeborg Drewsen's daughter, sixteen-year-old Jonna, is comic. The Countess, he said:

> dragged me over to the velvet sofa and asked me to sit down by her satin side – for she was dressed in the blackest of black, with jewels – and, holding my hand, she pulled Balzac, the author, by his hand to come and sit on the other side of her, and then exclaimed, 'How lucky I am, to be sitting here between two of the greatest men of our time!'

Andersen confessed to Jonna that his grasp of French was 'original.' When words failed him, he simply shrugged and said, '*C'est tout.*' The Collin family, he added, would be surprised at how well he managed – 'but then, the views of the Collins on languages are too severe and not those accepted by the world.' He smarted a little from knowing that the family laughed at his linguistic blunders, '*N'est pas?*' having become a catch-phrase among them. His need for the family's approval remained very strong, and when his thirty-eighth birthday had passed in Paris with no word from them, he had flown into a fury. 'Am mad with rage!' he had written in his diary that day. 'No attention from those at home.'

In fact, as Andersen knew, the family had just been struck by tragedy, for Edvard's little daughter had died. His first-born child, she could not have been more than six years old, and Edvard was distraught. Andersen felt himself excluded from his friend's distress, and was full of resentment. He remarked in a furious letter of complaint to Jonas Collin that 'even if I am not fortunate enough to be among the friends to whom he turns for consolation in his sorrow, he might all the same, once this grief is relieved, remember me by writing a few words.' He did not, he went on, write letters for the fun of it, but in order to get letters in return. Such an egocentric response must have seemed intolerable to the bereaved family, and Andersen wrote to Edvard's elder brother, Gottlieb, complaining of the 'cold air stream coming from the Home, which makes my mind sick and poisons my blood.'

The family had an endless power to wound him, and Andersen watched morbidly for any sign that he was not quite accepted as being of their own social status. In *Mit livs eventyr* he recalls how Jonas's brother-in-law objected to Andersen's invitation to a society ball on the grounds that he could not belong in such places. Andersen had pointed out that others of modest status had been invited, including a couple of students. Those young men came of good families, he was told – and what was Andersen's father? 'My father was a craftsman,' he had retorted, 'and I won my position through my own efforts and with the help of God, and thought you would respect that.'

For all his protests that he took no interest in politics, Andersen's struggles on a personal level to be recognised as a human being of equal worth with any other did much to advance the cause of democracy in Denmark. He stressed constantly that he was the child of a poor shoemaker, and those who admired his work were forced to accept that the despised underclass was capable of producing a great poet. This was easier for the aristocracy in their charitable security than it was for the rising middle class to which the Collins belonged. 'Knowing one's place' was for them an integral part of their moral code, and Andersen continually flouted it.

His difficulties with the family during his time in Paris were characteristically tempestuous and transient. Two days after his outburst to Gottlieb, his concerns had returned to his own affairs, as his diary for 4 April shows:

> Went at 8.30 to a concert in the salon of Mr Pleyel, where it was awfully elegant and brightly lit. The knowledge that my boots had no heels and that I was wearing my worst pair of trousers made me feel uneasy. Smartly dressed Frenchmen arrived. I looked at one of them carefully; his dress jacket wasn't as good as mine; the same went for the hat. I was feeling haemorrhoidal, terribly withdrawn into myself. A man came up and greeted me quite respectfully and familiarly. I've seen him before. Who is he? During the fifth number, I left. My thoughts had taken a different turn, and I was feeling good. Back home in my room, sick again. Fire burning hot in my veins; out − +.

By the end of the month, Andersen was reeling from a far worse blow than Collin displeasure. On 29 April, he heard that the *Berlingske Tidende* had reported that the operatic version of *Agnete and the Merman*, with music by Neils Gade, had been hissed off the stage in Copenhagen. To Jette Wulff, Andersen poured out a stream of invective about his native country and, in case she should discard the letter, copied it word for word in his diary (or, perhaps, copied the diary entry to Jette):

I hate those who hate me, I curse those who curse me! As ever, from Denmark come streams of cold air that turn me to stone when I receive them here! They spit on me, they trample me into the mud, and yet God gave them few Digters of my kind – and in my dying hour I shall ask God never to give them any others. Oh, what venom is flowing through my veins at this time! When I was young, I could cry, but now I can't! I can only be proud, hate, despise, give my soul to the evil powers to find a moment's comfort! Here, in this large foreign city, the best known and noblest among the spirits of Europe receive me with kindness and love, meet me as a kindred soul, and at home the boys are spitting on the best creation of my heart! Even if I come to be judged after my death as I am being judged now while living, I will still say, the Danes can be evil, cold, satanic! A people well suited to those damp, mouldy-green islands . . .

He seemed aware that Jette Wulff was probably the only person he could trust, for he remarked, 'If this letter were to be published, the whole of Copenhagen would roar with laughter.' And that, most certainly, was true.

Two days later, Andersen received a tightly self-controlled letter from Edvard which made no reference to his recent bereavement or to Andersen's outburst, but merely offered a formal assurance that Andersen might depend on him, as ever, for help when needed. Neither the implicit rebuke nor the steady dependability was taken on board by the irate poet, who lamented in his diary that Edvard had sounded 'as cold as a law book'. 'How strange,' he went on, 'that I cannot get used to his way of writing letters. In place of friendship he offers me willingness to render service.' Anyone else would have seen that Edvard's forbearance and patient stability did in fact constitute a most faithful friendship, but Andersen's intolerance of such mundane virtues reveal very clearly that he wanted, not support and service, but love.

He left Paris on 8 May and travelled reluctantly back to his homeland, finding on his way through Germany some consolation, for in that country his work was universally hailed with great enthusiasm. After a brief stay of only a few days in Copenhagen, Andersen retreated to the comfort offered by his aristocratic friends and their country estates.

On 9 June, a public holiday, while on his way across Funen to stay with a new host, Andersen happened to see Riborg Voigt, now Mrs Bøving, with her husband and children. 'It is thirteen years,' he noted in the small almanac he kept at the time, but made no further comment about the girl with whom he had claimed to be so infatuated. He went on to Fåborg – to stay with the Voigt family, ironically enough, to reflect with wry humour on the fate of their daughter.

The meeting with Riborg gave rise to a story called 'The Top and the Ball', sometimes translated as 'The Sweethearts', a wry tale in which the beautiful ball, admired by the humble top, ends up in the gutter while the top is given a coat of gold paint and brought into the living room:

> There, no one ever talked about the ball, and the top never mentioned his old love again. You get over it when your beloved has lain in a gutter and oozed for five years. You never recognise her in the rubbish bin.

The laconic ending contains a certain disgust as well as a weary sense of triumph. After thirteen years, perhaps the beautiful Riborg had become rotund and matronly, perspiring a little in the summer heat, a fleshy ball whom Andersen now found repellent – and yet the top, for all his fastidiousness and his fragile self-satisfaction, could not disguise his essential lovelessness.

Chapter 14
A Nightingale and a Grand Duke

In September 1843, just as Andersen's summer travels had ended, a young Swedish singer called Jenny Lind arrived in Copenhagen for a few days' rest after a concert tour with the tenor, Julius Günther. She stayed at the house of August Bournonville, who turned some of his children out of their nursery to make room for her. Bournonville had heard the young soprano sing as an eighteen-year-old in Stockholm and was both smitten by the beauty of her voice and shocked by the pittance paid her in her own country, and he suggested that she should while in Copenhagen sing in *Robert of Normandie* at the Royal Theatre. Jenny had sung in the Stockholm opera house, but the thought of appearing before an audience of critical foreigners so terrified her that she flatly refused.

Bournonville was a determined man. Realising that the girl's panic was genuine, he went round to Andersen's lodgings to appeal for his help in persuading her. Failing to get much response, Bournonville thrust his friend's stick into his hand, jammed his hat on his head and hauled him round to the house. 'Why not use the same tactics with her?' Andersen enquired. 'Just pick her up and dump her on the stage!'

He had in fact met Jenny Lind once before. Three years previously, she had stayed briefly at the Hotel du Nord, where Andersen was living, and he had called on her. Not knowing who he was, she found him foppish and peculiar. Her guarded response had not pleased the poet, and he now assumed that she was behaving like any other spoiled and temperamental prima donna, but when Jenny came forward, hand outstretched, her simplicity and lack of affectation impressed him at once. She told him she was frightened of being hissed off the stage, and Andersen understood her fear only too well. He said with honesty that he could not predict her reception without having heard her voice, but he thought a Copenhagen audience would be satisfied with quite a moderate performance.

Bournonville took Jenny to see a play called *Son of the Desert*, purely so that she could get an idea of the size of the auditorium, but she was further unnerved by the stunning performance given by Johanne Heiberg. Bournonville's ten-year-old daughter, Charlotte, afterwards said she was amazed to see a grown-up person wringing her hands and weeping with sheer terror – and the ballet-master sighed and gave in. Once the suggestion was dropped, Jenny began to suffer from pangs of conscience, and agreed to attend just one rehearsal.

Having heard her sing, even the orchestra gave her a collective ovation and Andersen was completely bowled over. To see her on the stage, he said in *My Life's Fairytale*, was to feel that she was 'a pure vessel, from which a holy draught will be presented to us'. He went on, 'Through Jenny Lind I first became aware of the holiness there is in art; through her I learned that one must forget oneself in the service of the Supreme.' And in these quasi-religious terms, he declared himself in love.

Although much has been made of the supposed affair between Andersen and Jenny Lind, there is no shred of evidence to show that either of them took it seriously. There was fellow-feeling between them, certainly, as both had emerged from deep poverty, and Andersen's brief almanac entries show that he saw her frequently during her three-weeks' visit. He gave her his poems, a briefcase and a portrait of himself, and noted a couple of times that he was 'in love', but Jenny laughed at his attempts to be alone with her, hurrying him up when he lagged behind the rest of the group on return from an evening party. 'Come on, Andersen, get your long legs moving,' she said, and ran ahead to join the others. Once, in a gesture which must have been infinitely painful to him, she interrupted his flow of talk by holding up a small mirror to his face. Whether she meant to remind him of his ugliness or reprove him for self-obsession, it was a blunt rebuff, impossible to dismiss as a piece of coquettish provocation. There was nothing of the flirt about Jenny Lind. Deeply religious, she was also very clear about the nature of her friendships, and while finding much in common with Andersen, she could not for a moment have any romantic feelings for him. As she wrote to a friend the following year, 'I need support! A man! A real, *strong, healthy* man!' [Her emphasis.]

Andersen, as in all his previous declared love-affairs, was establishing the reasons for its impossibility even as he proclaimed himself infatuated. 'Jealous of Günther' he noted in his almanac of 17 September as the Swedish tenor arrived in Copenhagen. It was widely rumoured that Günther hoped to marry Jenny, and Andersen's references to this sounded unperturbed. His casual note the following day was almost comically laconic, and in the sharpest possible contrast to the barely controllable passion which he had expressed for Edvard Collin:

> Visited her. Read the others' poems, thought of proposing. Had a swim. She is going to sing before the king.

As Andersen quite probably intended, it has been assumed that he showered Jenny with ardent proposals, but his own brief notes show only the pleasure of being in the company of a famous and wonderful young singer about whom the whole of Copenhagen was in raptures. Jenny left Denmark on 19 September, and Andersen handed her a letter 'which she will understand'.

There was no reply for a month. Andersen was busy with the three stories which were shaping themselves in response to her visit, and when he did receive a letter, seemed content that it was, as he wrote to Jette Wulff, 'extremely cordial and kind'. He went on:

> She is a great and lovely soul; may God see to it that her future husband makes her happy. I imagine it will be G.

Andersen seemed happy to regard Jenny Lind as an unattainable goddess, and took pleasure in a letter from her close friend, Frederika Bremer, the Swedish novelist, who wrote:

> Flowers are showered at her feet, poems too, suitors likewise (though not in such quantities), and she charms women just as much as men by her natural, modest, pleasant manners . . . If you want to see Jenny Lind's eyes shine and her entire face and personality taken over by the beauty of joy and inspiration, then speak to her about her art, about its beauty and innocence, about its beneficial influence on human souls. But if you want to see the deepest and most attractive side of her, then speak to her about the doctrines of religion, about the grace and will of God . . .

Andersen sent Jette Wulff a long quotation from this letter, and then made his own position clear:

> Do you see now how it is that all my thoughts are taken up with such a
> pearl? And yet, she won't be mine – cannot be mine, but will live in
> my soul as a good and kind spirit . . .

Jenny Lind had come very close to his impossible ideal, exemplified by
the blind girl from Paestum in *The Improvisatore*. As the hero of that
book, Antonio, had observed, ' "Our love is of the spiritual world!" '
Through this voice, Andersen had gone on to insist that the lift of the
spirit is the goal of human existence and therefore constitutes 'the
great reality'. Ironically enough, Jenny was far closer to Annunciata,
whom Andersen had modelled on the tragically short-lived opera
singer, Maria Malibran Garcia, whose brother Manuel had been
Jenny's tutor in Paris. For all her devoutness, Jenny Lind was a very real
woman. She formed a close relationship with Felix Mendelssohn,
though respecting utterly that he was married, but made no secret of
the fact that she wanted a husband and children. She became engaged
to Julius Günther for about six months in 1848, though that withered
in the face of a strange infatuation with a religious bigot called
Claudius Harris while Jenny was singing in England. On 5 February
1852, she married a seven-years-younger pianist, Otto Goldschmidt,
perhaps mainly because he had been a pupil of her beloved
Mendelssohn.

   Andersen himself had no hope of entering this world of courtship
and marriage, as he made clear to Ingeborg Drewsen. Stressing in a
letter to her that Jenny was engaged (which, at that time, she was not),
he underlined the salient word in a sentence which acted as the
epitaph to the whole affair. 'She is the loveliest *child* I have ever met.'

   After Jenny had gone, he sent her 'The Nightingale', a story about
the superiority of the natural singing bird to any artificial toy, together
with 'The Angel' and 'The Ugly Duckling'. It was six months before she
replied, and then only because Bournonville nudged her. She thanked
Andersen for 'the pretty tales' and exclaimed at the 'glorious gift to be
able to clothe one's light thoughts in words, to show mankind on a
scrap of paper how the noblest often lies hidden'.

   Andersen had moved into a new confidence about his stories. The
collection which he published on 11 November 1843 comprised the
three which he had sent to Jenny, plus 'The Top and the Ball', and for

1. Hans Christian Andersen's House, Odense. Lithograph, 1868.

Broholm Gaard

2. Broholm Castle. Gouache 1833.

3. Jonas Collin. Painting by J.V. Gertner, 1840.

4. Simon Meisling.

CHRISTIAN FRIEDRICH

Kronprinz von Dännemarck.

5. Christian VIII. Lithograph, 1830.

6. Elise Ahlefeldt-Laurvig.

7.   Edvard and Henrietta Collin. Painting by W. Marstrand, 1842.

8. Henrietta Wulff.

9. Drawing by Hans Christian Andersen. My Window in Rome, 1833.

10. Drawing by Hans Christian Andersen. Casino dell' Orologio I Villa Borghese.

11. Bertel Thorwaldsen, Self Portrait, 1810.

12. Hans Christian Andersen. Portrait by Albert Küchler, 1834.

13. Hans Christian Andersen. Portrait by C.A. Jensen, 1836.

JENNY LIND.

14. Jenny Lind, The 'Swedish Nightingale'.

Grand Duke Carl Alexander of Sachsen-Weimar-Eisenach. Litograph

15.   Grand Duke Carl Alexander of Sachsen-Weimar-Eisenach. Lithograph.

16.   Hans Christian Andersen. Photograph by C. Weller, 1865.

the first time, he deleted any reference to children from the title, simply calling the volume *New Fairy Tales*. He explained the change in a letter to B.S. Ingemann:

> Now I tell stories from my own heart, catching an idea for the grownups – then telling the tale to the little ones while remembering all the time that Father and Mother often listen, and you must also give them something to think about.

Five days after the book's appearance, Andersen went to Nysø, where Thorvaldsen had a studio provided by Baroness Stampe, and there he became deeply involved with the Baroness's son, Henrik, twenty-two years old to Andersen's thirty-eight. There is no diary for this period, but his small pocket almanac is full of references to a relationship which went on into 1844 and became increasingly passionate. On 11 December the two men drank a pledge to say '*du*' to each other, and Andersen began to refer to him in his notes as 'my beloved Henrik'. On 3 March, he wrote, 'Was at H's house, he sat with me, he cares for me.' He recorded outbursts of jealousy and a continuing struggle with his frustrated sensuality, and worried over a recurrently painful penis which was probably the result of his constant masturbation. This practice, too, was a cause for anxiety, for it was commonly held to be a cause of madness, the deepest of his fears.

Whether Andersen was simply unlucky in failing to find a male friend who would respond to him physically, or whether he was unable to contemplate any form of sexual love is impossible to tell, but in either case, the result was the same. He lived in ostensible celibacy and received no caresses but his own, despite his intense loneliness and need for love. Despite his attachment to Henrik, he had not lost his deep devotion to Edvard, and was profoundly touched to receive at the end of December 1843 a letter which at last spoke freely of the grief caused by his daughter's death. Andersen wrote back at once, overwhelmed by gratitude. 'My deeply dear Edvard, God bless you for the letter you sent me! It came so unexpectedly that I felt a real thump of the heart as I opened it . . .' He was too full of emotion to offer Edvard any real sympathy:

> I think this is the first time you have really revealed your friendship, which I have never doubted; you have told me of your grief in quite

casual terms – but I understand you. You have always been my first friend; what hurt me was that you never quite confided in me. Oh, dear, dear friend. Probably you will never quite understand how close to my heart your welfare lies and how deeply I have felt your sorrow, prayed to God in my loneliness to soften what could not be changed. This last year, you say, you have aged tenfold . . .

Andersen, too, had suffered, he protested – but his letter ended on a note of apology for being so obsessed with himself and his work. Bitter experience had taught him how empty all these self-seeking dreams had been, and he asked, 'Am I becoming more reasonable or less egotistical? I don't know.'

It was an honest admission. The pretext of ruthless ambition was beginning to wear a little thin now that the fairy stories were starting to win Andersen real recognition. Socially, his position was assured by the favour he had found with royalty, and striving for success no longer sufficed as a total self-description. He was a little uneasy, recognising that his underlying lovelessness and isolation could no longer be disguised as the fury of a neglected young poet. Increasingly, these qualities appeared in his work with a new nakedness, and in the years since they were written, countless readers have been uncomfortably aware that below the poetic surface lies the bleak pain of loneliness and exclusion.

On 13 March 1844, Bertel Thorvaldsen died with dramatic suddenness in the Royal Theatre in Copenhagen, having stood up during the overture to let another member of the audience pass. Andersen had dined with him that evening at Baroness Stampe's house, together with Henrik, plus Oehlenschläger, a botanist called Schouw and a young painter, Constantin Hansen, who was to do the frescoes for the Thorvaldsen museum. Andersen did not go with the others to the theatre because, as he admits in *My Life's Fairytale,* he had no free ticket – though in a letter he wrote at the time to Willhelm von Lenz, editor of the German newspaper, *Zeitgenossen Hamburg,* he claimed to have been unwell.

This letter is very much that of the journalistic 'stringer' communicating a juicy news item. Andersen claimed that Bournonville had come running from the theatre to tell him what had happened, whereas his autobiography recalled that he had first heard the news from a waiter at breakfast in the Hotel du Nord the next morning. Either way, he went at once to Nysø to pay his last respects to Thorvaldsen:

> There lay his corpse, stretched out on the bed; the room was filled with strangers who had forced their way in; the floor was wet from the melted snow on their boots; the air was stuffy. Nobody spoke a word. Baroness Stampe was sitting on the edge of the bed weeping. I stood there, shocked and deeply moved.

That day, Johan Vilhelm Gertner made a detailed pencil drawing of the dead sculptor, whose face looks calm and almost amused, and when Baroness Stampe had recovered a little she agreed that 'there had never been so beautiful a corpse'.

For the second time, Thorvaldsen changed the pattern of Andersen's life. His return from Rome had ended the convivial life there which his young admirer had hoped to rediscover on his second visit, and now his death brought to a close the cheerful bohemianism of Nysø. Andersen had loved the swimming, the walks in the woods, the silly conversations and the mad impromptu celebrations such as the one which had heralded Thorvaldsen's last birthday with a song accompanied on dinner-gong, fire-tongs, cutlery and bottles, but all of this was now gone. At the same time, Andersen's relationship with Henrik Stampe, which had been wearing thin, finally gave way. Henrik told him their close friendship must end but refrained from adding the true reason, which was that he had fallen in love with Jonna Drewsen, the daughter of Edvard's sister, Ingeborg.

In the bleakness following Henrik's rejection and Thorvaldsen's death, Andersen packed up his battered old trunk and carpet bag and set out on his travels again, staying first at Breitenburg, the Holstein estate owned by Count Rantzau. Here, too, the atmosphere was elegiac, for the old Count was frail and predicted that he would be under the green grass next time Andersen came. This proved to be true, for he died the following winter.

Andersen moved on to the duchy of Weimar, the legendary centre of German culture ever since the days of Goethe and Schiller, in response to an invitation from Carl Olivier Beaulieu-Marconnay, whom he had met briefly on a previous visit to Germany – and there, he stepped into a new world. Weimar society, steeped in art and music and literature, welcomed him as its own. He visited Goethe's daughter-in-law, whom he had happened to meet in Constantinople, and found Beaulieu a delightful host. As he remarked in *Mit livs eventyr*:

> There are people one can come to know and love in only a few days; in those days I believe I found a friend for all time in Beaulieu. He took care of me and introduced me to all the finest families . . .

Chief among these, of course, was the Grand Duke himself, who with the duchess invited the Danish author to dine. A few days later, Andersen drove with Beaulieu to a hunting lodge at Ettersburg where he met the ducal couple's son, Carl Alexander. His autobiography recalls the occasion with tenderness:

> a short distance from the lodge the coach came to a standstill and a young man with a frank face and magnificent, gentle eyes came and spoke to us . . .

This was the Hereditary Grand Duke, twenty-six years old, married to a princess of the Netherlands with whom he had a little son within a marriage which seems to have been an affair of State rather than of the heart. For the dazzled Andersen a bright new star shone in the empty sky of his loneliness. A strong friendship sprang up at once between the two men despite the gulf of difference in background, and Andersen wrote in ecstatic terms to various members of the Collin family about the glories of Weimar. He recalled in *Mit livs eventyr* how reluctant he had been to leave:

> As I drove through the gate, out across the bridge at the side of the water-mill and took a last look at the town and its castle, my soul was filled with a profound melancholy. It was as though a beautiful period of my life now belonged to the past.

In Dresden on 4 July he happened to meet up with relatives of the Drewsens, who let fall that Jonna was in love with Henrik Stampe. Andersen was incredulous. 'It's a lie!" he wrote angrily in his diary, and then, as the truth began to sink in, reflected on the irony of having been led on step by step until he arrived face-to-face with a girl to whom he was virtually an uncle. Jonna in her affectionate letters to him had refused to change to the formal '*de*' when she ceased to be a child, and at seventeen, continued to call him '*du*'; yet, just as Jette Thyberg had robbed him of Edvard, Jonna had robbed him of Henrik. The Weimar interlude had mercifully softened the worst of the blow, but his attitude to Jonna underwent a marked and permanent cooling.

The rest of Andersen's summer tour was a success. While in Dresden, he spent some time with the Schumanns, where he heard four of his own poems, translated into German by Chamisso, set to music by Robert Schumann. Clara accompanied the singer, Frau Frege, and it was, Andersen said, 'a beautiful and truly poetical evening'. Clara Wieck, as Frau Schumann had been before her marriage, was well known as a pianist, but the public had been slow to accept Robert's compositions. Andersen seemed unaware of this, but the practical and ever-generous Jenny Lind did a lot to secure Schumann's reputation by including his songs in her repertoire. Andersen, a very different character, had to be reminded by Schumann the following April that he had promised to send a sketch of the young composer which was due to appear in a German newspaper.

In Berlin, Andersen went to call, unannounced, on Jacob Grimm, one of the famous story-collecting brothers. On this occasion he had not thought a letter of introduction necessary – but Grimm stared at him blankly, having never heard of him. Explanations ensued and were gladly accepted, but the moment was an embarrassing one.

Andersen was hardly back in Denmark when he received an invitation to visit Christian VIII and his second wife Queen Caroline Amalie, (the exiled Charlotte had died in 1840) at their holiday residence on the small island of Føhr. He was a little dismayed, being short of funds as a result of his German tour, but there could be no question of refusal.

It is not easy to see why Andersen's presence should have been requested at such short notice. Some say it was because Christian Frederik wanted to set things to rights, both with Hans Christian, his illegitimate son, and with his daughter Fanny, whom Charlotte had borne to him before the royal couple's marriage, and who was reputedly also present on Føhr. Andersen's diary, which was increasingly given to the non-committal recording of events as his life progressed, gives no hint of this, but it is certainly evident that his visit to the king and queen in that summer of 1844 centred to some extent round the possibility of a financial offer.

Andersen's account of the whole affair is filled with unease. His journey across Jutland had been a grim one, though he had paused on Funen to stay in Odense with the Hancks, where Jette was completing a novel. After that, it had been like venturing into a wilderness as he worked his way down to what is now the German border, where Føhr (also now in Germany) lay off the west coast. It was a bleak and treeless place, and the journey to it had been appalling. In his diary, Andersen had complained about the poor hotels and the wretched state of the muddy tracks into which the horses sank as they struggled with the heavy coach, and he had been alarmed by a drive along an invisible causeway between flooded fields. The coach was an open one and he had left Flensburg at two in the morning, and on arrival at Dagebøl after the dreadful night, he found the place 'a miserable hole' where the people were unfriendly.

On the island itself, things were not much better. Andersen had not been invited to share the spa which the royal couple and their retinue occupied, and he seemed uncertain as to whether he had been invited as a friend or as a kind of court jester. He dined with the king and queen every night and was required to make himself available should his company be required, but during the day he spent a lot of time wandering about on his own. There was, he noted sadly on 30 August, 'something stiff about it all'. He read his stories and the king 'laughed a lot' and thanked him for coming – but a sour question of money lay not far below the surface. Henning Sally, a Court official, assured Andersen that the trip would be paid for, but this did little to soothe his feeling of being taken for granted. In Weimar he was welcomed with genuine love and made to feel talented and important, but here he seemed to merit only a casual kindness, and was in no way treated as an honoured guest. On the day of his complaint about the stiffness of the atmosphere, he had been summoned to dine and then told at the last moment that he could not come after all as there wasn't room.

On the following day, he was included among the guests on a trip in several small boats to the island of Oland, but again he found himself overlooked, relegated to the last boat and thus arriving on Oland just as the royal party was about to leave again. The king told him airily to take his time, but the place was less than attractive, and Andersen spent a gloomy hour there, gazing at a sea-washed cemetery in which exposed human bones and skulls lay about among the remains of rotten coffins. That evening, he chose for his readings 'The Swineherd' and 'The Nightingale', both of which are notably cutting about the foolish pomposity of royal behaviour, but evidently the sarcasm was not noticed, for Queen Caroline invited him to lunch the following day. Rather oddly, however, for this meal she 'ladled up porridge with cream'. This may have been an ironic effort to tease him out of his sulkiness, for on the previous day he had remarked that when visiting Bregentved he felt at ease, as though at home. 'But I should hope you are at ease here with us, too!" the queen had remarked.

On 5 September, Christian Frederik raised the subject of money, asking if Andersen had enough to live on. In his diary account of the exchange, itself very stiff, Andersen noted the king's offer ' "to be of assistance to you in furthering your literary endeavours" ', which he courteously turned down. Two days previously, he had recorded a conversation with a civil servant called Rudolf Christiani, who 'wishes that the king would do something for me, that everyone is expecting it' – but pride and resentment of being patronised prevented Andersen from accepting the help which he so much wanted. His diary entry for that day ended in disgruntlement:

> Rantzau, whom I accompanied home, said that the king had indeed been prompting me to make a request, but praised my noble feelings; promised, if the opportunity should arise, to put in a good word for me. I was a little dissatisfied with myself, but put my trust in God.

Later, he did in fact accept a cash gift.

The consolidation of his trust in Count Rantzau was one good thing gained by Andersen during his stay on Føhr, and another was a pressing invitation from Duke Christian August to visit him at Augustenborg Castle on the island of Als. Andersen accepted gladly, spending three weeks there immediately after the Føhr visit. He went with the duke and duchess in their gilded carriage to the Bishop's Palace, and on descending from this grand conveyance, found himself shaking hands with a familiar figure. The Bishop was none other than the former Dean Tetens, who had so reluctantly accepted the washerwoman's son into his confirmation class all those years ago in Odense. It was a moment of sweet satisfaction.

Other meetings were less reassuring. Also present on Als was Prince Frederik of Nør, the duke's younger brother, prince of Schleswig-Holstein-Sønderborg-Augustenborg. Thorvaldsen's bust of the prince as a young man shows him classically good-looking, full-lipped and wavy-haired, but Andersen found himself disturbed by the political movement which this Adonis represented. The Prince of Nør, who was Governor of Schleswig-Holstein, fervently supported the Prussian claim that these large, German-speaking duchies should belong to Germany rather than to Denmark. Andersen probably did not know of the personal Augustenborg bitterness which lay behind this disaffection for the Danish crown, but the fact was that the duke and his brother, who seemed to be grandsons of Christian VII, were the second-generation result of a liaison between the king's wife and Johan Friedrich Struensee, the doctor who had exercised a somewhat Rasputin-like influence in the royal household. The queen, Caroline Mathilde, gave birth to Struensee's daughter, Louise Augusta, who married the Duke of Augustenborg and gave birth to the Prince of Nør and his brother. Because of this illegitimacy (hushed up at the time, though it was not a well-kept secret), the Augustenborg line had no claim to the Danish throne and looked instead to a position of power within the Prussian empire. The Duke of Augustenborg's son, Frederik, did in fact become Friedrich VIII of Prussia.

During his time on Als, Andersen noticed with disquiet that people were not referring to the Danish king as 'his Majesty', but simply as 'the Duke'. The German-speaking population was openly in favour of becoming part of Prussia, and this preference troubled Andersen deeply. He saw that it must lead to conflict between Denmark and Germany, and hated the thought that his own loyalties would be split between the two countries, specially now that he had formed such an affectionate relationship with the ruler of Weimar.

On return to Copenhagen, he found a letter from Carl Alexander awaiting him, and wrote back at once:

> Your Highness can easily imagine my happiness on receipt of your warm and affectionate letter; it was as if we were again together at Ettersburg at the sad moment of parting. You pressed my hand, and said you would be a kind and sincere friend.

For the rest of that autumn, he busied himself with another instalment of stories, this time including 'The Snow Queen', that great fable of icy-heartedness and love, together with 'The Fir Tree'. This tale of the tree chosen for decorating at Christmas and afterwards burned in the yard is imbued with Andersen's new sense that fame and glory were after all transient things. A little boy runs about with the tree's golden star pinned to his chest, but the tree itself lies in ashes. 'Done with! Done with! That's what happens to all stories.'

At about the same time, Andersen also wrote a play, *The Flower of Fortune,* and submitted it to the Royal Theatre. Heiberg rejected it so quickly that Andersen suspected he had not even read it. He went to see Heiberg, who admitted the charge quite cheerfully and added that he could not resist the chance to take a rise out of the hyper-sensitive author. The play did in fact achieve a short run, but Heiberg was right in thinking that drama was not Andersen's medium. The absence of the third-person narrator who is so powerfully present in the stories left them wordy and uncertain, though Andersen never saw this. Of *The Flower of Fortune,* he said in his autobiography:

> I sought to show that it is not the immortal name of the artist nor the splendour of a royal crown which makes a man happy; happiness is found where one is satisfied with little, where one loves and is loved in return.

This shift of emphasis came too late to protect Andersen from a hurtful attack launched early in 1845 by a man he had counted as a friend. Carsten Hauch, in his novel, *The Castle on the Rhine,* included an instantly recognisable portrait of Andersen as a conceited poet, Eginhard, who by the end of the book has gone insane. It was this last element which particularly unnerved Andersen, and in a letter to Ingemann, he revealed the painful truth:

> My own grandfather was mad, my father became mad shortly before he died. So you will understand how the mental collapse of the unfortunate poet in Hauch's novel affects me – his dissolution is a picture of *myself.*

Ingemann, indignant on his friend's behalf, tackled Hauch, who would admit only that one or two of Andersen's characteristics might have crept into the character. As a token of apology, he wrote an appreciation of Andersen's work, but it was a half-hearted affair and did little to dispel Andersen's resentment. Sparked into a new and bitter energy, he wrote a comedy called *The New Lying-in Room* – and this time, letting no one but Jonas Collin and H.C. Ørsted into the secret, he submitted it to the theatre anonymously.

Heiberg fell unsuspectingly for the trick and declared the play a winner in an enthusiastic letter to the quietly chuckling Collin. It ran for a long time to great applause, and the director of the theatre, Privy Councillor Adler, ignorant of the facts, advised Andersen to try something similar, adding, 'but of course it lies quite outside your talents; you are a lyric poet and do not possess the wit of that man.' Andersen meekly agreed, and hid his amusement.

Although Jonas remained reliable and helpful, he and the Collin tribe had been determinedly unimpressed by Andersen's rapturous accounts of his social acceptance in Weimar. Ingeborg, ignoring the fact that her own daughter was about to move into the nobility through her impending marriage to Henrik Stampe, said, 'God! How boring it must have been, with so many famous men', and Jonas himself delivered a magisterial rebuke. Told of Andersen playing a game with Carl Alexander's little son, he remarked, 'I cannot tell you about a life with dukes and duchesses, and I do not crawl about on the floor with their children.' Edvard, who had commented on what a 'hell of a fuss' the Weimar family were making of Andersen, tried to explain in a later letter the reasons for the family's distaste:

> You are popular in Germany, in Weimar you are being spoilt, you are being kissed and hugged by all the distinguished people there. We who are your friends here at home and who do not happen to like the idea of kissing one another, will not melt away in sentimental joy over this, but we are sincerely pleased with the essence of the story, namely, that you are having a success, that you are acquiring friends, who for the time being I shall assume to be true friends, and that altogether you have been happy in this journey of yours.

Edvard, with far more political acumen than his friend, was evidently suspicious that the Weimar connection might crumble if the political tensions should lead to open conflict. He added with some dignity that the Collin family could offer only the humble comfort of the house in Amaliegaden, where Ingeborg teased him and Theodor tickled him and called him '*un pauvre pomme de terre*'. This, he suggested, was why Andersen thought himself despised in Denmark.

In his newly revised scale of values, Andersen was readily chastened, regretting the hubris of the letters he had written from Weimar, and he was doubly touched when, on the Sunday night of 19 May 1845, a messenger came to his door with an urgent summons: 'My dear Andersen, – My wife is very ill. All the children are here. Yours, Collin.' Warmed by his inclusion as a family member, Andersen watched Mrs Collin's death two days later with reverence. It was, he said, 'a great experience in my life'.

There was no longer so much need to impress the family with his success; it was beginning to speak for itself. That year, Andersen's annual stipend was increased to four hundred rixdollars, plus a personal gift from the king of half that amount again, perhaps as a tactful reimbursement for the Føhr visit. Foreign translations of his work were multiplying, including three English versions of his novels by Mary Howitt. She, despite professed fluency in Danish, translated from the German editions, and the sketch which prefaced *The Improvisatore* had been lifted from Marmier's biographical piece. Growing fame, however, did nothing to settle Andersen's restless way of life, and in June he set off once more for a summer of shifting from one aristocratic house to another.

That same month, there appeared in a magazine one of his most powerful stories, 'The Bell'. Ostensibly, this deeply personal parable centres on the mystery of an unseen bell which rings deep in the woods, but this serves merely as a pretext for a symbolic search involving two boys, one a prince and the other poor. It is the underlying theme of almost all Andersen's work, but here, he develops it into an ecstatic ending which is impossible to dissociate from the events of his own life. He was at the time of 'The Bell' filled with joy at finding himself equal in emotional terms with the young nobleman who would one day rule Weimar, and the closing paragraphs of the story give rhapsodic expression to his happiness:

> All nature was a great cathedral: the flowers and the grass were the mosaic floors, the tall trees and drifting clouds were its pillars and heaven itself was the dome. The red glow of the sky was fading, for the sun had set. The millions of stars were lit; millions of tiny diamond lamps. The prince opened his arms to it all; the forest, the ocean and the sky. But at that moment, from the other side of the cliff came the poor boy with his ragged tunic and his wooden shoes. He had arrived almost as quickly by going his own way.

The two boys ran to meet each other. There they stood, hand in hand, in the vast cathedral of nature and poetry; and far above them, the great invisible holy bell sounded in loud hosanna.

While in Germany the previous year, Andersen had told the composer, Giacomo Meyerbeer, about the glories of Jenny Lind's voice, and partially as a result of this, Jenny was to sing in a Christmas season of opera in Berlin. She told Andersen about this during a brief autumn visit to Copenhagen, during which she selected him to be her escort and 'brother' at her own dinner party, and he decided to go to Germany to hear her. 'Jenny is kind and loving towards me,' he wrote in his almanac; 'I'm happy and hopeful – although I know – !'

He set out on the last day of October on a leisurely journey, again staying at the houses of friends, though avoiding Nysø, having quarrelled with Baroness Stampe during the summer. He spent ten days at Glorup, and was frankly bored. After an early dinner between four and five in the afternoon, there was nothing to do but write letters and listen to the sound of a servant playing a flute somewhere, 'badly', as he commented in his diary. Things were not much better downstairs with the family, where he found himself the only one who wanted to converse. 'Miss Lise's stomach rumbles,' he noted sourly. He went on to Augustenborg, where he fell foul of the prevalent political discussions, and took refuge in sitting for a watercolour portrait by Carl Hartmann, who also painted him reading aloud to the ducal family, Prince Frederik of Nør included.

In Hamburg Andersen went to see the illustrator of his stories, Otto Speckter, with whom he was very friendly, and at that time his story, 'The Little Match Girl' appeared in Denmark. He reached Berlin on 19 December and this time was warmly welcomed by the Grimm brothers, with whom he held long discussions on the writing and collecting of folk tales. He dined with Friedrich Wilhelm IV of Prussia, who a week later dubbed him a knight of the Red Eagle – his first decoration. The main point of his visit, however, was to see Jenny Lind, and he took the extraordinary step of getting himself taken on as a member of the chorus so that he might hear her sing at close quarters. This move proved disastrous, for on the first night he was so overcome by the beauty of her performance that he burst into tears on the stage and was dismissed forthwith.

Jenny, who at this time was yearning for Julius Günther, had more concerns than Andersen's welfare. The season was a demanding one, and a multitude of admirers besieged her with social invitations. She forgot to send Andersen the promised ticket for her performance on Christmas Eve, and his diary the following day sounded aggrieved:

> Have heard nothing from Jenny. I feel hurt and sad. She is not like a sister to me in Berlin. If she had wanted me to be a stranger here, she could have told me, and I would have been so. – She did once fill my heart – I do not love her any more. In Berlin she has carved out my sick flesh with a cold knife. I wonder what thoughts are filling her mind since she pays so little attention to me, I who came to Berlin mainly for her sake, I who might have spent a much happier Christmas Eve.

He claimed in *Mit livs eventyr* to have waited in the whole evening, hoping for a message from Jenny, but in fact he went out to a party. Jenny sent him a note the following day, but by this time he was sunk in gloom:

> Is it because she is afraid for her reputation that she pays so little attention to me? "I do not hate you, for I have never loved you," she once told me.

When Jenny Lind realised how offended he was, she seemed surprised, saying she had assumed he was spending his time with kings and princes, but she laid on a little post-Christmas party for him and gave him some eau-de-cologne and a bar of soap in the shape of a piece of cheese. He sensed that he was being patronised, recording irritably that she 'patted me, called me a child' and when on 30 December he did receive a ticket for her performance, he remained unmollified, commenting that 'her voice didn't quite move me'.

For all his pique, Andersen's Christmas was in fact far from lonely. When he got home from Jenny's compensatory party, he found an invitation to dine with the king of Prussia, and set off at three in the afternoon to the palace. 'The king was very gracious,' he noted in his diary for that day; 'talked a lot about *Only a Fiddler*, said that when he was in Copenhagen he had at once asked about me. He wasn't familiar with my tales.' The queen expressed sympathy for the illness of Frederik, the Crown Prince of Denmark, and chatted warmly about other members of the Danish royal family, and the king asked Andersen to call next time he was in Berlin. Altogether, it seems to have been a relaxed, informal evening, uninhibited by the presence of the Lord Chamberlain and other notabilities.

The following day, Andersen sent the king a copy of his stories, and went to see Jenny Lind again. While they were eating ice-cream, a sudden twang sounded from the piano. Andersen demanded to know what note it was, and Jenny, investigating, told him it was a C. He was filled with superstitious terror:

> "My God, Collin!" I exclaimed, and a fear came over me which forced tears into my eyes. I told Jenny the name, saying I had always been scared of visions . . .

On setting out from Copenhagen, Andersen had been perturbed that he had not seen 'beloved father Collin' and given him a farewell kiss. 'I'm so worried that I'll never see him again,' he noted on that day. In fact, by the time Jonas Collin did come to the end of his life, Andersen's whole attitude towards him had changed – but in 1845, he was still shaken by the death of Mrs Collin, and needed all the security his friends could offer.

His moment of alarm soon passed, and he wrote triumphantly to Edvard's wife, Jette Collin, 'I'm a lion, a Berlin lion, a male Jenny Lind, I'm in fashion!' The German aristocracy were flocking round him, Mendelssohn praised his work extravagantly, and publishing houses were competing for rights to his stories. His decoration at the hand of the king on his final day in the city came as the climax of his success. He had hoped to get a similar recognition from his own country, noting on 31 October, the day of his departure, that an audience with the king and queen had been disappointing. 'Did not get it.' He needed royal permission to wear the Prussian order in Denmark, and wrote to Jonas Collin to ask him to intercede with the king, adding, 'if a tiny Knighthood of the Dannebrog were to accompany it, I wouldn't mind.' He added quickly that he was only joking.

There was some political sensitivity about wearing a Prussian order, as even Andersen realised, for hostility between Denmark and Germany was mounting. Meeting the sons of the now-dead Chamisso, he was a little shaken to find the young men in the uniform of Prussian army officers, and was relieved when Henrik Stampe's younger brother, Holger, turned up in Berlin as a safely Danish companion.

From Berlin, Andersen moved on to Weimar, where Jenny Lind had been invited to join them when her concert season ended. He arrived on 8 January 1846, and was from the start in a state of rapture:

> At 10 I went to the hered. grand duke, in those splendid rooms. He came towards me, pressed me to his bosom, kissed me several times, thanked me for my love for him; arm in arm we walked to his room, sat talking for a long time until he was called to the Council of State, then he walked, arm in arm with me, to the furthermost door.

Small signs showed the coolness of the duke's marriage. On 17 January, when he took Andersen to see his little son, Carl August, it was only after Carl Alexander had left the room that his wife came in to greet the visitor. They appeared to lead very separate lives, and during Andersen's visit, the Hereditary Grand Duke asked him to take up permanent residence in Weimar.

In view of the discontent he had so often voiced about his lack of critical acclaim in his own country, it might be thought that Andersen would accept this invitation – but the political implications forbade it. He told his friend that he loved his native land, and Carl Alexander said he would in that case have to alternate between the two countries. He went on, as Andersen's diary noted, "'Give me your hand!" He held it so firmly in his, told me he loved me and pressed his cheek to mine.'

On 22 January, Jenny Lind arrived from Berlin, and that evening there was a grand dinner, to which Andersen was carried in a sedan chair. For such occasions he was dressed in a three-cornered hat and wore a rapier at his side, but most of his conversations with Carl Alexander were conducted in much less formal circumstances. On 7 February, he wrote:

> Went to the hered. grand duke at 8 o'clock in the morning, he received me in his shirt, with only a dressing-gown over it; 'I can do that, we know each other.' He pressed me to his bosom, we kissed one another. "Think of this hour," he said, "as though it were yesterday. We are friends for life." We both wept.

Jenny Lind, meanwhile, was finding life at Weimar a strain. On the day after her arrival, she had been required to sing an evening concert for the sumptuously dressed ladies and gentlemen of the court, and Andersen noted that she

> sat completely alone by a window, looking down at her lap, like an animal waiting to be slaughtered. I stood at the front, next to the hered. grand duke who had pulled me forward. During the Mendelssohn *lieder* Jenny's eyes fell on me, and I think she kept looking in that direction.

One need hardly wonder why. The following morning, when Andersen went to see her accompanied by Beaulieu, Jenny pleaded a headache, and Beaulieu commented as they left that she had not been very gracious.

That night, Jenny was performing again, in a first performance of *Norma*, and at an afternoon concert two days later, Andersen noted that Carl Alexander's wife was almost unbearably moved. She embraced Jenny and kissed her, and Jenny burst into tears. Both women were suffering from emotional strain. The young duchess, watching her husband's possessive behaviour towards Andersen, must have been newly aware of his sexual ambiguity, and Jenny Lind, worked remorselessly hard by her aristocratic hosts, was exhausted. Despite having sung that afternoon, she was due to play the lead in *La Somnambula* that same evening, and this was not untypical of her Weimar schedule. Also, she missed the company of Felix Mendelssohn, with whom she would undoubtedly have been in love had she not suppressed it sternly because he was married. The pair of them enjoyed such empathy that they capped each other's stories and had a private language incomprehensible to anyone else. In the overheated emotional atmosphere of Weimar, she must have longed for his humour and understanding.

Andersen, far from being any help to her, was showing signs of jealousy. The self-styled 'male Jenny Lind' did not like to be upstaged, and on the day following *La Somnambula* he was annoyed that his reading from *Picture Book Without Pictures* was followed by Jenny, who 'had to sing'. His diary is frank about his spleen, though not about its cause:

> I was in a bad mood, said so, was unkind; towards midnight we drove home. I was ill. Beaulieu told me I was falling in love with Jenny; I told

him it wouldn't happen. He told me his own love story, I thought of mine and wept.

Weimar's opulence and formality was riddled with ambiguities. On the day after Jenny Lind left, the Hereditary Grand Duke told Andersen that he wanted the Swedish singer to come and live permanently at the Court as his wife's companion. Had his proposals been accepted, Weimar might have seen a foursome of quite extraordinary decadence and artistry – but Andersen dared not get involved in the political maelstrom which was brewing, and Jenny had fled back to Berlin and Mendelssohn, and at his urging, planned to go on to Vienna.

She wrote a careful letter to Andersen, asking him to convey her thanks to her hosts and praising them for their 'genuine and honest souls', but the following week she admitted in a letter to her guardian that at Weimar she had been 'working like a slave and subjected to the most shameless demands in the world.'

Andersen left Weimar on 7 February and travelled south, without great enthusiasm. He visited Mendelssohn and heard Wagner's *Tannhäuser* overture for the first time, and made contact with Niels Gade, the Danish composer with whom he had long been friendly but who since 1844 had been living in Germany, but nostalgia for Weimar made it hard to be happy anywhere else. Arriving in Rome on the last day of March, he lamented in a letter to Carl Alexander that the city was 'not the Rome of thirteen years ago – everything is modernised, even the ruins.' He moved on to Naples, but even here he was discontent, complaining in the same letter of the 'never-ending Sirocco' and the scorch of the sun.

Naturally enough, his mind ran back to his first visit, and his falling-out with Edvard over *Agnete and the Merman*. Seeing it fresh in the light of his loving friendship with Carl Alexander, Andersen seemed able to acknowledge how furious he had been, yet without the terror of rejection which had at the time so paralysed him. Thinking over it now, he wrote to Edvard on 26 April and raised the '*du*' question once again, to say that if he ever had a son, the boy would refuse to say '*du*' to Edvard's son, young Jonas. Edvard wrote back affably, describing the idea as a piece of 'excellent nonsense', but the theme of revenge had taken firm hold of Andersen's thoughts, and he needed to give tangible shape to this sullen ghost which had lain for so long at the back of his mind.

In the hot Italian sun, the notion of a shadow so sharp-edged and substantial that it could be tripped over was once again part of his thinking, and this provided a persona which could embody all Andersen's long-held fury and resentment. 'The Shadow' is story of violent revenge, featuring its author as the helplessly subservient shadow which at last breaks away from its master and steals his princess-wife. The master is in his turn reduced to a shadow, and the wife and his former dependent agree that he is worthless. Together, they kill him.

The story is packed with personal references, including the spa in which Andersen had joined the Collins before going on to Italy. The shadow is there because, like Andersen, it could not grow a beard until it was turned twenty-five years old. The '*du*' question is raked over exhaustively, and yet the story holds together perfectly in its own terms for the reader who comes to it with no knowledge of the background. The simmering anger gives it a powerful and sinister atmosphere, but raises no curiosity about a more personal underlying truth. Andersen, in this story as in so many others, was a master of self-disguise. He did not shrink, however, from sending the story to Edvard, who refers to it in his later book, *H.C. Andersen and the Collin Family*, with a weary lack of surprise.

In that summer of 1846, Andersen was miserably lonely. He stayed in Naples until 23 June, then took a steamer to Marseille. The crossing was rough and the boat desperately overcrowded, the deck passengers sheltering with their baggage and livestock as best they could under their shackled-down carts, and Andersen, always a nervous sailor, thought he was going to die. He met Ole Bull on the same boat, but merely felt jealous of the violinist's bragging about his popularity in the United States, from which country he had just returned. Bull revealed, too, that Mary Howitt's English translations of Andersen's novels were sold widely in America, the copies having been pirated with no royalties to publisher or author, and this depressed Andersen further.

In France, wilting in the summer heat, he wandered through Nîmes and Arles, took a boat to Sète and went on through Beziers and Perpignan to Vernet, but gave up the idea of crossing the border into Spain and wrote instead to Carl Alexander, declaring himself wretchedly homesick for Weimar. He amends this in *My Life's Fairytale* to a mere desire for cooler weather, declaring himself 'a son of the North, whose flesh, blood and nerves have their roots in the snow and the cold winds'. This sits oddly with his constant grumbling about Danish weather and his yearning for southern sun, but he was understandably careful about what he said concerning his relationships with Weimar and its ruler.

Carl Alexander wrote back at once, suggesting a date for a further visit, and Andersen began to move northward, through Montpellier, Nîmes and Avignon, up the Rhône by river boat to Lyon and thence across Switzerland. From Geneva he took a steamer across the lake to Vevey and paused for some Byronic musing at Chillon, then went on the Fribourg and Berne. During this time he was working intermittently on an autobiography expanded and developed from the pages he had given to Louise Collin so many years ago, and it was now almost finished.

He arrived in Weimar on 19 August and resumed his happy relationship with Carl Alexander, as his diary for the following day confirms:

> In the evening the hereditary grand duke walked arm-in-arm with me across the courtyard of the castle to my room, kissed me lovingly, asked me to love him always as though he were just an ordinary person, asked me to stay with him this winter. – Unhappy me, who in the midst of this great love has the feeling that it cannot possibly last. Fell asleep with the melancholy, happy feeling that I was the guest of this strange prince at his castle and loved by him.

While Andersen was still at Weimar, a letter came from Edvard with an offer to edit the autobiography which had been arriving in instalments from Andersen's various stopping-places in other countries. He would, he said, correct mistakes and copy the whole thing in more legible handwriting. It was a big task, for the book, called in English *The True Story of My Life*, was a long one, and Andersen was overwhelmed with gratitude. On 25 August he wrote back:

> I read your letter last night and learned that you have taken on this work. My God, it's such a terrible lot, whatever can I do for you? I'll never forget this proof of your brotherliness, it's an embrace, it's a kiss, it's a – a "du" pledge; you know what I mean. Thank you!

From this time on, partly because 'The Shadow' had relieved Andersen of a poisonous burden and partly because Edvard had proved himself to be imperturbable and ever-generous, relationships between the two of them settled into a calmer and steadier state. Andersen's passionate letters, though couched in suitably respectful terms, were now reserved for the young duke of Weimar.

On his return from Weimar in 1846, Andersen stopped off in Odense, where he learned that Jette Hanck had died on 19 June. She had been two years younger than himself, full of life and gaiety – and, as the Iversens' granddaughter, she had represented the only real link between Andersen and his Odense childhood. Her two novels, *Aunt Anna* and *The Daughter of an Authoress* did not make her famous, but to Andersen she had been a 'sister' whose irreverent liveliness he had enjoyed, and he missed her.

Ironically, his real sister, Karen Marie, died the following month, on 14 October, though he was probably not aware of it. She died as she had lived, in poverty and obscurity. Peder Kaufmann had been her common-law husband, as the Copenhagen register revealed in its description of him as 'unmarried labourer', and if he was still living, he did not attend her funeral. She was buried in a pauper's grave.

Andersen, by contrast, was now indisputably famous, having on his return to Denmark at last been given his coveted Order of the Dannebrog by Christian VIII. All personal interest apart, the king could hardly do otherwise now that Andersen had been honoured by the Prussian monarch, but Andersen ignored the political implications and busied himself with a new volume of stories. This included the terrifying tale of 'The Red Shoes', centred round a girl called Karen.

Andersen's notes make no reference to his half-sister, ascribing the story to his memory of how his new boots had squeaked during his confirmation, thus distracting his thoughts from a proper contemplation of God. His meeting with Dean Tetens had certainly reminded him of this, for the same incident features in 'The Bell' but this new story, in which the irreverent girl is punished by the new shoes themselves, has a terrible aptness to his thoughts about Karen Marie. The red shoes condemn their wearer to dance endlessly until, in desperation, she goes to the public executioner to cut off her feet – and Andersen could hardly have found a more powerful image with which to lay the ghost of his sister than by stopping her dance for ever.

In the same collection was 'The Jumping Competition', a surprisingly astringent tale about royal favour from a man who had just been knighted by the king. The flea, the grasshopper and the jumping jack compete to produce the highest leap and win the hand of the princess, but this simple structure is full of gritty little asides. The flea, who knows he jumped the highest but lost to the jumping jack who merely hopped into the princess's lap, sighs, 'in this world, it's only appearance that counts'. He joins the army and is killed, leaving the grasshopper to repeat his words. The tale ends with a typical Andersen disclaimer, assuring the reader that the story was told to him by the grasshopper and may for all the author knows be a pack of lies. Far from wanting to step into the limelight as some critics have insisted, he frequently constructed an escape-route through which he could get out of it. The tale suggests a deep and well-hidden resentment, and makes sudden sense if Andersen knew that he himself was of a quality which nobody could or ever would perceive. It is not hard to imagine that in the closed, favour-seeking world of the court, he often felt himself slighted, and if he held an ace card which he knew he must never play, his bitterness is clearly explicable.

In October, Andersen received a letter from William Jerdan, editor of *The Literary Gazette,* telling him how popular his novels were in England. Having felt since his meeting with Ole Bull on the Marseille steamer a little concerned about the handling of his English translations, Andersen wrote back with a strong hint that he would like to come to London. He sent greeting to Ainsworth who had been with him in the Danube quarantine station, and to his translator, Mary Howitt, but in his general cordiality there was one note of dissent. Jerdan was quite wrong, he said, in his comment that Andersen was 'always against the Jews'. In fact, as any present-day reader will be aware, his novels are notably pro-Semitic, often featuring a Jewish heroine and, as in *The Improvisatore,* giving horrified accounts of racial harassment. 'You cannot point out a single passage in which I have uttered any ill-feeling towards that gifted but unfortunate people,' he insisted.

Jerdan's next letter contained a firm invitation to visit London, and Andersen at once began his preparations. Worried about the cost of the visit, he spoke to Edvard about the possibility of pawning a valuable ring – perhaps even the diamond-set one given to him by the king – but Edvard recoiled from the idea, assuring him that credit facilities could be arranged. Through the Danish banker Joseph Hambro, who had gone to England because, as a Jew, he was unable to trade in his own country, Edvard established that Andersen could obtain cash as he needed it, and the king personally offered to provide funds should any financial embarrassment occur. Thus reassured (though he turned down the royal offer with dignity), Andersen set about organising the social side of his visit. English newspapers were contacted to ensure 'a friendly reception', and Baroness Stampe was roped in to give some lessons in basic English. Carl Alexander, too, was approached:

> You, my dear friend, would not wish me to go to England without your distinguished protection. Will your Royal Highness give me a letter to Prince Albert? . . . The house of Weimar is so closely related to the Queen of England that I venture to beg this of your Royal Highness, and trust that you will not be angry.

A postscript conveyed the details of Andersen's proposed journey and ended, 'In Hamburg, at the end of this month, I will find your Royal Highness's letter poste restante, won't I?'

Carl Alexander went one better. He planned to visit London himself, he said, the dates coinciding with those when Andersen would be there. His friend would be welcome to come and visit him every morning between eleven and twelve, at Marlborough House.

The trip was not to take place until the following summer, and Andersen passed the winter months contentedly, working on his wildly ambitious history of the world in verse, *Ahasuerus*. A portrait of him was commissioned by a court official, Jorgen Hansen Koch, (who was married to Jette Wulff's sister, Ida), and Andersen sat for this to the painter C.A. Jensen. The Kochs had been good friends to him ever since his impoverished early days, and he was a frequent visitor to their house.

On 13 May 1847, Andersen went to Glorup on the first stage of his journey to Britain, and spent three weeks there, finishing off *Ahasuerus*. Edvard, on receiving the completed pages, was baffled, and wrote back to say it was either the best thing Andersen had done or it was completely mad. Andersen, serenely convinced of the first interpretation, made his way to Rotterdam, pausing in The Hague for a party to celebrate his presence in Holland, then on 22 June boarded the *Batavier* for the overnight passage to London. He described her as 'a real snail of a ship', and was hardly more complimentary about the passengers:

> A number of emigrants to America were travelling on deck, and the children were romping about merrily. There was a German, as fat as Falstaff, walking up and down with his thin wife who was practically seasick already and was terrified of the moment when we would sail out of the River Maas into the great North Sea. Her greyhound was trembling just as much as she was, even though it had a coat on, tied with big bows.

They had to wait for eight hours for the ebb tide to fill again, and the sun was setting as Andersen retired to his bunk. When he came back on deck in the morning, they were sailing into the Thames estuary, and the river was full of maritime traffic, as his diary records:

> The ships come running under full sail, pluming themselves like swans. Thousands of fishing boats, like a teeming marketplace, like a brood of chicks, like confetti. Steamer after steamer, like rockets in a great fireworks display. At Gravesend it looked like a widespread marsh fire, and it was the smoke from the steamers!

Once disembarked and in London itself, the city astonished him with its congestion. 'All was movement, as if half London was trying to get to one side of the city and the other half to the other', he wrote in *Mit livs eventyr*. He was not impressed by St Paul's, which he said looked more impressive from outside than in, but the small details of London life amused him:

> A gentleman on the street very politely gave me directions! This is a remarkably polite nation, very different from the individual Britons you meet abroad. I was reminded of the insufferable Englishman I put in *A Poet's Bazaar*. – Drove home for the first time in one of those small cabriolets, where the coachman stands on the back and drives the horses . . . Oranges and omnibuses are the only inexpensive things in London.

On the evening of his arrival, Andersen checked in at his hotel, the Sablonière in Leicester Square, a district which, to his embarrassment, he found to be frequented by prostitutes. It was to be his home base throughout his stay in Britain, even though 'the windows had so much soot on them that my sleeves were blackened'. He had chosen the hotel on the recommendation of H.C. Ørsted, who had stayed there when in London, but the Danish ambassador, Count Frederik Reventlow, was somewhat shocked, and advised Andersen to say if asked that he was staying with him.

Andersen went round to Marlborough House on his first morning for a reunion with Carl Alexander, but after the usual hugs and kisses, the young duke confessed that he did not share his friend's enthusiasm for London. In his diary for that day, Andersen sounded concerned for him:

> We sat together; he told me he felt restricted here. It was impossible for him to meet with literary figures; you didn't even dare mention that you wanted to see Lady Blessington. Everything was cliques. Dickens had written in *Punch*, and therefore you couldn't talk to him. They'll die from etiquette, he said. The Queen herself was bound by it two breakfasts and dinner in the evening at eight o'clock. Everyone else was outside in the lovely parks, but the queen had to be home by 8 o'clock. Because of the etiquette she couldn't enjoy herself the way one does in Germany.

It was Andersen's first intimation that England was bound by a class snobbery quite absent from the bohemian freedom of the Continental aristocracy, and he was astonished. Surely, he suggested, the queen could do as she chose? But Reventlow, the Danish ambassador, confirmed Carl Alexander's impression. In England, he explained, royalty did not associate with artists. He confessed that he himself found the lack of democracy tiresome. His own quarters were in a street barred to the common people except for necessary deliveries, and he recounted with some pleasure that a cow had slipped and fallen outside his house on one occasion, thus giving a splendid excuse for non-diplomatic persons to come in and stare.

Reventlow advised Andersen to pick carefully among the many invitations that had come in. At one man's house he might find a well-laden table, at another's, the best of company; this was a society in which it did not pay to be modest. Andersen, by virtue of his fractured English and his strange, foppish appearance, managed to move through London society with ease, greeted as an exotic foreign guest wherever he went, and he noted with surprise that the eminent 'D'Israeli' did not enjoy the same universality of welcome.

Jenny Lind was also in London, living in Clairville Cottage, Old Brompton, which Andersen thought 'infinitely far out', though he liked the 'lovely little garden with mown grass, flowers and shady paths'. She promised him a ticket for the opera, which in London was 'ridiculously expensive' at something between three and five pounds - which, by the standards of the day, it was. Despite an invitation to come and eat with her whenever he chose, Andersen saw little of the singer during his visit.

He was, however, grateful for the opera ticket, as he was running short of cash and noted on 30 June that he had borrowed two sovereigns from Grímur Thomsen, a young Icelandic author. A first meeting with Hambro reassured him, for the banker confirmed that open-ended credit was available. Andersen told him that Mary Howitt had been to see him and offered ten pounds for translation rights of his new works, and Hambro was outraged by the paltry sum mentioned. He would, he said darkly, 'take care of the matter'.

With the Howitts, Andersen had fallen into something of a literary wasps' nest. Mary Howitt and her husband William had learned German while living for a few years in that country, and had now set up what amounted to a translation industry, largely based on re-translation of German editions in the case of Scandinavian authors. As Mary herself observed in her autobiography, 'We are like a piece of machinery that works well; one day is just like another, week after week, month after month . . . ' A Puritan by upbringing, she was not merely careful about money but fanatically mean with it, and in Germany had sacked all her servants after working out that she and her family could live more economically by eating at cheap hotels. She was notably crisp in her opinions of authors and, writing to her sister, Anna as she had done about the efficient Howitt machinery, she said, 'I am tired of Sir Walter Scott and his imitators, and I am sick of Mrs Hemans's luscious poetry, and all her tribe of copyists . . . a thousand books are published, and nine hundred and ninety nine are unreadable.' When her husband had been writing his book on *The Rural and Domestic Life of Germany*, begun after only a few weeks' residence in that country, she was clear about their purpose in being there, explaining to Anna:

We can perceive that it will be both new and rich, and will in the end make an excellent return, still our want of the language must of necessity keep us working for the first six months for nothing . . . My thought is therefore to begin a series of translations for some periodicals and thus combine the two objects.

Compared with such beady-eyed business acumen, it is hardly surprising that the preface to her translation of Andersen's autobiography sounded a little over-fulsome:

No literary labour is more delightful to me than translating the beautiful thoughts and fancies of Hans Christian Andersen. My heart is in the work, and I feel as if my spirit were kindred to his, just as our Saxon English seems to me eminently fitted to give the simple, pure, and noble sentiments of the Danish mind.

The book was published by Longmans while Andersen was in London, entitled *The True Story of My Life,* but he was irritated to see that Mary Howitt's preface ended with a public statement that she had arranged through her publisher to pay Mr Andersen 'a certain sum'. Even more annoyingly, she had, without consulting Andersen, dedicated the book to Jenny Lind. This abrogation of what should be a very personal gesture seems to have confirmed Andersen's growing dissatisfaction, and, with Hambro and Richard Bentley, who had published his previous novels and was prepared to cap the Longman offer of ten pounds, he drove down to The Hays, the Howitts' house in Clapton, in early July. There, he said in some embarrassment that he did not want to talk about money to 'such a good friend', and handed over the negotiations to the professionals.

Hambro and Bentley did indeed 'take care of the matter', and Mary Howitt was furious. She sent Andersen a series of letters, alternately cajoling and peremptory, demanding that he pay her a further visit on his own, but when he reluctantly did so, several weeks later on 31 July, a Saturday, the occasion was not a pleasant one. That very morning, Andersen received a note from Charles Dickens, the much-admired hero-figure whom he had met briefly a few days previously, suggesting a call at two o'clock. Obliged to turn this down, Andersen set off in a bad temper and accompanied by Hambro on the bus to Clapton where 'we ate, rather modestly'. The assembled company then went in an overcrowded one-horse carriage to see a friend of the Howitts', where children flocked round Andersen as he sat 'in a sun-hot gazebo making picture cut-outs'. He felt himself neglected by the adult company and 'got very nervous and had to lie down on a sofa. Was fearful and profoundly exhausted.'

These scant diary excerpts evoke only too clear a picture of the veiled English hostilities and Andersen's inability to deal with them except through what must have appeared to be a fit of the sulks. C.R. Wooding, in his somewhat sycophantic biography of the Howitts, described the Dane as 'a wearing egotist', clearly being guided by Mary Howitt's contention that Andersen was offended because the children had gone to play with someone else. In fact, she herself was probably annoyed by Hambro's presence. Having written to Andersen in the heat of their previous meeting to tell him she was withdrawing her translation services, the purpose of her pressing second invitation can only have been to attempt a re-negotiation without the presence of his business advisers, for she was too shrewd not to realise that she had thrown away a valuable client.

From that time on, Mary Howitt ceased to praise Andersen's 'beautiful thoughts and fancies', and referred to him in disparaging terms. In *The Literature and Romance of Northern Europe,* published in 1852, she described him as 'but an average sample of a numerous and giant race', and poured scorn on his 'sighing after princes'. In her autobiography, Mary Howitt excused her loss of the translation rights to Andersen's work by saying that she had been 'deeply engrossed in other literary work', but admits that her decision had been foolish. As she had remarked in a letter to her sister, 'Everything in the literary world is done by favour and connections' – and that summer, Andersen's connections were rather better than hers, for he was the lion of London society.

Andersen himself admitted later in a letter to Carl Alexander that he had found the fuss 'so excessive that I could bear it no longer'. At Lord Palmerston's he had felt faint with heat and exhaustion and was irked that he could not get away until two-thirty in the morning, and a party given by Lady Duff-Gordon was equally tiresome:

> I had to speak English. Lady Stanley spoke Italian with me. Got into a bad mood because I was no linguist, and went home. There were no carriages to be found; a servant went after one.

Carl Alexander was forced by protocol to ignore his friend when appearing in public. Andersen saw him from a distance at the opera, in a box with Queen Victoria. Overcome with heat or impatience, Andersen went out in the third act, glancing up to make an explanatory gesture of fanning himself, and the young duke had 'nodded slightly'.

Gradually Andersen began to withdraw from the excesses of society life, turning down invitations and spending more time with people of his own choosing. Grímur Thomsen was a fairly constant companion, and so was Charles Boner, Andersen's new translator. An author himself, he had taken a liking to the lanky Dane, and together they went to see publishers and booksellers, viewing London from the top deck of omnibuses and taking a river trip to Hampton Court.

Andersen's meeting with Charles Dickens took place at Lady Blessington's house which, despite its grandeur and its 'servants in silk stockings and with powdered hair', acted as a meeting-place for artists and writers. In *Mit livs eventyr*, he still sounded impressed by the occasion:

> We shook hands, looked deep into each other's eyes, talked and understood each other. We went out onto the verandah, and I was so moved and delighted to be speaking to the one living English author I loved more than any other that tears came to my eyes.

Lady Blessington, too, was a favourite of Andersen's, being the first person who had taken the trouble to make sure he understood what she was saying. She was, he said, 'so careful to speak slowly, held me by the wrist firmly and looked me in the eyes all the time at every word.' However, he found himself in trouble a few days later when he commented at Lady Duff Gordon's on how moved Lady Blessington had been by Jenny Lind's performance in *La Somnambula*. There was a collective gasp of outrage from the assembled ladies, and the blundering Dane was given to understand that a woman who lived in open sin with her son-in-law as Lady Blessington did was far too coarse a creature to pass opinions on someone as pure as Jenny Lind. Andersen, who had merely thought of Lady Blessington as a kind of English Madame de Stael, was perplexed and irritated. The English class system baffled him completely.

On 17 July, Andersen left the Leicester Square hotel and went to stay with Hambro at his 'place in the country'. There was a hint of tension in his diary entries there:

> Thursday, July 22nd. Am beginning to feel like going into town. "Just give your laundry to the maid, if you have any!" Hambro said. I gave it to her, and today I got the bill . . . Bad mood because people in Denmark don't make enough of me. Beautiful sunset. Toothache.

Back at the Sablonière on the following day, Andersen was mildly annoyed that Reventlow had not got him a ticket for the close of Parliament, but happening to run into the author, Leigh Hunt, whom he had met a few days previously, he found himself taken into a Whitehall building from which he had a good view of the procession:

> Queen Victoria arrived in a tremendously large, old-fashioned carriage with colossal figures on it and gilding all over. She was in white satin. Prince Albert and a few others were in the carriage . . .

For some reason, all this had the effect of making Andersen agitated and upset:

> I was so nervous that I could hardly stand, threw myself into a carriage, came home, ate, drank beer and got the most appalling toothache. While I was lying on the sofa, the famous tragedian Macready came; I didn't recognise him, out of my head with pain, sent him packing and then realised who he was. I was terribly upset; tried to take a short walk but was quite disorientated by my feverish toothache.

The following day, he drove to Macready's but found that he was away from home; Hambro told him of a letter from Mary Howitt in which she said she was deeply offended – and Carl Alexander had gone back to Weimar, leaving a note in which he regretted that he and Andersen had not said goodbye to each other.

The next day was a depressing British Sunday. Despite having received an invitation from the Athenaeum Club as 'the famous traveller', Andersen admitted in his diary that he was tired of London. Its stark social contrasts disturbed him, as his entry for that day revealed.

Yesterday a neatly dressed man was standing with some children – five of them, each one smaller than the next – all of them in mourning and holding bunches of matchsticks. Was it a plan to attract attention? I don't think so. People glanced at them and went on.

By the time he came to write his later biography, *Mit livs eventyr*, Andersen had understood a little more about British poverty and the restrictions laid on its expression:

> I remember beggars, both men and women, who carried on their breasts a large, stiff piece of paper on which was written the words, "I am dying of hunger. Have pity on me." They dare not speak, for they are not allowed to beg, and so they glide past like shadows. They stop in front of people and stare at them with an expression of hunger and sadness on their pale, thin faces. They stand outside cafés and restaurants, choose one of the people sitting there and stare fixedly at them with such eyes, oh, such eyes as only misery can give. Then a woman might point at her sick child and at the words which are written across her breast – "I have not eaten for two days." I saw many of them, and yet I was told that there were only a few in my district, and none at all where the rich people lived; that part of the town was closed to the poor race of pariahs. Everything in London is turned into business; so is begging . . .

and, with hindsight, he concluded that the black-clad man and his five children were showing a certain professionalism in their desperation.

Before his departure, Carl Alexander had invited Andersen to visit Weimar, but Hambro had also offered to pay his fare on a trip to his house in Edinburgh and a tour of the Scottish Highlands. Andersen was badly torn – but his desire to see Scott's birthplace, combined with the generosity of Hambro's offer, tipped the balance in favour of Scotland. The decision made, he spent a few days with Richard Bentley at his house in Sevenoaks. Coming back with Bentley on 6 August, he was confronted in Bromley, Kent, with all the razzmatazz of a General Election – the first he had seen, but which he predicted in *Mit livs eventyr* would probably become a feature of his own country:

Amid the crowds of people men were walking about with voters' lists on their backs and chests so that people could read the names on them. Banners were waving, and were carried about in procession. Scarves and great flags with slogans were waving from wagon-loads of voters. Shouting and yelling, crowds of badly dressed people went past in elegant carriages, often with elaborately dressed servants; it looked as if the gentry had fetched the meanest of their servants, as though it were the old heathen festival where the masters wait on their slaves. Around the platform is a throng of people and a clamour of voices, and sometimes rotten oranges and even carrion are thrown at the speakers.

Andersen had expected to set off for Scotland the following day, but Hambro was ill with a gastric infection and could not travel. Killing time in London, Andersen wrote his customary quantity of letters and grumbled that a sovereign for the opera was more than he could afford. The hotel, too, was costing him a pound a day, 'so nothing has been gained by the free trip'. On the 'terribly boring' Sunday of 8 August, he noted:

Did not visit Jenny Lind to say goodbye, though I might have done. What a mystery I am to myself! Wrote her a farewell note.

Carl Alexander – or even the King of Denmark – had perhaps put in a word for him with the royal couple, for Andersen received an invitation from the Court Secretary, Dr S. Meyer, to join Prince Albert and the queen at Adverikie, their holiday residence in Abbotsford, near Loch Laggan. There had already been a suggestion that he might visit them on the Isle of Wight, but Andersen had declined on the grounds that he was exhausted. Considering his enthusiasm for the crowned heads of Europe, his reaction to the British monarchy was strangely muted. His diary contains so little reference to these invitations that the reader is left guessing as to his real feelings. A visit to Knole while he was with Bentley in Sevenoaks provoked the comment that Henry VIII looked 'bestial' and certainly the snobbish, essentially philistine London social set had repelled him with its bitchiness and prejudice. One gets the impression that he found the royal invitation to Abbotsford embarrassing, but could not bring himself to square up to a refusal. As he set off for Edinburgh with Hambro, who was still unwell and beginning to suffer from gout, he had still made no decision.

After a night spent at the Black Swan in York, breaking a railway journey which had begun on 10 August, the pair went on through the town by bus, picking up their train journey on the north side of the river, since the railway viaduct had not yet been completed. Travel in England, Andersen noted, was like everything else, dominated by questions of class. He and Hambro had missed 'an express train put on for gentlemen who were going hunting with their dogs in Scotland' and now had to compete with the commoners:

> All the first class carriages were occupied, and so we had to travel in the second class which is as bad as can be imagined, with wooden seats and shutters like those which other countries have in their fourth class. The track was not finished over some of the deep valleys . . . we could look down through the open timber-work to the depths below where people were working on the river bed.

At Berwick, too, there was a break in the track, but the travellers reached Edinburgh that night, although a lot of people got off before the final tunnel, being convinced that it might collapse.

Hambro's son, Carl Joachim, met the pair on arrival, and looked after Andersen well in the following days, escorting him round the city and introducing him to some of the Scottish literati. Among them was Elizabeth Rigby, a veteran of the Grand Tour who had written extensively about her travels. Her diary entry for that day is hardly flattering in her impression of the visiting Dane. She described him as:

> a long, thin, fleshless man, wriggling and bending like a lizard with a lantern-jawed, cadaverous visage. Simple and childlike, and simpletonish in his manner.

It is a mark of Andersen's curious ability to charm that even this beady-eyed critic admitted later that he seemed very affectionate. 'No wonder he finds people kind; all stiffness is useless with him, as he is evidently a simple child himself.' It was perhaps part of his self-disguise that the watchful, shrewd observer lying behind the simplicity so often remained undetected.

During his stay in Edinburgh, Andersen was invited to the house of Dr James Young Simpson, professor of obstetrics, who would twelve years later deliver a child in Castle Street called Kenneth Grahame. Simpson was much in the public gaze for having pioneered the use of chloroform in childbirth. The idea of gas anaesthesia was not new, for Sir Humphrey Davy had explored the pain-relieving properties of nitrous oxide as long ago as 1799, and ether had been used by an American surgeon for an operation in 1842 – but to Andersen and his fellow-guests, these magic agents were more a fascinating novelty than a scientific breakthrough. Simpson was happy to demonstrate their effect, and Andersen watched in some horror as two of the lady novelists present took ether and 'laughed with open, dead eyes'.

He was happier with the more conventional aspects of Edinburgh, which, he said, reminded him of Athens in its setting. He particularly enjoyed a visit to Heriot's Hospital, then an orphanage for poor boys, and was touched when the porter assured him that all the young inmates were familiar with his work. The man had been surprised that it was Andersen, rather than the white-haired Hambro, who was the famous author, and said with Scottish frankness that well-known people were usually either old or dead.

The Hambro family took him on the promised tour of the more accessible fringes of the Highlands, through Stirling and Callander and by steamer down Loch Katrine, where he encountered the 'little white gnats' known to all Scottish travellers. The midge-plagued track that led across the hill to Loch Lomond was a rough one, and although the tourists were in a carriage, the driver walked beside his horse and requested his passengers to get out and walk whenever the downward slope became dangerously steep.   Andersen noted a little apprehensively that people seemed wilder in Scotland, reminding himself that they were Celts. He was appalled by the unexpected expenses of the journey – 'every other minute a two-shilling toll for our carriage.' Landlords of the large estates were evidently beginning to cash in on the tourist trade.

From Loch Lomond they returned to Dumbarton – and there Andersen woke the following morning to the full bleakness of the Scottish Sunday. 'No one on the street; doors closed; curtains closed in most houses. They are reading the Bible or getting drunk. Scotland is the only country where there is no train service on Sundays.' At this point, Andersen's indecisiveness about the royal invitation began to cause him trouble. The Hambros, evidently assuming that he would be making his way to Abbotsford, went on to the spa town which was their destination and left him to his own devices. He always hated the departure of friends, and finding himself alone in Dumbarton on a Sunday was particularly unpleasant. He had heard during the tour that Louis-Philippe of France had been killed – a baseless rumour, as it turned out – and had promptly assumed his own problem to be solved. The queen and Prince Albert would have to go to the funeral, so there could be no question of his visit. On learning that Louise-Philippe was alive and well, his dilemma was worse than ever, for his failure to reply was highly discourteous, and he now had either to arrive unannounced at the royal residence or make a rapid apology. He wrote in desperation to Dr Meyer to ask his advice, giving Glasgow as a poste-restante address.

Two days later, no reply arrived. Andersen hung about in Glasgow, which he had begun to dislike because of his difficulties, and on 24 August was round at the Post Office as soon as it opened in the morning – but Meyer was in fact still in the Isle of Wight and had not received his letter. 'Desperate,' Andersen wrote in his diary that day, 'and in a morbid frame of mind, gave up the trip to Loch Laggan. Wrote my regrets to Meyer.' He then paid a reluctant twelve shillings for a first-class seat on the train from Glasgow to Edinburgh, and booked himself into the North British hotel, which stands just above Waverley station. He seemed hardly able to believe that he had deprived himself of going to Abbotsford, for this, all royal interest apart, was where Sir Walter Scott lay buried in the ruins of Dryburgh Abbey, a place he had specially wanted to visit. His continuing diary entry records a kind of mental paralysis:

> I have enough money, but no desire to travel any more. I'm longing for home and work. When you must make a decision, sometimes you feel as if you are in a magic circle. You are aware of thinking, "I can; I will do it," but you are held by invisible bonds; you are faced with a struggle. You are at the outer limits of your freedom, the limits set by God.

The next morning, he still seemed bound by those limits, even though he toyed again with the thought of retracing his steps and heading north for Abbotsford. He 'wandered aimlessly' round the streets for a while, then found himself buying a ticket for London. Once on the train, his agony was completed by reading a newspaper report that he had accepted an invitation from the queen to join her at Abbotsford. In a sweat of embarrassment, he spent the night in Newcastle, still wondering whether he should go back, and boarded the London train. Never one to suffer in silence, he had told his fellow-passengers from Edinburgh who he was, and they assured him gleefully on meeting again that the Scottish papers were full of his intended visit to Her Majesty. Even *Punch* had received what was evidently a Court hand-out and had written up the impending visit with some venom, remarking that in order to win royal favour, one evidently had to be a poet from 'some dirty little Duchy on the Continent'.

Andersen was so distraught that he almost hoped there would be a train accident. In London, he crawled into the Sablonière, where he was received with open arms, and, inconsolable, went round to see Rudolphe Bielke – a Court official who had previously been helpful – where he burst into tears.

A letter from Dr Meyer arrived the next morning, regretting that he had been delayed in the Isle of Wight. Andersen had been wise not to risk his health, he went on smoothly; the weather in Scotland had been dreadful. A letter from Prince Albert would assuredly follow.

It did not, but the trauma was over, and Andersen's spirits rebounded when he again made contact with Charles Dickens. On the tiresome day when the visit to Mary Howitt had prevented their meeting, Dickens had left a complete set of his works for Andersen, inscribed 'from his friend and admirer', and such a token seemed to offer an open door. Andersen wrote a pleading letter to the Dickens family home in Broadstairs, explaining in his mis-spelt English that he would be in the Royal Oak Hotel in Ramsgate the day before his return to Denmark. To see Dickens and thank him would be 'the last flower for me in the dear England!'

Dickens duly invited Andersen to supper with his family in Broadstairs, and in the morning walked to Ramsgate to see the Danish author off on the boat. 'He was the last person to shake my hand in England,' Andersen's diary recorded proudly. And then, with what seemed like a sigh of relief, he headed for Germany and the comforts of Weimar.

Andersen's trip to Britain had done nothing to improve his reputation in Denmark – rather the reverse. Goldschmidt's *The Corsair* had carried a sarcastic piece about 'Andersen, the Lion', accompanied by biting cartoons depicting him as a grovelling toady. Edvard Collin had shown William Jerdan's enthusiastic report of Andersen's visit to the editor of *Berlingske Tidende*, a Danish newspaper named after its founder in 1745, suggesting that he might reprint it from the *Literary Gazette*. He was met with a firm refusal – not, the editor explained, through any malice, but because Jerdan had equated Andersen's greatness with that of Jenny Lind, and such a ludicrous overstatement would make him a laughing-stock in Denmark.

This assessment seems to have been right, for Andersen had only been back in Copenhagen a few hours when a mortifying incident occurred. Looking out of his window, he saw two well-dressed men pass by:

> They saw me, stopped, laughed, and one of them pointed up and said in such a loud voice that I could hear every word, "Look! There's our orang-outan who's so famous abroad!"

By contrast, the modest Jonas Collin had been made a titular privy councillor, and H.P. Holst, who had been Andersen's somewhat reluctant companion in Rome before Andersen's Greek trip, had been knighted for his services to poetry.

On 4 November, Felix Mendelssohn died. His disintegrating health had been partly responsible for Jenny Lind's preoccupied mood in London, for she knew, as Andersen must also have done, that the composer had been so distressed to hear of the sudden death of his beloved sister in May of that same year, 1847, that he himself had lost consciousness, having suffered a stroke from which he never fully recovered. Although he had written the F minor String Quartet that summer during a period of remission, a further attack in September led to his death in under two months. Jenny Lind, grieving for him even before he died, had told Andersen in London that she would never be the same again.

Ahasuerus appeared on 16 December 1847. If Andersen had intended this ambitious verse drama to be a clinching proof of his status as one of the world's great writers, it failed abysmally. He had talked to Oehlenschläger about the idea before he started writing, and the wise old professional had warned him not to attempt it. 'There are such things as form and limits, and one has to respect them,' he advised – but Andersen had ignored him. When he sent Oehlenschläger a copy of the finished book, it earned him a sharp reproof:

> The whole work makes an unpleasant and disorderly impression on me; you must forgive me for putting it so bluntly . . . the entire structure consists of aphorisms, fragments, sometimes stories, all of which are loosely connected. It seems to me that there is too much pretension and too little achievement in this poem.

Andersen reproduced his long letter in its entirety in *Mit livs eventyr,* but persisted in defending *Ahasuerus* as a new stage in his development. Early in January 1848, the king asked Andersen to come and take tea with him, and bring something to read. It was not an unusual request, for he had long been on easy terms with the older man who could have been his father, but this time, as Andersen read, he knew that his listener's vitality was failing, and realised with distress that this might be the last time the two of them would meet. Christian VIII was suffering from kidney cancer. Some theorists hold that an early diagnosis of this lay behind his sudden decision to ensure Andersen's welfare in 1844, on Als during the last holiday he took – and now, his remaining days were running out.

The king died on 20 January. He had ruled for only nine years, a steady, far-sighted monarch who had wisely retreated from the nervy absolutism of his predecessor, Frederik VI. They had been good years for Andersen, whose relationship with the king was warm and familiar. He put no thoughts on paper, but Christian VIII remained in his mind for a long time, referred to months later with regret.

The king's death cut the bonds on the demand for democracy which had been swelling in Denmark as it had in the rest of Europe.

Christian VIII had been riding this turbulent force with a light hand, yielding to the liberalism of such men as Anders Sandøe Ørsted (brother of the physicist who so strongly influenced Andersen), well aware that his predecessor had come close to causing an embarrassing high-level rebellion in his move to censor the press, which he had been forced to drop. Had Christian lived longer, the new Constitution which was being prepared might have been less confrontational; as it was, his son 'Fritz' (Frederik VII) was left to sign a document which attempted, hopelessly, to bind the duchies of Schleswig and Holstein to Denmark.

The revolutionary urge which was infiltrating Europe in the wake of the French upheaval was essentially nationalistic in character, and the southern duchies seized the opportunity of Christian's death to demand their independence.

Frederik, often written off as 'the mad king' had none of his father's rational intellectualism. He had charm and could always say the right thing to the right person, which caused him to be known in his own time as Frederik the Popular, but he was essentially a lightweight, quite unable to withstand the huge cultural and political authority of Germany. As tension between the two countries rapidly worsened, Andersen, like almost every educated Dane, grieved that the land of Goethe and Schiller and the great composers was closing off and becoming a hostile camp. For years, young Danes of the upper classes, together with the odd maverick like Andersen and Thorvaldsen, had assumed it a vital part of their education to study in Munich or Dresden, Dusseldorff or Weimar, or at least to become familiar with these places on the long trek to Rome, and now, impending war threatened to block off this great cultural hinterland and set friend against friend.

On 22 February, revolution broke out in Paris for two violent days, followed by an uprising in Vienna on 13 March. Widespread famine throughout Europe brought the desperation of starving people to explosion point, and Schleswig-Holstein followed the Viennese example two days later when it staged armed insurgence. Two men whom Andersen knew well were leaders of the revolt; one was the Prince of Nør and the other was his brother, the Duke of Augustenborg, who went to Germany to enlist military support for the rebel movement. Andersen watched in horror as the Prince of Nør, too impatient to wait for the results of his brother's mission, launched an armed attack on the Danish garrison of Rendsburg. German troops supported him, precipitating a war which would rumble on for the next three years.

Lord Palmerston, whom Andersen had met in London, is reputed to have remarked years later that only three men ever fully understood the Schleswig-Holstein conflict; 'One was Prince Albert, who is dead, the second was a German professor who went mad. I am the third – and I have forgotten it.' For Andersen, no such levity was possible. To him, it was an agonisingly intimate war, and the thought of Weimar was particularly painful. Only six months previously, on 4 October 1847, he had written an ecstatic letter to Carl Alexander about his recent visit. Following his trip to Britain had come

> the beautiful days at Ettersburg, with our reunion, our life together there, and our parting. Yes, yes, my noble friend, I love you as a man can only love the noblest and best. This time I felt that you were still more ardent, more affectionate to me. Every little trait is preserved in my heart. On that cool evening, when you took your cloak and threw it round me, it warmed not only my body, but made my heart glow still more ardently.

With the death of Christian VIII, Andersen had suffered a great loss of warmth and friendship. The visits to Amalienborg stopped, and there were no invitations from the new king, a man three years younger than Andersen himself, to come and read.

Carl Alexander's father, the Grand Duke, awarded Andersen the Order of the White Falcon in February 1848, as if in a token of faith before the conflict which was boiling up. At almost the same time, Andersen, together with Oehlenschläger's son William, was honoured with the Swedish Order of the North Star. Oehlenschläger himself gave Andersen as a personal present the miniature replica of his own Danish North Star, confirming his affection and admiration despite his criticism of *Ahasuerus*. Andersen was touched by all this, but the assurances of friendship which they represented seemed a frail defence of decency in the face of what was happening all round him. The Prince of Nør's intervention had led to the Battle of Schleswig on 24 April, leaving countless dead and wounded, and ten days later, Andersen wrote to Carl Alexander in anguish:

> Denmark, my native country, and Germany, where there are so many

whom I love, are standing opposed to each other in enmity! Your Royal Highness will comprehend how much all that pains me! I believe so firmly in the nobility of all men, and feel certain that if they only understood each other, everything would blossom in peace . . . How is it in Weimar? When shall we meet, my noble friend? Perhaps never again! And as I think this, all the dear memories of every hour of our life together, the warmth of our meetings, flash through my mind, and my heart melts.

In a kind of horrified fascination, Andersen set off for Glorup shortly after writing this letter. The manor was not far from the scene of the action, and his journalistic instincts prompted a first-hand view of what was going on. A week before the disastrous battle had taken place, he had written a vivid account of Denmark's preparations for war and sent it to Jerdan, well aware that it would be printed in the *Literary Gazette*. In this piece, he had been forthright about the treachery of the Duke of Augustenborg who, despite his support for the German attack on the Danish garrison, had turned and fled in the thick of battle, enraging the troops on both sides. The Moltke mansion of Glorup, on Funen, just north of Schleswig, was visited frequently by officers who had taken part in the action, and Andersen's diary was full of appalling details:

> Heard a good deal about the battle; the men shot in the chest or head lying as if they were asleep; those shot in the abdomen had been almost unrecognisable because their faces were so convulsively distorted with pain. One had lain literally 'biting the dust' with his teeth; his hands had been clutching at the turf.

Some of the stories were about men whom Andersen knew personally. The artist Johan Lundbye, thirty years old, died with tragic absurdity as he leaned on his rifle, which went off when a passing farmer happened to trip over it. Lieutenant Høst wept as he told the story.

The defeated and disorganised Danes were scattered across the countryside and found scant hospitality from frightened villagers who feared Prussian reprisals if they offered food or shelter. The invading troops were pillaging their way across the land, and Andersen wrote on 24 May to his publisher, Richard Bentley, in the hope of stimulating British sympathy:

> You will know that the Prussians have penetrated into the country itself, have occupied Jutland and are daily requisitioning foodstuff, wine and tobacco, are sending out troops to take away whole herds of horses, cloth from the factories, in short, they are oppressing this poor country in the harshest possible way, impounding the civil servants if they refuse to give in to their demands. And just in these last few days – this really is the limit – they have levied a forced contribution of four million rixdollars, to be paid before May 28th, otherwise it will be extorted by the power and terror of war! Jutland cannot pay this sum, not even half of it can be found; so the Prussians intend to plunder and set the towns on fire. That such things can happen in our time, that such things can happen in civilised nations, seems to me like a nightmare.

He went on to make a passionate appeal to Britain for help, and it may have been that his intervention had some effect on public opinion, for, having seen Sweden and Norway lend their support, the British government, together with Russia, weighed in on the side of Denmark. The Prussian leaders prudently withdrew their troops and refrained from pressing the demand for four million rixdollars, and an armistice in September brought about a fragile and uneasy peace.

In that same month, Andersen's new novel, *The Two Baronesses,* was published in England, two months prior to its appearance in Denmark. While in London, he had realised that the only way to stop the pirating of his work in unauthorised translations was to corner the market with an original publication, and from that time on, this became his standard practice. That international copyright became established was largely due to the campaigning of Charles Dickens, but it was Richard Bentley who had prompted Andersen to his self-protecting course of action.

Andersen himself sent Dickens a copy of his new book. He had already sent him his latest collection of tales, dedicated to Dickens and entitled *A Christmas Greeting to my English Friends,* but this had elicited no response, and neither did the new book. Until prompted by Andersen nine months later, the great man remained silent. It may well have been that he found himself unable to say much about *The Two Baronesses,* even if he read it, for the book is completely lacking in all the qualities which Dickens regarded as valuable. Its storyline is wandering and confused, without humour or identifiable characterisation, and its heroine is so closely modelled on Jeanie Deans in Scott's *Heart of Midlothian* as to border on pastiche. Andersen's diary records his reading of this novel on 17 May 1848, early in the writing of his own book.

As a mosaic of elements from his own life, *The Two Baronesses* holds a certain interest to present-day readers. The usual theme of making good from poverty-stricken origins is there, together with the friendships between young men, a shoemaker called Hansen, a girl who wears Hansen's red boots, a childhood dream of living in castles, a child with a wonderful voice and a reference to the magnificent acting of Johanne Heiberg. It may have been Jonna Drewsen's pending elevation to the rank of baroness through her engagement to Henrik Stampe which had sparked off the idea of a contrast between the young woman of non-aristocratic background and the older, more secure one, but numerous role-models have been suggested. Whatever its origins, the plot is so diffuse and lacking in organisation that it fails to hang together. Despite these shortcomings, the book was lighter in tone than Andersen's previous novels, and proved popular. Heiberg even went so far as to send its author his congratulations.

During the summer months of 1848, discontent continued to simmer in Schleswig-Holstein, the German-speaking inhabitants having been denied their wish to break away from Denmark, and Andersen saw that the armistice could not hold much longer. He wrote to Carl Alexander, voicing his fears that the duchies, already unwilling to abide by the terms of the peace settlement, would explode into further violence – 'then we will have no postal connection in winter at all'. His concerns were always essentially personal.

Without apparent awareness that his friend's allegiances lay with the other side, Andersen's letter went on to give a description of the Swedish detachment that had been billeted on Count Moltke of Glorup while he had been there. He made it sound more like a cultural delegation than an army. There had been, he said:

> a colonel, eight officers, a chaplain, a surgeon and forty bandsmen, besides a large number of soldiers . . . the officers are still cultured and mostly talented men (I met a pianist among them, a friend of Liszt). Every day the band played during dinner, and there were promenade concerts for the whole neighbourhood in the long avenues of the garden.

The Swedes had not actually engaged in the war, since the armistice had been declared shortly after their arrival, but they gave a hand with the harvest in the absence of so many Danish men, and were warmly welcomed.

At the end of that troubled year, Andersen was commissioned by the Royal Theatre to write a play for performance at its hundredth jubilee gala. After his years of struggle and disappointment in the theatrical world, it was a touching gesture of confidence, and Andersen produced a patriotic piece called *The Groundwork of Art,* in which he claimed that Denmark's greatness lay in her collective intellectual power rather than in military strength. It was an elegant explanation of his country's losing situation in Schleswig-Holstein, and the play ran to great public acclaim.

On 3 April 1849, as Andersen had feared, the fragile peace broke down and Denmark was again at war with Germany. This time, he had no desire to be a witness, and instead headed north to Sweden, leaving Copenhagen on 17 May. He stayed away for four months, finding himself heralded with much celebration wherever he went. He had only one unnerving moment; when taken to visit an insane asylum, the minister in charge of it asked on hearing Andersen's name, 'Will he be staying here permanently?' If meant as a joke, it was less than hilarious, and Andersen, morbidly sensitive on the subject of madness, could find no reply.

In the renewed fighting, the Danish forces were again losing heavily, as might be expected when the sympathies of the population lay with the opposing side, and Andersen found himself touched personally by the conflict as letters from his beloved friend in Weimar ceased to arrive. Finally he heard that Carl Alexander had himself led a contingent of troops into battle, and recognised at last that the man he cared for so deeply must be counted among Denmark's enemies.

Following a further defeat in a battle on 6 July, an armistice was again declared, and Andersen ventured to write to his friend. In a letter dated 18 August, he commented that the young duke had 'certainly experienced sad days this summer'. He did not post the letter until 8 September, by which time he had added a rash postscript:

> Your noble heart, and every noble German heart which loves the truth, will feel that Denmark is blameless and good, and has suffered injustice . . .

Carl Alexander felt no such thing. In a letter written shortly after the latest armistice, he had, as Andersen told Edvard, stressed that their friendship should have nothing to do with politics. It was a clear warning not to overstep the mark, and Andersen did his best to keep his patriotic feelings out of their continued correspondence, even though the armistice broke down once more.

On 14 November 1849, he wrote a song called 'Poetry' for the public celebration of Oehlenschläger's seventieth birthday, little suspecting that the man he had admired so long was almost at the end of his life. At eleven o'clock on 20 January 1850 'at the same hour of the same day as Christian VIII' Andersen noted, Adam Oehlenschläger died, with immense dignity. He kissed his family goodbye and assured them that he felt no pain, and when Andersen saw his body, he commented that the jaundice which had killed him had conferred 'the appearance of a bronze statue rather than of a corpse. The forehead was beautiful, youthful and clear.'

People from all walks of life followed the poet in a long procession to his burial-place at Frederiksberg, where he had been born. Once again Andersen ('and old Grundtwig' as he told Carl Alexander in a long letter) had been commissioned to write suitable words, and Andersen's funeral song was set to music by Christophe Weyse. In the same letter to the young duke, he had spoken with excitement about H.C. Ørsted's newly published book, *Soul in Nature,* which revealed the world to be 'so splendidly great, so intelligible, so sacred'. Ørsted, though renowned for his innovative practical work in physics, was based very much in the tradition of Goethe, writing about natural phenomena with a perceptive curiosity which is only beginning to re-emerge in our own time from an age of artificial and restrictive division between the arts and the sciences.

On 2 February, the marriage between Jonna Drewsen and Henrik Stampe took place, and Andersen's diary contained no comment. On his forty-fifth birthday, 2 April 1850, he wrote to Carl Alexander with a long description of his new verse play, *Ole Lukoie,* which had just been staged. The eponymous hero is a figure not unlike the legendary Scottish Dream Angus, a bringer of the heart's desire to the sleeping mind, and the plot addressed the question which was beginning to trouble Andersen so much; when a man has all he could wish for, why is it that he still senses an inner emptiness and despair?

The play was widely misunderstood. Andersen quoted in his letter a critic who had taken the point to be a political one and assumed the author to be rebuking those who held 'false notions of a perfect equality in worldly circumstances for all'. Nothing could be further from the truth. As always, Andersen's concerns were purely personal, and while he retained a fellow-feeling for the underdog, he showed no signs of envisaging a society free of the gradients which were so material to his life and to his writing. The dismaying blankness which accompanied his success came from realising that admiration is no substitute for love. Edvard was lost to him, reduced to the status of a sensible and supportive friend, and the continuing war had made Weimar and Carl Alexander seem remote. His play was parodied in the newly established Casino Theatre, a popular and irreverent rival to the Royal, and Andersen wrote in distress to Ørsted's daughter, Mathilde. Ørsted himself replied, pointing out that 'almost all men of distinction are subject to attacks of that kind'. Very gently, he told Andersen that *Ole Lukoie* was not the best thing he had ever done, and cautioned him on no account to try to defend himself.

Andersen took his advice – but by the summer, he was sinking into depression. At Glorup, his fellow-guests made it clear that they knew about his friendship with the Hereditary Grand Duke of Weimar, and needled him constantly about this and about his effeminacy. His diary entries in June record a multitude of provocative remarks. ' "Isn't that a handkerchief from Schleswig-Holstein?" '. ' "You're not writing to the Duke of Weimar, are you?" '. On 25 June, he had a particularly bad time:

> Mr Lindegaard was boorishly witty at my expense – talked about my courage with bulls and so forth, and later, at home, about my having made the cloth flowers for the chandelier. I ignored him, but felt uncomfortable about it. Afterwards . . . Countess Scheel came out with some drivel – that I was supposed to have said I didn't have the heart for war but would go along as a troubador! I was angry to have such nonsense pinned on me and objected to such 'unnatural talk'.

The next day, he went out to pick forget-me-nots for Miss Raben and Countess Moltke, and felt a little better, but toothache began to plague him, with an abscess which had to be lanced. 'Melancholy;' he wrote on 1 July, 'my progress as a writer is a thing of the past.'

Four days later, as Andersen was out walking alone in a 'dark and sombre mood', a servant rushed up with the news that there had been a cease-fire:

> Tears sprang to my eyes; I ran in to His Excellency; saw the announcement on the leaflet sent to us from Nyborg by the merchant Suhr. It isn't official; I don't dare give myself over to my joy.

The peace treaty was signed on 2 July 1850. 'Peace! Peace with Germany!' Andersen wrote to Carl Alexander. 'It rings through my heart.' He rushed on to voice his hope that he could visit Weimar again, and lamented that Beaulieu had entirely ceased to write to him.

His letter met with a hostile silence. Andersen seemed unaware that Germany had technically lost the war, since the treaty had given Denmark continuing, though conditional, rule over the duchies. The Schleswig-Holstein insurgents ignored the cease-fire and continued to fight on against the Danish troops, but without their Prussian allies they had no real hope of victory, and were finally crushed in January 1851. Their defeat left the duchies in a state of sullen resentment, under a Danish hold much weakened by conciliatory clauses in the peace treaty – and Germany was biding its time, well aware that the business had not been concluded. In such continuing tensions, Andersen's gushing letters to Weimar must have seemed blunderingly insensitive, and Carl Alexander remained silent.

Home concerns occupied Andersen. Jette Wulff, an intrepid traveller despite her small, deformed body, embarked on 12 September on a year's trip to the Danish West Indies aboard the brig *Mercurius*, of which her brother Christian had just taken command. Like several Danish women of the time, she was a skilled painter, depicting landscape and genre scenes with a fluent, easy technique and clear perception. Shortly after her departure, Andersen began sitting to another woman artist, Elizabeth Jerichau-Baumann, for a portrait.

On 7 November, Copenhagen University honoured H.C. Ørsted with a celebration of his fiftieth jubilee as a lecturer there. At seventy-three, with an untidy shock of white hair and an enthusiasm for the mystery and excitement of physics which was as strong as ever, he was adored by his students, who staged a torchlight procession for him. Andersen described the whole thing in yet another letter to the silent Carl Alexander, chatting excitedly about the second part of Ørsted's

Soul in Nature and its effect on his own latest book, *In Sweden.* He added that the Moltkes' son, Jerichau, who had served as a hussar in the Danish army, had died of typhus. The silence from Weimar continued.

As the unofficial war finally came to an end in January, Andersen watched the victorious troops returning to Copenhagen, exhausted rather than triumphant. His publisher, Reitzel, gave him thirty copies of the book of patriotic songs Andersen had written during the war, including the famous *In Denmark I Was Born,* for distribution to the soldiers. Andersen gave them to the wounded men first, then to the youngest, and lamented that he had not enough. What the men said is not recorded.

There was a waspish reference to this public benevolence in Meier Goldschmidt's new publication, *North and South,* but it was caused in part by a foolish discourtesy of Andersen's towards the editor. He had been invited to Goldschmidt's house on 12 February for a celebration of Ole Bull's birthday but decided not to go 'as I so often do', he admitted in his diary. The indignant Goldschmidt took him to task for sending no apology or excuse and accused Andersen of being jealous that somebody other than himself was being feted.

It was the kind of social gaffe which Andersen, ever locked within his own concerns, was particularly prey to. Now that the victory celebrations were over, the anticlimax was setting in, and there was little to distract him from his growing bleakness. On 21 February he wrote, 'No joy about the future. The wreaths and garlands have been taken down; only a few hang here and there like flowers after a ball.'

An old friend, Emma Hartmann, died on 6 March, and a worse blow followed three days later. H.C. Ørsted, after only a few months in the country residence provided for him, caught a cold which led quickly to a chest infection, and he was dead in a matter of hours. A great procession went to his house and laid a silver wreath on his coffin, then the mourners carried it on their own shoulders to the University, where he lay in state until his burial on 18 March, very close to the main door of the University, in the courtyard which separates it from the Church of our Lady. Andersen's new book, *In Sweden,* came out the next day, as if in tribute to the man who had so heavily influenced it.

Ørsted's death deepened Andersen's sense of solitude, and he sent the still-silent Carl Alexander a bust of himself, following this by a letter to Beaulieu-Marconnay in which he asked tentatively whether a visit to

Weimar might be possible, or whether his pro-Danish views might make him unpopular. Beaulieu reacted like a poked lion, snarling that if Andersen was so one-sided as to consider Denmark right in all things, he had better stay away. Recovering himself, he added that his correspondent would of course be welcome as 'a dear, worthy poet with whom one may go for a walk but not discuss politics'.

Andersen forwarded this sharp reply to Edvard Collin for advice, and received a closely reasoned response tinged with sheer fury. Beaulieu should not forget, Edvard said, that his token support of a democratic uprising in Schleswig-Holstein must be set against a regime of press prosecutions, civilian oppression and political imprisonment in his own country. Denmark had been forced to oppose 'German arrogance', and the fact that the new Danish government of the duchies was described in Germany as a 'Casino-Cabinet' showed a continuing contempt:

> It might perhaps interest Herr Beaulieu to learn that there are four noblemen in the Cabinet, among them two counts, and that the President of the Council is one of our highest and most distinguished aristocrats.

Edvard, as a deeply conservative civil servant, had an ingrained respect for aristocracy and regarded the radical changes which were sweeping Europe as utterly distasteful. Describing himself as 'an official of the *ancien régime* and no friend to democracy', he was outraged that Beaulieu should regard himself as a virtuous progressive where Schleswig-Holstein's affairs were concerned, and hoped that Andersen would utterly refuse to be regarded by such a man as 'a dear, worthy poet with whom one may go for a walk but not discuss politics'. His repetition of the phrase showed how offensive he found it, and he offered to make his entire letter available to Andersen to send to Beaulieu as it stood.

Andersen could not take such a drastic step. It would have meant the final breaking-off of all contact with Weimar, and while Edvard would have thought this a good thing, Andersen could not face it. He wrote in conciliatory terms to both Carl Alexander and Beaulieu, explaining that he had merely feared that the 'lower orders' might show some ignorant prejudice. He had no fear of coming into conflict with 'the cultivated classes', he went on:

> We have so many other interests in common which are dear to us, so
> much that is good and beautiful to talk about and entertain ourselves
> with, that I would unhesitatingly come to my friends.

A slightly stiff contact was resumed – but Andersen abandoned any
thoughts of going to Weimar that year. Nevertheless, after the
restrictions imposed by the war, he was chafing to go abroad again,
and on 17 January, set off on a modest European journey. This time,
he took with him Ingeborg Drewsen's youngest son, Viggo, knowing by
now that loneliness was a constant hazard of his travels.

Viggo, now twenty-one years old, found Andersen's fussiness over
details irritating and, with the impatience of youth, probably seldom
understood why his companion seemed so set in his ways and easily
upset. For Andersen, the journey was a disturbing one. He was
troubled by the evidence of warfare that lingered in the embattled
duchies and 'did not breathe freely until all Holstein, including
Hamburg, had been left behind'. To travel through Germany without
visiting Weimar was equally painful, and by the time the pair got to
Prague, Andersen was suffering from persistent and excruciating
toothache. In Dresden, Viggo headed for home alone, leaving
Andersen to stay with his old friends, the Serres, at Maxen.

In the autumn of the same year he was made an honorary professor
of Copenhagen University, to his great delight, and through the winter
of 1851–2 he worked on a new volume of stories. The bulk of what are
now considered his classic fairy tales had by now been written, but he
continued to produce short pieces which have much to say on the sad
comedy of human life and his own experience of it.

A week before Christmas, he wrote to Jette Wulff, who was now in
America. She had told him the voyage was perfectly easy, and urged
him to come over and sample the delights of the New World. 'You can
travel about with the Lind,' she suggested. Jenny Lind was indeed
about to start an American tour with that great showman, Barnum –
but Andersen would not cross the Atlantic. He had always been afraid
of long sea voyages, which Jette knew, but he fell back on the excuse
that he could not afford it. He was interested, however, in the
question of his books circulating in the States in cheap and un-paid-for
editions, and gave Jette strict instructions to bring sample copies back

with her.

He was still obsessed with the idea of going to Weimar, and in March 1852 wrote a politely insistent letter to Carl Alexander, fishing for an invitation. It duly came, and he set out in mid-May, full of nervous hope. The visit was not a great success. He stayed with Beaulieu, a little surprisingly in view of their previous correspondence, but was only one of several guests, and found the atmosphere difficult. Beaulieu was now married, with two children, and had his cousin staying with him. This young man, Ernst Beaulieu-Marconnay, had been an officer in the Prussian army and still suffered from the effects of a severe head-wound, complaining constantly of pain and sometimes almost fainting, and in fact died three years later. He was a walking reminder of the war, and Andersen found him unnerving. 'He is lying in the room outside mine,' he wrote in his diary on 23 May, 'I'm completely shut in by him, and the thought occurred to me that he might go mad during the night and come in and murder me. Can't lock my door.' He spent some time during the days that followed in listening to the young man reading his poems aloud and admitted eventually that he could be quite pleasant, but he never quite recovered from his first impression that Ernst was sinister and not to be trusted.

Carl Alexander himself proved elusive. His first meeting with Andersen had taken place on the neutral ground of his mother's house, and although the two men had embraced and kissed as old friends would expect to, he seemed otherwise occupied for most of the visit, only seeing Andersen on formal occasions, with other people present.

There were substantial reasons for his preoccupation. The Empress of Russia, Alexandra Feodorovna, arrived during Andersen's stay, necessitating a shift round of rooms. Her husband, Tsar Nicholas I, was the brother of the Grand Duchess of Wiemar. The Empress was frail and almost blind, having to be carried upstairs. Andersen found it pitiable and, as he admitted in a letter to Ingeborg Drewsen, slightly absurd that such a frail invalid should be head of a country 'the size of the surface of the moon'. He was not feeling welcome, and increasingly occupied his time with visits to artistic friends, and on 25 May wrote with some astonishment of Liszt, who was living in sin with the Princess of Wittgenstein, that the pair of them seemed 'like fiery spirits blazing, burning – they can warm you at once, but if you get too close, you will be burned.'

Liszt was full of enthusiasm for the music of Wagner, which Andersen failed to admire, as he made clear in *Mit livs eventyr.*

> In Wagner I see an intellectual composer of the present day; he is great because of his understanding and his will; he is a tremendous innovator, rejecting everything old, but I feel that he lacks that divine element which was granted to Mozart and Beethoven.

He sat through a performance of *Tannhäuser* and remarked in his diary that the music was competent but lacking in melody. 'What Weber or Mozart couldn't have done with it!' he added, in a somewhat comic lumping-together of unlikelihoods. *Lohengrin* failed to change his opinion. When Liszt came bounding into his box at the theatre to demand what he thought now, Andersen merely said limply, 'I feel half dead.' He was happier with Flotow's light opera, *Martha*, with its indisputably tuneful theme-song, 'The Last Rose of Summer'.

Despite its evident shortcomings, Andersen wrote rapturous descriptions of his Weimar visit to his friends. At the end of three weeks he moved on, and in Munich he met King Maximilian of Bavaria, generally known as 'King Max', together with the old king, Ludwig I, Max's father. Andersen went on a boat trip with them to their island villa, and after dinner sat chatting with the younger monarch on a bench. He then joined Viggo Drewsen in Leipzig and travelled with him to Milan. Rather strangely, he wrote from Frankfurt on the way home to Beaulieu, saying that he would have liked to call again at Weimar, but his companion 'wished to return home without making a stay anywhere'. It seems doubtful that there had been a specific invitation, but Andersen could not stop worrying at the Weimar question, as if he could somehow shake it into the real welcome he so desperately wanted.

In Frankfurt, some German friends tried to take him to Homberg, where the Duchess of Augustenborg was anxious to see him, but here Andersen dug his heels in. He could not forgive that family for its involvement against Denmark during the war, and wrote in his diary on 14 July, 'they have brought misfortune and unhappiness to my native land. I'm not judging them, but I cannot bear the thought of meeting them.'

In the spring of 1853, Andersen arranged a large-scale deal with Reitzel for four thousand copies of his *Illustrated Stories* and two thousand of his *Collected Works* to be reissued. It was to be his last meeting with the publisher, who died shortly afterwards and was succeeded by his son. In May he went to Sorø for a long stay with the Ingemanns, and wrote to Jette Wulff on 5 June about the daily good-natured wrangles with the poet about the meaning of creativity:

> He sets poetry high above science, but I don't. He admits that our time is a great era of inventiveness, but only in the field of the mechanical and the material, which is constantly expanding. I think of this as a necessary support for what is spiritual, a great branch from which poetry can blossom . . .

The Ørsted influence was still strong. Two days previously, Andersen had written in great excitement to Carsten Hauch about the electric telegraph which had just been installed between Elsinore, Copenhagen and Hamburg, due to open for public use the following year. Andersen had stood beside Peter Faber, the operator, and heard him contact Elsinore with the news that a great poet was in his office – whereupon a whole stanza of one of Andersen's earliest poems had come back from that distant place. It was, Andersen said, 'as if I stood under the wingbeat of an eternal, mighty spirit'. He added that, had he discovered science twenty years ago, he might well have followed that discipline, which could have been 'a better one'.

A few days later, cholera broke out in Copenhagen. It was an appalling epidemic, causing nearly five thousand deaths during the summer months, and Andersen fled for safety to Jutland. There, he heard that Carl Alexander's father, the old Duke of Weimar, had died, leaving his son to inherit the title. 'In the new activity of your life I shall probably hear from you less often,' he wrote in his letter of sympathy and congratulations, 'but I firmly believe in you, and that I live in your thoughts as you have grown into mine.'

During the two months of his self-imposed exile, Andersen began work on an extended version of *The True Story of My Life*. This new autobiography was to occupy him for the next two years, and would eventually appear as *The Fairy-tale of My Life – Mit livs eventyr*.

By the time Andersen thought it safe to return to Copenhagen, the epidemic had killed Edvard's mother-in-law, Oline Thyberg, and also a cousin on old Mrs Collin's side of the family, Emilie Hornemann. The newspapers declared the city to be free of the disease, but Andersen, ever fearful and hypochondriac, lived for some time in the dread of being stricken down.

His sensibilities were deeply offended in January 1854 when he read a book called *Mimona*. This was the work of a young actress known as Clara Raphael, her real name being Mathilde Fibiger, and it dealt uninhibitedly with incest and other sexual aberrations. Andersen was deeply shocked that a young woman could, as he wrote to Ingemann, 'live, think, write and read about something like that'. Such confrontation with female interest in sex repelled him, and he described the book as 'bestial'.

That year, he took Viggo's younger brother, Einar Drewsen, with him on a trip to Germany and Italy. In Vienna they dined with Jenny Lind, now married to Otto Goldschmidt, who had gone out to America to be her accompanist there. He had converted to Christianity in order to appease his wife's increasing religiosity, and the first of their three children, a little son called Walter, had been born in the previous September. Jenny had now become convinced that to sing in a theatre was sinful, and restricted her appearances to concerts and oratorios sung in churches. Andersen remarked that it was 'a sin against the spirit, an abandonment of the mission God gave her', and his disappointment soured his mood and may well have added to the difficulties of his relationship with Einar, who became fretful and unwell. Andersen did not tolerate other people's malaises easily, and in Munich the pair of them quarrelled. Whether by pre-arrangement or as a result of their falling-out, Andersen went on alone, first to visit King Max and then to Weimar, and this time found a warmer reception.

For all Carl Alexander's cordiality, politics lurked not far below the surface, and when Andersen was asked to visit the Duchess of Augustenborg and resume the friendship, he flatly refused. Carl Alexander accused him of bearing a grudge, pointing out that ladies were above politics, but Andersen was not to be moved.

In the spring of the following year, he was fifty. Oddly enough, it was a muted birthday; after a meal with the Drewsens he went home and spent the evening correcting the proofs of *My Life's Fairytale*. He was living at this time in a couple of rooms in Nyhavn, an adequate base for such tasks, but essentially he remained as homeless as a stray cat, shifting from one hospitable house to another and travelling abroad at least once a year. No longer young, he retained extraordinary stamina, seeming unaware that few people could cope with such constant moving about, and yet he fretted obsessively over every ache or itch or stomach upset. At Christmas he had gone home from the Collins' house because of a stye on his eye and had sat alone, holding a compress over the affliction. Winter was always a bad time for him, and he looked forward to the better weather which heralded another travelling season.

In June, after attending the funeral of Neils Gade's wife, Sophie, he set off again, and while passing through Nuremberg, heard that King Max and his queen were in the town. He at once put off his journey, as he wrote to Jette Wulff:

> and as soon as the Majesties heard that I was here, I was received most warmly, most beautifully. We dined at the castle in the large banqueting hall, where the wood panelling is beautifully carved, walls and windows medieval, and immediately outside, the old town lay down below in the sunshine.

Andersen had arranged to meet another young member of the Collin tribe in Munich, this time Edgar, the nineteen-year-old son of Edvard's elder brother, Gottlieb. Edgar's mother, Augusta, was the sister of Andersen's friend from his days in Rome, Fritz Petzholdt, who had been so tragically killed. With this young companion, Andersen spent four days in Wildbad – and discovered to his alarm that the Prince of Nør was also present. 'I saw him from behind,' he wrote to Jonas Collin – 'I do hope we won't meet!' He managed to avoid this enemy of Denmark, and headed for a far more congenial meeting, though one which filled him with some nervousness. Edvard and his wife, together with their son, Jonas, then fifteen, happened to be visiting a spa in Wildbad, and Carl Alexander had also come to the town in order to see Andersen, bringing with him Karl Schiller, son of the poet. This rather oddly assorted company was to meet, and Andersen was well aware of Edvard's feelings about Weimar and its rulers.

He need not have worried. Whatever Edvard's private opinions, he was nothing if not diplomatic. He was also a royalist, and was much taken with the duke, telling Andersen afterwards that he would like to know Carl Alexander better. Relieved, Andersen went on with Edgar into Switzerland, where they climbed Rigi-Kulm.

On return to Zurich, the pair spent half an hour with Wagner. The composer was then living in exile from Germany, having been much involved in the revolutionary movement, but Andersen, with his customary political blindness, seems not to have understood the implications, or even to have realised that it was Liszt who, because of Wagner's poverty and lack of recognition, had personally funded the productions of *Lohengrin* and *Tannhäuser* in Weimar.

At the beginning of September, Edgar had to go back to Copenhagen, and Andersen missed him. He was upset, too, by meeting a Dane who told him that *My Life's Fairytale* newly published in Denmark, had been badly reviewed. His diary recorded that he felt 'physically and spiritually ill', and he fled to Weimar to take refuge with Beaulieu, Carl Alexander still being away. It was not a happy visit. The weather turned cold and Andersen was bored and chilly. 'I have my winter clothes on and sleep with a down comforter. Not in a good mood.' Peevishness exudes from his entry on 11 September 'At home alone at the tea-table with Mrs Beaulieu-Marconnay.'

In practical terms, however, the stay was a productive one. Andersen talked to Liszt about staging his two musical plays, *The Raven* and *Little Kirsten*, in Weimar, and Beaulieu helped him to translate *Little Kirsten* into German, promising that it would appear early the following year.

Back in Copenhagen, Andersen found that his autobiography had not received the savaging he had feared. His sharpest critic, in fact, was Jette Wulff, who had seen the book in proof form. She was even more critical than the Collin family of her friend's hobnobbing with the nobility, for whereas the Collins' objections sprang from a respect for the social divisions and a feeling that one should know one's own place, hers were briskly political. Her nature, she told Andersen, was 'definitely democratic and egalitarian', and his liking for the aristocracy baffled her. Before the book's publication, she had written to him with some severity:

> I am surprised when someone like you, Andersen – recognising that God has given you special gifts – that you should feel happy and honoured to be placed – well, that's what you say here – at the table of the King of Prussia or some other high-ranking person – or to receive a decoration of the same kind worn by the greatest scoundrels, not to mention a horde of utterly insignificant people. Do you really place a title, money, aristocratic blood, success in merely mundane matter,

above genius – spirit – the gifts of the soul?

Jette, the daughter of an Admiral who was also a renowned man of letters, had a well-founded confidence underpinning her refusal to be impressed by the trappings of wealth and class, and could not see why her admired friend was incapable of the same mental freedom. For Andersen, disillusion about the follies of the rich was more than outweighed by the sense of security he derived from each mark of acceptance he was given, not to mention the possible implications of an actual royal connection. His was the classic paradox of the self-made man, simultaneously measuring himself in terms of the favours he could win while resenting the power of those whose approval he sought.

As if to mark how far he had come, he sent a copy of *My Life's Fairytale* to Fedder Carstens, the teacher who nearly half a century ago had patted his cheeks and protected him from the rough boys and then so abruptly disappeared. One can only wonder anew what memories had stayed in Andersen's mind to prompt such a gift. Carstens had clearly been important to him.

In the following year, 1856, Jette Wulff left Denmark again on a further transatlantic voyage – but this time, she was overtaken by tragedy. In America, her much-loved brother, Christian, died of jaundice. Jette made her desolate way home alone, leaving Christian to lie in his grave in South Carolina.

Andersen, by contrast, seemed increasingly concerned with petty detail. He had begun another novel, titled *To Be Or Not To Be,* in which he was exploring the question of Christian faith, floundering a little as he grappled with the holism of Ørsted's thinking in the great man's absence. As if in recoil from these large ideas, his mind took refuge in trivia; his diary entries plunged into a long saga about being overcharged for some postage stamps, and another stye on his eye reduced him to 'sitting with half a boiled egg on my eye; can't get out at all, can't read and have difficulty in writing'.

Little Kirsten had been staged as promised in Weimar during January, and Andersen, who had been travelling between manor-houses for some months, set off in June for another visit to Germany. He stayed with the Serres in Maxen, and found that a fellow-guest was the author Karl Gutzkow. Andersen had met Gutzkow the previous year and described him as 'cold, cautious, not very charming'. The dislike was clearly mutual, for Gutzkow at Maxen missed no opportunity to pour scorn on the Dane's work and to imply that he was effete. On 17 June Andersen recorded furiously that his enemy had been 'so tactless as to ask me whether I had ever been in love – one couldn't tell from my books, where love came in like a fairy; I was myself a sort of half-man!'

Gutzkow's point was a valid one, as Andersen knew. His objection is to the tactlessness rather than to the accusation itself. As a man of over fifty, craggy and yet dandified, he had begun to look what would nowadays be recognised as 'an old queen', but he relied on the decencies and inhibitions of the time not to say so – and, perhaps, to refrain from forcing his own recognition of his nature. The status of poet had long protected him from any such incursions into his privacy, and he fought off Gutzkow's attack with an intensity that left his hosts distraught. 'Mrs Serre was crying, said she'd like to thrash Gutzkow, who was now chasing her dearest friends away. Serre came and spoke with me in an effort to restore harmony . . . ' Some kind of uneasy truce was achieved, but Andersen took himself off a couple of days later and fled to the more reliable Weimar.

To Be Or Not To Be was published on 20 May 1857 in simultaneous German and English editions with the Danish. It is one of Andersen's least readable novels, mulling inconclusively over the religious conflicts which he himself could never quite resolve. The simple Lutheran belief inherited from his mother was at odds with a kind of instinctive Judaism, whether present by blood or not, which made him feel it his duty to play the hand of cards dealt by God as successfully as possible. At a deep level, he felt as his father had done, that there was nothing supernatural about Jesus Christ, and his chosen hero, Niels Bryde – a name very close to that of his composer friend, Niels Gade – worries his way through the almost plotless book, pausing only to express his dislike of Kierkegaard, Grundtvig and dogs.

Andersen dedicated the new novel to Charles Dickens, with whom he had kept in touch sporadically since his visit to London a decade ago. Writing to his fellow-author in sending him the book, he described it as marking 'a stage in my development which I have not previously reached'. He also took up a polite invitation issued by Dickens the previous autumn, announcing that he would like to visit him in the coming summer of 1857.

Chapter 17
Five Weeks With Dickens

Andersen's friends had misgivings about his visit to the British author. Andreas de Saint-Aubin, who wrote as Carl Bernhard, admitted in a letter to Countess Mimi Holstein that he feared Andersen would be disappointed, remarking that the personalities of the two writers were 'too divergent for any real friendship to exist'.

For Andersen, the visit was one of the few ambitions left unfulfilled. With new editions of his work constantly appearing in a variety of European languages, and with a reliable income both from his annual stipend and the profits from his books, it was beginning to seem that he had nothing left to aim for. He was the darling of royalty and could count on a welcome in aristocratic houses all over Europe – and yet he was haunted by a suspicion that his best years were behind him. Dickens, the most famous writer of the era, was virtually the only man who had remained difficult to bring into actual friendship, responding to letters belatedly if at all – and yet Andersen could not forget the warmth that had seemed to exist between them, and the great man's willingness to walk into Dover on the day of his departure, apparently for the sole purpose of giving him a fond farewell embrace. Andersen, without a shred of hypocrisy in his being, had no means of understanding what an Englishman will do in the name of good manners, and how big the gulf is between his behaviour and his private opinion.

The trip to London was not without its difficulties. The language, to start with, presented a problem. English was not commonly spoken in the Europe of the nineteenth century, and Andersen's sketchy grasp of it had faded during the decade of disuse. His travel instructions, too, were scant. Dickens had written to explain that the family would be spending the summer at Gadshill, their country house in Kent (now a girls' school), but beyond advising Andersen that the nearest railway station was at Higham, he had given no directions.

Andersen set out on 30 May for a fortnight's journey through various congenial stopping-places, pausing in Brussels to write to Dickens and ask him to leave a note at Higham station, or suggest a nearby hotel where Andersen could meet him. In the same letter, he promised that his stay would not exceed a week or a fortnight.

After a night crossing from Calais which laid him flat with seasickness, Andersen arrived in London and made his way to Higham. There, he was met by a man sent by Dickens to carry the visitor's luggage, who silently shouldered the trunk, the carpet bag, the hat-box and other bits of paraphernalia which Andersen considered essential, and trudged the mile and a half to Gadshill.

They arrived a little after ten, and Andersen joined Dickens and his wife for 'brackfest' as his diary recorded. A combination of his dyslexic tendencies and the illogicality of English spelling very nearly beat him, but he tried hard. On that first morning, another visitor was present. Miss Angela Burdett-Coutts had inherited a fortune from her grandfather and was one of Britain's greatest philanthropists, helping Dickens extensively in his efforts to do something to redeem the 'fallen women' in whose welfare he was so interested. She remembered Andersen from a previous visit and had a genuine liking and sympathy for him perhaps – the more so because of the comment Dickens had added when inviting her:

> Hans Christian Andersen may perhaps be with us, but you won't mind him – especially as he speaks no language but his own Danish, and is suspected of not even knowing that.

Mary Howitt, by Dickens' own admission, was responsible for spreading this rumour. Now living in a cottage on the borders of fashionable Highgate, she was very much part of the literary scene, and she had never forgiven Andersen for failing to remain one of 'her' authors.

Andersen had an unorthodox approach to foreign languages, but he tackled them with great verve and flair, and could make himself understood in German, Swedish, Italian, and French as well as having a schoolboy grasp of Latin, Greek and Hebrew. His diary for the early days of his Dickens visit is full of the delight he found in the similarities between Danish and English, recording that everyone understood *der er en graeshoppe in den høstak* ('there is a grasshopper in the haystack'). When stuck for a word, he worked his way round it with great ingenuity. Wanting to describe a plant as poisonous but lacking the word for 'poison', he invoked the death of Socrates to make his meaning clear.

His efforts brought him little credit, though he may not have realised this. Dickens, though unfailingly polite to his guest, made it clear to various correspondents that he regarded him as rather stupid. Andersen had been relieved when on the second evening of his stay Dickens' son, Charles junior, revealed that he spoke German, having been to school in that country. The long conversation in German which followed failed to impress the monoglot Charles senior, who wrote to William Jerdan after Andersen's departure, 'My eldest boy swears that the ear of man cannot recognise his German.' In a further letter to Miss Burdett-Coutts, he reiterated his insistence that Andersen could not speak his own language correctly: 'his Translatress declares he can't – is ready to make an oath of it before any magistrate'.

It was true that Andersen's spelling had the inconsistencies of all dyslexics and that his style, by the standards of the day, was punchy and laconic rather than elegant, but Mrs Bushby, who had replaced Mary Howitt, had no complaint about his linguistic ability, and her contact with him during his visit was frequent and friendly.

William Jerdan, at whose insistence Andersen had first come to Britain, found himself sadly ignored on this second occasion, as his letter to Andersen at Gadshill reveals:

> Bushey Heath, Herts.
> 25 June 1857

My dear friend,

Learning from the Newspapers that you are again in London I cannot resist the wish to hear of your "whereabouts" and to have the great pleasure of meeting you occasionally during your stay. I am, unfortunately, farther from Town than when we used to be much together on your former visit, and am besides at this moment confined to my Cottage by indisposition; but I hope to be able to go out within a few days, and to make some arrangements for seeing you. I observe that you are with our mutual friend, C. Dickens, to whom I had the gratification of making you personally acquainted, and I rejoice in your sojourn under such congenial auspices. Your riper fame and his universal connections will no doubt lead to the full occupation of your time, but I still look to your Portrait now before me with the loved inscription "the excellent kind hearted Jerdan from his true friend H.C. Andersen", and trust not to be forgotten . . .

Whether Andersen asked anyone to translate the letter is impossible to prove – but poor Jerdan was forgotten, for this visit was concentrated solely on Charles Dickens.

Even the most august invitations were turned down so that Andersen could be with his hero. Within a few days of his arrival, the First Secretary to the Danish Legation, Count Alfred Reventlow-Criminal, not the same man who had been so helpful on Andersen's previous visit, wrote to him with the suggestion that he should be presented to Queen Victoria. 'You must be in uniform or court dress,' he advised, 'but it is worth the trouble, and you will then be invited to the Court balls.' After the trauma of his previous misunderstanding with the royal couple, Andersen might have been expected to jump at the chance to get his stripes back, but he had no desire to be embroiled in London society on this visit. He declined the suggestion very firmly, somewhat to Reventlow's consternation, and wrote a frank letter to the Danish dowager Queen Caroline Amalie explaining his decision. He grew sick of these London invitation last time, he said, and found the city unpleasant: 'The air is so heavy, coal smoke so oppressive, and the heat not to be borne. I cunningly arranged, therefore, to stay in the country on this visit.' To Jette Wulff, he wrote a happy letter on 8 June about the family which he admired with unsuspecting wholeheartedness:

My reception was very warm, Dickens took me in his arms, later his wife and children came . . . Mrs Dickens I find beautiful this time, and the eldest daughter Mary takes after her, the second, Kate, has on the other hand absolutely Dickens' face, as you know it in his portrait; there are three sons over in Boulogne and four in this house; the youngest, Edward Bulwer Lytton Dickens, appears to be five years old. All the children are named after writers. The eldest is called Charles Dickens, the second, Walter Landor (he is leaving in four weeks for Calcutta, where he will become an officer and will remain away for seven years); then come the sons in Boulogne, Francis Jeffrey, Alfred Tennyson, Sidney Smith, and here at home the two youngest, Henry Fielding and Edward Bulwer. Of them all the little Henry was the first to show kindness to me.

> The family life seems so harmonious, and a young Miss Hogarth, who has been living in this house for many years, pours tea and coffee, plays with the young Misses Dickens and seems to be a most kind and cultured lady.

In fact, far from being harmonious, the Dickens family life was a slowly ticking time bomb. The Georgina Hogarth Andersen mentions was the younger sister of Dickens' wife, Catherine, and within the year, Georgina would be presiding over a house from which Catherine, despite the ten children she had borne her husband, had been banished, while Dickens himself was conducting an affair with a young actress called Nelly Ternan. Andersen had arrived in the closing weeks of the family's apparent harmony, and within a few days, he began to realise that things were not quite so idyllic as he had first thought them.

His own behaviour did not help. Used to the services he could take for granted in the houses of his aristocratic friends, he noted with surprise on the first morning that 'nobody came to pick up my clothes'. He called the maid, and was then annoyed to discover that there was no barber available to shave him. He made the huge mistake of asking the eldest son to perform this service, which he refused with some indignation. Every day after that, as Henry Dickens recalled in his memoirs, the visitor had to be driven into Rochester to be shaved by a barber, being apparently incapable of doing this for himself. Rochester was fourteen miles away, meaning that the carriage horses had to be harnessed and a member of the family (usually Charles junior) had to accompany Andersen – but his diary entries show no sign of unease about the trouble he was causing. On the day when he went with Dickens and young Charles to London, he complained that there had been no time for his shave and that he had gone round with a growth of stubble all day.

Dickens was busy at this time with a charitable undertaking which kept him in London a lot. One wonders whether Andersen's presence at Gadshill had anything to do with this sudden impulse, but the nominal cause was the death of Douglas Jerrold, dramatist and editor of *Lloyd's Weekly Newspaper*. Dickens, having heard that Jerrold's widow had been left destitute, decided to stage a performance of *The Frozen Deep* by his friend, Wilkie Collins, in order to raise funds for her.

Several members of the Dickens family were to take part, and Dickens himself, as actor-manager, was busy drumming up a suitably wealthy and generous audience.

The play was due to open on 4 July, well beyond the expected date of Andersen's departure, but on Sunday, 20 June, Dickens suggested that he should stay on for the performance, and Andersen unhesitatingly accepted. It was, of course, an offer which Dickens felt obliged to make, and which Andersen should have turned down with a smile of regret, but the guileless Dane was only too ready to believe himself genuinely wanted for another two weeks. In fact, he stayed on for a further ten days after *The Frozen Deep*, and began to see signs of stress in the family – but at first, he thoroughly enjoyed the entertainment laid on for him.

At Catherine Dickens' invitation, he went to a late afternoon performance of *Messiah* at the Crystal Palace, and was enchanted:

> The Crystal Palace is like a fairy city, with wide, floating paths; a great marble basin was there, with red, white and blue lotus, creepers wound their way up from the earth round pillars; statues and flowering trees everywhere . . . the sun was shining on the glass roof; an awning was stretched out within against the sun's rays. The wind whispered outside, and when the singing and the music rolled it reverberated in my head; I was near to tears. When we came out later, fountains were playing; it was as if we were in Undine's gardens; rainbows played, there must have been over a hundred fountains. Only the Blue Grotto had exerted such a magic power over me.

The event had been a large-scale one, with two thousand singers and ten thousand in the audience, and Andersen was startled at the high cost of the tickets at two guineas each – more than twenty rixdollars, he calculated, perhaps remembering that he had lived for six months on eighty rixdollars when he first came to Copenhagen.

From the Crystal Palace, he went on to a theatre, and spent the night at Dickens' London residence, Tavistock House. 'Walked arm in arm with Dickens to the office of *Household Words*,' he noted the next day, referring to the periodical which Dickens had started up in 1850, largely as a medium for his own work. Its premises in Wellington Street, just north of the Strand, included a couple of rooms which Dickens used as a private retreat. From there, Andersen spent the day about his own affairs, visiting Mrs Bushby to talk about translations and spending some time with Hambro, Reventlow and Richard Bentley, with whom Dickens had quarrelled in 1839 over the terms of a contract. Since then, he had referred to the publisher as 'the brigand of Burlington Street'.

Andersen went on from these engagements to the large house owned by Miss Burdett-Coutts, who had invited him to stay overnight. This comprised not only number 80, Piccadilly, but the adjoining building in Stratton Street, and Andersen, used as he was to opulence, found it incredibly grand. His diary is full of admiration for Miss Burdett-Coutts, who had turned down all suitors in case they were after her money. She was indeed fabulously rich, having inherited the money because her grandfather's widow, an actress, had bequeathed the fortune to her, feeling that it should remain in the family. Andersen respected Miss Burdett-Coutts for her charitable enterprises and her evident authority, but the house overawed him, and he described it to Jette Wulff as the most elegant he had ever seen. The servants were so daunting in their superiority that he dared not ask them for a couple of extra pillows, but put his request to his hostess herself. Miss Burdett-Coutts, with exquisite understanding, made up his bed herself as he wanted it.

On Monday 22 June, the first signs of strain on the Dickens family started to show. Sharing the larger of the family carriages with young Charles and two of his friends who were going to town, Andersen realised that his presence was not entirely welcome, and returned 'in a very bad mood which I couldn't conceal'. At Mrs Bushby's a few days later, he heard that *The Athenaeum* was about to carry a very adverse review of *To Be Or Not To Be*. This worried him, but he was reassured when *The Times* gave the book a favourable notice, and resumed his noting of minor details:

> Very expensive, these carriage rides, half a souvereigns [sic] already. It is hot here, and I am lonely. Went into a humble-looking eating house and paid four shillings for a cutlet and soda water.

When the *Athenaeum* notice did appear two days later, it was as severe as he had been led to expect. Andersen read it on his way back to Gadshill after a night spent at Richard Bentley's house, and was deeply upset. One of Bentley's sons had driven him to the station after he had seen the review, and had done his best to console the distraught author, but by the time the train left in the early afternoon Andersen had worked himself into a terrible state. 'It was oppressively hot; shut up in the carriage I came near to being sick, the sweat streamed off me . . .' He was met at Higham station by Walter Dickens and the son of the *Household Words* publisher, F.M. Evans, but neither of the young men made any move to help Andersen with his luggage. They walked ahead, leaving him to find a lad who would carry his bags the mile and a half to the house, and he arrived at Gadshill 'dripping with perspiration'. After dinner he read the offending article again and was further upset:

> I was heavy in the head, tired and confused, had the feeling that no-one sympathised with me, so I told Mrs Dickens and Miss Hogarth that I was very tired, and went to bed at nine o'clock.

This diary account was much elaborated by Kate Dickens in her verbal account transcribed by Gladys Storey in her book, *Dickens and Daughters*:

> One morning Mrs Dickens found him prostrated face downwards upon the lawn, in tears and clutching a newspaper received that day from Denmark which contained an adverse criticism regarding his latest book.

Such mythologising tends to become accepted as fact – but the *Athenaeum* review hit hard at the weaknesses in Andersen's book, and came uncomfortably close to stripping away his rather woolly intellectual pretensions. The *Hamlet* quotation of the title was itself irritating to the British reviewer, inviting as it did an assumption that Andersen's hero, Niels Bryde, was of Shakespearian status. The author's failure to establish this was 'absolute':

> We may go further, and say, – in his anxiety to appear impartial, and allow each side its hearing, he has stated many arguments, stereotyped and usual, but plausible – which he has left unanswered. With great force and clearness he has put together all that science, half understood, is imagined to oppose in the way of natural fact or reasonable inference to the religious belief of mankind. These

statements are left to produce an impression; – and in the end they are vaguely met by an assertion that faith is a gift, not an acquisition. In his hands, the worse is allowed to appear the better reason.

The reviewer quoted a long excerpt from the book in illustration of his point, but ended with the opinion that Andersen's blundering explorations of science and atheism could lead 'some young intelligence, some susceptible heart' away from the path of righteousness. 'In one word, the book is dangerous.'

Andersen should have been flattered that anyone thought his book to have so much potency, but he was devastated. Mrs Bushby wrote him a consoling letter in which she said the reviewer was 'stupid', but he was inconsolable – and Dickens, the one person whose opinion he valued, was away in London. 'I am not happy,' Andersen wrote in his diary, 'cannot be so, and feel myself a stranger among strangers; if only Dickens were here!'

When Dickens came bowling cheerfully in for dinner that same evening, he brought with him Shirley Brooks, a leading contributor to *Punch,* and dismissed Andersen's anxieties with careless ease. 'You should never read the papers, except for what you have written yourself,' he said, adding that he himself had read no criticism of his own books for twenty-four years. After dinner, he took his still-tremulous guest out for a walk and told him, 'God has given you so very much, go your own way and give what you have in you, go your way, you are head and shoulders above the little men!' Tracing a few marks in the sand with the toe of his shoe, he said, 'That is criticism.' A dismissive wipe obliterated them. 'This is it gone.'

Those few hours alone with his hero were a compensation to Andersen for all his suffering:

> Up by the monument we lay the whole evening; a mist came up from the sea; the sun shone upon the windows in Rochester; we drank mixed wine up there; later there was lightning.

Dickens, for all his toughness and his secret impatience with Andersen, was always kind to him, at least to his face. As master in his house, he controlled his family's behaviour while he was present but his escape routes were well in place, and he often left his guest in the tetchy atmosphere of Gadshill while he went about his own affairs.

The following day, 29 June, Andersen read in *The Times* (which he variously rendered in his diary as *The Temps* or *The Tamps*) of a horrific railway crash on the line from London to Higham. Two trains had collided, killing fourteen people and injuring forty. That same day he passed the place on his way to London with the family, most of whom were involved in rehearsing *The Frozen Deep*. Andersen spent the rest of the day alone. Taking a cab to Tavistock House, he became alarmed when the driver took a route through 'one of the poor quarters' (in fact, Clerkenwell), where he thought he might be attacked and robbed. Dickens recorded in his letter to Jerdan that the Dane had stumbled in with all his personal property stuffed for safety into his boots, including, he said maliciously, 'a Bradshaw, a pocket-book, a pair of scissors, a penknife, a book or two, a few letters of introduction . . .' Andersen never travelled without a certain amount of paraphernalia. In a letter to Miss Burdett-Coutts, Dickens omitted this fanciful account, but noted more soberly, 'We are suffering a good deal from Andersen.'

His guest, too, was suffering. 'Wish to leave England,' he wrote in his diary the following day. 'Not really happy with my visit.' *The Literary Review* had not improved his mood by remarking of his new novel that he would be better advised to stick to fairy tales. Andersen was still disconsolate the next morning, ('Too little sugar in the tea') but cheered up during a trip with Evans to *The Times* printing press:

> It was as if I stood in the midst of a roaring waterfall when the great machines began to move. The gallery on which I stood shook, I was alarmed, giddy. The big, white sheets moved like lightning and absorbed the printed word and fell from hand to hand . . .

Relationships with the Dickens family worsened from day to day. Andersen did not improve things with his sulkiness. He refused to go with them to hear Charles give a reading from *A Christmas Carol*, seeming unaware that this was a discourtesy – and complained in his diary that they had little to say to him on return. 'Mrs Dickens tired, the daughters without thought for me, the aunt even less. Went to bed out of humour.'

Dickens hardly ever returned to the house as *The Frozen Deep* neared its production date. Andersen noted a press report that his old enemy, Christian Molbech, had died, but made no comment. 'Little Kate sarcastic, the aunt is certainly weary of me,' he wrote.

The première of the play on Saturday, 4 July came as a relief. Andersen visited Bentley, who showed him a scathing notice of *Little Dorrit* in the *Saturday Review* and pointed out that he was not the only one to be criticised. He spent the afternoon in the British Museum then made his way to the Gallery of Illustration in Regent Street, where the play was to be performed. This odd venue had been chosen because the Queen wished to be present, and could not for reasons of protocol enter a private house. Because Dickens' daughters, who were acting in it, had not been presented at court, they could not enter Buckingham Palace, where the play might otherwise have been staged – and Her Majesty would not attend a crowded theatre because she got too hot.

Andersen was so moved by Dickens' acting in the death scene that he burst into tears. The French farce, *After Midnight*, which completed the programme, featured Mark Lemon, the editor of *Punch*, and Dickens again, and while Andersen admitted in his diary that their acting had been 'a joy', he noted also that he himself had not been in a good mood the whole evening. The euphoric company had gathered in the *Household Words* office after the show to drink champagne until two in the morning, but, as Andersen confessed in a letter to Jette Wulff the next day, he had been afflicted by 'the spleen . . . my old heavy mood'.

He was perturbed by Jette's intimation that she intended to emigrate to America, where her brother Christian lay buried after their last tragic journey, and did his best to dissuade her:

> It is true that you have friends there, but believe me, even the best of friends in the long run do not put on their Sunday best if one comes too often. People are the same everywhere; better that you were nearer hearth and home.

He went on to express his disillusion with his current hosts:

> I have not in fact found the wonderful spirit I had expected to breathe in during my stay in England; but the days are interesting, and Dickens can still be seen in the same beautiful light which I had imagined before I came.

Even to Jette, whom he knew so well, he offered excuses for his own truculence. It had been Dickens, he said, who suggested that he was too tired to attend the *Christmas Carol* reading, and a combination of late nights and London air were responsible for his despondency.

On the Monday morning Andersen took himself off to Bentley's house for a few days, noting that the sons and daughters were 'extremely charming, more approachable and sympathetic than Dickens' children'. He also observed with some concern that the publisher and his family were 'less than well off ' a fact which Dickens confirmed, without much sympathy. Bentley was, he said, 'a nefarious rascal who expected to publish serials for his own benefit and authors to acquiesce in toiling to make him rich.' Ten years previously, when Andersen had visited Bentley in Sevenoaks, he had written to Jette Wulff about the 'fine house with plenty of elegance . . . that is indeed a publisher!' – but now, there had been a change of fortune, and he noticed that the Bentley girls, although assiduous in finding him a carriage after an outing, went home themselves on foot to save expense, and always took buses rather than cabs. 'Friendly, decent people,' Andersen observed. He was still trying to dissuade Jette from going to America, and was exploring the possibilities of finding her a home in England instead.

As the final days of his visit ran out, Andersen did the rounds of his acquaintances to say his farewells and attended another performance of *The Frozen Deep*, which was followed by another party, this time in a marquee. Andersen complained about the heat, fretted over a sore throat and developed toothache. On Wednesday, 15 July, he was up at six in the morning and left the house at half past eight, driven by Dickens in a little carriage, 'we two quite alone', to catch the boat train from Maidstone. 'I spoke but little,' he wrote to Jette Wulff:

> I was unhappy. He was to the last minute like an affectionate brother, looked quite sadly at me on parting, kissed me, and – I went alone onto the steam dragon to Folkestone, waited a few hours on the steamship before it sailed away, and reached France some hours later, dejected, deeply dejected, as if I had left someone dear to me whom I should never see again . . .

Andersen's premonition was correct. When *The Frozen Deep* transferred to Manchester, professional actresses replaced the women of Dickens' family, and these included Nelly Ternan. At eighteen, she was the same age as his daughter, Kate, but such was Dickens' infatuation with Nellie that within three months he had bricked up the door between what had been the marital bedroom and the small dressing room where he now slept. Kate told Gladys Storey that 'nothing could surpass the misery and unhappiness of our home', and Catherine Dickens was banished to a small house in Gloucester Crescent. Her husband paid her £600 per year for the rest of her life, but forbade the children to have anything to do with their mother, this interdict being challenged only by young Charles, who chose to make his home with her.

London hummed with gossip over the scandal. Thackeray quarrelled with Dickens over his behaviour, describing him as 'abominably coarse, vulgar and happy', and Dickens severed contact with anyone who expressed any sympathy for his wife's cause. Andersen unwittingly dropped into this category, having as usual written up his travel notes for publication, this time, perhaps in imitation of Dickens himself, in serial form under the title, *A Visit to Charles Dickens in the Summer of 1857*. In all innocence, he wrote in glowing terms of Mrs Dickens' understanding and kindness, and a German translation of the piece found its way to Britain. Bentley pounced on it with glee and printed it in his *Miscellany*, though not without a word of disapproval for what he regarded as the author's treachery:

> A man can hardly attain a decent amount of literary celebrity ere a chile's [sic] among his household taking notes, and faith he'll print them. The last and most striking instance of this nature is supplied by the Danish poet Hans Christian Andersen, who having spent a portion of 1857 at Charles Dickens's hospitable house at Gadshill, has recently put forth his experiences . . .

Andersen never realised that the ensuing silence could have been caused by his own actions. Having left London, he had spent five days in Weimar at the insistence of Carl Alexander, who wanted him to be present at the centennial celebrations of his grandfather's birth and the unveiling of statues of Goethe and Schiller. The latter poet, Andersen remarked a little complacently, 'looks like me'. He had sat through a Liszt concert, reading and re-reading a letter from Jette Wulff, and admitted in his reply to her that otherwise the music 'would have killed me'. He seemed far from London and Dickens, but in writing to the Grand Duke afterwards, he was unguarded in gossiping about his host, even though his intentions were merely to praise Dickens for his charitable efforts:

> When I stayed in his house I saw how generously and zealously he worked to raise a few thousand pounds for Douglas Jerrold's widow. He arranged recitations, dramatic performances and similar entertainments, but received very poor thanks for his trouble. The son of the deceased Jerrold has, I hear, intimated that it was unnecessary to carry the hat round to collect money for his mother, as she was not left in straitened circumstances. This is written after everything had taken place and all the trouble been spent on it. How ungrateful!

It may well have been that Dickens had rushed into a high-handed assumption, but it was typical of Andersen not to realise that such tittle-tattle might well get back to his host. To Dickens himself, he wrote in effusive thanks:

> It is as if I am standing in your parlour in Gadshill, seeing, as I did on the day I first arrived there, roses in bloom round the windows, and the green fields stretching away towards Rochester. I am aware of the smell of apples from the hedge of wild roses out by the field, where your sons are playing cricket. Oh, how much may lie between now and the time when I shall feel and see it in reality again, if indeed that will ever happen! But whatever time may reveal, my heart will cling to you faithfully, lovingly and gratefully, my great, noble friend. Make me happy with a letter, and when you have read *To Be Or Not To Be*, tell me what you think of it. Forget in friendship the dark side of me which proximity may have revealed. I would so much like to be remembered well by one whom I love as a friend and a brother.

It was a month before Dickens wrote back, excusing the delay by saying he had been busy in Manchester – a fact which his unfortunate wife might bitterly have confirmed. He made such scant reference to Andersen's novel that it seems certain that he had not read it, despite his assurance:

I have read "To be or not to be" and think it is a very fine book full of good purpose admirably wrogt out – a book in every way worthy of its great author.

> Good by, dear Andersen,
> Affectionately your friend,
> Charles Dickens.

The spelling is his own.

In saying goodbye to Andersen, he seems to have meant it quite literally, for he never wrote to him again. Andersen supplied letters of introduction to various friends who intended to visit Britain, and some critics have held that the arrival of Grímur Thomsen and Elizabeth Jerichau-Baumann so irritated Dickens as to cause the rift. In view of the fact that the whole pattern of the British author's life was changing dramatically at this time, this seems a minor factor – but whatever its cause, Andersen was saddened by the silence. It was a year before he heard through newspaper reports that the Dickens marriage had broken up, and he wrote in anxiety to Jette Wulff, asking if she had any further news. Elizabeth Jerichau-Baumann would probably have the full story when she returned from Britain, he added.

In fact, Andersen knew more than he chose to admit. On his way back to Denmark after the London visit, he had written to Edvard, 'I have much to tell you and your wife of Dickens and his private life, but I do not like to put such private matters on paper; one never knows what may be printed in the course of time.'

He did not know, either, that after his departure, Dickens had stuck a card above the dressing-table mirror in the room he had occupied. It said, 'Hans Andersen slept in this room for five weeks which seemed to the family AGES!' To the last, Andersen always believed they had been friends.

After his return from England, Andersen entered into a period of bleakness. There now seemed no unfilled ambition to give shape to his life, and he was beginning to feel old. 'As I am now,' he wrote to Jette Wulff, 'I must make shorter journeys.' Jette herself was still set on emigrating to America, and this, too, depressed him.

A renewed outbreak of cholera in Copenhagen sent him off to Sorø to stay with the Ingemanns, but he was back in the capital on 19 October, occupied with the preparation of a collected edition of his stories and fairy tales which was to appear in the spring. Edvard, who took care of Andersen's accounts, gave him a year-end statement which showed him to possess 6,462 rixdollars, some of which, at least, had come from Christian VIII either officially or personally. From this amplitude, Andersen lent Edvard 2,500 rixdollars at 4% interest, most probably to assist young Jonas, Edvard's son, with the purchase of a house.

In January 1858 the weather was unexpectedly fine, and Andersen wrote to Carl Alexander to say that he was longing for the south and a return to 'the land of the *Improvisatore*'. By the time his summer travelling season came round, however, Italy was in turmoil, with rebellion rising against the Austrian-dominated regimes, and Andersen plumped for safe, tranquil Switzerland instead. He dared not visit Weimar, for the conflict over Schleswig-Holstein was flaring up again. Despite desperate and increasingly draconian measures to force the duchies into speaking Danish and becoming part of the 'whole-state' constitution, the populace felt itself to be German, and was merely further infuriated by the Copenhagen government's banning of public meetings and outlawing of all foreign press productions. Although Andersen's letters to Carl Alexander remained as affectionate as ever, he knew that his friend would tolerate no defence of the Danish position. The political gulf between them now was so wide that there seemed little hope of resuming further contact until the tension between Denmark and Germany was resolved.

Andersen's journey to Switzerland began on 15 June, and this time he took with him the youngest of the Drewsen boys, Harald, then twenty-two years old. It was a free trip for the young man, for Andersen always paid his companion's fare, but Harald showed no sign of appreciating it. 'Harald is difficult to rouse in the mornings,' Andersen complained in his diary, 'and awkward to have around he won't call on people, won't speak German, very heavy-going, like Viggo.' The Drewsen brothers probably agreed that travelling with Andersen was a tiresome duty rather than a pleasure and Harald was obviously bored by his older companion's relentless socialising.

Jette Wulff, too, had begun her travels, leaving Copenhagen a little after Andersen had done. She was making her way to Hamburg, there to board the steamer for New York. Andersen had written to her from Sorø on the first stage of his own journey:

> It was with a heavy heart, I think far more than you realised that I said goodbye to you, although I am quite sure we will meet again more than once in this world.
>
> Thank you for your faithfulness to me, in spite of the fact that we are, as you say, and rightly I think, so different in many ways. Thank you for being so indulgent with me in all my irritability.

Arriving in Dresden, a town safely distant from forbidden Weimar, Andersen found a letter from Jette awaiting him. In Hamburg, she had discovered that the first available ship to America was the *Austria*, sailing on 1 September. She thus had a month to wait, and suggested that Andersen might like to call at Eisenach, where she was staying, and spend some time with her on his way back to Denmark. She put her request as a light-hearted command; 'I think it is almost your duty to come and see me once more and give me your brotherly blessing.'

Eisenach, as Jette pointed out, was only a six-hour train ride from Dresden – but it was also perilously close to Weimar, and Andersen could not face the idea that Carl Alexander might find out that he had been so near and yet had made no contact. He admitted this in his reply to Jette, but backed it up with the second excuse that Harald particularly wanted to return via Brunswick, as he was interested in old buildings.

Jette was dismissive of the Weimar question, knowing that the Grand Duke was himself away on a journey to other parts of Germany, but she accepted the second plea without hesitation. 'Please forget *altogether* my inconsiderate little plan, which I should never have suggested . . .' Her letter was a touching exploration of her feelings towards Andersen. In the warmth of her affection, she often forgot, she said, that he was 'what is called a famous man'. She went on to express a kind of need for him which was as close to love as Jette, with her bent and deformed little body, could hope to come:

> I read your letter with my heart – this one is written with my heart, please read it that way – but I <u>know</u> you will; I know your heart, it is a safe anchoring place, it will not betray the trust I have in it, of that I am fully and firmly convinced, <u>even though</u> appearances might give a different picture sometimes.

She wrote to him one further time, asking him not to forget her and giving him her blessing, and then sailed for the New World. Twelve days later, as the *Austria* was nearing New York, fire broke out on board, and the ship sank with a loss of four hundred and seventy lives. Jette Wulff was not among the few who were saved.

News of the tragedy did not reach Andersen until 7 October. He entertained no hope that she had been among the ninety survivors. Writing to Ingemann before the final confirmation came, he was already elegiac. 'You have seen her; in her small, deformed body a great and strong spirit reigned.' Her loss was a devastating blow which filled him with nightmares and guilt, expressed in a letter to his old friend, Mrs Laessøe:

> Day after day the terrifying vision of it stirs in my imagination; the vivid clarity of it all in my feverish mind frightens me; for several weeks I have been unable to work . . . She was one of the few people who really and truly loved me; she appreciated and overrated me. She gave her feelings fully, and I did not return them with the same generosity – this is something for which I reproach myself. I am grieved that in Germany, on my journey last summer, I did not make the detour she wanted . . .

It was to be two years before Andersen ventured abroad again. The summer which followed Jette's death saw war break out in Italy between Austria and the combined forces of France and Sardinia. The

Austrians were rapidly defeated, and the rebel forces in other European countries rose with new courage against their oppressive regimes. Denmark managed to stave off the continuing unrest in the duchies, largely because Germany was too busy with her own troubles to bother overmuch with the disputed border territories, but the coming explosion was inevitable.

Andersen wrote prolifically during this time, but the tales he poured out were charged with grief and darkness. His streak of black humour saves them from turgidity, but the only gleam of hope which they offer is vested in the belief that a spiritual life may continue beyond death. In 'Anne Lisbeth', a woman, hearing that the son she abandoned in infancy has drowned at sea, is haunted by the peculiarly terrible grief of those whose loved ones lie somewhere unburied and unknown. 'Bury me, bury me,' the ghost of the dead boy calls, as perhaps the unquiet spirit of Jette Wulff called to Andersen in the recesses of his own mind.

He was still deeply troubled when, ten months later, he went to stay with Ørsted's daughter, now Sophie Dahlstrom, in northern Jutland. There, he was told by Bishop Kierkegaard, brother of the philosopher Søren, that Børghum Monastery, lying just across the river, was haunted. The next day, Andersen took a barge across to the mysterious place, where he understood that visitors were catered for, and asked to stay overnight in the same room which the bishop had occupied. His diary records how he searched the room from floor to ceiling before going to bed, though finding nothing unusual. He woke a little after midnight, his mind full of uneasy thoughts about Jette, and still saw nothing, but on settling back to sleep, was certain that a misty figure stood in the room's far corner. He seemed satisfied rather than scared, though the apparition was too transient for him to be quite sure what he had seen.

During the same period he wrote 'The Dead Child', again featuring a bereaved mother. The woman in this tale is so distraught that she herself wishes to die, and it is the spirit of her little son which insists that God wills her to take up her tasks again, promising her that they will meet in heaven.

Despite his established fame, there were some mutterings from the public about the gloomy tone of these stories, and Andersen's notes on their origin are defensive, contending that people only preferred the earlier ones because they had read them when young and had now lost their mental receptivity. It was an ingenious argument, and one which revealed obliquely that Andersen himself was aware of a lack of freshness. Vilhelm Pedersen, whose evocative pencil drawings had so gracefully illustrated the early tales, had died six months after Jette Wulff, and the spring of 1859 brought no respite from the loveless emptiness of his life. A devoted fan called Anna Bjerring had made contact with him during his stay in Jutland and wrote him countless letters, but such adulation did not touch his private grief.

Europe was still in a state of turmoil, and Andersen had temporarily lost his taste for travelling. He shifted from one Danish host to another during the summer, increasingly concerned over small details of his physical health, and came back to Copenhagen in low spirits. On 18 February 1860 he made a will, leaving his entire estate to Edvard Collin. Constantly tormented by toothache, he had a number of teeth extracted during that winter, necessitating an upper denture which did not fit properly and continued to cause him discomfort.

Even more disturbing than his bodily failings was Andersen's constant fear of insanity. He had noted shortly before his visit to the haunted monastery that he had been greeted on the street by a man said to be immensely wealthy but who 'had lost his mind from masturbating'. As this had for years been Andersen's only form of sexual activity, he had good cause to dread the commonly believed result.

As the political climate in Europe began to stabilise, Andersen hoped to renew his acquaintance with Carl Alexander, but the duke was away in Baden Baden. Andersen went instead to Oberammergau for the Passion Play, where he happened to meet two young members of the Copenhagen Royal Theatre company, Lauritz Eckardt and Harald Scharff. He took a strong liking to Scharff, a ballet dancer, and was bereft when the time came to go on alone to Le Locle and then Geneva. 'Wanted to go home,' he noted on 1 September. 'Wrote a letter in that frame of mind to Edvard and asked for his advice.'

On the following day, Andersen read that Heiberg had died, and a letter from H.P. Holst containing the same news awaited him at the Post Office. He was plunged into renewed misery and felt 'a demonic urge' to throw himself into the rushing water of the Rhône as he walked by the river. A few days later was 5 September, the anniversary of his arrival in Copenhagen, a day he celebrated as always with friends who provided 'a lovely supper', but he could hardly enjoy it for the morbidity of his thoughts.

Towards the Christmas of that year, his mind turned back to memories of Charles Dickens, and he wrote 'The Dung Beetle' based on an Arabic saying which Dickens had quoted, 'When the emperor was shoeing his horses with gold, the dung beetle also stretched out his legs.' Andersen's tale has the beetle eventually riding the horse (after adventures which centre round a narrow escape from the dreaded trap of marriage), and feeling convinced that his mount has earned its gold shoes only because it carries so important a personage. This tale, Andersen's note to it remarks, applied to many things which he had not consciously realised while writing it. Jette Wulff's gentle derision of his need for royal favour in order to prove his own worth was harder to forget now than when she had lived.

At the New Year of 1861 Edvard again asked Andersen for a loan, this time suggesting that he should invest a thousand rixdollars with him at 5% – which was 1% above bank rate – as a fund for 'a mutual acquaintance', who in fact was Henrik Stampe. Since Edvard knew by now that Andersen's whole estate would come to him, the request was a reasonable one, and the terms generous, for Edvard was a man of scrupulous, if unimaginative probity.

On 20 February, Andersen read aloud to a large audience of working people as part of an innovative university series which responded to the new demands for democracy. It was a new experience for Andersen. 'Artisans, with their wives and children filled the large hall, and it was of psychological interest to note the impression which the lecture made,' he wrote to Carl Alexander. Denmark was moving towards a new liberalism with startling speed and with little of the civil unrest which had erupted in the less progressive countries of Europe. Italy, however, now liberated from Austrian domination and, united in a Sardinian-led national identity, was regarded as the shining light of democratic modernity and Andersen at last shook off his depression in a renewed desire to visit Rome again.

He set out on 4 April, taking with him Edvard's son, young Jonas, now twenty-one years old. Once again, he found his companion irritating. Jonas, a true Collin, had little patience with what he called Andersen's 'egoism', and Andersen felt this to be an injustice. 'I am staying in Rome for his sake alone,' he confided to his diary on Sunday, 5 May, 'may never leave here. I'm feeling despondent, unwell. Sat in tears on my bed.' He was suffering from haemorrhoids, and made frequent reference in his diary to passing blood, and yet his appetite for sightseeing and socialising was relentless, and it was Jonas who flagged and became bored.

On Ascension Day the pair of them went to church, but when Andersen saw the size and density of the crowd waiting to be blessed by the Pope he said he did not feel well, and left. Jonas stayed on to get a glimpse of the Pope, and when he returned, to the waiting Andersen, a battle of wills took place. Jonas wanted to go back and watch the rest of the ceremony, while Andersen insisted that he felt ill and needed the younger man's company. 'I had the hope that he would care enough about me to stay,' he recorded, 'but he went.' It then began to rain with sudden Italian violence, and Andersen was forced to follow Jonas into the church for shelter. In doing so, he tripped over a stool and fell, causing several people to tumble over him in turn, and Jonas was furious, making it clear that he found such behaviour ludicrous and embarrassing.

Andersen's friends were well used to episodes of this sort, and Bjørnstjerne Bjørnson, a Norwegian poet whom he met in Rome and liked was quick to perceive the truth. Writing later on to Andersen, he was amused to note his foibles:

> Whenever I read your letter it makes me laugh, because wherever you go it seems that you find yourself in a draught or being pushed about by crowds. I imagine you'll turn round to St Peter the minute you enter Heaven and ask him to shut the door against the draught that is, unless you've decided at the doorway to go back because you are being pushed by crowds.

Bjørnson added good-humouredly that there wasn't a man in Denmark about whom so many jokes were told – or who told so many himself. At his best, Andersen could be very funny, but there was always a danger that he would fail to be amused, as Bjørnson had found out. At their first meeting, the Norwegian had remarked as a joke that Uncle Peppo, the beggar on the Spanish Steps whom Andersen had named in *The Improvisatore*, was angry about being depicted as such a villain because nobody gave him their spare coppers any more. Andersen's diary revealed that he took this perfectly seriously. 'I was highly affected; this man, who doesn't understand me but hates me all the same, wants to hurt me. I shall be killed . . .' He was half inclined to leave Rome at once, and it took all Bjørnson's persuasion to convince him that the story was not true. The Norwegian became sincerely fond of the gaunt, now greying Andersen, and wrote to him later with real kindness, saying he had found him

> so full of character, with so much behind you, with such a glorious love in your way of speaking and behaving – and – please forgive me! – with so many weaknesses which one must take into account and pay tender regard to all the time . . .

Jonas, on the other hand, was too young and impatient to find Andersen's failings amusing, let alone loveable, and his dissent was expressed in oblique terms which passed as debating points. On 14 May he expressed admiration for his cousin Viggo Drewsen because 'he worked on his own development and had nothing to do with other people'. Andersen regarded this as quintessentially selfish, and admitted in his notes that it provided him with the material for the story he wrote at that time called 'The Snail and the Rosebush'. Following their argument, Jonas had gone out, not returning until after midnight, and Andersen had been so angry that he wrote in his diary, 'My legs are shaking under me; my head is burning hot'.

The tale he produced contrasted his own natural, if thorny blossoming of poetry with Jonas's mollusc-like coldness. The boy was in fact busy collecting snails to ship home to Copenhagen as part of his zoological studies, so the protagonists were very lightly disguised. Asked what it can give that is of value, the snail/Jonas/Viggo reply is unequivocal:

> "What will I give?" snarled the snail. "I spit on the whole world. It's worth nothing to me, and means nothing. Go on creating your roses, since you can't stop, anyway . . . "

Having completed the story, Andersen read it out to Jonas, who said it showed 'great malice'. Certainly it demonstrated that Andersen was not unaware of the meaning of his own allegories. In the previous decade, he had made it very clear to Edvard that 'The Shadow' was meant for him, despite the unvarnished malevolence of its ending. Lest the meaning should be missed, he had referred to it in a letter to

Edvard from London just after the story's publication, and Edvard found it necessary years later to append an explanatory note to the reference in his book of posthumously published letters.

Not unnaturally, relations with young Jonas worsened during their stay in Rome, and by 18 May, Andersen was on the verge of total breakdown. He went to bed 'without supper, terribly depressed, spiteful and in tears, jumping out of bed and ranting, beside myself.' Jonas was, he said, 'quiet'. The next morning, a Sunday, Andersen got up early and went out for a long walk, trying to subdue his mood of manic fury, and lapsed back into despondency. In the afternoon he drove with Jonas to St Peter's, and there he was temporarily lifted from his heaviness:

> In one of the chapels the castrati were singing. One of the voices was resonant and moving; it was a handsome young man. The whole Pentecost celebration was held in the Sistine Chapel, but Jonas was not allowed in there wearing his jacket and straw hat, so we went out of the church and changed clothes. He looked funny in my big coat . . . I went home with his short-sleeved jacket.

They lunched with Niels Ravnkilde, a Danish composer who was teaching music in Rome, and afterwards, Andersen went for a walk with him alone and told him about his state of mind. The composer sensibly advised him to go off somewhere on his own for the afternoon, and by the end of the day his anger and depression had abated. 'Later, when Jonas came home,' he wrote in his diary, 'I put my arms round him, said a few kind words; and he was moved and agreeable. It made me happy. The heavy clouds had lifted . . .'

Andersen's unrest sprang in part, it seems evident, from frustrated sexuality. In Italy he was always 'sensual,' as his diary entries recorded, and the stories he wrote at this time increasingly held veiled references to this. On 8 May, ten days before his crisis with Jonas, he had been to the Bonaventura monastery to see his friend Albert Küchler, now a Franciscan monk there. Küchler had figured in *The Improvisatore* as an ambiguous presence strongly associated with sexuality, and the fact that he had now retreated into the purity of the church held a great attraction for Andersen. Catholicism, since his first contact with it, had moved him deeply with its concept of chaste masculinity and the inbuilt distaste for female physicality which underlies the worship of a mother who is also a virgin. This paradox, formalised into a tenet of faith, must have seemed to Andersen a religious ratification of his own most fundamental instincts. During his visit to the monastery, Küchler introduced him to a friend, Brother Ignatius, who had heard a lot about Andersen and said they had much in common.

Andersen referred to Brother Ignatius by name in the story called 'Psyche' which he wrote while still in Rome. Very obviously, the tale is an exploration of sexual identity, featuring a young sculptor who is urged by his friends to enjoy the Roman girls as they themselves do. In his own mind, the idea of feminine perfection resides in the marble statue of the nymph, Psyche, which he has just completed, and he finds the prompting of his friends repugnant. However, by the end of a roistering night he is in a state of sexual arousal and goes to a prostitute.

Andersen cannot quite bring himself to describe what happens but makes it plain that the result is terrible:

> A strange, foul smell of corruption mingled with the perfume of roses, it lamed his mind and blinded his sight. The fireworks of sensuality were over and darkness came.

The young sculptor, sick with self-disgust, is rescued by Brother Ignatius and the purity of the church, which he embraces with relief:

> How kindly, how happily his new brothers greeted him, and how like a festival on a high holy day it was when he took his vows . . . Everything melted into one, everything spoke of peace and beauty; a fairy tale, everything was a dream!

Nevertheless, he continues to be troubled by 'unclean, evil thoughts':

> What were these strange flames that seemed to set his body on fire? Where did the evil come from that he wanted no part of, yet that seemed always to be present within him? He punished his body, but the evil did not come from the surface but from deep within him.

Andersen probes carefully into the nature of this perceived evil. The sculptor dismisses the thought that the outer world, with all its enjoyments and temptations, has provided him with his personal devil, both in sexuality and the pursuit of ambition – but then he comes to the ultimate test of faith, and fails it. 'I search for happiness and comfort in the consolation of religion. But what if it is only consolation? If everything here, as in the world I left behind, is but vain dreams . . .' He comes to the conclusion that it was, after all, God's intention that he should have continued to work as a sculptor. On entering the monastery he had buried his statue of Psyche deep in a well, but at the end of the story it is discovered and admired long after the bones of its creator have crumbled to dust.

It is an immensely skilful structure, double-layered as so many of Andersen's stories are. The investigation into his own psyche is hidden within the romantic symbolism of marble and godliness, and readers were happy to see it merely as a parable of the artistic muse and its triumph over temptation. 'Psyche' was published, together with 'The Snail and the Rosebush' and two other stories, at Christmas 1861, and Andersen was furious that Bentley, without seeking his permission, dedicated the book to the Princess of Wales. 'I'm not at all pleased to have a story like 'Psyche' dedicated to a young woman,' he noted, making it clear that his objection was on the grounds of gender rather than personality.

While in Rome, Andersen visited the Brownings, and met their twelve-year-old son, Pen. Elizabeth Barrett-Browning was mortally ill, and would die a few weeks later, but she was amused by Andersen, and wrote to a friend the next day, 'Pen says of him, "He is not really pretty. He is rather like his own ugly duck, but his mind has developed into a swan." That wasn't bad of Pen, was it?' The last poem she ever wrote, 'North and South', ends with a reference to her Danish visitor:

> And thus to Rome came Andersen.
> – 'Alas, but must you take him again?'
> Said the South to the North.

As always, Andersen's social life was busy, and on 13 May he and Jonas went to a get-together in the Palazzo Barberini, the home of a wealthy American sculptor, William Wentworth Wetmore Story, whom he had met two days previously. In a cosmopolitan gathering of expats and their children, Andersen was pressed into reading 'The Ugly Duckling', but could not manage it in English and had to hand over to Story. Browning recited 'The Pied Piper of Hamelin' while Story played the flute as the piper, followed round the room by the excited children. Henry James mentions the episode in his book about Story, claiming that Andersen let the children believe he kept every one of the tin soldiers and toys which they gave him. 'Beautiful the queer image of that great benefactor moving about Europe with his accumulation of these relics.'

On 29 May, Andersen and Jonas began their journey home. In Lausanne a month later, a letter from Adolphe Drewsen broke the news that Jonas Collin senior was seriously ill. It warned Andersen that he might not find the old man alive when he got home. From the same town less than a year ago, Andersen had written to Edvard in distress about a dream which had caused him to think Jonas might have died ('My God! What has happened at home? Have I lost him?') – and yet now, with that dream about to come true, he made no attempt to speed up his journey. He and young Jonas made long pauses in Brunnen, Munich and Dresden despite frequent letters from the family about the old man's worsening condition. Even as close to home as Hamburg, Andersen declared his intention to make a detour through Basnaes and Sorø. Young Jonas said he would go straight to Copenhagen – and on their last evening together, a peace was made between the travellers. As Andersen recorded:

> I did what I had all along meant to do; I suggested to him that he should say "*du*" to me; he was surprised, but said a firm 'Yes!' and thanked me. Later, after I had gone to bed, he came in before retiring himself and took my hand, again repeating a deeply felt 'Thank you!' so that tears came to my eyes; he pressed a kiss on my forhead and I felt very happy.

There is something deeply poignant in the fact that Edvard's son gave Andersen the reassurance of friendship which Edvard himself had denied a generation previously. Elias Bredsdorff points to the fact that Edvard allowed his son to travel with Andersen as proof that there could have been no question of homosexual interest, but Aksel Dreslov quotes a later letter from Andersen to young Jonas which tells a different story. Having spoken of the liking he has had for the boy since childhood, Andersen goes on to describe the delight it gave him to see Jonas coming into the room 'with that blessed face which the dear God has given you. I long for you, dear friend'; he continues – 'I need you to become lighter and happier in mind – you are so charmingly young!' In the same letter, he adds, 'you will hardly guess how I constantly long for you and wish you were here with me.' His later anger with the young man, for which he gives no specific cause, may well have been due to a firm rebuttal on Jonas's part on realising the strength of Andersen's feelings.

Where Jonas Collin senior was concerned, the emotional situation was even more complicated. As Johan de Mylius points out in his masterly overview, *H.C. Andersen – Liv og vaerk: en tidstavle, 1805–1875,* Andersen had long been trying to liberate himself from the moral debt which he felt he owed Collin. Despite the recognition he had earned with almost everyone else, where Collin was concerned, he had never quite managed to throw off the sense of inferiority which was a relic of having been rescued from destitution – and neither had he been able to express the deep resentment which this caused. Now that the financial debt, at least, was amply repaid, with money flowing the other way in the form of large loans to the Collin family, Andersen's self-respect demanded that he take up a more independent attitude towards his former benefactor. His diary note about the news that Collin was ill referred to Jonas senior not as 'the father', as he was accustomed to, but merely as 'old Collin'. With his reluctance to be there at his death, it seemed that Andersen was testing his own precarious independence.

When Jonas Collin died on 28 August, Andersen answered Edvard's letter informing him of the fact with a steadiness which was slightly precarious:

> The news of his death did not overwhelm me as it would have done previously, but throughout yesterday, even last night and today, it has filled my thoughts. I want to be with you, to talk to you.

Despite his apparent calm, while reading for his hosts at Basnaes that night, he 'felt faint and went to bed before 10 o'clock.' He had no hesitation in describing it in his diary as 'a physical reaction'.

The Collin family must have found his attitude extraordinary and more than a little hurtful, and the terse words of Andersen's diary for 1 September expose the distance which had opened up between him and what he used to call 'the home of homes':

> In Amalie Street they are still holding open house today and tomorrow. The atmosphere tolerable. Mrs Drewsen was prepared to go to Jonna, who is expecting a baby. She'll have to drive all night. Saw old Collin's body. He looked as if he were sleeping peacefully. His beard was very red.

The funeral took place the following morning, on Monday, 2 September. After it, Andersen noted, he 'ate at a restaurant and felt very alone.'

Chapter 19
Spain, and a Danish Defeat

For all his determination to find emotional independence, Andersen was doggedby depression in the autumn and winter of 1861. He was living a grand life, attending Court balls, and his relationship with the new king, Frederik VII, had warmed into liking, resulting in many palace visits – and yet insecurity haunted him. There was no obvious reason for it; he was welcomed in the book-lined library room which the dowager queen Caroline had established at Amalienborg, and his diary showed an increasing intimacy with the man who could have been his half-brother. On 27 January 1862 he recorded an evening which had given him evident pleasure:

> The king himself put sugar and water in front of me and three times gave me his hand, which I kissed; he was very open and warm. "But how can you think up all these things?" he said; "How does it all come to you? Have you got it all in your head?"

He had been invited to meet the Italian minister at a state dinner, and was publicly welcomed home from his own Italian journey by the king, but Frederik VII was a little surprised that Andersen thanked him for having invited him.' But of course I wanted you to come, old chap,' he said. 'You know that.'

At some deep level, Andersen did not know it, and the royal cosiness did nothing to allay his irrational fears. After a banquet at the palace in October, he took home as a souvenir a red flower which had been part of the table decoration, and then felt overwhelmingly guilty about it, convinced that the theft would be discovered and that he would be 'dragged down into the mud, mocked and despised'. His diary entries spoke of 'this madness' as an almost perpetual state, from which he escaped only for brief spells.

Things worsened with the shortening of the days to mid-winter and although the king gave Andersen a gold box inlaid with precious stones in February, the mental shakiness persisted. At a ball given a few days later by Prince Christian, who was to succeed Frederik as Christian IX, he agonized over finding himself the only person present to be wearing black gloves instead of white ones. However, at about the same time, his friendship with Harald Scharff, the young ballet dancer whom he had met at Oberammergau, blossomed into a love-affair. Clutching at this emotional life-line, Andersen was evidently too relieved and excited to be discreet about his relationship with the young man, for Edvard's brother, Theodor Collin, commented on 17 February that the strength of this friendship was becoming noticeable and was 'ridiculous'. Theodor was Andersen's doctor, and spoke not merely as a member of the Collin clan but as a medical man who was probably well aware of his patient's proclivities. His warning put Andersen into 'a very bad temper', as he admitted in his diary for that day, and his passion for Scharff continued to be so prominent in his mind that he seemed hardly moved by the death of Bernhard Ingemann on 24 February.

Andersen was perhaps sated with grief after the loss of Jette Wulff and the unadmitted trauma of Jonas Collin's death, but Ingemann had provided him with friendship and a welcoming home ever since the days at school in Slagelse, and there is something strangely cold about Andersen's reaction. Past affections had little hold on him now, for after the funeral in Sorø, he came straight back to Copenhagen and went to a court ball the same evening. By 5 March he was recording in his diary how he had told Einar Drewsen about his passion for Scharff and their exchanging of 'all the small secrets of the heart'. Scharff gave him a silver toothbrush engraved with his name for his birthday, and in the weeks that followed, Andersen's diary held several more references to his longing for the young man. It seemed that he had almost dropped the guardedness which had been the habit of a lifetime. With the confidence of a man secure in court favour, he may have felt his standing to be proof against gossip – but he was also free for the first time from the stern presence of Jonas Collin senior. That father-figure, for all his kindliness, had been severely conventional, and Andersen was deeply in awe of him. The old man had exercised a controlling authority which, for a gutterboy who owed him his whole life's success, was impossible to challenge. Now that he was gone, Andersen was more alone than he had ever been, but he was also relieved of a judgmental presence. As his life's remaining problem defined itself with increasing clarity as one of lovelessness, Andersen felt newly able to address this and to accept the risks inherent in doing so.

Despite his involvement with Scharff, he planned a long trip to Spain in the summer. Travel marked the seasons of his year as essentially as the flight of a migrating bird, and he could not look ahead without allocating journey-time. He set out on 23 July 1862, again taking young Jonas with him. The young man had obtained leave of absence from his zoological studies on the grounds that this would be a 'field trip', but the bottles of alcohol which he brought along for preserving specimens fell foul of the first Customs inspection, and were promptly confiscated.

Edvard and Jette Collin, together with Edvard's sister, Louise, were visiting Switzerland, and joined Andersen and Jonas for a month's leisurely touring in that country. It was not until 6 September that the longer-distance pair reached the Spanish border, and there, Andersen found himself confronted by conditions that were a step back in time, as he related in his subsequent travel-book, *In Spain*:

> At Perpignan, I had to revert to the travel of olden days, to take my seat again in the poetical conveyance of our poetic old times. I am not poet enough to enjoy going back to the past, I prefer the present with all the blessings of a modern life.

He was dismayed to hear the Spanish diligences described as 'torture boxes, great heavy omnibuses with an entrance on one side only, so that there was no escape if the coach overturned'. And, he added grimly, they always overturned.

He had to admit that the twelve mules which pulled their carriage set a cracking pace, even fording a river where the water was up to their chests and the passengers had to lift up their feet as the water flooded in across the carriage floor. At Gerona, he was glad of the 'modern magic' of the train which took them on to Barcelona. There, he was delighted by the cafés and the narrow, awning-shaded streets where jugglers and musicians performed, and wrote an evocative account of it in his book:

> A little black-eyed child danced and shook a tambourine before being tied half in knots by its half-naked papa. In order to see better I mounted a couple of steps in the entrance to an old house with a single Moorish-style window and two horseshoe arches supported by

slender marble columns. Behind me the door was half open; I looked in and saw a thick hedge of geraniums growing round a dust-dry fountain. An enormous vine overshadowed most of the place, which seemed forsaken and dead; wooden shutters hung on one hinge in loose window frames, as if ready to fall. Inside it looked as though the place were given over to bat-filled twilight.

Andersen was in a dilemma about the onward journey to Valencia, reluctant to venture further by diligence. During his two weeks in Barcelona he had seen a sudden flood engulf the town, and two people had told him how lucky he and Jonas had been to survive their fording of the river in the mule-drawn coach, for exactly at that place, two passengers had recently been drowned when a carriage overturned. The alternative was to go by ship round the coast to Valencia, but the ships were reputed to be dirty and unreliable, and the nightmare of Jette Wulff's death haunted him and made him more than ever afraid of the sea. A Danish friend, Herman Schierbeck, poured scorn on his fears and said there could be no question of attempting an overland passage. He took Andersen along to the shipping office and supervised the buying of a ticket for the *Catalan*, which had, he said, a good engine and a competent captain.

The overnight voyage down the coast was rough. Jonas went happily down to dinner, smoked a cigar then turned into his bunk, but Andersen, wretched with nerves and seasickness, huddled on deck in the wind. He got into conversation with a young German from Mannheim who, on hearing Andersen's identity, could not do enough for him:

> He busied himself doing all he could to make me more comfortable – put his own woollen scarf round my neck and his cloak over my feet, because there was a cold breeze and the rolling of the ship prevented me from going down to my cabin to unpack . . .

Such solicitude was exactly what Andersen would have liked, and never got, from Jonas.

Safely docked, the pair made their way into Valencia, where Andersen cheered up after a good lunch. He said during a conversation about mutual acquaintances that a certain girl would make him a good wife, but Jonas did not take this to be a joke.

According to Andersen's diary, he declared the idea disgusting and said it should be protested against 'for humanitarian reasons'. Andersen found this offensive, and complained in his diary that Jonas seemed to regard rudeness as 'manly'. Tension began to build up between them, but Jonas now had the good sense to go off on his own whenever they were staying in a place for some days, and serious conflict was avoided.

Andersen was glad he had opted for the sea voyage when he saw the diligence from Barcelona arrive:

> It was smelly, dusty, and only a ghost of the coach we had seen two days ago. The horses were dripping with sweat, the vehicle itself was macadamised withdust and the passengers limped out like hospital patients.

An additional reason for his impatience with coach travel was the prevailing fashion for the crinoline, a garment which he hated because of the space it took up. *In Spain* contains a contemptuous description of this ridiculous contraption which, he said, enclosed a woman as if she were the clapper in a bell. It had been invented by a young empress who wanted to disguise the fact that she was pregnant, and in his view, proved the stupidity of those to wore it for reasons of mindless fashion.

He opted for sea travel again on the next leg of their journey to Málaga, but although it was calm, Andersen was still panicky. As the only first-class passengers, he and Jonas had a cabin each, but he found his pillow 'too greasy to touch', and covered it with a piece of clean linen taken from his trunk. During the night his lamp burned out, and in the darkness Andersen became convinced that the sound of the ship's screws was so noisy that it must be scraping over rocks. He went up on deck and encountered the ship's captain, who ordered his cabin lamp to be relit and reassured him, but Andersen was still too nervous to sleep.

In Málaga, Andersen found a thriving Scandinavian community, and was much happier, admitting in his diary that 'sympathetic, kind-hearted people' were much more important to him than any picturesqueness of landscape or architecture.

On 5 October Jonas persuaded him to go to a bullfight, and although it was a modest affair in which most of the bulls had their horns wrapped and were there merely as a preliminary canter to the real thing in Seville or some other big centre, Andersen still found the whole thing disgusting. He seemed relieved to be setting out the next day for Granada, even though this journey was in a coach which had to be accompanied across the stony mountain roads by armed guards to defend it from bandit attacks.

Granada was well worth the hazardous journey. 'The famed, enchanting Alhambra, the object of our whole journey' was all Andersen could have expected, and he wrote a rapturous account of it. A Colonel Larramendi looked after the travelling pair assiduously during their stay in his city, and although he spoke no Danish or German, Andersen noted with some surprise that Jonas had 'made great strides in Spanish'. Supplemented by Andersen's 'invention and mine', they got on well. Queen Isabella was in the city that day, but the pleasure of meeting her was dimmed by Andersen's discovery on return that he had been robbed of a gold chain on which he wore replicas of his many decorations. It had included the miniature Order of the North Star given to him by Oehlenschläger.

On 30 October, Andersen and Jonas crossed from Gibraltar to Tangier, where they were bodily carted ashore from small boats by a wading crew who dumped them on the beach. They spent a week of 'unforgettable, untroubled days' as the guests of the British Consul, General Sir John Drummond Hay and his Danish-born wife. Andersen was disconcerted to find that the only toilet provision consisted of three holes dug in a corner of the garden. 'As I was squatting there, a yellow dog came by,' he recorded – 'I thought it was a lion!' The assumption was not as wild as it seems, for his hosts had mentioned seeing a lion the previous year and seemed unconcerned that the garden was visited by a wild boar, not to mention jackals and mongooses.

Jonas, with an eye to obtaining specimens, joined a hunting party during their stay, riding a horse with a pedigree that named five hundred ancestors, a present to Drummond Hay from the Emperor of Morocco. Andersen, who detested the idea of hunting, was taken by a wealthy Jewish friend of the Consul's to his opulent house. Andersen remembered enough of his schoolboy Hebrew to read the first verse of Genesis aloud and spent a happy day with these new friends, but recorded having met a very different Jewish family the previous day. A poorly dressed man had smiled at him, beckoning, and Andersen had followed him a little nervously, to be led into a small house where a woman lay with her recently born baby. The man held the child out for Andersen's inspection, he said, so that he could see it was 'a real son of Abraham' – by which he presumably meant that it was circumcised – and he gave the child some money as he thought the custom demanded. The room had contained, he said, nothing but a few rags and a large pitcher.

Jonas came back from his expedition with a 'bag' of several animals, and was up late that night skinning them, declaring his intention to bring the heads home as trophies. He had also collected two live tortoises which duly accompanied them back to Denmark and, Andersen later noted, were still alive when they got there.

On return from Morocco to Spain, the pair went from Cadiz to Seville, where Andersen commented that dirt and dust from the famed tobacco factory fell like snowflakes over the town. They moved on, but Santa Cruz looked so dirty and disgusting that a plan to stay overnight there was quickly abandoned in favour of the ten-hour train journey to Madrid.

Spain's capital city proved a complete failure. It was snowing when Andersen and Jonas arrived there, and nobody knew the whereabouts of the Danish legation where letters should have been waiting. The Swedish minister eventually rescued the pair and found them accommodation, but Andersen's impression of Madrid was a bad one, not improved by another visit, at Jonas's insistence, to a bullfight. This was a much bigger affair than the one he had seen in Málaga, and it made a 'shattering, unforgettable impression' on the squeamish Andersen. He left after the fifth bull, having seen a score of horses disembowelled, describing it as a 'brutal, horrible form of entertainment'. He claimed in his book that many Spaniards shared his opinion, and seemed to think that a pending petition against it was likely to be successful. Madrid's art gallery and opera house earned a grudging approval, but in the main, he had consigned the city to a mental waste paperbasket in which Venice already belonged. Madrid reminded him, he said, of a camel that has fallen down in the desert.

A large part of Andersen's disappointment stemmed from the fact that his books were not known in Spain. In most European countries, his fame unlocked doors for him with no effort, but among the small, dark Iberians, his lanky height and odd appearance merely caused him to be stared at, and his diary recorded more than once that he was laughed at in the street. He and Jonas spent the New Year in Bordeaux then moved on to Paris, where they stayed for two months, Jonas being particularly keen to explore it.

As so often during the dark days of winter, Andersen lapsed into despondency. Bjørnstjerne Bjørnson, whom he had met in Rome, happened to be passing through the city on his way back to Norway and organised a celebratory dinner for the Danish author with the Scandinavian expat community, but even this failed to spark Andersen into much enthusiasm. In a letter to Edvard, he remarked that Bjørnson's speech had been so effusive that he had felt as if he were hearing a funeral oration spoken over his coffin.

Back in Copenhagen, Andersen found that Harald Scharff's affection had not survived the long absence. The affair did not lapse immediately, but Andersen at fifty-eight wrote gloomily of the falling-off in his physical energy and youthful spirit. He made no plans for further travel abroad that year, and by 27 August he knew that he was alone again. 'Scharff's passion for me is now over,' he wrote in his diary, 'he has set his sights on someone else.' He added bravely that he was not as cast down by this as he had been by 'other disappointments', but a fortnight later he wrote, 'I cannot exist in my loneliness'. He began to drink more heavily, having a taste for sweet fortified wine, and brooded bitterly on those who failed to show him the degree of friendship he wanted. After an unidentified episode of what he called 'the Collin brand of unpleasantness', he referred in his diary to Jonas as 'an insolent little brat on whom I have wasted the kindness of my heart'.

On 16 October, the day following this remark, he walked out to Vesterport where Copenhagen's grand new railway station was being completed, altering the whole appearance of the old entry through the city's ramparts, and was overwhelmed by the unfamiliarity of it all. He felt 'strange', he said, and 'had the feeling I might lose my way'.

International events were adding to his unhappy sense of bewilderment. The Prussian king, Wilhelm I, bent on increasing the size of the army, had appointed Otto von Bismarck as Prime Minister, a man of massive military ambition who was prepared to flout the constitutional rules by wildly exceeding the approved budget for rearmament. Mistrust between Denmark and Germany was intense.

At this point of national crisis, in an ironic repetition of his father's demise in the run-up to the Three Years' War, Frederik VII died on 15 November 1863. He had been an odd, essentially incompetent king, and after two failed marriages had taken as his third bride Louise Rasmussen, a former ballet dancer who, to the horror of the Court, had a child by another man. None of these liaisons brought Frederik a child of his own, and with his death ended a royal line which went back to 1426. Andersen mourned him as a lost friend, and mourned too for the dynasty which had gone, leaving him more than ever aware of his solitude.

The question of succession was a complex one. The Augustenborg family had a tenuous claim, but Struensee stood as a skeleton in their cupboard, and in any case, their pro-German sympathies made them an impossible choice. A young duke of Glücksberg had long been selected as heir to the throne when it became obvious that 'Fritz' would die without issue. Christian IX, as he became, was on his mother's side the nephew of Frederik VI's queen Marie whose six sons had all died, and when Christian's own father died the boy was sent to Frederik and Marie to be brought up as a brother to their two daughters.

Christian IX inherited an appalling situation. Like his father before him, Frederik had made a dying agreement to a new constitution which, again, sought to bind the duchies of Schleswig and Holstein irrevocably to Denmark, but died before he had signed it. Christian saw the dangers which it embodied, but was pressurised by the ruling politicians and by the upsurge of patriotic Danish feeling (at least in the northern part of the country which included Copenhagen) against Germany. As newly crowned monarch, he was urged to show a strong hand. He signed − and Bismarck saw his chance. As the duchies screamed in protest at being yoked to a country which they did not regard as their spiritual mother, an obvious opportunity presented itself to lend strong support to a Danish uprising. A successful war would take the mind of the German public off the tricky question of Bismarck's high-handed disregard of his own government and bring him into a position of unassailable power. He at once drew up his troops along the border, and Denmark began hastily to mobilise. As the year of 1683 ended, Andersen wrote with foreboding, 'the outlook is pitch black, sorrowful, bloody . . . '

The Prussians invaded in the early weeks of February, supported by Austrian troops, and routed the ill-prepared Danes at Dannevirke. It was a time of personal pain and grief for Andersen, who, beside his fear that the sons of his friends might be injured or killed, underwent the distress of having more teeth extracted. The period of waiting for six weeks, as was then necessary, before he could be fitted for his new dentures, was a misery ('better dead and buried'), and even after that, he felt unhappy and self-conscious, trying to get used to his 'role as an old man'. When his fifty-ninth birthday came round on 2 April, he could see nothing to look forward to:

> First, Jonas Collin behaved badly to me – he is now out of my heart. The king died. The war is threatening Denmark with destruction. I have become old. I have false teeth which torment me. I'm not in good health. I'm heading for death and the grave.

Meeting Johanne Heiberg on 3 May at a performance of his two-act play, *He Is Not Born,* he talked to her of old times and told her how desperately lonely he was. The great actress knew how he felt, agreeing that she, too, could not get used to the loneliness that had followed her husband's death. A brief rumour ran round Copenhagen that she and Andersen might make a match of it – but they knew each other better than that, and the gossips were disappointed.

Andersen had not seen Carl Alexander since his visit to Weimar on his way back from Charles Dickens in 1857, and he knew now, as Denmark struggled on in the new conflict, that he would probably never see him again. This time, there was little chance that a Danish victory would enable him to re-establish a friendship with a defeated enemy, and on 16 April his diary entry recognised that the end had come:

> I feel each kindness people in Germany have shown me, acknowledge friends there but feel that I, as a Dane, must make a complete break with them all. They have been torn out of my heart; we will never meet again; a beautiful past cannot be renewed. My heart is breaking!

Two days later, the Prussian army reached Als, destroying bridges and killing scores of officers and men. The war was coming terribly close, and Andersen was horrified to hear that Viggo Drewsen had been wounded and captured. It turned out that his injury was not serious, but things were going badly for Denmark. France and England had both refused their support in the struggle, and the odds were hopeless. Bismarck's weaponry was superior, and he had the huge advantage of knowing that the people of Holstein were on his side.

After a conclusive Danish defeat in June, a cease-fire was declared on 20 July 1864, and the duchies were formally handed to Germany. It was a catastrophic loss of territory comprising about a third of the land and population of Denmark. On the night when the peace terms were signed, Andersen had a dream that was to recur often, in which he nursed a child in his arms but found that it had died, leaving him holding nothing but its empty skin.

As the defeated army came straggling home, Andersen kept up the poetry readings he had been giving throughout the war, and his patriotic verses were still popular. A continued round of social visits still marked the pattern of his days, and on 22 July, just after the peace declaration, he went to Elsinore to meet the Swedish Prince Oscar. Clara Raphael, who had written the erotic book which so offended him, was there as well, and so was Harald Scharff, with whom Andersen spent a couple of days before returning to Copenhagen.

During a visit to Nysø, Andersen was furious with Jonna Stampe when she said the Danish king was pro-German and accused Andersen of the same sympathies. That she should have so little appreciation of his personal sacrifice in giving up the friendship with Carl Alexander grieved him even though Jonna was probably not aware of the depth of his feelings, but he had striven to prove his patriotism in every conceivable way. At a dinner with the British attaché, Robert Bulwer-Lytton, he had even preferred to struggle through the evening in his inadequate English rather than speak German, a language so charged for him now with 'the sound of cannon and the shouts of enemies'.

As the days shortened into autumn, nothing could ward off his sense of empty finality. On 16 September he attended a soirée at which Queen Victoria's son, the Prince of Wales, later to be Edward VII, was present with his Danish-born wife, Alexandra. She was one of the six children of Christian IX, most of whom made extraordinarily brilliant marriages. Alexandra's elder brother would become Frederik VIII of Denmark and a younger one, Vilhelm, was called to the throne of Greece as George I. Her sister Dagmar married Tsar Alexander III, entering the star-crossed dynasty of Romanovs, and as Empress Maria of Russia, managed to survive when in 1918 her son and his wife and all their children were murdered by the Bolsheviks. No hint of such tragedy darkened the Copenhagen occasion which Andersen attended however, and he should have revelled in the glittering assembly which met in the palace of the king and queen, known for good reasons as

'Europe's in-laws' – but he failed to respond. As the days shortened toward winter his gloom increased, and by 20 November, as his diary for that day makes clear, he thought he was finished:

> Low spirits, the tumour in my hand will probably lead to an operation and I shall die as a result. It is time for me to die anyway, and as I think about this, it seems to me that I have not enjoyed life, not accepted the gifts God gave me. My good fortune is over now; the war has separated me from many friends whom I can never meet again, and here at home I must just wait to be buried.

Fame had failed to make Andersen happy, and the new royal regime at Amalienborg, though it welcomed him as an honoured citizen, lacked the homely warmth towards him of the family which was now, with such appalling finality, extinct. Never skilled at comforting himself, Andersen did not reflect that this was a period of shock and mourning from which he would slowly recover. The only way in which he could harness his emotions was through writing, and at this point when he was too fraught to contemplate any work, his feelings took charge of him like a team of runaway horses.

To make matters worse, in the icy winter of that year, water leaked from a frozen gutter through the ceiling of his bedroom, soaking the walls, bedclothes and floor. His landlady, Mrs Anholm, 'flew into a temper' when Andersen mentioned this. He took refuge with Edvard and Jette Collin while the necessary repairs were done, and seemed unconcerned about his homelessness, but his friends began to worry about him. He was nearly sixty, and still lived like some impoverished student in cheap lodgings, relying on his friends to feed him on the rota basis which he had never abandoned. Jette Collin in particular began to urge him to settle down and take more care of himself – but the most practical help and support came from an entirely new source in the form of two Jewish families with whom Andersen had often dined.

Moritz Melchior, a businessman and head of the Copenhagen Wholesalers' Association, had with his wife Dorothea taken a great liking to Andersen, and invited him frequently to their mansion called Rolighed ('Tranquillity') which lay to the north of Copenhagen. This great house and its grounds had at one time been a home for

H.C. Ørsted, and Andersen felt at home there. Dorothea Melchior had been born a Henriques, and the link with this other family remained strong. Her brother Martin was a banker and so was one of his sons, though the other children were artists and musicians.

Andersen's relationship with these families was free of the shadow of moral debt which had always darkened his liking for the Collins. The Melchiors and Henriques had never known him as a poor boy, and they accepted him as he was, with no disapproval. Very slowly, with their encouragement, he began to pull out of the trough of melancholy which had dogged him through the winter and had made it impossible to write. On 2 April 1865 he spent his sixtieth birthday at Rolighed, and from that point on, he began to feel a little better.

Edvard Grieg arrived on the day after Andersen's birthday, bringing with him a new composition, *The Heart's Music,* which he had dedicated to Andersen. The fairy stories were translated into Sanskrit, a new version of *The Raven* was staged at the Royal Theatre, and Anna Bjerring, Andersen's faithful fan, arrived with her mother and stayed in Copenhagen for a week. She gave Andersen a bouquet of flowers when he said goodbye to them at the railway station, but his diary makes virtually no reference to her.

During the dark days of the winter, Andersen had been invited to visit Portugal. The brothers Jorge and Carlos Torlades O'Neill, who had lived with the Wulffs in Copenhagen for a while as boys, had been back to Denmark and pressed Andersen to come and see them in the spring. Jette Wulff had paid them a visit in early 1845, and had brought a message back then to say that Andersen would find himself very welcome there, and he now began to toy with the idea. However, an outbreak of cholera in Lisbon made him dismiss it from mind, and he went instead to Basnaes for three weeks in late May.

In the quiet of this country estate, he at last began to write again. His story called 'The Bog Witch' is an engaging example of how to tackle 'writer's block' by writing about the condition itself. He begins with a frontal assault.

> Once there was a man who was well acquainted with fairy tales. They used to come knocking at his door. But lately he had not had any such visitors, and he wondered why the fairy tales didn't come any more.

Having established the bereft writer as a fictional character, Andersen was then free to unleash some of the anger which had underlain his depression, while disclaiming any personal involvement. With his usual self-protecting technique, he allowed the fictional author to talk to the even more fictional witch who brewed up her potions beneath the marshy landscape. In this disguise, he mused that every nation could make its own soup, according to its requirement. There was, for instance, 'old German blood soup with thievery dumplings . . . ' He moved on to protest in the witch's name about the draining of swamps to produce profitable farm land, warning that the flickering marsh-gas which is seen in all fenny country would take revenge for its dispossession by infiltrating the minds of people, causing them to lose all truth and decency. The witch shrugs, saying she must be mad to tell this to a poet who will spread it far and wide. Andersen, too, was able to shrug within this format, claiming disingenuously that such opinions did not originate with him.

The story broke the deadlock, and during the summer he wrote six more, to be published at Christmas in the same year. He went to Sweden for a month in mid-September, renewing his acquaintance with Frederika Bremer and the Swedish royal family, and on return moved into the Hotel d'Angleterre in Copenhagen. Coming back there after spending Christmas at Basnaes, he found Ole Bull in residence and, not for the first time, was slightly irritated by the violinist's ebullience:

> Last night, or rather, this morning at 1.30, I was woken by the sound of "hurrahs" shouted nine times in Swedish. It was for Ole Bull . . . I slept until 9 o'clock, then went up to see Bull at eleven. He was just about to leave, kissed me on both cheeks and said, "I always get an ovation when I'm staying in the same hotel as you! Do you remember Marseille?"

Goldschmidt had been right when he observed that Andersen did not like to be upstaged. Three days after the nocturnal cheering, having heard Bull play at the Royal Theatre, Andersen noted in his diary, 'I was bored. I can't stand violin music – if I was once moved by Ole Bull, it must have been my imagination.'

During the year's events, he had not forgotten the O'Neill brothers' invitation, and on 31 January 1866 he set out for Portugal.

Chapter 20
Peace in Portugal

Dining with the Henriques a week before his departure, Andersen looked with weary envy at the enthusiasm of the two young fellow-guests who were also about to set out on a journey abroad, but for the first time. His description of them was disillusioned and resigned:

> Here was Carstenen, physically though not intellectually attractive, going on a trip to Holland, Paris and Germany with young Holmblad. He was very excited about it. We'll run into each other for sure. Went to the theatre to see <u>Faust</u>, about four acts. Home and drank some port for my stomach and sat in sweet indolence, thinking about my trip. It seriously occurred to me to turn to God for mercy, for this one would be my <u>last</u>.

His diary entry for the following day, 22 January, showed deeper misgivings:

> Rainy weather. Didn't feel so well. Felt like an old man! Wrote with the old man's fear of travelling abroad, his pining for this and that from home, then mentioned the young person's expectations and rosy view of everything. Went to see Bramsen since his false teeth were cutting a hole in my mouth.

When Andersen's visa arrived from the Foreign Office it had been stamped for the wrong countries and had to be sent back, and efforts to ship a consignment of his books to Portugal failed as no ships were heading that way. However, Reitzel assured him that reissues of several of his works would more than pay for the trip, and Edvard supplied letters of credit for the supply of money. As a forerunner of travellers' cheques, he also obtained four certificates of a hundred rixdollars each from the Private Bank. Always obsessively careful, Andersen sewed banknotes into the lining of his clothes.

The Melchiors fussed anxiously over him. On his final day in Copenhagen, Moritz turned up with a selection of fur boots explaining that his wife wanted to be sure that Andersen would be warm enough on his journey, and emphasised that he must get in touch if there should be any financial difficulty. Much reassured, Andersen set off. He would not be back for seven months.

His route was carefully planned to bypass Germany as far as possible, and not merely for personal reasons. Following the victory over Denmark, a quarrel had broken out between Prussia and Austria about division of the spoils, and Bismarck was squaring up to attack his former allies in what would be the Seven Weeks' War. From Hamburg, Andersen headed west for Holland, where he stayed for six weeks, moving from Utrecht to Amsterdam and then to The Hague. He was welcomed with great enthusiasm and met Ten Kate, the Dutch writer who was to translate some of his stories. Andersen stayed for a while with Georg and Andreas Brandt, Danish businessmen who also held office at the Embassy, and settled happily into a life of being feted. The only thing which upset him was the sight of the Jewish ghettoes, and he got embroiled in a religious argument when he voiced his objections at a dinner party. For someone so anxious to be thought well of, Andersen was notably and almost recklessly courageous in his defence of Judaism.

At the end of March he moved on through Belgium to Paris, and here, too, he enjoyed himself, going to the races with Crown Prince Frederik of Denmark and visiting the composer Rossini, whom he thought 'rather grubby' in appearance. Although invited to a concert the next day as Rossini's guest, he did not go, and he failed to meet George Sand, although she waited in for him.

Crossing Spain from the train terminus in Madrid was again a return to what Andersen called 'the Middle Ages'. He could have gone by boat from Bordeaux to the Portuguese coast, but instead chose the overland route, enduring sixty hours of virtually continuous travel in a mule-drawn coach. He had been warned that there would be no hope of rest and refreshment until they reached Badajoz, and supplied himself in Madrid with bread, wine and a whole roast turkey, but the O'Neill brothers were astonished that he should come by the stony and little-used mountain road. They had confidently expected that he would be on the French steamer which had docked that afternoon, and were a little startled when their guest turned up at four in the morning, having completed his journey by train from the Portuguese border and taken a cab from Lisbon station to the house. However, as

Andersen recorded in his book, *A Visit to Portugal*, his hosts were unruffled and hauled his luggage indoors with smiles of welcome.

He stayed for a month with Jorge O'Neill and his family in the 'old, somewhat tumbledown, two-storey building', 'Pinheiros', 'The Pines', then transferred to Jorge's brother, Carlos, in Sebutal, for a similar time, returning in mid-July to the Lisbon house. As so often, he became impatient with his easy-going hosts when they did not fall in at once with his plans, cavilling at a delay in visiting Cintra because the younger brother, Jos, was not well. 'This is a bit too much!' he fumed in his diary. The visit took place in its own good time, and Andersen was bowled over by the spectacular beauty of the place, writing a lyrical description of it to Edvard Collin – and yet, the travel book he produced later catches little of this enthusiasm, sounding dutiful rather than spontaneous.

The muted quality of *A Visit to Portugal* may be largely due to Andersen's growing anxieties about the political situation in Europe, through which he had to pass in order to get home. The Prussians had decisively beaten the Austrians, and following a peace treaty on 3 July, had become masters not only of Schleswig-Holstein but of four small German states which had been rash enough to side with Austria. Bismarck, his high-handedness forgiven in his own country, was now secure as an immensely powerful military leader, and Andersen feared that he would turn greedy eyes on France. Meanwhile, Spain had exploded into rebellion with a mutiny of non-commissioned officers in June which had been put down with the execution of sixty-eight men, and General Narváez was presiding over a brutal regime of suppression and imprisonment. To Andersen, it seemed that Portugal was the only country still existing in 'blessed, lovely peace', and he toyed with staying on throughout the winter, then reminded himself of the old proverb that even the dearest guest becomes a burden if he stays too long. 'I always awoke with this thought in my head when I was a guest,' he remarked in his diary on 24 July, evidently oblivious of the exasperation he had caused in the Dickens household by his over-staying. The time of his departure drew nearer, and he agonized over the travel arrangements.

He was almost literally between the devil and the deep blue sea, for only two choices were available; either to return across Spain, now in the grip not only of August heat but of civil unrest, or to sail from Lisbon to Bordeaux, a passage of three nights and four days across the

Bay of Biscay. The idea terrified him.

Unaware of the nightmares which Jette Wulff's death had left in their visitor's mind, the O'Neill brothers told Andersen he would be mad to contemplate the mountain road across Spain. They took him down to Lisbon, booked him a passage on the *Navarro* and installed him in a hotel to await the ship's arrival. As it happened, the French ship was delayed by storms on her way across from Rio and was three days late in arriving, but on 14 August, almost sick with terror, Andersen together with a few other passengers was rowed out to climb the rope ladder to the steamer's deck. There, about five hundred people had already been travelling for three weeks in a kind of makeshift shanty town with all their children, animals and belongings crowded under whatever shelter they could improvise.

Andersen was as usual travelling first class, so he and Jorge O'Neill, who had accompanied him on board, lunched with the captain while the ship rolled gently at anchor. Orders were then given to get under way, and Andersen was filled with dread as he watched Jorge rowing nonchalantly back to shore. The notoriously treacherous Bay of Biscay lay ahead, and that evening, convinced that he would not be able to eat, Andersen sat near the door in the crowded dining room, and got no further than the soup before seeking fresh air. He was too tense to go to his cabin that night and lay in the saloon alone:

> The memory and terror of Jette Wulff's death on this same sea became more and more alive . . . I thought of shipwreck and could not help picturing how we would sink, the water breaking in through the walls, all the lights extinguished – one would know that this was the moment of death, but how long would one remain conscious?

When the ship happened to hit a heavy wave and shudder a little, Andersen ran out onto the deck in terror – and there he saw something that astonished him. In the darkness, the waves were breaking into phosphorescence, and the ship rode through them as if through a sea of flame. In that moment, Andersen came to terms with his fear:

> The danger was neither greater nor less than it had ever been but now I gave it not a thought . . . were I to die that night or in some years'

time, was it really so necessary for me to live longer? Death comes in the end and here it would come in grandeur and glory. I stood for a long time in the star-clear night and looked at the great rolling ocean, and when at last I went back into the saloon and stretched myself out on a sofa, my heart and mind were refreshed and glad in surrender to God.

A Visit to Portugal picks up pace during this closing chapter, as if reflecting its author's relief. It records how one of the ship's officers the following day showed Andersen how to measure his step with the rhythm of the ship's movement and thus achieve balance, and in his new confidence he was able to explore, even venturing into the engine room where 'flame burned under the steam-kettles [and] the crew worked half naked. If one walked over into the second class,' he continued:

> it was difficult to move, with groups of passengers stretched out on deck and goods of all kinds stowed everywhere – monkeys in cages, parrots and cockatoos rocking to and fro, swarms of children, a confusion and noise and racket just like that of a market-place.

In the dreaded Bay, where the sea was remarkably calm, Andersen saw the wreckage of ships drift past, at one point noticing a large red-painted chest. He remarked merely that 'it went its way, we went ours'. He had, perhaps in mind as well as body, found his sea legs.

It may have been his new confidence which drove him to what was for him an extraordinary step. Pausing in Paris on his way home, and conscious of the sexual restlessness which had as usual assailed him during his travels in the south, he went to a brothel. He paid the Madame five francs, but when an eighteen-year-old girl stripped naked in front of him, he could do nothing but gaze at her. She seemed, he noted in his diary, 'surprised'.

Waiting for his train the following day, it was Andersen's turn to be surprised as Alexandre Dumas approached him on the platform, and he regretted that there was only time for a brief conversation. The Melchiors met him when he finally arrived back in Copenhagen on 9 September, and took him out to Rolighed, where he stayed for three weeks. He was touched by their kindness. As he remarked in a letter to Mrs Henriques, a home, a real home, is the greatest of blessings. I shall never get it on this earth, and that is why I am so restless, feeling a desire to be on the move all the time, which – if I am to be completely honest – does not really satisfy me.

Andersen spent a further month in visits to Basnaes and Holsteinborg, the home of Countess Mimi Holstein, and when he returned to Copenhagen in late October, he took new lodgings at number one, *Lille Kongensgade* (Little King's Street), across the square from the Royal Theatre. The house was owned by a Miss Hallager, who happened to be a keen photographer, and she took many pictures of Andersen during his time there. He, enamoured of all modern inventions, never tired of posing before the wonderful black-draped box with its magic eye.

Jette Collin resumed her efforts to cajole Andersen into some measure of domesticity. She made him buy a bed of his own, though he was horrified by the price, remarking to the composer J.P.E. Hartmann that, at a hundred rixdollars, it had better serve him as a deathbed or it wouldn't be worth the money. In his diary, he grumbled in more general terms:

Now I am to have a house, even a bed, my own bed; it terrifies me! I am being weighed down by furniture, bed and rocking chair, not to mention books and paintings.

If he could be young again, he went on, he would travel the world with nothing more than a pen, a couple of shirts and a pair of socks. It seemed that the finding of his sea legs had brought him a belated confidence which was very much at variance with his customary mode of travel, burdened with trunks, carpet-bag, hat-box, stick, umbrella and a coil of rope with which to escape from burning buildings. He was in the habit of carrying with him far more than he ever left behind.

His mental baggage, however, seemed to have lessened, and in January 1867 he wrote to Jette Collin to say that he intended to 'fly out immediately' to enjoy whatever life-span was left to him. The situation in Germany had stabilised since the war with Austria albeit under a regime so rigidly undemocratic that Andersen could not approve of it. Prussia had passed a retroactive bill approving all Bismarck's illegal spending, and this had effectively silenced any liberal opposition – but at least Europe was safe for travellers. On 11 April, Andersen set out for Paris and the World Fair.

It was, naturally, a big international occasion, and Andersen found himself involved in a busy social whirl. A somewhat riotous group of Danish visitors was headed by Robert Watt, editor of *Figaro* as well as the *Danish Daily News*. At thirty-two, he also managed the Folk Theatre and Tivoli, a successful, hard-boiled young man well known as a womaniser, and Andersen noted with disapproval that he 'dives into the muck with too much youthful abandon'. On that same day, 4 May, his diary continued with an account of his own somewhat curious approach to the ladies:

> After dinner, I paced to and fro in a sexual frenzy. Then went impetuously up to the meat market – one of them was covered with powder, the second was common, a third, quite the lady. I talked with her, paid twelve francs and left without having sinned in deed, though I dare say I did in my thoughts. She asked me to come back, said I was very innocent for a man. I felt so happy and light when I left that house. Many would say I was gullible – was I?

Andersen seemed not to begrudge the twelve francs he had paid to sit and talk to a prostitute, although on the previous day he had jibbed at a three-franc cab fare back to his hotel although he had been 'about to collapse with exhaustion' after a day at the huge exhibition. The year-end statement produced by Edvard had shown that he had funds of 12,506 rixdollars, but he always grumbled at the cost of life's necessities, preferring to feel that the whole of his income was available to spend on the things he really wanted. He evidently found it fascinating to go into a brothel and be surrounded by the sinfulness which had for so long repelled and frightened him, but there is no evidence to suggest that his claim of continued innocence was untrue. At sixty-two, he showed little concern about his sexual image; by contrast with his early and highly publicised infatuations with inaccessible women, he made no mention to others of his visits, perhaps content to be thought 'past it'. He was continuing to see something of Harald Scharff, who had given him 'an incomparably beautiful' white azalea for his birthday, but, as if realising that his diary would one day become public, his entries were non-committal.

The brief glimpses into the lives of the young prostitutes he met had sparked Andersen into beginning a story called 'The Dryad', sometimes translated as 'The Wood Nymph'. It was based on the idea that the spirit of the chestnut tree which grew outside his hotel window was a dryad who would sell her soul for a single night of human pleasure in the city. It was a ticklish subject, for he did not want to outrage public opinion, and he made his way home in May with the story unfinished. In Switzerland on the 26th, he heard that he had been made a Titular Councillor in the Danish king's silver wedding honours list.

During the rest of the summer he finished his Portuguese travel book, working mostly at Rolighed, but the new insights he had tantalisingly gained in Paris continued to demand his attention. Evidently he talked to Moritz Melchior about this and explained that he felt a need to go back and do some more research, for the businessman gave him three hundred rixdollars towards the cost of a further trip. On 1 September Andersen set out for Paris a second time, accompanied by Robert Watt.

The choice of companion is curious. Andersen had been a little scandalised by Watt's veniality during his previous stay in Paris, but it may have been precisely this which interested him. 'The Dryad', though impeccably circumspect in its final form, was about the seamy side of city life, and Watt, with his fund of tall tales about his sexual conquests, was a rich source of information. Andersen stayed for three weeks in Paris and again went to a brothel, accompanied by Watt, though he himself wanted only verbal contact with the girl he chose. He noted in his diary for 9 September that he felt sorry for the 'poor child'.

Although some of Andersen's stories had been translated into French as *Contes Danoises*, he was aware that France did not have a great admiration for him. Its literary traditions were very different from the Nordic and Germanic ones from which Andersen sprang, and La Fontaine had brought Aesop so thoroughly into French culture that there was little interest in adding further fairy stories to the established canon. Andersen may have hoped that a tale set in contemporary Paris would spark a new interest in his work – but in order to do that, he would have to demonstrate that he knew what he was talking about.

Returning from his second trip, he was still unable to complete 'The Dryad', but other events demanded his attention. As he had done on his previous Paris visit, he paused in Odense on his way home, staying in the house of Bishop Engelstoft – and the bishop reiterated his report that the city wanted to honour its most prominent son by conferring on him honorary citizenship. It was the first – and, to date, the only – time that Odense had taken this step. After some discussion, it was agreed that the ceremony would take place that same autumn.

Andersen seems to have been unnerved by the proposal. He postponed the first date suggested, and by the time he eventually travelled on 3 December to Odense he was in a state of wretched nervousness. The journey had chilled him, and he complained of aches in his back and chest, and the dental troubles which so often assailed him at times of stress flared up again. 'Bothered by the stumps of my teeth, which are hurting, and by my false upper teeth which are loose,' he noted. It seemed that he was plunging into an excuse that would let him out of having to confront the assembled populace of Odense, the town where he had been so insignificant and so tormented.

He was appallingly isolated. Although the *Funen Bulletin* recorded that every seat for the ceremony had long been sold and that everyone in Odense wanted to come, Andersen himself knew nobody. An old cabinet-maker had come up and expected to be recognised, announcing himself as a school-fellow from the days with Fedder Carstens, but Andersen's old friends were dead and nobody from Copenhagen had come with him to share the ordeal which should have been a crowning honour. He struggled through the formal dinner and the speeches and the presentation, and was invited like royalty to present himself to the crowd outside:

> I stepped over to the open window; there was a blaze of light from the torches, the open square was completely filled with people, the sound of singing came up to me, I was overcome in my soul, but was also physically overcome and unable to enjoy this climax of happiness in my life. My toothache was intolerable; the icy air which rushed in through the window made it blaze up into a terrible pain and so instead of fully enjoying the happiness of these minutes which would never recur, I looked at the printed words of the song to see how many stanzas were left before I could slip away from the torture which the cold air was sending through my teeth.

He went across the next day to look at his old home. The yard was just the same, he noted, except that a shed had been built in the middle of it. 'A couple of gooseberry bushes were there, probably remaining from my childhood.' There was nothing else.

Some critics protested about the honour shown to Andersen, pointing out that there were greater writers, but his friends stuck by him. Bjørnson said that Andersen, together with Grundtvig, was Denmark's only national poet, and Georg Brandes, who was to become Europe's leading literary critic, made a first contact with him in March 1868.

On the day following this approach, Andersen received a letter from a young American editor, Horace Scudder, who wanted some original stories to publish in his *Riverside Magazine.* It was not his first request, but this time Andersen wrote back to him, beginning a correspondence which would last until the end of his life. In the wake of the Odense honour, he was content with the small immediacies of life, enjoying the novelty of a magic-lantern show at the Melchiors' and attending a concert given by the German tenor, Julius Stockhausen (no relation to the later composer), accompanied on the piano by Johannes Brahms. Andersen approved of the singer but found Brahms's playing 'dry and monotonous'. His opinion may have been coloured by the rumour that Brahms held strong pro-German views, confirmed when the composer was tactless enough to praise Bismarck for his 'great character', thereby deeply offending his Danish hosts. When remonstrated with, he was unapologetic, contending that Denmark had nothing of any value except the Thorvaldsen museum, which ought to be shipped to Berlin.

Andersen's sixty-third birthday on 2 April brought a mass of presents and flowers and telegrams. Mrs Melchior sent him a comfortable chair to go by his desk and her daughter Louise had embroidered a strap to go round the plaid blanket which he always carried as part of his luggage. Being now so famous, he also received a lot of begging letters, which he ignored.

Within three weeks he was off again to Paris in further pursuit of material for 'The Dryad'. In the French capital he met up with Einar Drewsen, who accompanied him on a further brothel visit where, Andersen said firmly in his diary, 'I only sat and talked with Fernanda, the little Turkish girl, while E. amused himself.' This entry for 17 May recorded a long conversation about Constantinople, Fernanda's birthplace, and how Andersen had seen it illuminated for the birthday of Mohammed. 'She was very insistent that we should make love,' he went on, 'but I told her I was only there for the talking, nothing else. "Come again soon," she said, "but not tomorrow, that's my day off." Poor girl.'

Back in Copenhagen, Andersen resumed his dealings with Horace Scudder, who was punctilious about sending bankdrafts for any stories printed in his magazine. Charles Dickens had by this time been over to America, using his position as a feted author to insist that it was time for the United States to honour an international copyright agreement, but Andersen knew that much of his own work was still circulating free of any royalties, and was grateful for Scudder's honourable intentions. Asked to supply the complete bulk of his stories for a collected edition, he pointed out that many of them were too Danish in character to be suitable for translation, and he also insisted that Scudder must not use the Mary Howitt version of his autobiography as he had suggested. Instead, Andersen proposed to extend *My Life's Fairytale*, adding an account of the last thirteen years to bring it up to the Odense ceremony. From being purely businesslike, the letters between him and Scudder soon loosened into a lively correspondence.

'The Dryad', finished at last, was published in a single slim volume at the end of that year, and three thousand copies sold out at once. By twentieth-century standards, the tale of a wood-nymph, typically 'both child and maiden', who ventures into the red-light district of Paris is so cautious as to leave the reader aware merely that the visitor to a certain house where the young women have no escorts finds his blood 'rush more quickly' – but every age is able to interpret its own conventions of language, and there can be little doubt that many a Copenhagen matron found 'The Dryad' agreeably shocking. In the essentially Faustian story, however, sin has to be paid for, and with the death of the dryad on the steps of a church, the chestnut tree, now bereft of its spirit, droops its leaves and dies. 'This all happened,' Andersen ends, 'I saw it myself, during the great World's Fair of Paris, in the year 1867, in our own wonderful times, the age when fairy tales come true.'

In the winter that followed, Andersen was occupied by domestic troubles. Convinced that an unpleasant smell was coming from under the floor of his room, he insisted that the tiled stove must be taken to bits. This yielding no result, he had the floor torn up, and found to his satisfaction that the gas pipes were leaking. Vindicated, he told the Melchiors and Henriques all about it while spending Christmas and the New Year with them.

On 12 January 1869, Andersen was summoned to the palace of Amalienborg to meet the Princess of Wales, who was visiting Denmark with her children. Niels Gade had been invited as well, and as they were leaving the place he and Andersen saw the royal offspring drive up to the door in a carriage, and turned back to talk to them. It was much more fun, Andersen said, than being presented to them formally.

Georg Brandes had come to see him twice more, in October and November, and as a result of his interviews, a series of lectures on folk and fairy tales was given by Brandes' erstwhile teacher, Professor Rasmus Nielsen, at Copenhagen University early in 1869.

On the first day of that year, Andersen had received an engaging letter from a little girl called Mary Livingstone, addressed merely to Hans Andersen, Denmark. She said how much she liked his books and sent him the autograph of her father, who was the famous explorer, Dr David Livingstone. Mary, whose mother had died in Africa, was a self-possessed child. She wrote to Andersen for five years, until her father, too, died in what is now Zambia. Her final letter included a calm description of the Westminster Abbey funeral which followed the return of his embalmed body from Africa, and ended with the information that she herself was about to be sent away to boarding school.

Mary's use of only half Andersen's Christian name in addressing him was a common mistake in English-speaking countries, as Andersen pointed out to Horace Scudder. His name was Hans Christian, and no Dane would dream of trying to abbreviate it. Scudder, who now understood enough Danish to read Andersen's letters in the original, quite understood – but to this day, it is a common mistake, although nobody would refer to 'Jean Sartre'. Hans Christian is as much a single name as Jean-Paul, but the Danish absence of hyphens can easily cause misunderstanding.

Andersen protested also about a profile of him written by an anonymous Dane who had evidently allowed his imagination full play. His letter to Scudder was firm:

> This dear compatriot, who clearly has the best of intentions toward me, can hardly have known me or ever have had a good look at me. It would never occur to any Danish child on the street to pull my coat

tails and fall upon me like that. The little folk might give me a mild and friendly greeting, nod at me from a window, or the parents might bring them out into the street to tell me something or other – how much the child liked me, or rather, liked 'Andersen's Tales'.

During this contented winter, Andersen was again enjoying the company of Harald Scharff, who was a frequent visitor during the early weeks of the year. He began to plan a journey to Vienna in the summer with the dancer as his companion – and then, on 10 February, Scharff suddenly announced that he was about to get engaged to a girl called Camilla Pedersen.

The shock was considerable. 'My young friend has left me,' Andersen wrote in a bleak diary entry that day. All plans for the Vienna trip were abandoned, and he suddenly felt very old, complaining of a nervousness and a weakness in the legs which made him feel as if he might fall down. Scharff, like many homosexuals of his day, had evidently felt it necessary to make a conventional gesture of conformity. The engagement lasted only nine months, giving way to further male friendships, but it went through the necessary celebrations. Andersen attended the engagement party, still feeling ill and shaky. On the previous day, he had been to one of Rasmus Nielsen's lectures and heard his work discussed without any reference to him as a living person, which had increased his sense of disembodiment. A renewed distaste for the destructive capacities of the female sex was compounded when he heard that Caroline David, who had lived for a long time with Georg Brandes, had left him after a tempestuous row, and was being sheltered by the Collins.

Nielsen's lecture had featured Andersen's story called 'The Snowman', ironically enough. What the professor had made of it is difficult to imagine, but any present-day commentator would be forced to recognise it as a parable of the different kinds of love. The innocent snowman asks why a girl and her lover walk hand in hand round the garden, and the disillusioned old yard dog sniffs. 'They are engaged,' he explains. 'Soon they'll be moving into the same kennel and sharing each other's bones.' The snowman has quite a different idea of love, being enamoured of the kitchen stove. When spring comes and he melts away, he is found to have been built round the old kitchen poker. It is a homoerotic image of such potency that a failure to spot it seems inconceivable – and yet, the thinning feathers of Andersen's fan-dance still succeeded in showing the watching audience only what he wanted it to see.

Georg Brandes was more perceptive than most. Following a further long interview with Andersen, he published a critical essay which was reprinted in his book, *Creative Spirits of the Nineteenth Century*, and in it he put his finger on the fact that Andersen's imagination operated within a field of self-protective imagery. Without suggesting any reason why such caution should be necessary, he observed that it resulted in a disengagement which made Andersen's work superficial. His imaginative perception, Brandes alleged,

> does not penetrate far into the innermost recesses of things; it occupies itself with trifles; it sees ugly faults, not great ones; it strikes, but not deeply; it wounds, but not dangerously; it flutters about like a winged butterfly.

Such refusal to be personally involved with his own material was, Brandes saw, a serious handicap to any writer. It must therefore serve some different purpose:

> A form that for anyone else would be a circuitous route to the goal, a hindrance and a disguise, becomes for Andersen a mask behind which alone he feels truly free, truly happy and secure.

It is fairly evident that Brandes had spotted the truth about Andersen, but was either too humane or too mindful of the furore it would cause to voice his conviction. He wrote all round it, but stopped short of putting a name to Andersen's central quality – and for very good reasons. He had no wish to destroy a famous writer by involving him in huge public scandal, nor to get involved himself in a libel action which would reverberate throughout the literate world. Considering the dangers, he sailed incredibly close to the wind, commenting on the effeminacy which contrasted so oddly with Andersen's rough-hewn appearance. He was too fastidious to take a straight look at anything coarse or unpleasant, Brandes contended, and recoiled 'a hundred times in his works from some wanton or outrageous deed with the maidenly expression, "We cannot bear to think of it!" ' Instead, he created a world of extended metaphor in which 'egotism, violence, coarseness, vileness and persecution can only be called so in a figurative way'.

Brandes was perfectly correct in his perception. Andersen's short stories almost always operate within notional quote-marks which hand the responsibility over to a character contained within the tale and leave the author observing from a distance, but uninvolved. Within this detached, microscopic observation, the events and passions often unfolded with condensed, crystalline clarity, but the same could not be said of the novels, where the broader scope would not permit the use of the same device. Here, Brandes contended, Andersen failed because he lacked 'the cool, calm power of observation of the man of the world'. He went on to investigate further the quality of manhood and Andersen's lack of it. 'His men are not manly enough, his women not sufficiently feminine.' He continued:

> I know no poet whose mind is more devoid of sexual distinctions, whose talent is less of a nature to betray a defined sex, than Andersen's. Therefore his strength lies in portraying children, in whom the conscious sense of sex is not yet prominent. The whole secret lies in the fact that he is exclusively what he is, – not a champion, as many of our great writers have been, not a thinker, not a standard-bearer, but simply a poet. A poet is a man who is at the same time a woman.

The final definition was clever, channelling all suspicions exactly the way Andersen would have wanted, into the assumption that what he himself called 'the poetical being' must be androgynous and so lit with spirituality as to be barely of the physical world. Brandes described 'The Bell', that haunting parable of love between two young men, as 'the crown of Andersen's work', and there can be little doubt that he understood him very well.

Brandes also understood how vulnerable Andersen was to criticism, and how unhesitating in attack when he felt himself wronged. Before the first part of his long essay appeared in the Danish *Illustrated News*, he wrote Andersen a pre-emptive letter designed to ward off any screams of protest:

> Dear Sir,
> Among all writers you are the one who has been most unjust to literary criticism, having lent your support to every vulgar prejudice

against it, brought it into contempt and disrepute.

To me literary criticism is a branch of learning and a passion, and of course, along with others, I naturally imagine that everyone else must be able to see the excellence of my profession.

In the *Illustrated News* for tomorrow I have begun a series of articles about your fairy tales. I shall ask you not to judge them until you have finished reading them, and – if you find I have refrained from taking revenge on you for your many slurs on literary criticism – to let yourself have a little faith in this aesthetic branch of learning, and not to forget the kindness you have previously shown.

Your sincere and cordial critic,
G. Brandes.

Andersen did not wait as asked to see the whole series of instalments, but wrote straight back with a broadside against all critics which showed just how necessary Brandes' move had been:

No one in the past has been more harshly and ruthlessly treated by what is called criticism than I have; it did all it could to annihilate and destroy me; . . . Now the younger generation is compensating for the crimes committed by its predecessors, and you, my dear friend, are among the young men whom I trust and appreciate. I have hit out against empty, evil, pernicious criticism for its yelping, and I intend to go on doing so; old debts must be paid . . .

Brandes stood his ground, pointing out that Andersen should discriminate between good and bad criticism, and when the whole long essay had appeared, Andersen seemed nonplussed. It was perhaps too close for comfort, but the 26-year-old Brandes had run rings round him, even thanking him for his 'true spiritual enrichment'. Andersen grumbled a little that he had been misunderstood, but he had no real comeback.

For no specific purpose, he embarked on another long journey that autumn, having celebrated the fiftieth anniversary of his arrival in Copenhagen at a banquet attended by 244 people. He travelled alone, having found no replacement for Harald Scharff and it was in Vienna, where he had planned that the two of them would be together, that he heard of Scharff's broken engagement.

He spent Christmas in the Pension Suisse in Nice, and in a letter to

Edvard Collin, sounded moved by what had happened when the
candles on the tree had been lit:

> A gentleman came forward, saying, 'We are gathered here from all
> parts of the world, and amongst us is a man who has given all of us
> many happy hours. Let us thank him, in our own name and in the
> name of our children' – whereupon a little girl came over to me with a
> big laurel wreath, with fluttering silk ribbons in the Danish colours;
> they all applauded.

Edvard was touched by the simplicity with which his old friend told him
this, and said so:

> I went to my study at once to write to you with tears in my eyes, for
> your description moved me deeply, not because your human vanity
> had been flattered but because God's strange ways with you were
> revealed in it again and again.

Andersen had not planned to spend Christmas at the Pension
Suisse. The original intention had been to come to the south of France
with the Melchiors and share a house with them for the whole winter,
but their daughter had fallen ill, and they had moved across to Algiers
in search of a warmer, drier climate for her. Andersen admitted in a
letter to Scudder on 11 January 1870 that it was a 'heavy
disappointment'. He was acutely lonely, and had written to Edvard as
early as the end of November with an offer of three hundred rixdollars
if Jonas would come down and keep him company.

Despite his previous references to Jonas as an 'insolent young
puppy', Andersen was profoundly glad to see the young man when he
arrived on 18 January. The pair travelled back to Paris together, but
Andersen confessed in a letter to Mrs Melchior that the whole trip
seemed to have been a waste of time and money.

There were good reasons for him to feel unnerved at the thought of
going to Paris on his own, for the city was seething with tension. The
old and ailing Napoleon III had been making enfeebled efforts to find
a compromise between those who favoured war with the Prussians who
were mobilising along the frontier and those moderates who
advocated conciliation, but he had succeeded only in alienating both
sides against a vacillating and ineffectual leader. The government was

hopelessly split as a result between the progressives, who were stoutly republican, and the monarchists, themselves divided between the few who still backed the Emperor and those who sought more effective leadership. The freedom of speech that had already been won was being used to voice justified complaints about the increasing repressiveness of Napoleon's regime, but this had hardly been reflected in the elections of the previous year. Only twenty-six per cent of the population held the right to vote, and although this was by far the highest proportion in Europe, it represented a wealthy, powerful section of the community which had unsurprisingly returned a government committed to authoritarian, pro-war policies. The official line was in favour of proving through battle that the French Parliamentary Empire could see off the threat of Bismarck, and Andersen, in common with many people all over Europe, looked at the unstable situation with terror, and wondered what the effect of the inevitable war would be.

He was relieved to be safely back in Denmark, even though he heard on his way through Hanover that his old friend, Henrik Hertz had died. Since the Melchiors were still in Algiers, he moved into their vacant flat in Højbro Plads, 'this lovely home where I have all the conveniences,' as he described it in a letter to Scudder. He would stay there 'until the woods are green and I can move out to the country where other dear friends will welcome me'.

During those early spring months he met an old friend, Wilhelm Dinesen, whose daughter would become famous as Karen Blixen, and resumed his acquaintance with Grieg, whose young wife sang some of her husband's settings of Andersen's poems. At the end of May, the woods now green, he went to Basnaes, and was still there when he read on 11 June of the death of Charles Dickens two days previously. 'So we will never meet again on this earth, nor speak together', he wrote in his diary. 'I shall not have any explanation from him as to why he did not answer my later letters.' Robert Watt wrote to suggest that Andersen might compose some verses to Dickens, or a short prose piece about him, but Andersen chose not to. In a letter to Jette Collin a couple of days later, he quoted the closing words of his story, 'The Fir Tree', as a dry epitaph. 'Done with! Done with! That's what happens to all stories.'

His visit to Basnaes was proving difficult. Although his hostess, Mrs Scavenius, was among Andersen's oldest friends, odd tensions were springing up. He felt misunderstood and wrote tetchily in his diary about the 'contradictions' that gave rise to frequent petty arguments. He disliked his hostess's son, Otto, and wrote on 10 June that he felt 'a little uprooted since Otto came home'. He added, 'God knows whether this will be the last time I come to Basnaes, where otherwise I feel so at home.' He developed shingles, which he was advised to rub with almond oil, and slept badly, dreaming of Meisling and his schooldays. On 14 June, things came to a head in what he called a 'big, unpleasant argument' about religion. Throughout his life, Andersen had inclined towards his father's view that there was nothing intrinsically supernatural about the birth and status of Jesus Christ. Ørsted's scientific theism had reinforced this opinion, and so had the Judaism for which Andersen felt so much sympathy. It may have been that his close friendship with the Melchiors and the Henriques had caused tongues to wag speculatively about his own religious background, and certainly the dispute at Basnaes centred on this question. The Scavenius family protested that the teachings of Christ would be meaningless without a belief in the holy circumstances of His birth and death, and if Andersen had no faith in these, he could not call himself a Christian.'

Clinging to a perilously narrow point, Andersen said he believed in them as concepts but not as people. 'They almost gave up on me,' he noted. 'However, when I left, Mrs Scavenius squeezed my hand with warmth and sincerity. She is a dear soul but . . . '

From Basnaes he went on to Holsteinborg, where he began his novel, *Lykke Peer* (*Lucky Peter*) which he wrote astonishingly fast. After a shift back to the Hotel d'Angleterre, he moved on to the Henriques at their big house, Petershøj, and completed the book on 15 July, having written it in only three weeks. The plot was close to that of his story, 'The Bell', centring on two boys born into different social circumstances, but essentially Andersen had written his own story once again, detailing how the poverty-stricken one of the pair triumphs after unpleasant years at school and vain efforts to become a singer and then a dancer. Even Lucky Peter's death was lifted straight from the author's own experience, mirroring that of Thorvaldsen, who had expired in the Royal Theatre. The music of Beethoven is all that is added.

On the day of the book's completion, the French declared war on Prussia. Bismarck, only too ready for an excuse, had managed to escalate a squabble over Prussian claims to the Spanish throne, sending a telegram so worded as to cause certain offence, and the French walked into the trap. Prussian soldiers surged across the country towards Paris, and Andersen was distraught, as his letter to Mrs Scavenius shows:

> I am completely overwhelmed by all the fighting and the shedding of blood. If I hadn't been able to finish my latest book about Lucky Peter in your quiet, peaceful home, I would probably never have completed it at all.

The death of his 'motherly friend', Mrs Signe Laessøe, on 24 July, further depressed Andersen, and he was not able to rouse much interest when thefamous Norwegian playwright, Henrik Ibsen, came to the Melchiors' house. Hehad ploughed through *Peer Gynt* as a matter of duty, but refused to see any virtue in it. On 18 August he noted:

> It's as if it were written by a mad poet! You go insane yourself trying to understand that book. The poetry is not good, either – there is something wild and unwholesome about it. Regret having read it, specially as Ibsen will be here this evening for the first time. I have never seen him. He is supposed to be gloomy and taciturn.

Andersen had in fact met Ibsen briefly in 1852, but had evidently forgotten this. His behaviour on the evening at the Melchiors' was extremely odd, as Ibsen himself remembered. The Dane had stayed upstairs in his room and would not be coaxed down until Ibsen went up to fetch him. According to the account in John Paulsen's *Samliv med Ibsen*, it took only an embrace and a casual compliment to break through Andersen's reserve. 'So you really like me?' he asked, beaming, and went arm-in-arm with Ibsen down the stairs to join the rest of the company. From that point it was, Ibsen said afterwards, one of the pleasantest evenings he had ever spent.

Andersen's diary made no reference to the incident, remarking only that the Norwegian had 'made a good impression – we all liked him'. The prejudice he had shown might in part have been linked to his growing dislike of the violinist Ole Bull, at whose theatre Ibsen had begun his career as resident playwright, but it reveals more fundamentally how easily he could be knocked off balance, despite all his fame.

A month later, on 19 September, the siege of Paris began. It would be four months before the Prussians finally broke into the city, and Andersen's diary that autumn was full of horrified imaginings as his sympathies went out to both sides. On 15 October, he wrote, 'I see myself stabbed by bayonets, the city is burning, friends are dying, or I dream of being thrown into prison'. A couple of days later, in more objective mood, he was still concerned:

> My mind is overwhelmed as I keep thinking of the terrors suffered by the French people, and of the mortal suffering experienced by the German soldiers . . .

On 19 November, a week after the publication of *Lucky Peter*, Andersen attended the centenary celebration of Thorvaldsen's birth, and dwelt on his thought in some detail:

> With bared heads, we walked round the grave. I was saddened, but felt free from the unhealthy despondency, the unending depression and particularly the hopelessness that had engulfed me as a result of the appalling, bloody course of the war, the domination of the cannons which had reduced me to a snivelling idiot, turned me away from God. It was as if I had woken strong and healthy from a fevered dream. I need not conceal on these pages – which will never be published but stem from my daily thoughts – that I have felt myself to have much in common with Thorvaldsen – our low birth and our struggle and our great world recognition. Without doubt, I am as well known in the world as he, even though our countrymen do not perceive this truth. But I think his name will live longer than mine. I am sure my name is better known round the world than his is at present, but mine will be forgotten and his will live. Is this vanity? Will I ever know?

On the same theme, Andersen was morbidly interested in a conversation between two people in the crowd which had been overheard by one of his young friends, a would-be writer called Nicolai Bøgh. He transcribed it into his diary word-for-word as Bøgh had retold it:

"Andersen's a great man, I suppose. Some say Oehlenschläger was greater, but he's harder to understand. I can understand Andersen – I suppose there'll be a hundredth birthday celebration for him, too. Yes, they'll hold it in Odense, illuminating the city will be cheaper over there, most of the houses are only one storey high. But then, we won't be able to go to his grave. I don't suppose anyone knows where it'll be."

Despite the flicker of optimism he had felt during the Oehlenschläger ceremony, Andersen soon relapsed into melancholy. A lukewarm review of *Lucky Peter* upset him, particularly as he happened to read it on a day when the Henriques and the Melchiors had gone to a wedding, leaving him to eat alone at a restaurant rather than at their hospitable table. Two days later he was still 'embittered and angry' and noted that he felt inclined to give up writing. 'If I were young and rich, I would live to embrace life.' The thought provoked a febrile eroticism that caused him to mark the day's date, 17 November with one of his small crosses, but he looked ahead without joy. He spent Christmas with the Henriques and the New Year with Edvard and Jette Collin, but in a final diary entry, summed up 1870 in a few, bleak words; 'Blood-filled, horrible year.'

In the early days of 1871, Andersen spent a lot of time 'lying on the sofa doing nothing.' The cold winter was afflicting him with aches and stiffness, and the worsening news from France depressed him.

On 27 January, Paris at last capitulated after months of siege, and Prussian troops entered the city in a three weeks' armistice. Louis Napoleon, having surrendered at Sedan the previous summer, was still a prisoner, and his wife Eugenie had put together an imperialist government which fell almost at once in a bloodless revolution. An infant Republic had straight away had to cope with the continuing war and the siege, but was now politically split. As the Assembly removed itself to Versailles, there to co-operate with the triumphant Bismarck, a dissenting populace, which included the armed *Garde Nationale*, set up the Paris Commune, a self-governing city which would act in accordance with its own democratic decisions.

Andersen, along with millions of others in Europe, watched in horror as the appalling results of this action took place. The Versailles governments unleashed a savage attack on the Communards, and the streets which Andersen knew so well ran with blood. In the week of 22–28 May alone, 25,000 Parisians were killed, more than had died in the whole eighteen months of the 1789 revolution. The butchery was incredibly intense. At the prison of La Roguette, 1,900 people were shot in two days of concentrated killing, and Adolph Thiers, head of the Versailles government, remarked with satisfaction that 'the ground is paved with their corpses.' Vast funeral pyres burned in the public parks, and the stench was said by a witness to be so noxious that birds fell dead from the sky.

Andersen seemed paralysed. Foreign travel could not be contemplated, and all inclination to write had deserted him. In May he ventured out to his friends the Moltkes and then, despite his misgivings, spent some time at Basnaes. There, he began to write a story about the affliction of toothache which had for so long been his enemy, but he was unable to find a suitable alter ego through which to shape the tale, and abandoned it. The Melchiors were about to celebrate their silver wedding, so Andersen returned to Copenhagen and the Hotel d'Angleterre, where he composed a cantata for the occasion. The piece was set to music by the Norwegian composer J. Hägg, but there was a silly argument with members of the choir who insisted that 'cantata' should be spelled with the correct Danish 'k' rather than Andersen's 'c'.

The sense of being cluttered with irritating detail caused Andersen to wish he could escape from the whole thing, and he was relieved when Bjørnson invited him to Norway for a month. That country seemed further from the troubled heart of Europe, and the rapturous welcome he received did much to soothe Andersen's spirits. Coming back through Goteborg, he was intercepted by his devoted fan Anna Bjerring, who to his embarrassment forced herself on him with loud reproaches that he had not been in contact for a long time.

Return to Copenhagen brought renewed irritations. Clearly, his religious views had become the subject of scandalised gossip, for at a dinner party in October, Andersen was attacked by Anna Kiellerup, a devout follower of Grundtvig's brand of Nordic Christianity. Taking him to task for his lack of belief, she openly accused him of being Jewish in his religious outlook. Andersen countered by referring her to a book called *Nathan der Weise* by the German thinker, Gotthold Ephraim Lessing, in which it was pointed out that those of truly noble character can easily tolerate people of different doctrines, and seemed unaware that this could be said to constitute a tacit agreement with her contention.

At the end of October Andersen moved back to Miss Hallager's house in Nyhavn. Horace Scudder was still trying to persuade him to go to America, but the idea had no appeal. 'I don't have the physical resources for such an undertaking,' he wrote in his diary on 15 November. 'I'd rather die in Denmark.' At sixty-six, he was tired and peevish. His restless way of life was utterly unsuited to increasing age, and he could find no compensations for the gradual loss of physical strength and energy. As winter approached, he was temporarily diverted by small sparks of interest – a letter from Jenny Lind after twenty years, a new illustrated edition of his stories, a Bournonville ballet based on his work called *Fairy Tales in Pictures* – but lightness of heart evaded him, and on the last day of the year he came back to his lodgings early after a meal with the Henriques, and saw the year of

1872 in alone.

He toyed with an intention to burn all his papers, perhaps having heard of the devastating bonfire which Charles Dickens had made of all his correspondence, consigning to the flames countless letters from the notabilities of the day in a gesture which caused his family's protests and the grief of generations of biographers. Andersen, however, had for years been careful about what he put in his diary and his letters, knowing that it was only a matter of time before unknown eyes would scrutinise them. For all his protests that his records would never be published, he was too assiduous a dissembler to destroy any part of his own chosen image, though his notes became increasingly non-committal. It was as though he felt himself to be already addressing the public, using this medium to defend himself from unjust attack or explain his point of view while refraining from comment on personal matters. Thus his entry for 22 February 1872 recorded the mere facts that Jette Collin was ill with typhus and that Harald Scharff had 'turned up alone, with a walking-stick. It's his first visit to me in Nyhavn.' If any inferences are to be drawn, they will be the invention of the reader.

The following day, however, Mrs Melchior warned Andersen that his failure to turn up to read to Crown Prince Frederik as promised had caused considerable royal annoyance. This threw him into a torrent of protest, and he explained that he had been unwell – but he had too often ignored invitations for this excuse to impress anyone, and a week later, tales of his rudeness were still circulating. Jonna Stampe reproached him, saying that even if he had been truly unable to go, he must at least see the Crown Prince and offer his apologies.

Andersen felt badly used, and said so without reservation in his diary:

> I hadn't done anything wrong except to be ill. I've gladly visited these people, and nobody has spoken about them more warmly than I have. What was I supposed to apologise for?

He was so upset that he couldn't sleep. 'Worked myself into a froth,' he admitted – but he was fond of the young couple, Frederik being then twenty-nine and his wife, Louise, twenty-one, and the next day he went to the palace to apologise. The Crown Prince was not in, so Andersen left a message and on return felt so exhausted that he fell asleep in his chair. Naturally his apology was accepted. A visit to Amalienborg a few days later passed amicably, and yet a faint sense of sourness remained. The order of things seemed to be changing, and not for the better. The Royal Theatre, which had been so intimately bound up with Andersen's career, was being torn down to make way for a larger, purpose-built structure, and when he passed by the demolition site, he could not help regretting the old, inconvenient building that had started life as a bell-foundry but had, with its tallow candles and tiny orchestra pit, given life to many of his plays.

A minor uprising in Copenhagen during the spring alarmed him, but by this time, in mid-April, Andersen was once again out of the country, and heard of the workers' rebellion only through a letter from Mrs Melchior. He had taken with him William Bloch, younger brother of the painter Carl Bloch, whom Andersen had known for several years, having met him first during his Italian trip of 1861. Avoiding France, they travelled through Germany and Switzerland to Vienna, and William afterwards wrote his own account of the nine-weeks' trip in a book called *A Journey with H.C. Andersen.*

In July Andersen went to Rolighed, still working intermittently on his story about toothache, and on the 22nd of that month, he was run to earth by a young Englishman, Edmund Gosse, then twenty-three years old. Gosse had been working since 1867 as an assistant librarian at the British Museum, and was keenly interested in Nordic culture. He was gathering material for his *Northern Studies,* a survey of Dutch and Scandinavian poets, and was naturally anxious to interview Andersen.

Gosse was on friendly terms with Swinburne, Hardy, Stevenson, Henry James and sundry other literati, and was a little startled to find Andersen, as he put it, 'shielded by a bodyguard of friends, against the incursions of the Philistine'. Once admitted, however, he found the Melchiors perfect hosts, and was impressed by their fluent English. His account of the afternoon in the book he wrote later, *Two Visits to Denmark,* gives one of the most evocative pictures of Andersen ever written:

> There appeared in the doorway a very tall, elderly gentleman dressed in a complete suit of brown, and in a curly wig of the same shade of snuff colour. I was almost painfully struck at the first moment, by the grotesque ugliness of his face and hands, and by his enormously long and swinging arms; but this impression passed away as soon as he

began to speak. His eyes, although they were small, had great sweetness and vivacity of expression, while gentleness and ingenuousness breathed from everything he said. He had been prepared to expect a young English visitor, and he immediately took my hand in his two big ones, patting and pressing it. Though my hands have no delicacy to boast of, in those of Hans Andersen they seemed like pebbles in a running brook, as E.B.B. [Elizabeth Barratt Browning] might say.

The face of Hans Andersen was a peasant's face, and a long lifetime of sensibility and culture had not removed from it the stamp of the soil. But it was astonishing how quickly this first impression subsided, while a sense of his great distinction took its place. He had but to speak, almost but to smile, and the man of genius stood revealed. I experienced the feeling which I have been told that many children felt in his company. All sense of shyness and reserve fell away, and I was painfully and eagerly, but with almost unprecedented success, endeavouring to express my feelings to him in Danish.

Andersen led his young guest on a tour of the house, ending 'in his own bright, high room open to the east'. From the balcony he pointed out to Gosse the ships that went to and fro in the Sound between Denmark and Sweden, then sat down to read a story – 'and as he read,' Gosse said, 'he sat beside me, with his amazingly long and bony hand – a great brown hand, almost like that of a man of the woods – grasping my shoulders.'

The story Andersen read was 'The Cripple', one of the last he ever wrote and one he was particularly proud of. As he was explaining to Gosse how the plot, concerning a crippled boy whose life is changed by the gift of a book of stories, was in fact an apologia for the fairy tale itself, his voice began to grow hoarse and after a few minutes failed him altogether. 'The bell was rung, and servants summoned the family, who looked at me as though I had blotted one of their black-letter volumes or dropped one of their splendid vases,' the unfortunate Gosse related. The continuing drama was not without a certain humour:

It was, however, decided that the great man had lost his voice by the imprudence of reading aloud in the evening air, and he was conducted to his bed with infinite precautions. I could not help being amused by the languishing way in which Andersen lent himself to all this fuss, gazing silently at me while they supported him from the room.

Andersen recovered in time for the evening meal, and made no mention of the incident in his diary, merely noting a visit from 'an Englishman from the British Museum, an admirer of mine'. He added, 'I gave him my photograph, and he stayed for supper.' In their subsequent correspondence, he warmed to Gosse, addressing him as 'my dear young friend'.

Gosse for his part, despite his genuine liking for the famed writer, could not refrain from commenting in his *Studies in the Literature of Northern Europe* on Andersen's obsession with his royal connections:

> It was impossible to be many minutes in his company without his referring in the naivest way to his own greatness. The Queen of Timbuctoo had sent him this; the Pacha of Many Tails had given him such an Order . . .

Whatever its underlying cause, it is clear that at some deep level, Andersen depended on these signs of recognition to reinforce his sense of identity. He knew by now that he was widely regarded as an exasperating show-off, and made no attempt to modify his behaviour. This had become his accepted public persona, and whatever lay below it was his own business.

Celebrating the September anniversary of his arrival in Copenhagen, Andersen went with Harald Scharff to the Tivoli Garden where he noted with satisfaction that his bust had been given pride of place among the others. Three days later, he sent a cast of this bust to Fedder Carstens, though there is no record of any correspondence between them since Andersen's sending of his autobiography in 1855.

In the months that followed, he became seriously ill. For all his hypochondria, Andersen had been extraordinarily fit throughout his life, suffering from nothing worse than haemorrhoids and the occasional cold. Toothache had been his worst affliction, plus the attacks of shingles a couple of years previously, but now he was gripped by severe abdominal pain and nausea, with alternating bouts of constipation and diarrhoea. Theodor Collin was at first inclined to regard the copious bleeding which accompanied these symptoms as a further result of the haemorrhoids, and Andersen sought a second opinion from professor Emil Hornemann. He, too, was dismissive, and saw no reason why Andersen should not attend the premiere of his play, *More Pearls Than Gold*, rather than stay at home 'sunk in self-pity'. Accordingly the sick man tottered out to the performance at the Casino Theatre on 18 November, accompanied by Hornemann himself and William Bloch – but the effort was too much for him. In the days that followed he was too ill to get out of bed, suffering from what was in fact cancer of the liver.

His final four stories were published on 23 November, including the last one of all, the grim tale of 'Auntie Toothache'. Andersen had solved the problem of finding a form for this saga of pain by personifying the affliction into a witch-like figure, an Auntie whose own teeth are of unnatural whiteness, though she used to complain so much of toothache that she earned her nickname through it. At the beginning she simply feeds the children 'jam and sugar sandwiches', but as the boy of the story gets older, she appears as the nightmare figure who conflates the pain of his efforts to write poetry with his constantly worsening toothaches. 'For a great poet a great toothache,' she tells him, 'and to a small one a small pain.' There is, it seems, no escape:

> Every tooth leaves you again, and that out of turn, before the need for its service is over. That day when the last tooth leaves is no day of rejoicing; on the contrary, it is a day of mourning. Then one is old, even though one's spirit may be young.

Andersen's 'day of mourning' arrived on Sunday 19 January, as his diary recorded:

> Dr Voss came at about 3 o'clock and pulled out my last tooth. It was anaesthetised, but I could still clearly feel the wrenching. He stayed with me for a good half hour. I was light-hearted at the thought that I was now rid of all my teeth, but not quite as jubilant as the other day, when he extracted the first of the four loose ones. Well, now I am completely toothless . . . when was it I lost the first one? Wasn't it done at school in Slagelse by Dr Hundrup?

Two days later, all euphoria had evaporated. 'I'm in a very depressed mood,' he wrote, 'with all this sitting about indoors, and I don't feel, moreover, that I'm getting any better.' His young friends William Bloch and Nicolai Bøgh were in constant attendance through the winter weeks, and King Christian IX and the Crown Prince visited Andersen several times. As the weather began to improve, Mrs Melchior took to sending her carriage round to his rooms in Nyhavn, and he went on a few small outings.

Hornemann, who had still not come to a diagnosis about Andersen's condition, suggested that a cure at a spa might help. Of the potential establishments put forward, Andersen chose one in Switzerland, and three weeks after his new dentures had been fitted on 18 March, he set off with Nicolai Bøgh. They stopped off in Berne for a consultation with a Dr Henri Dor, who thought Andersen was suffering merely from 'excessive excitability'. After three weeks at the spa in Glion, drinking the whey which was regarded as an infallible cure, Andersen was no better. He and Bøgh spent five days with Jules Jürgensen in Geneva and then, almost incredibly, continued to travel for a further eight weeks, moving from town to town in Switzerland and then heading down through the Italian Alps, returning via St Moritz and Munich. They paused en route for excursions to places of interest and at last made their way back to Denmark through Nuremburg, Kassel, Hanover and Hamburg.

By the time he returned to Copenhagen on 28 July, Andersen could hardly stand. The horrified Melchiors watched in consternation as he emerged from the carriage leaning heavily on Nicolai Bøgh, and took him straight to Rolighed, where he stayed until 9 September. At that point he declared himself well enough to return to his lodgings, but the Melchiors insisted that he must have a night-nurse.

The Nyhavn house had been taken over by a Miss Ballin, who proved to be a more sympathetic landlady than the brisk Miss Hallager, and Andersen's health improved a little during the next few weeks. By October he was able to get out and about again, but he knew the respite was a temporary one, and he was lonely and frightened. On 1 November, he wrote in his diary, 'I want to die and at the same time I fear it.' There was only one person to whom he felt able to communicate these secrets of his heart, and that was Edvard Collin. He wrote to him on the same day, in desperate appeal:

> It is becoming obvious to me that I shall not get well, but God only knows how long I shall have to stick it out. I feel terribly lonely, and

my thoughts are becoming more and more morbid. Please come and see me soon.

Edvard came at once. The two old friends talked for a long time, and Edvard confessed that he, too, often felt irrationally worried, sometimes getting out of bed at night to see that no lights or fires had been left burning, even though he knew these had been properly attended to. His concerns were pedantic ones compared with Andersen's fear of death, but the conversation was comforting, and Andersen recorded that it left him with his mind at ease, feeling 'as if reborn'. For all his dependence on the Melchiors and their family, Edvard had been his first love, and still occupied a special place in Andersen's thoughts. As he had told him in a letter from Switzerland on 22 May, 'You are infinitely dear to me, and I shall pray to God for you to survive me, for I cannot think of losing you.'

Ever since his return from the trip with Nicolai Bøgh, Andersen's diary had dwindled into an account of microcosmic travel, detailing his small forays into the foreign land that lay outside his room, and the return journeys up the stairs, noting meticulously how often he had to sit down and rest, or pause to get his breath.

In November, after a lifetime of fruitless investment, he won five hundred rixdollars in the National Lottery. He had over 23,000 rixdollars in the bank, and yet he worried constantly about how he would support himself should he live for another ten years. It was a completely irrational fear, for there was no question that the country's foremost writer would be allowed to sink into poverty. Christian IX and his family had in their turn brought Andersen closely into their personal friendship, so much so that the king had lent him own travel bag for the Swiss journey – and yet an insecurity remained. All the kindness Andersen had received, all the money and all the recognition, could not alter his evident feeling that these things were not his by right. His instincts whether by birth or not, were essentially aristocratic, founded on the idea that one did not have to justify the claim of personal greatness through the squalid process of work. His output as a writer had been concerned with the expression of his own deeply hidden feelings, and the fact that he made money at it had been secondary to a very uncommercial need to engage in art for urgent psychological reasons. Unlike Dickens, who turned himself into a profitable and efficient word-factory, Andersen had never charged for public readings and had never written anything in which he himself was not personally interested. Now, facing the fact that he was too tired and ill to work any more, he was thrown back into the plain state of his own existence as a man who had come from nowhere – and who, his worst fears told him, might return there.

Andersen stayed in the Nyhavn rooms during the Christmas holidays, looked after by the two theology students who lived on the floor above his own, Erik Lassen Oksen and Mathias Weber, and the early weeks of 1874 were calm ones. He spent his days in the congenial task of decorating a folding screen with an intricate collage of photographs and illustrations cut from magazines and booklets, most of which were provided by his publisher, Reitzel. It is now in the Odense museum, an extraordinary piece of work in which the careful grading of each component results in a strong sense of perspective, as if a vast crowd of people receded to the far extremes of an open space. Andersen seemed to have returned to the world of his boyhood in which, oblivious to any tiresome realities, he cut and arranged and pasted his toy figures. After a lifetime spent in the company of the famous, the scraps he pushed about were the faces of great men, and yet their juxtaposition makes them as decorative as roses or stars or cherubs. The young students from upstairs continued to look after him during these winter weeks, and sometimes Erik Oksen would take him out for a little walk if the weather was kind.

As the days lengthened, Andersen managed to go to the theatre once or twice, but he knew now that he had a liver complaint, noting this in his diary on 7 March 1874, and he was weepy and irritable. As he wrote to Jette Collin, 'if this is old age, it's terrible.' His sixty-ninth birthday happened to fall on the Thursday of Easter Week, as had the second of April in 1801, the terrible day when Nelson had defeated the Danish fleet, and all the flags were at half-mast in commemoration of this fact. Andersen, always superstitious, saw this as 'a symbol of death' – but was reassured a little by the fuss made of him during the rest of the day. The king awarded him the title of Privy Councillor, and in the evening the Melchiors held a dinner party in his honour.

Anna Bjerring, his devoted but slightly oppressive fan, came to the city for a stay of two weeks to celebrate Andersen's birthday, and visited him several times – and, out of the blue, a telegram of congratulations arrived from the Grand Duke of Weimar. Andersen was deeply moved. There had been no communication between him and Carl Alexander since the second outbreak of war ten years ago, and it touched him that his eminent friend should be the one to resume contact. He cabled back at once, and followed this with a letter written in German, which he submitted to Edvard before despatch, to check that the spelling was correct.

In May, Edmund Gosse made a second visit to Denmark. He knew Andersen had been ill, having kept in touch with him by letter but he was clearly not prepared for the tremendous change that had taken place. Having received a 'tremulously scribbled' note inviting him to call, Gosse went round to the house in Nyhavn, and after some difficulty in persuading the landlady to admit him, climbed the stairs to Andersen's rooms:

> Hans Christian Andersen was coming in from an opposite door. He leaned against a chair, and could not proceed. I was infinitely shocked to see how extremely he had changed since I had found him so blithe and communicative, only two years ago. He was wearing a close-fitting, snuff-coloured coat, down to his heels . . . This garment, besides being very old-fashioned, accentuated the extreme thinness of Andersen's tall figure, which was wasted, as people say, to a shadow. He was so afflicted by asthma that he could not utter a word and between sorrow, embarrassment and helplessness, I wished my self miles away.

Gosse assumed the adjacent room to be a bedroom, and begged Andersen to return to it and lie down, but the old man was determined to be hospitable. Leaning heavily on Gosse's arm, he stumbled back into what turned out to be a library, and sank down on a sofa holding the visitor's hand affectionately between his own. Gosse then saw that Nicolai Bøgh was also in the room, as he related in *Two Visits to Denmark*. Bøgh was, he said,

> a good-looking young fellow, with a very refined expression. Andersen introduced him, saying, "You read so much Danish that I dare say you know his poems. He is like a son to me, God bless him!" He went on to say that Bøgh had never left him since his last severest attack of illness, and that he hoped he never would. "I should have died without him!" and still holding me by one hand, he affectionately pressed that of his young friend with the other.

Andersen went on to relate how he and Bøgh had gone out to the
wood at Sondermarken, and Bøgh, as Gosse remembered, speaking
for the first time, looked at him reproachfully and said, 'You ought not
to have gone! It has tired you too much! 'Gosse stood up to take his
leave, conscience-stricken and acutely aware that Bøgh was regarding
him 'with unmitigated displeasure'. The last minutes of the visit were
poignant:

> Hans Andersen, who was now certainly less feverish, insisted on
> rising, and, with his great emaciated hand laid again upon my wrist,
> accompanied me slowly into the outer room, where several boughs of
> sparkling young beech stood in a vase. He broke off a spray, and gave
> it to me, half solemnly with his poet's blessing; and then Mr Bøgh
> came, peremptorily this time, and led him back again.

To Gosse's surprise, he received a further invitation from Andersen,
and this time found the old man dressed to go out and posing for a
photographer. All about them, servants were busy packing, for
Andersen was on the move again. On 23 May he would depart for a
month at Holsteinborg, and Gosse's final recollection of him was one
of calm:

> He was sad, but not agitated; he said farewell with much tenderness;
> his last words to me were, "Remember me in your dear and distant
> country, for you may never see me again!"

Nicolai Bøgh, whose jealousy of Gosse had been so evident, had
during the early months of 1874 been assiduously sifting through
Andersen's correspondence in order to retrieve his own letters, for he
planned a book on the great man, and clearly did not welcome any
incursions from another author. He knew, as Gosse did not, the other
side of Andersen's apparently sweet nature, having seen how furiously
angry he became when his landlady, Miss Ballin, put the rent up by five
rixdollars a week. Andersen had never accepted the idea of paying to
maintain a home during a time when it was not lived in, for which
reason he had always moved out of his lodgings before beginning a
long journey, and usually came back either to take up residence in a
cheap hotel or stay with friends. As he had grown older, Jette Collin
and the Melchiors, among others, had seen to it that he was equipped

at least with a modicum of furniture and the trappings of domesticity, and a photograph taken in 1874, possibly the very one at which Gosse was present, shows Andersen sitting by a desk with all the expected array of framed photographs and portraits on the wall behind him. He intended to return to Nyhavn after his usual peripatetic summer, and was particularly annoyed that Miss Ballin had not mentioned the rise in rent until it was too late to change his mind. He wrote a raging letter to Jette Collin in which his estimate of his living expenses was almost hysterically high, and complained vigorously to all his friends, almost falling out with the sensible Mrs Melchior, who thought the increase quite reasonable.

Through the summer, Andersen moved from one mansion to another, arriving at Rolighed in September. He had ceased to write but continued to read with perceptive interest, and was outraged by Georg Brandes' book, *Hovedstrømninger* (*Leading Trends*), in which the young critic advocated free love. Andersen would have been delighted by the piece of gossip about Brandes which Gosse picked up from August Lassen, the chief clerk at Gyldendahl, Copenhagen's leading publisher, and quoted in his book, *Two Visits to Denmark*. 'All our youngest writers seem to be trotting after him, like performing dogs after the circus-man with the whip. But the big-wigs do hate him, and as for the clergy – well, you'll see for yourself.'

Andersen had finished the Brandes book by 4 August, and wrote in his diary that day a protest which came straight from his own being rather than through literary chit-chat. A German poem lay between the pages like 'an obscene flower', he complained, evidently objecting to its sexual frankness, though it was merely about a young woman who longs to be embraced by '*ein süsser knabe*' and grumbles at her mother for not letting her display her charms.

While still with the Melchiors, Andersen received a letter from America, written by a little girl who enclosed a dollar bill and said she had read in the paper that Hans Christian was now old and poverty-stricken. The article had gone on to urge all children to spare what they could in order to bring the destitute writer some little comfort. Andersen was appalled – and the more so when Moritz Melchior was visited by the American ambassador, who had handed over two hundred rixdollars collected by children in the United Stated.

It may well have been that Andersen's constantly voiced complaints about small expenses had become the subject of common gossip. In the previous year, on 16 October 1873, his diary had contained an irritable outburst about a fan-letter from America, remarking that it 'would be better if they made a collection over there and sent me a sum of money in my meagre old age'. The obsession with poverty belonged in deep-rooted fantasy rather than fact, for Andersen was to lend Edvard a further two thousand rixdollars at the year's end in a few months' time, to help Viggo Drewsen in his turn with the expenses of building a house, and he was deeply embarrassed when his psychological chickens came home to roost. He asked Melchior to tell the ambassador that he had a perfectly adequate pension and was in no need of help, but the story proved hard to kill. A second newspaper got hold of the story of two small girls who had sent the old writer their pocket money, and Andersen was upset all over again. Nervy and irritable, he admitted in his diary that he felt a 'strange, febrile resentment' which made him dislike almost everyone, particularly Jonna Stampe's children. He found them spoilt and insolent, specially 'that rude little Jeanina.'

At the same time, his general state of health was improving, in one of those mysterious remissions which cancer will sometimes permit. He was able to drive into town to visit the hairdresser, being still vain about his appearance, and even began to plan another trip abroad. He talked to Jonas Collin about this, and was pleased that the younger man agreed to accompany him and be of whatever help he could. A chesty cough was continuing to trouble Andersen (not to mention a constant itchy soreness of the penis), and he decided that he must go south to Menton, possibly to stay there over the winter.

On 23 August he sounded much cheered by the arrival home of Christian IX and his family from a trip abroad. Three days later he went to see the dowager queen and then drove over to Bernstorff Castle, where the royal family was staying. On arrival, he learned that a Captain von der Maase was in audience with the king but the doorman added that Andersen always had access to the royal family. He found the Princess of Wales there, together with her children. 'She took both my hands,' he recorded. 'They received me with such warmth and such friendliness, as if I were visiting the family of any of my good friends. We talked about the king's trip to Iceland – ' Christian had by now joined the party – 'and he was excited about it . . . and said he had conveyed my greetings when at Geysir'.

Andersen also confided his concern over the money collected for him by the children in America, wondering whether to return it. The king pointed out that such a move would cause great offence and suggested that the fund should be diverted to needy children in Denmark. Andersen's diary goes on with a rather touching account of royal hospitality:

> The king wanted me to have something to eat and a little port. He also suggested some "red fruit pudding" and junket. I replied that I didn't feel like anything and that Mrs Melchior had given me a lunch basket. "It's not proper," said the king, "to bring a lunch basket when visiting the royal family." I answered that I hadn't been sure of getting to see any of them.

He wrote a firm letter to the Philadelphia *Evening Bulletin* stating that he was in no financial distress, and this at last checked the flow of money into the Children's Fund – and yet, the gesture had not, for all his protests, been entirely repugnant to him. His diary the following day mused that a sense of kinship with America had

> become precious to me because of the love flowing out to me from the hearts of its young people. The children of America have broken open the piggy banks to share what they have with the old Danish writer they believe to be living in need. It has been a whole page in the fairy tale of my life.

He moved back to his room in Nyhavn on 10 September, and almost at once his cough grew worse. He began to rely heavily on a morphine syrup to help him sleep, and complained of general lassitude and debility. Old dreams returned to plague him, including the terrible one of the child who became a lifeless strip of skin, but one night he dreamed that Meisling came to him with new respect, and awoke refreshed and happy.

People did what they could for him. A brewer called J.C. Jacobsen, who in fact founded the Carlberg breweries, sent him twelve bottles of an export ale which Andersen particularly liked, promising to keep him supplied throughout the winter from his own cellar.

On 15 November, Andersen was visited by a small committee about a proposal to erect a statue of him in Copenhagen in time to celebrate his seventieth birthday in the coming year. Two artists, he was told, would be asked to prepare drawings, and he would be asked to state his preference – and a public subscription list would be opened in order to raise the necessary funds. On the same night as this visit, there was a gala opening for the newly rebuilt Royal Theatre, but Andersen felt too tired and unwell to go.

He spent Christmas with the Melchiors, and in the early months of 1875 managed to write half a dozen poems and even started revising his opera based on Scott's *Kenilworth*, but his cough was worsening, and severe abdominal pain returned. Plans to commemorate him after his death were a torment to him as he struggled to stay alive. He was asked to sanction the founding of a Hans Christian Andersen orphanage, but when he agreed to this the committee in charge of the statue-erecting project complained that the public could not be asked to contribute to two funds simultaneously. They insisted that the statue must come first, and Andersen then agonised over the thought that people might assume him to be more interested in perpetuating his own image than caring for orphaned children. It was obvious in any case, he argued, that the statue was not going to be ready in time, for the sculptors had not even submitted their drawings yet. The orphanage project went ahead.

His seventieth birthday on 2 April 1875, was a large-scale event. Andersen had on the previous day been invested with the Order of the Dannebrog, first class, the king having sent his own carriage to bring him to the palace, and his birthday itself was filled with festivity. Dorothea Melchior and Jette Collin came to his Nyhavn rooms to act as hostesses and deal with the mass of presents and flowers and entertain the many visitors, and that evening, after an early dinner-party at the Melchiors, he went with his friends to the theatre, where two of his own plays, *Little Kirsten* and *The New Lying-in Room* were performed in the splendidly reconstructed building.

Andersen was particularly delighted by the publication of a celebratory book containing his 'Story of a Mother' in fifteen different languages. 'What a wonderful, magnificent day,' he wrote in his diary that night. A week later, he mentioned the praise he had received in the London *Daily News*, which had compared him with Shakespeare and Homer. It had ended with the words, 'It is only a writer who can write for men that is fit to write for children,' And on 2 May, Andersen heard that the Grand Duke of Weimar had made him a Commander of the White Falcon.

A week later, the two sculptors asked to produce drawings for the projected statue presented their sketches. Andersen preferred those of Otto Evens, but was given to understand that the committee was strongly in favour of the other artist, A.V. Saabye. Andersen was too tired to argue. His condition was deteriorating and he was taking morphine almost daily, and such tiresome details as decisions over a statue merely irritated him. He found it easier to let his mind run ahead in the customary travel plans which were natural to him in the spring, and on 21 May he wrote a firm note in his diary about his journey to France. He would need relays of four travel assistants, all of whom had already been approached, to help him on the way to Montreux, where he would spend the summer, and then further south as the weather turned cooler, at least one of them remaining with him as a companion through the winter in Menton. 'I won't get away with less than 3,000 rixdollars,' he estimated.

One of his proposed co-travellers was Johan Krohn, a young friend who had offered on the very day of Andersen's diary note about the French trip to come and sleep outside his door in case he needed help in the night. A clear and rather touching picture emerges of a gravely ill old man who nevertheless remained central to the affections of a close circle of young admirers.

Despite his increasing weakness, Andersen flew into a rage when the sculptor Saabye came to see him the following week with further sketches for the proposed statue. These now showed the famous author reading from a book while surrounded by children – and Andersen was horrified. His diary for 29 May has no hesitation about declaring the reason. To have a 'tall boy leaning right up against my crotch' was unpleasantly reminiscent of 'old Socrates and young Alcibiades' and, by inference, their homosexual relationship.

Andersen had not spent his life in denial of his deepest instincts only to be commemorated by a statue which seemed to confirm them, but he was thrown into a dilemma. As his diary entry continued, he could not explain the reason for his fury to Saabye. The sculptor, he knew, had drawn up his designs in all innocence; it was the general public which might take a malicious delight in offering a more scandalous explanation. Andersen's immediate reaction was to refuse to have any further contact with Saabye. He would not, he noted, pose for him again or even speak to him.

By 3 June Andersen had realised that some explanation would have to be made. He needed a plausible reason for turning down the proposed design without revealing the special sensitivity which lay behind his true objection. He saw Saabye again, and the next day recorded the interview in his diary and also copied the entry virtually word-for-word in a letter to Jonas Collin:

> Saabye came to see me again last night. My blood was boiling and I spoke clearly and plainly, saying that neither of the sculptors knew me, that nothing in their efforts showed that they had seen or realised the characteristic thing about me, that I could never read aloud if anyone was sitting behind me or leaning up towards me, and even less so if I had children sitting on my lap or my back, or young Copenhagen boys leaning between my legs, and that it was only in a manner of speaking that I was called 'the children's writer' my aim being to be a writer for all ages, and so children could not represent me; innocence was only part of the fairy tale, humour, conversely, was its salt, and my written language was based on the folk language, that was my Danishness.

His panic is evident in the stumbling progress towards an alternative reason for the rejection. Only towards the end of his outburst does Andersen write himself into a different stance – that of the writer for all ages rather than merely for children.

He had not arrived at this rationale while Saabye was still present, for he had to venture out the next day to the sculptor's studio with this fresh explanation. The children were duly abolished, and the statue sits to this day in Kongens Have surrounded by its own solitude, a hand upraised as the author reads from his open book to invisible listeners.

Still set on the trip to France, and responding as urgently as a swallow to the seasonal need to migrate, Andersen began to pack up his things in early June, just a few days after his set-to with Saabye. He proposed to begin his journey with a stay at Bregentved. Theodor Collin had gone on holiday, but his other doctor, Hornemann, was concerned about his condition and advised that he should be in hospital rather than planning a year's European journey. Andersen, fretful and determined, would have none of this idea. Obsessed by money as always, he was set on removing all his belongings from the rooms in Nyhavn before the next month's rent should become due. Mrs Melchior, arriving to help with the packing, was distressed to find him so feeble and agitated, and suggested that a further month's rent would be money well spent, for other people could then deal with the removal and storing of his belongings while he was away. Andersen could not encompass such an idea, and went on bundling and tying his letters and papers. That night, he complained in his diary that the morphine syrup didn't seem strong enough.

His friends rallied to the task of packing, joined on 9 June by Jonas Collin, and by four o'clock on the afternoon of the 10th, it was all done, and Andersen was ready to depart. At that moment, a message came via the agitated Johan Krohn – Count Moltke had just told him that a change of cabinet ministers had meant an unexpected meeting in town. There would be nobody at Bregentved for at least a week, and Andersen must postpone his trip.

Whether the excuse Moltke gave was true must remain a matter of speculation. It seems unlikely that a vast manor house such as Bregentved should be incapable of entertaining a visitor while the master was away, and it may well have been that Moltke realised, like everyone else, that Andersen was dying on his feet, and did not want the responsibility of coping with his last days.

Andersen, 'utterly put out' by being so abruptly let down, stood among his packed trunks with nowhere to go. In desperation, he wrote a note to Mrs Melchior, asking if he might come to Rolighed for a few days instead, and she responded magnificently.

Quite obviously, the Melchiors knew that Andersen would not leave their house alive. They nursed him and took care of him, but after nine days he was no longer able to write in his diary. The last words in his own hand were simple ones, inscribed on 19 June 1875. 'The sun is shining, but I am cold all the same, and have a fire in the stove.' After that, he dictated his entries, either to Dorothea Melchior or one of her daughters, Harriet and Louise. The words were perfectly coherent at first, recording the correspondence he had received and the day-to-day indignities of being ill, and on 2 July he revised his will, adding some specific bequests.

From that point on, the dictated diary notes began to disintegrate into the ramblings of one who is starting to move away into dream. Most of what the Melchior women faithfully wrote down was an incoherent mixture of the people and events which moved through his memory, but there was one rather poignant reference to 'a silk-clad young girl with a crooked back' who came to ask him to write a poem for her mother's birthday, and frightened him by saying, ' "You are my poet; I adore you!" ' In this dream, she became 'terribly aggressive' and asked him to embrace her. The conflation of Mrs Meisling and Jette Wulff suggests itself – but this faint hint that the intelligent, radical Jette could have been the one woman in his life who genuinely loved him for himself is deeply touching.

By the end of July the rambling dreams had ended, and Andersen lay quietly, sometimes able still to get out of bed and venture as far as the balcony. From 27 July, Mrs Melchior wrote her own notes in his diary. 'His mind is beginning to wander,' she noted two days later, 'he repeats the same thing over and over.' The following day, he said to her, 'don't ask me how I feel – I don't understand a thing now.' On 2 August, he woke in the morning and stretched out his hands to Mrs Melchior and the servant she had hired for his exclusive care, and said, 'Oh! How blessed, how beautiful! Good morning, everyone!' He was aware that death was very near, and felt 'strange'. Although able to get out of bed and sit on a chair while his sheets were changed, he was concerned with the state of death rather than life, and worried, as he so often had for others, that the appearance of death might conceal a continuing consciousness. He asked Mrs Melchior to see that his arteries were severed, and then was horrified by the thought that this might be done prematurely. Gently, Dorothea Melchior pointed out that he had already pencilled a note – which he left on his bedside table while sleeping – 'I only look dead.'

Andersen smiled. Two days later, on Wednesday, 4 August, at five past eleven in the morning, he slipped into death from a deep sleep which had lasted from the previous night. It was, Mrs Melchior noted before she closed his diary, 'a happy death'.

Afterwards, people behaved as they so often do when the living person has gone and only the fame remains. Andersen left his entire state to Edvard Collin, except for specific bequests to the orphanage that would bear his name, and to such people as the Melchiors. Edvard, with the cool practicality which had so often caused his friend distress, tried to sell his correspondence with Andersen to Horace Scudder, who fortunately could not afford the price asked. Scudder pressed somewhat insistently for a memento from the great writer's desk, and Edvard eventually sent him an ornamental paper clip. The letters were rightly retained in Denmark.

Nicolai Bøgh wrote a biography of Mrs Signe Laessøe in which he was plainly opportunistic about his famous friend, referring to Andersen's quarrel with Heiberg and to his irrational rages which in retrospect sullied his reputation. A reaction against Andersen, he claimed, was now 'treading on the dead man's heels'.

Edvard wrote a furious letter to Bøgh:

> Has anyone known Andersen better than I? Have I not been as perceptive as anyone regarding his weaknesses, and have I not pointed these out to him with the utmost firmness? . . . But, to write these things down for others – no!'

In his own later book about Andersen, Edvard was faultlessly supportive of his friend's chosen self-presentation. He had, he said, 'wanted people to know even the smallest detail of his life from cradle to grave, even his inmost thoughts'. This insistence that there had been no pretence and no guardedness was not quite consistent with Andersen's own statements. In his diary of 9 May 1870, five years before his death, he had written what amounted to a public statement:

> If this diary should be read at some time, it will appear empty and indifferent. What happened within me and around me I don't put on paper, out of consideration for myself and my friends.

By Andersen's special request, Edvard Collin was laid to rest beside him when he died eleven years later, and there was a space reserved, too, for Edvard's wife, Jette, who lived until 1894. The other members of the Collin family did not demur, even though the family plot was to be established in Frederiksborg. That mysterious friendship was too strong for its final expression to be denied.

As a writer, Andersen lives on in the few perfect stories which have entered the world's collective unconscious as only the greatest myths can do. His sad, strange existence as a man is perhaps best given its own epitaph in the words he wrote in his diary on 15 January 1866:

> My time has passed; gone and forgotten, except perhaps to be torn apart by the mob, but they can only get at the surface which bears the imprint of my reputation.

Bibliography

PRIMARY SOURCES
Andersen's works in Danish

Breve til Henriette Wulff 1829–1857, Skandinavisk Bogforlag
Dagboger 1825–75, København, Det Danske sprog og Litteraturselska, 1971–76
Der To Baronesser, København, Gyldendal, 1903
Digte, København, Gyldendal, 1929
Eventyr: Anden samling, Boghandlerforlaget A/S, 1995
Eventyr og historier, illusteret af Vilhelm Pedersen, København, Gyldendal, 1930
Fodrejse fra Holmens Kanal til Østpynten af Amager in Aarepe 1826 og 1829, København, Reitzel, 1829
I Sverrig, København, Jespersen og Pios, 1941
Kun en Spillemand, København, Glyndendal, 1901
Levnedsbog, København, Det Schønbergeke Forlag, 1971
Lykke Peer, København, H. Hagerup, 1925
Mulatten, København, Reitzel, 1878
Ole Lukøie, København og Kristiania, Gyldenalske Boghandel Nordisk Forlag, 1905
O.T., København, Gyldendal, 1902

SECONDARY SOURCES
Andersen's works in translation

The Andersen-Scudder Letters, Berkeley and Los Angeles, University of California Press, 1949
The Complete Fairy Tales and Stories, trans. Erik Haugaard, London, Gollancz, 1974
The Diaries of Hans Christian Andersen: A Selection, ed. and trans. by Patricia L. Conroy and Sven H. Rossel, Seattle and London, University of Washington Press, 1990
The Fairy Tale of My Life, trans. W. Glyn Jones, Copenhagen, London and New York, Nyt Nordisk Forlag, 1954

Hans Christian Andersen's Correspondence: A Selection, ed. by Frederick Crawford, London, Dean & Son

The Improvisatore: or, Life in Italy, trans. from German by Mary Howitt, London, Richard Bentley, 1847

To Be or Not To Be, trans. Mrs Bushby, London, Richard Bentley, 1857

The True Story of My Life, trans. Mary Howitt, London, Longman, 1847

A Visit to Portugal 1866, trans. Grace Thornton, London, Peter Owen, 1972

A Visit to Spain and North Africa, trans. Grace Thornton, London, Peter Owen, 1975

Bibliographies, critical studies and background

Avery, Gillian, *Behold The Child: American Children and their Books*, London, Bodley Head, 1994

Blackham, H.J., *The Fable as Literature*, London and Dover, New Hampshire, The Athlone Press, 1985

Bligaard, Mette, *The Face of Denmark: The Danish Portrait from 1750 until the Present Day* , Frederiksborg, Det Nationalhistoriske Museum, 1997

Bomholt, Julius et al, *Hans Christian Andersen: His Life and Work*, Copenhagen, Det Berlingske Bogtrykkeri, 1955

Brandes, Georg, trans. Rasmus B. Andersen, *Creative Spirits of the Nineteenth Century*, London, T. Fisher Unwin, 1924

Bredsdorff, Elias, *Hans Christian Andersen: A Biography*, London, Souvenir Press, 1993

Bredsdorff, Elias, *Hans Christian Andersen and Charles Dickens*, Copenhagen, Rosenkilde and Bagger, 1956

Britten, James, *Mary Howitt*, London, Catholic Truth Society, 1890

Bulman, Joan, *Jenny Lind*, London, James Barrie, 1956

Burnett, Constance, *The Shoemaker's Son: The Life of Hans Christian Andersen*, London, George G. Harrap, 1943

Christiansen, Rupert, *Paris Bablyon: The Story of the Paris Commune*, London, Viking, 1995

Collin, Edvard, *Hans Christian Andersen og det Collinske Hus*, København, C.A. Deitzel, 1929

Cronin, Vincent, *Napoleon*, London, Collins, 1971

Dreslov, Aksel, *A River – A Town – A Poet*, Copenhagen, Skandinavisk Bogforlag, c.1955

Dreslov, Aksel, *Hans Christian Andersen og "denne Albert Hansen"*,

København, Samleren, 1977

Friedenthal, Richard, *Goethe*, London, Weidenfeld, 1963

Godden, Rumer, *Hans Christian Andersen*, London, Hutchinson, 1955

Goldstein, Robert Justin, *Political Repression in Nineteenth-Century Europe*, London, Croom Helm, 1983

Goldthwaite, John, *The Natural History of Make-believe: A Guide to the Principal Works of Britain, Europe and America*, Oxford and New York, Oxford University Press, 1996

Gosse, Edmund, *Studies in the Literature of Northern Europe*, London, C. Keegan Paul, 1879

Gosse, Edmund, *Two Visits to Denmark, 1872, 1874*, London, Smith and Elder, 1911

Hein, Jørgen, *The Royal Danish Collections, Amalienborg*, København, De Danske Kongers Kronologiske Samling, 1997

Hellsen, Hanry, *Journalisten Hans Christian Andersen*, København, Det Berlinske Bogtrykkeri, 1954

Hobsbawm, Eric, *The Age of Revolution 1789–1848*, London, Abacus, 1997

Howitt, Mary, *Autobiography*, London, Ibister, 1889

Høybye, Paul, *Andersen et la France*, Copenhagen, Munksgaard, 1960

Hude, Elizabeth, *Frederika Bremer og hendes venskab med Hans Christian Andersen og andre danske*, København, G.E.C. Gad, 1972

Jørgensen, Jens, *Hans Christian Andersen: En sand myte*, Hovedland, 1996

Kierkegaard, Søren, trans. Alexander Dru, *Journals 1834–53*, London, Fontana, 1965

Kjersgaard, Erik, *Danmark historisk Billedbog Vol III*, Hillerød, Dansk Histroisk Faellesforening, 1971

Kjølbye, Bente, *Hans Christian Andersen og Kvinderne*, København, Ejlers Forlag, 1997

Lee, Amice, *The Life of William And Mary Howitt*, Oxford, Oxford University Press, 1955

Merriman, ed., *Consciousness and Class Experience in Nineteenth-Century Europe*, New York and London, Holmes and Meier, 1979

Mitchell, P.M., *A History of Danish Literature*, Copenhagen, Gyldendal, 1957

Moltke, Count, *Notes of Travel* (extracts from Journals), London, Keegan Paul, 1880

de Mylius, Johan, *Hans Christian Andersen, Liv og vaerk: en tidstavle 1805–*

1875, Odense, Aschehoug, 1993

Naydler, Jeremy, *Goethe on Science: An Anthology of Goethe's Scientific Writings*, London, Floris, 1996

Oxenvad, Niels, et al, *Jeg er i Itlaien! Hans Christian Andersen på rejse 1833-34*, København, Thorvaldsens Museum og Hans Christian Andersen hus, 1990

Ørsted, H.C., *The Soul in Nature* (trans. from German), London, Bohn's Scientific Library, 1847

Ørsted, H.C., *Aanden i Naturen*, København, Vintens Stjerneboger, 1978

Papayannis, Nicholas, *The Coachmen of Nineteenth-Century Paris: Service Workers and Class Consciousness*, Baton Rouge and London, Louisiana State University Press, 1993

Roberts, John, *The Penguin History of Europe*, London, Penguin, 1997

Roscoe, Will, *Queer Spirits: A Gay Men's Myth Book*, Boston, Beacon Press, 1995

Rosendal, Axel, *Var Hans Christian Andersen ordblind?*, saertryk af en artikle I Ordblindebladet no. 2, København, 2 juni 1975

Ruse, Michael, *Homosexuality*, London, Blackwell, 1988

Sandemose, Aksel, *En flygtning krydser sit spor* (*oversat fra norsk af Ane Munk-Madsen*), København, Schonberg, 1994

Scavenius, Bente, ed., *The Golden Age Revisited: Art and Culture in Denmark 1800-1850*, Copenhagen, Gyldendal, 1996

Skjerk, Jørgen, *Hans Christian Andersen og Edvard Collin*, Aarhus, Aarhus teknieke Skole, 1985

Skjerk, Jørgen, *Hans Christian Andersen som hjemme-digter*, Aarhus, Bogtrykskolen, 1997

Spink, Reginald, *Hans Christian Andersen and his World*, London, Thames and Hudson, 1972

Taylor, A.J.P., *From Napoleon to the Second International: Essays on Nineteenth Century Europe*, London, Hamish Hamilton, 1993

Thestrup, Poul, *Mark og skillig, krone og øre: Pengeenheder, priser og lønninger i Danmark i 350 år (1640–1989)*, København, Arkivernes Informationsserie Rigsarkivet G.E.C. Gad, 1991

Toksvig, Signe, *The Life of Hans Christian Andersen*, London, Macmillan, 1933

Ulrichsen, Erik, *Hans Christian Andersen og Hjertetyven*, København, Samleren, 1991

Williams, Rosalind, *Dream Worlds: Mass Consumption in Late Nineteenth*

Century France, Berkeley and Oxford, University of California Press, 1982
Wilson, Angus, *The World of Charles Dickens*, New York, Viking, 1970
Winding, Kjeld, *Danmarks Historie*, København, Fremad, 1958
Woodring, Carl Ray, *Victorian Samplers: William and Mary Howitt*, Kansas, University of Kansas Press, 1952

Index